SQL/400

A Professional Programmer's Guide

Tim Martyn

Tim Hartley

Richard Johnson

McGraw-Hill, Inc.

New York   San Francisco   Washington, D.C.   Auckland   Bogotá
Caracas   Lisbon   London   Madrid   Mexico City   Milan
Montreal   New Delhi   San Juan   Singapore
Sydney   Tokyo   Toronto

Library of Congress Cataloging-in-Publication Data

Martyn, Tim.
    SQL/400 : a professional programmer's guide / Tim Martyn, Tim
Hartley, Richard Johnson.
        p.   cm.
    Includes index.
    ISBN 0-07-040799-1
    1. IBM AS/400 (Computer)—Programming.   2. SQL (Computer program
language)   3. Database management.   4. Relational databases.
I. Hartley, Tim.   II. Johnson, Richard, date.   III. Title.
QA76.8.I25919M37   1994
005.75'65—dc20   94-38608
                                                                      CIP

1 2 3 4 5 6 7 8 9 0   DOH/DOH   9 0 0 9 8 7 6 5

ISBN 0-07-040799-1

*The sponsoring editor for this book was Jerry Papke, the editing supervisor
was Christine H. Furry, and the production supervisor was Donald Schmidt.
It was set in Century Schoolbook by North Market Street Graphics.*

Printed and bound by R. R. Donnelley & Sons Company.

Contents

Preface

A number of books have been published which introduce SQL, the most popular language used with relational database systems. Many of these books attempt to provide the reader with a general overview of standard SQL as it applies to a variety of commercial database products. However, each database product really supports a unique version of SQL because it will include vendor-specific enhancements (or restrictions) to standard SQL. The authors of this text have elected to focus their attention on the AS/400 version of SQL.

This text is based on our previous texts, *DB2/SQL: A Professional Programmer's Guide* (McGraw-Hill, 1989), and *ORACLE/SQL: A Professional Programmer's Guide* (McGraw-Hill, 1992) which, respectively described IBM's DB2/MVS version of SQL and the ORACLE version of SQL. This text will introduce SQL as it exists in the AS/400 database product. It will also present some of the new features to be included in the forthcoming version of the AS/400 database product which will be called DB2/400.

This text has specific objectives and is written for a specific audience. We describe these objectives and audience below.

SQL OBJECTIVES

SQL is a complete database language. It has statements to

1. Initially create a database

2. Create underlying physical objects

3. Create application-specific logical objects

4. Define authorization and other management controls

5. Retrieve and manipulate data in the database

This text will focus on the last task, the retrieval and manipulation of data in the database. It will present a comprehensive discussion of SELECT, INSERT, UPDATE, and DELETE statements. Other SQL statements (e.g., CREATE TABLE, CREATE INDEX, CREATE VIEW) are presented to provide insight into the rules and behavior of the SELECT statement and other data manipulation statements.

Any SQL statement can be issued interactively using some front-end interface to the database system. (This book will describe the Query Manager front-end interface.) The same SQL statement (with minor modification) can be embedded within an application program written in some traditional programming language (e.g., RPG, COBOL). In fact, a desirable feature of SQL is that it allows a programmer to test a statement in an interactive environment before embedding the statement within an application program. This text will restrict its attention to "interactive" SQL. Professional programmers who need to learn the additional SQL statements relevant to "embedded" SQL will find some information on this topic in Chap. 25. However, a detailed discussion of embedded SQL is beyond the scope of this text.

QUERY MANAGER OBJECTIVES

Query Manager is a relatively simple front-end software tool which allows users to submit SQL statements and display the results. It also supports some report formatting facilities and other useful facilities which allow users to save and re-execute SQL statements. This text introduces many of these facilities. We chose to present Query Manager because it is representative of the interfaces that are often used with IBM's DB2 family of database systems. Our presentation will be at an introductory level. Our intention is to present just those Query Manager concepts and facilities necessary to execute the SQL examples and exercises described in this text.

AUDIENCE

A wide variety of people may interact with an AS/400 database. These may be database administrators, systems analysts and designers, systems programmers, application programmers, and users (the "customers" who hope to benefit from the system). This book is specifically written for professional programmers and users. Programmers require an in-depth knowledge of SQL's data retrieval and manipulation statements. Users can often use "simple" SQL statements to satisfy ad hoc data retrieval objectives.

In general, this text can be read by any person who has attained a basic level of computer literacy. As such, it can serve as an introduction to SQL for anyone interested in the subject. The authors have used a preliminary version of this book as a supplemental independent-study tutorial in a graduate-level database course where the content and primary text focused on the theory of relational database. The positive criticism provided by students has helped the authors to prepare the current version of this text.

ORGANIZATION OF TEXT

This book adopts a tutorial format. A topic is presented by introducing a sample query and the SQL statement that satisfies the query. Usually this is enough to give the reader a basic idea about the syntax and behavior of the SQL feature under consideration. Thereafter, a list of pertinent comments is presented. These comments present details on syntax. However, *the primary intention of the comments is to highlight the more important, and sometimes subtle, logical issues relating to the semantics of a SQL statement.* This will be a constant theme throughout the text. SQL's syntax is easy. But, logical errors can occur when formulating SQL statements. Where appropriate, our comments will emphasize the possible semantic difference between (1) the query you may have intended to execute and (2) the query actually executed by the system in response to your SQL statement.

This text is organized into an introduction and seven major parts, some of which can be skipped depending on your background knowledge, your status (user or programmer), or your particular objectives. We briefly outline each part below.

Introduction: The Database Environment

The Introduction is written for the reader who has no previous exposure to relational database concepts. It describes the fundamental concepts of relational database systems and the evolution of SQL, and it introduces SQL/400. This section is strictly conceptual. There are no behavioral objectives to be mastered by doing exercises. These concepts are important but are not critical. If you have no previous exposure to relational databases, you are encouraged to read this introduction. However, you should not be discouraged if you have a problem understanding some of the concepts. Just carry on. This book really begins in Chap. 1.

Part 1: Selecting Data from a Single Table

This section introduces the SELECT statement. In particular, we restrict our attention to retrieving data from a single table. You will learn how to retrieve specific rows and/or columns from a table, specify the sequence of the result, utilize the Boolean operators (AND, OR, and NOT), and perform basic calculations.

Many users may only display, but not modify, data in a database. Also, some users will be restricted to displaying data from a single table. Such users should find practically everything they need to know in these chapters. For this reason, the chapters in this part of the text have more of a tutorial flavor than subsequent chapters. We expect that most professional programmers can skim the sample queries and bypass the narrative comments.

Part 2: SQL/400 Built-in Functions

SQL/400 provides a collection of built-in functions which serves a variety of purposes. Each function performs a specific task such as a computation or a string manipulation. The special topic of date/time processing using built-in functions is also described.

Part 3: Query Manager

This part of the book describes the Query Manager front-end to the SQL/400 database system. No new SQL statements are introduced. Instead, we introduce Query Manager features and commands which facilitate report formatting and other housekeeping tasks.

Part 4: Data Definition and Manipulation

This section introduces the CREATE TABLE statement to provide background information on the SQL/400 data types and the basic concepts of database integrity. This information is necessary for a proper understanding of the INSERT, UPDATE, and DELETE statements which are described in detail.

Part 5: Accessing Multiple Tables

This section covers all aspects of the SELECT statement that were omitted in Parts 1 and 2. In particular, it introduces queries that require access to multiple tables. This part of the text presents a comprehensive discussion of the join operation, subqueries, and the union operation.

Part 6: More About SQL/400

This section introduces the SQL statements that allow you to share your data with other users of the system. It covers the CREATE VIEW statement and the GRANT and REVOKE statements. It includes a brief examination of the transaction concept and SQL/400 collections.

Part 7: SQL/400 Joins the DB2 Family

As this book was going to press, IBM announced a major enhancement to the database manager for the AS/400. It revised and renamed the SQL/400 product. It will be called DB2/400 in the OS/400 Version 3 system. The authors were able to obtain some preliminary information on DB2/400 which is presented in this part of the text. This part of the book will introduce new database integrity features, client-server issues, and application programming.

PHILOSOPHY

The primary objective of this text is to present a comprehensive examination of SQL's data retrieval and data manipulation statements as they exist in the AS/400 product. Our intention was to write a book that teaches these few (but very important) topics in a clear and organized manner. We solicit your feedback in the form of positive criticism regarding errors or enhancements that might be made to future editions of this text. Your comments can be addressed to the authors at The Hartford Graduate Center, 275 Windsor Street, Hartford, CT 06120.

Tim Martyn
Tim Hartley
Richard Johnson

Acknowledgments

We gratefully acknowledge the following individuals who played various roles in helping us bring this book to press. They are Fran Ehrmann, Beverly Leach, Tony Troy, and Christine Furry.

Tim Martyn again expresses his appreciation to members of the Arch Street Institute. Special acknowledgment is accorded to Dr. John H. Farrell, Dr. James Hynes, and Rev. Timothy Jones.

Introduction

This section introduces the following topics:

- Basic concepts of a Database Management System (DBMS)
- The characteristics of a "relational" DBMS
- The evolution of SQL
- SQL and the AS/400

This introduction provides a conceptual background by presenting the history and evolution of database technology. There are no behavioral objectives for this chapter. The intention is to set a context for our discussion of the AS/400 version of SQL. Users with some SQL/400 experience or experience with any other SQL-based relational DBMS may choose to skip this section and begin reading Chap. 1.

We use the term *SQL/400* generically to represent the SQL interface available on the AS/400. This book was developed on an AS/400 system running SQL/400 V2.2 utilizing the native file system. In IBM's continuing efforts to provide consistency between software products, the AS/400 database implementation is evolving to be consistent with the DB2 database family. This strategy will result in the emergence of the next release of SQL/400 under the name of DB2/400. The final chapter of this book will discuss some of the important developments in DB2/400. From a learning perspective, the SQL content of this book is compatible with either environment.

RELATIONAL DATABASE CONCEPTS

What is a database?

Many people use the terms *file* and *database* as though they were synonymous. However, there is an important difference. A file is a collection of records where each record is composed of multiple data items called *fields*. A database usually encompasses many files and, furthermore, provides facilities to capture relationships that exist between records. Hence, a database system transcends a file system by providing the designer with facilities to represent relationships between records. We present a simple example to illustrate this point.

Consider two files, an EMPLOYEE file and a DEPARTMENT file. An EMPLOYEE record contains fields for employee number, name, address, and department name. A DEPARTMENT record contains fields for department name, location, and phone number. (See Fig. I.1.) Now consider a request to retrieve the name and address of every employee, stored in the EMPLOYEE file, and their respective departmental locations and phone numbers, stored in the DEPARTMENT file. In a traditional file system this query would involve considerable effort. Both files would first have to be sorted in department-name sequence. Then an application program would follow a match–merge process to extract the desired data. The key point is that considerable work is required by application programs. This is because a file system cannot capture the employee-works-in-department relationship which exists between the two record types. A database system can.

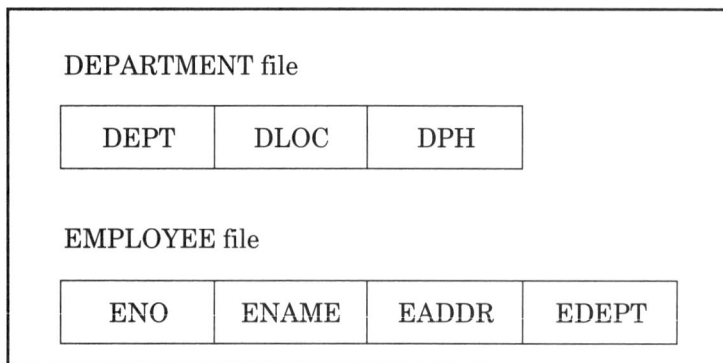

DEPARTMENT file		
DEPT	DLOC	DPH

EMPLOYEE file			
ENO	ENAME	EADDR	EDEPT

Figure I.1   Traditional file system.

Traditional database products, which evolved during the 1970s, captured relationships by allowing the database designer to represent the data and relationships as a tree or network structure. (A tree is just a special type of network.) Figure I.2 reflects such a network structure for our simple example. The figure denotes a database consisting of two record types which are related on a one-to-many basis. A department may have many employees, and an employee works for one department. The database system would usually implement this relationship by using internal pointers to link together a given department record with all its associated employee records. Then an application program would issue commands to the database system which effectively instruct the system to follow the pointers and return the desired data. This process, whereby the application program "navigates" its way through the network, is better than the sort–match–merge process of traditional file processing. However, there are a number of negative issues associated with network databases.

A network structure is often too rigid from the database designer's point of view. And the navigation process is complex from a programmer's point of view. Finally, because the application programs which navigate the database are written in traditional high-level languages (COBOL, FORTRAN, etc.), it is obvious that these early database systems are not at all user-friendly. The current generation of relational database systems addresses these problems.

What is a relational database?

The relational approach to database was proposed by E. F. Codd in 1970. However, commercial products did not appear in the marketplace until the early 1980s. The remainder of this section presents the basic concepts of relational database. We describe these ideas from a user viewpoint. Codd and others have developed a solid theoretical foundation of relational theory.

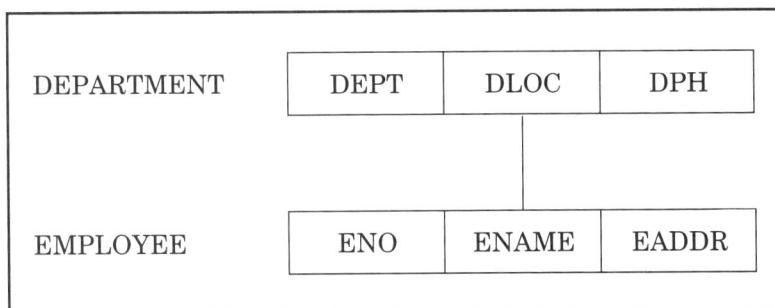

Figure I.2 Network database.

A relational database must fulfill at least two objectives. The first is that the system must present the data in tabular format to the user. In the simple example described previously, the user would see the database as a collection of two tables. Figure I.3 illustrates an EMPLOYEE table and a DEPARTMENT table. We have two tables instead of two records types. An individual row in a table corresponds to a record occurrence; a column in a table corresponds to a single field in a record. In fact we will often use the terms *row* and *record* interchangeably. Likewise we will use the terms *column* and *field* interchangeably.

Note that unlike the previous network design there is no explicit mapping between the tables. Instead the EMPLOYEE table contains a column (EDEPT) to indicate which department the employee works in. This observation might lead to the mistaken conclusion that a relational database is just a friendlier presentation of the old classical file concept. However, this is definitely not the case. The second major feature of relational databases clearly distinguishes relational database systems from file systems and earlier network-type database systems.

DEPARTMENT table

DEPT	DLOC	DPH

EMPLOYEE table

ENO	ENAME	EADDR	EDEPT

Figure I.3   Relational database.

The second major feature of any relational database is its support of a set-at-a-time query language. This requires some explanation. With traditional systems the query language was record-at-a-time–oriented. This meant that the query language was capable of expressing a query to retrieve only a single record. Therefore, in order to retrieve a set of records, the programmer would have to write code to repeatedly execute a query statement. For example, if you wanted to retrieve all the employees in the data processing (DP) department, and there were 200 such employees, a query statement (to get the "next" record for an employee in the DP department) would be executed 200 times. Each execution would retrieve one record and return it to the application program.

With a relational system the process is considerably easier because the query language is much more powerful. The language is powerful enough to request any subset of rows and columns. When the user issues a query, the system collects all the data and returns it to the user. The user issues only one query (without multiple iterations), and the system returns all the desired data.

Another important point is that relational languages for commercial database products are user-friendly. One does not need to be a professional programmer to access the database. A computer-literate user can sit at a workstation and enter a statement in the query language. The system will extract the desired rows and place them on the display screen.

A number of query languages for relational databases have been developed. This book presents a tutorial on SQL, the most popular relational language. The user will find that SQL is indeed a simple but powerful set-at-a-time database language. Before we describe the evolution of the SQL language, we present a simple SQL statement to illustrate the aforementioned points.

Figure I.4 shows a SELECT statement which will retrieve specified rows from the EMPLOYEE table. In this case it retrieves only those rows where the EDEPT value is "DP". You would enter this statement if you wanted to display all information about employees who work in the DP department. We will discuss the details of the SELECT statement in Part 1 of this text. For the moment we merely note that this command is indeed quite simple and would retrieve and display all the desired rows.

```
SELECT *
FROM EMPLOYEE
WHERE EDEPT = 'DP'
```

Figure I.4   Sample SQL statement.

SQL: A DATABASE LANGUAGE

Evolution and standards

SQL (Structured Query Language) was initially defined by D. D. Chamberlin and others during the late 1970s. It was originally called SEQUEL (Structured English QUEry Language) and was developed in conjunction with IBM's relational database prototype, System R. System R is the ancestor of IBM's commercial relational database roots in DB2, SQL/DS, and SQL/400. SEQUEL is the ancestor of all the different commercial versions of SQL.

Over the past decade many vendors have introduced SQL-oriented relational database products. Earlier versions of these products had a strong SQL flavor but were quite idiosyncratic. In response to this situation, the American National Standards Institute (ANSI) has established an "official" standard.

This book will present a discussion of SQL which is specific to the SQL/400 product as implemented via Query Manager. It will not examine the ANSI SQL standard. (In fact, some database authorities believe that any attempt to entice or force vendor conformity to the ANSI standard is a lost cause. We believe there is merit in their argument.)

Embedded SQL

SQL/400 supports "embedded" SQL. This permits application programs written in RPG, COBOL, C, PL/I, etc., to contain SQL statements. This means that a production-information system with batch and/or on-line programs can also interface with SQL/400.

Embedded SQL statements are similar to the interactive SQL statements presented in this text. However, there are some significant differences. For example, an embedded SQL statement must identify a memory location where the data are to be placed after being extracted from the database. Furthermore, because these traditional programming languages are record-at-a-time–oriented, special SQL statements are required to process a query that returns multiple rows. (This detracts from the previously mentioned set-at-a-time advantage of SQL. Note that the source of this problem is the host language, not SQL.) As mentioned in the Preface, this book restricts its attention to interactive SQL. However, we note that a knowledge of SQL statements as presented in this book is a necessary prerequisite for writing embedded SQL.

Efficiency considerations

Ideally, in a relational database environment, application programmers and users do not have to concern themselves with the machine efficiency. This task falls to the database administrator who establishes the database and specifies possible data access paths by creating indexes. Each SQL statement is processed by a system component, called the *optimizer,* to determine the most efficient way to satisfy the objective of the statement. This is an ideal scenario. To date, no vendor of any relational DBMS product produces a perfect optimizer. In particular, this applies to SQL/400 and has implications for those who write SQL statements.

We will see that a single query can have many different SQL solutions. Hence a programmer/user occasionally has some options in writing SQL statements. This might be desirable if the optimizer would always choose the most efficient data access path. However, this is not the case. Therefore, the SQL/400 reference manuals contain documentation describing SQL efficiency techniques. This documentation will reflect changes (presumably improvements) in future product releases.

Some of the comments in this text will address these SQL efficiency considerations. However, we do not elaborate on this issue because the optimizer improves with each new release of the system. Our objective is to teach SQL per se. This text will present the various ways of expressing a query objective. After reading this text you are advised to consult the SQL/400 documentation to become aware of the idiosyncratic behavior of the current optimizer.

SQL AND THE AS/400

Many of the building blocks for the effective use of SQL in the AS/400 world will not be foreign to the experienced AS/400 user. This is because the basic foundation for the AS/400 is built around an integrated relational model.

The use of SQL on an AS/400 system represents another interface to the "native" DBMS that is supported by the hardware and operating system software. This integration is unique when compared to other commercial implementations of database systems that bundle the database on top of other system functions. The most significant benefit of this integration is that it allows one to access the same data in a file system format (e.g., using RPG) or by an SQL interface. This flexibility allows you to process data in a "record" mode or "set" mode as your processing requirements dictate. Figure I.5 shows the various levels in the AS/400 atop which SQL/400 sits.

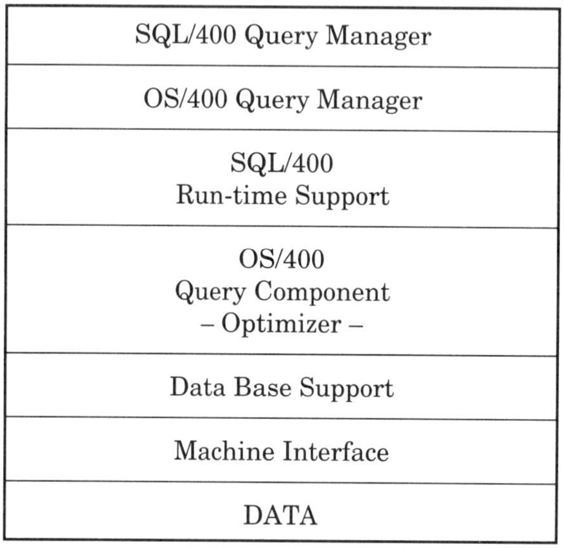

| SQL/400 Query Manager |
| OS/400 Query Manager |
| SQL/400
Run-time Support |
| OS/400
Query Component
– Optimizer – |
| Data Base Support |
| Machine Interface |
| DATA |

Figure I.5   SQL interface layers.

The top layer shown in Fig. I.5 illustrates the SQL/400 Query Manager. This is the user interface to the database. There are other user interface software tools which serve a similar purpose. Some are listed as follows.

Query/400	A decision support tool used to access database files
Open Query File	A Control Language that selects a subset of records for processing by a high-level programming language
PC Support	A utility that transfers data from the AS/400 to a PC using an SQL-style interface
OS/400 Query Manager	Provides the SAA Query/CPI support for the AS/400
SQL/400	A programmer facility to query and manipulate data with SQL commands
SQL/400 Query Manager	A part of SQL/400 that provides result formatting along with query and data manipulation

Although each of these tools provides useful features, the authors have chosen to use the SQL/400 Query Manager to introduce SQL. Regardless of which user interface you select, we are confident that the concepts presented here will be beneficial to you.

A COMMENT ON TERMINOLOGY

The terminology integration between the native data management functions and SQL includes the following.

AS/400	**Relational**
Physical File	Table
Record	Row
Field	Column
Keyed Logical File	Index
Nonkeyed Logical File	View

The inherent relational nature of the AS/400 provides for reduced duplicated code and increased system efficiency. However, this integration can make it difficult to get a complete understanding of the pieces involved. Some of the key issues to be aware of for individuals that have been exposed to other SQL implementations are:

- Referential Integrity is not implemented in SQL/400 (available in DB2/400).

- Stored Procedures are not available in SQL/400 (available in DB2/400).

- Optimization does not use a catalog to obtain statistics for query optimization. That information is stored with the data objects.

- Performance is a complicated issue because SQL queries have a longer access path than "native" file access.

Some of these issues will be addressed in Part 7 of this text.

SELECTing Data
from a Single Table

Practically every user and programmer will be required to retrieve data that were previously stored in the database. For this reason, Part 1 of this text is devoted to introducing the SELECT statement, which is used for database retrieval. More specifically, we restrict our attention to selecting data from a single table. This is because many users will be limited to the relatively simple task of querying data located in a singe table. Therefore, we have endeavored to encapsulate everything this audience needs to know in this part of the text. Discussion of queries that reference multiple tables is postponed until Part 5 of the text.

THE SAMPLE DATABASE

This text introduces the reader to SQL by presenting a series of sample queries against a small but realistic application database. This is an academic database designed to support the information-processing requirements of a mythical college. This design consists of seven tables that will be introduced as we progress through the text. (See App. B for a summary of this design.) All sample queries in the first six chapters will reference the same table. This is the COURSE table, which contains one row for each course in the curriculum. It is necessary that you understand the structure and content of this table in order to avoid any confusion pertaining to the illustrated sample queries.

THE COURSE TABLE

The entire COURSE table is shown in Fig. P1.1 along with a description of each column indicating its name, data type, length, and content. You should simply assume that this table exists in the database and that you have been granted permission to examine its content. You are advised to scan Fig. P1.1 and then note the following points:

- *Any reference to a column requires that you know and correctly enter the precise column name.*

- *References to some columns require a knowledge of actual stored values. For example, the CDEPT column will contain "THEO" to represent the theology department, "PHIL" to represent the philosophy department, and "CIS" to represent the computer and information science department.*

- *The description of data type and length is informal. A more formal presentation of SQL data types is given in Chap. 12. A proper understanding of the topics covered in Part 1 requires only that you comprehend the following points pertaining to SQL data types.*

INTRODUCTION TO SQL DATA TYPES

In general, the database can contain three kinds of data: (1) numeric, (2) character, and (3) date/time. The COURSE table contains two numeric columns, CRED and CLABFEE. The other four columns, CNO, CNAME, CDESCP, and CDEPT, contain character data. Date/time data types will not be introduced until Chap. 9.

We will see that certain types of database operations can be applied only to certain data types. In particular, arithmetic should be performed only on numeric data, and pattern matching should be applied only to character data.

Different numeric columns can vary in length. This determines the range of values which may be stored in particular numeric columns. Chapter 6 will address specific issues involving operations on numeric columns.

Columns defined as a character data type may also be of different lengths. Chapter 5 will address specific issues which involve the processing of character string data.

COURSE Table Description

Column Name	Data Type	Length	Content
CNO	Character	3	Course Number: A unique "number" used to identify each course
CNAME	Character	22	Course Name: The name of each course will also be unique (variable-length)
CDESCP	Character	25	Course Description: Each course should have a unique description (variable-length)
CRED	Number	not specified	Credits: An integer value which represents the number of credits a student earns by passing a course
CLABFEE	Number	5 (max.)	Course Labfee: A decimal value that represents the labfee paid by each student who takes the course (Maximum value = 999.99)
CDEPT	Character	4	Department Identifier: This identifies the academic department that offers the course

COURSE Table Sample Data

CNO	CNAME	CDESCP	CRED	CLABFEE	CDEPT
T11	SCHOLASTICISM	FOR THE PIOUS	3	150.00	THEO
T12	FUNDAMENTALISM	FOR THE CAREFREE	3	90.00	THEO
T33	HEDONISM	FOR THE SANE	3	.00	THEO
T44	COMMUNISM	FOR THE GREEDY	6	200.00	THEO
P11	EMPIRICISM	SEE IT-BELIEVE IT	3	100.00	PHIL
P22	RATIONALISM	FOR CIS MAJORS	3	50.00	PHIL
P33	EXISTENTIALISM	FOR CIS MAJORS	3	200.00	PHIL
P44	SOLIPSISM	ME MYSELF AND I	6	.00	PHIL
C11	INTRO TO CS	FOR ROOKIES	3	100.00	CIS
C22	DATA STRUCTURES	VERY USEFUL	3	50.00	CIS
C33	DISCRETE MATHEMATICS	ABSOLUTELY NECESSARY	3	.00	CIS
C44	DIGITAL CIRCUITS	AH HA!	3	.00	CIS
C55	COMPUTER ARCH.	VON NEUMANN'S MACH.	3	100.00	CIS
C66	RELATIONAL DATABASE	THE ONLY WAY TO GO	3	500.00	CIS

Figure PI.1   COURSE table information.

ORGANIZATION OF CHAPTERS

The first four chapters provide an introduction to the structure of the SELECT statement and the fundamentals of using Query Manager. You will learn the basic structure of the SELECT statement (Chap. 1), how to enter SQL statements and format the output display using Query Manager options (Chap. 2), how to display the output in some desired sequence (Chap. 3), and how to specify complex retrieval conditions using the Boolean operators (Chap. 4). Professional programmers will be able to skim these chapters. The narrative comments are primarily directed to the rookie user who needs to learn the logical aspects of query specification in addition to the syntax of the SELECT statement.

The next two chapters concern pattern matching (Chap. 5) and arithmetic expressions (Chap. 6). Professional programmers may also skim these chapters. However, the narrative addresses subtle points that should be read in order to obtain a comprehensive understanding of these topics.

The SELECT Statement

This chapter introduces the fundamental concepts and structure of the SELECT statement. This is by far the most frequently used SQL statement. Its purpose is to retrieve data from the database. In this chapter you will learn how to display an entire table or display just some specific rows and/or columns of a table. You will find that the sample queries are almost self-explanatory. In fact, some are so "obvious" that you may be tempted to skip reading the comments pertaining to each sample query. This might be appropriate for experienced professionals. However, users should not yield to this temptation. The commentary on each sample will highlight subtle issues which are important. Understanding these points will prove beneficial to those users who choose to master the more advanced topics covered later in this book.

This chapter covers only the SELECT statement. Chapter 2 will present the details of using SQL/400 Query Manager to execute SELECT statements. We recommend that rookie users adhere to the following sequence:

- Make sure that you read the Introduction, which places SQL/400 in the context of the AS/400 architecture.

- Read Chap. 1 for conceptual purposes only.

- Read and execute the examples in Chap. 2 to get acquainted with using Query Manager to execute SQL/400 statements.

- Return to Chap. 1 and, using your knowledge of Query Manager, execute the sample queries and exercises.

- Proceed to Chap. 3.

DISPLAY AN ENTIRE TABLE

The goal of the first sample query is to display the entire COURSE table (i.e., display every column in every row). This can be achieved by coding the simplest of all possible SELECT statements.

Sample Query 1.1   Display the entire COURSE table.

```
SELECT        *

FROM          COURSE
```

CNO	CNAME	CDESCP	CRED	CLABFEE	CDEPT
T11	SCHOLASTICISM	FOR THE PIOUS	3	150.00	THEO
T12	FUNDAMENTALISM	FOR THE CAREFREE	3	90.00	THEO
T33	HEDONISM	FOR THE SANE	3	.00	THEO
T44	COMMUNISM	FOR THE GREEDY	6	200.00	THEO
P11	EMPIRICISM	SEE IT-BELIEVE IT	3	100.00	PHIL
P22	RATIONALISM	FOR CIS MAJORS	3	50.00	PHIL
P33	EXISTENTIALISM	FOR CIS MAJORS	3	200.00	PHIL
P44	SOLIPSISM	ME MYSELF AND I	6	.00	PHIL
C11	INTRO TO CS	FOR ROOKIES	3	100.00	CIS
C22	DATA STRUCTURES	VERY USEFUL	3	50.00	CIS
C33	DISCRETE MATHEMATICS	ABSOLUTELY NECESSARY	3	.00	CIS
C44	DIGITAL CIRCUITS	AH HA!	3	.00	CIS
C55	COMPUTER ARCH.	VON NEUMANN'S MACH.	3	100.00	CIS
C66	RELATIONAL DATABASE	THE ONLY WAY TO GO	3	500.00	CIS

Comments

1. The asterisk (*) following "SELECT" is an abbreviation for "all columns." The left-to-right column sequence of the output is the default left-to-right sequence. This default sequence is determined by the order in which the columns were initially specified in the CREATE TABLE statement. (The CREATE TABLE statement will be described in Part 4 of this text.)

2. The "FROM COURSE" clause identifies the table. Your system will undoubtedly have many tables. Each table has a unique name. This name follows "FROM" in the query.

3. "SELECT" and "FROM" are keywords in SQL. A keyword always has a specific unalterable meaning in the language. For this reason keywords are also called *reserved words*. Your SQL/400 reference manual will contain a list of SQL keywords.

4. You could have entered this statement as a one-line statement. Entering the following line would produce the same result.

```
SELECT * FROM COURSE
```

Throughout this text we will usually begin the FROM clause on a new line. This will enhance readability of the SQL code. In practice you may find it easier to type just one line. The key point is that, regardless of how you type the statement, it is interpreted as a single statement.

5. Observe that the rows of the displayed output are not sorted. This is because

   a. Tables do not have any predefined sort sequence.

   b. The SELECT statement does not contain an ORDER BY clause.

   In general, you can never assume the displayed result will be in any particular sequence unless you explicitly designate some sort sequence by using the ORDER BY clause. We will examine this clause in Chap. 3.

6. This statement does not contain a WHERE clause. In the next example we will see that a WHERE clause is used to select just some of the rows from a table. The point we wish to emphasize here is that the absence of a WHERE clause means that SQL/400 will retrieve all rows from the table.

7. The result table is displayed using a "default" format which specifies decimal accuracy, column headings, etc. Chapters 2 and 10 will show you how to customize the format of your display.

WHERE CLAUSE

Most real-world databases have tables which contain too many rows to be examined visually by the user. With the exception of small tables, you will rarely want to display an entire table. Instead, you will use the WHERE clause in the SELECT statement to display just those rows that you want to see. (WHERE is another SQL keyword.) The next sample query illustrates this clause.

Sample Query 1.2   Display all information about any course with a zero lab fee. (More precisely, select just those rows from the COURSE table where the CLABFEE value is zero. Display every column of these rows.)

```
SELECT        *

FROM          COURSE

WHERE         CLABFEE = 0.00
```

CNO	CNAME	CDESCP	CRED	CLABFEE	CDEPT
C33	DISCRETE MATHEMATICS	ABSOLUTELY NECESSARY	3	.00	CIS
C44	DIGITAL CIRCUITS	AH HA!	3	.00	CIS
P44	SOLIPSISM	ME MYSELF AND I	6	.00	PHIL
T33	HEDONISM	FOR THE SANE	3	.00	THEO

Comments

1. The WHERE clause follows the FROM clause. Again, we could have entered the SELECT statement in one line. The following statement is equivalent to the previous one.

    ```
    SELECT * FROM COURSE WHERE CLABFEE = 0.00
    ```

2. The syntax of the WHERE clause is

    ```
    WHERE condition
    ```

    The condition in our example is "CLABFEE = 0.00". It is the condition which specifies which rows are to be retrieved. Examine the entire COURSE table and then observe the result. Four of the rows in the COURSE table have CLABFEE values equal to zero. These rows form the displayed result. Only rows which match the WHERE condition are displayed.

3. CLABFEE was defined as a numeric field. Hence, this is an example of a *numeric* compare. This means the system compares on mathematical value rather than on a character-by-character basis. The following WHERE conditions are all equivalent and would select the same four rows as the original example.

   ```
   WHERE CLABFEE = 0
   WHERE CLABFEE = 0.0
   WHERE CLABFEE = 00.00
   ```

4. Numeric values can contain a leading minus sign (−).

5. Our example compares on an "equals" (=) condition. Other comparison operators are

   less than <

   greater than >

   less than or equal to <=

   greater than or equal to >=

   not equal <>

   The logical not symbol (¬) can also be combined with comparison operators to negate conditions. For example,

   not less than ¬<

   not greater than ¬>

   not equal ¬=

6. Our example illustrates a "simple" WHERE condition. It references only one column (CLABFEE) and does not contain any Boolean operators such as AND, OR, and NOT. We will study the Boolean operators in Chap. 4.

The next sample query contains a WHERE clause to select rows based on CDEPT value. This query is similar to the previous one, with one important exception. The CDEPT column contains character data. This means that the comparison value must be enclosed within apostrophes.

Sample Query 1.3   Display all information about any course which is offered by the philosophy department. (More precisely, select just those rows from the COURSE table where the CDEPT value is "PHIL". Display all columns.)

SELECT	*
FROM	COURSE
WHERE	CDEPT = 'PHIL'

CNO	CNAME	CDESCP	CRED	CLABFEE	CDEPT
P11	EMPIRICISM	SEE IT-BELIEVE IT	3	100.00	PHIL
P22	RATIONALISM	FOR CIS MAJORS	3	50.00	PHIL
P33	EXISTENTIALISM	FOR CIS MAJORS	3	200.00	PHIL
P44	SOLIPSISM	ME MYSELF AND I	6	.00	PHIL

Comments

1. Syntax: The character string must be contained within apostrophes. Our example illustrates WHERE CDEPT = 'PHIL'. (Note that this is not the case with numeric data. The previous example referenced CLABFEE. That WHERE clause did not contain apostrophes.)

2. Character string data are compared on a character-by-character basis. Two strings are equal only if all corresponding characters match. You should note whether the two strings being compared are the same length. In the preceding example, because we are comparing CDEPT (a four-character column) to "PHIL", we have a simple case of comparing two strings of the same length. Each character of CDEPT must exactly match "PHIL" for a row to be selected.

   A special case occurs where the strings being compared do not have the same length. When this occurs, the same character-by-character comparison applies; however, the system assumes that the shorter string has blanks appended to its right side. The system action means that you do not have to type trailing blanks at the end of character constants placed in WHERE clauses. For example, if you wanted to display information about courses offered by the CIS department, you could use either of the following WHERE clauses:

   ```
   WHERE CDEPT = 'CIS'
   WHERE CDEPT = 'CIS '
   ```

   It should be emphasized that two strings are considered to be equal only if all corresponding characters match. This means that you have to be careful about leading and embedded blanks. Note that the following WHERE clauses would not match the left-justified four-character CDEPT value of "CIS".

   ```
   WHERE CDEPT = ' CIS'
   WHERE CDEPT = 'C I S'
   ```

3. CDEPT is a fixed-length column. (This is why the system stores trailing blanks in CDEPT when a user enters a string which is shorter than four characters. See Chap. 13.) The same comparison rules apply to columns which contain variable-length character data. Fixed-length columns utilize storage for the total size of the column. Variable-length columns utilize storage for only the size of the data entered. See the next sample query.

The next sample query references CNAME, a column which contains variable-length character data. Observe that the character string comparison process is the same as described for fixed-length character strings.

Sample Query 1.4 Display all information about the course with the CNAME value of "COMMUNISM".

SELECT	*
FROM	COURSE
WHERE	CNAME = 'COMMUNISM'

CNO	CNAME	CDESCP	CRED	CLABFEE	CDEPT
T44	COMMUNISM	FOR THE GREEDY	6	200.00	THEO

Comments

1. Because CNAME contains variable-length character data, the system will not attach trailing blanks to any data value which is smaller than the maximum column length.

2. Although there is no good reason for doing so, you can still attach trailing blanks to a character string. The following WHERE clause is valid:

   ```
   WHERE CNAME = 'COMMUNISM '
   ```

3. The previous examples illustrate "full" character string comparisons. This means that a row is selected only if every corresponding character matches the other. In Chap. 5 we will discuss "partial" character string comparisons. This will help you search for any character string pattern regardless of its position within the column.

4. *Reminder:* Very often something called "number" is defined as a character string. Such is the case with the "course number" (CNO) column. Real-world systems contain part numbers, policy numbers, Social Security numbers, etc., stored as character data simply because no calculations are to be performed with these values. Also, they sometimes contain alphabetic characters. When these "numbers" are stored as character strings, you must use apostrophes in the WHERE clause.

Exercises

1A. Display all rows where the lab fee is less than $150.

1B. Display all rows where the number of credits exceeds 3.

1C. Display all information about courses offered by the theology department.

1D. Display all information about the Relational Database course.

1E. Display the row for course number P44.

Usually we compare character data using the equals (=) condition. Occasionally we would like to compare character data using the other comparison operators (<, >, <=, >=, <>). Consider the following sample query which requires such a comparison.

Sample Query 1.5   Display all information about courses having CNAME values which follow "HEDONISM" in alphabetic sequence.

```
SELECT       *

FROM         COURSE

WHERE        CNAME  >  'HEDONISM'
```

CNO	CNAME	CDESCP	CRED	CLABFEE	CDEPT
T11	SCHOLASTICISM	FOR THE PIOUS	3	150.00	THEO
P22	RATIONALISM	FOR CIS MAJORS	3	50.00	PHIL
P44	SOLIPSISM	ME MYSELF AND I	6	.00	PHIL
C11	INTRO TO CS	FOR ROOKIES	3	100.00	CIS
C66	RELATIONAL DATABASE	THE ONLY WAY TO GO	3	500.00	CIS

Comments

1. The system will compare each CNAME value with the character string "HEDONISM". All CNAME values contain just the standard characters (A to Z). This means that the evaluation will be based on the conventional alphabetic sequence.

2. A special case exists when the character strings being compared contain digits, special symbols, and both upper- and lowercase letters. SQL/400 will evaluate a character sequence according to the sequence specified by the EBCDIC codes. These codes specify the collating sequence for all characters found within the system. Figure 1.1 summarizes the EBCDIC sequence.

The EBCDIC code is used by IBM systems. Almost all other systems (DEC, SUN, IBM PC, etc.) use the ASCII code set.

Within the EBCDIC character set you will note that special characters (&,?,+, etc.) will sort before lowercase letters, which in turn sort before uppercase letters, which in turn sort before the digits.

When comparing character data using an operator other than equals, the system examines the two strings on a character-by-character basis beginning with the left-most character of each string. Comparison continues until an inequality is encountered or, if the strings are of unequal length, one of the strings has been exhausted. In this case the shorter of the two strings is considered to be less than the longer string.

Listed below are some character strings sorted according to EBCDIC character sequences.

```
!!!FIDO!!!
jessie
julie
Jessie
JEssie
JULIe
JULIE
Zeek
3M
77aaaaaaaAAAAAAAAA
```

Exercises

1F. Display every row where the course number is less than "P01".

1G. Display every row where the course name is greater than "RATIONALISM".

(Low)	Symbols:	. < (+ . . .
	Lowercase:	a b c d e . . .
	Uppercase:	A B C D E . . .
(High)	Digits:	0 1 2 3 4 . . .

Figure 1.1 Hierarchy of EBCDIC characters.

DISPLAYING SPECIFIED COLUMNS

All of the previous examples selected every column. This was because the statement began with "SELECT *". In practice we usually want to examine just some specified columns. The current example illustrates how to achieve this objective. We simply specify the column names after "SELECT". Only those specified columns are displayed.

Sample Query 1.6 Display the CNO, CNAME, and CDEPT values (in that order) for every row in the COURSE table.

```
SELECT      CNO,  CNAME,  CDEPT

FROM        COURSE
```

CNO	CNAME	CDEPT
C11	INTRO TO CS	CIS
C22	DATA STRUCTURES	CIS
C33	DISCRETE MATHEMATICS	CIS
C44	DIGITAL CIRCUITS	CIS
C55	COMPUTER ARCH.	CIS
C66	RELATIONAL DATABASE	CIS
P11	EMPIRICISM	PHIL
P22	RATIONALISM	PHIL
P33	EXISTENTIALISM	PHIL
P44	SOLIPSISM	PHIL
T11	SCHOLASTICISM	THEO
T12	FUNDAMENTALISM	THEO
T33	HEDONISM	THEO
T44	COMMUNISM	THEO

Comments

1. *Syntax:* Each column name must be separated by a comma. You may optionally include one or more spaces before or after the comma.

2. You must know the names of the columns. Usually you are working with a familiar database, and therefore this will not be a problem. Otherwise you must do one of the following:

   a. Ask somebody who knows. ("Poor show.")

   b. Issue a statement beginning with "SELECT *". The output will display all the names of the columns. (Again, "poor show." You are wasting computer resources, especially if the table has many rows.)

   c. Examine the documentation that the database administrator should have produced and made available to you. This should contain the names of the columns that you can access.

   d. You can use the SQL/400 Query Manager DRAW command (see Chap. 2). This will create a default SQL SELECT statement.

   e. Information about tables and columns is stored in the Data Dictionary. Certain dictionary features will be presented at appropriate points in our examination of SQL.

3. This example happens to select the three columns in the same left-to-right order as the default column sequence. This is the same order which is displayed when you issue a query beginning with "SELECT *". This is not required. Columns can be displayed in any left-to-right order. (See the next sample query.)

4. Note that the current query does not have a WHERE clause. Hence all rows of the COURSE table are retrieved. But only the three specified columns are displayed.

This next example produces essentially the same result as the previous example. The content is the same. The only difference is the specification of the left-to-right column sequence.

Sample Query 1.7   Display the CDEPT, CNAME, and CNO values (in that order) for every row in the COURSE table.

```
SELECT      CDEPT,  CNAME,  CNO

FROM        COURSE
```

CDEPT	CNAME	CNO
CIS	INTRO TO CS	C11
CIS	DATA STRUCTURES	C22
CIS	DISCRETE MATHEMATICS	C33
CIS	DIGITAL CIRCUITS	C44
CIS	COMPUTER ARCH.	C55
CIS	RELATIONAL DATABASE	C66
PHIL	EMPIRICISM	P11
PHIL	RATIONALISM	P22
PHIL	EXISTENTIALISM	P33
PHIL	SOLIPSISM	P44
THEO	SCHOLASTICISM	T11
THEO	FUNDAMENTALISM	T12
THEO	HEDONISM	T33
THEO	COMMUNISM	T44

Comments

1. The SELECT clause specifies the left-to-right ordering of the displayed columns. The example shows that CDEPT is the leftmost column, followed by CNAME and then CNO.

2. Again, we have no WHERE clause. Hence all rows are retrieved.

3. You can specify any valid COURSE column name after "SELECT" as long as the COURSE table is referenced in the FROM clause. You can even enter the same column name more than once. This means that the following query is valid:

```
SELECT CDEPT, CNAME, CLABFEE, CLABFEE, CLABFEE
FROM COURSE
```

This is obviously redundant. But it is valid and will produce three identical CLABFEE columns. (There is a situation where this does make sense. In some situations you may wish to wish to use Query Manager to perform different calculations on the same data.)

Exercises

1H. Display course name and description, in that order, for every course.

1I. Display department, course number, lab fee, and credits, in that order, for every course.

DISPLAY SOME SUBSET OF ROWS AND COLUMNS

This next example combines the previously described techniques to select some subset of rows (using the WHERE clause) and some subset of columns (by explicitly specifying column names after "SELECT"). The example does not introduce any new concepts or SQL reserved words.

Sample Query 1.8 Select the CNO, CDEPT, and CLABFEE values for every course with a CLABFEE value less than $100.

SELECT	CNO, CDEPT, CLABFEE
FROM	COURSE
WHERE	CLABFEE < 100.00

CNO	CDEPT	CLABFEE
C22	CIS	50.00
C33	CIS	.00
C44	CIS	.00
P22	PHIL	50.00
P44	PHIL	.00
T12	THEO	90.00
T33	THEO	.00

Comments

1. This example illustrates the general format of a typical **SELECT** statement. This is

```
SELECT col1, col2, ..., colN
FROM table name
WHERE condition
```

2. In the current example the WHERE condition referenced CLABFEE, and we happened to select CLABFEE to be displayed in the output. It is not necessary to display a column used in a retrieval condition. The following example which retrieves all three credit courses displays only the course name and description. It may not be reasonable to display the CRED column because it will be the same for all displayed rows.

```
SELECT CNAME, CDESCP
FROM COURSE
WHERE CRED = 3
```

3. Remember that no punctuation is allowed in numeric constants. Therefore, even if we were comparing on 100 dollars, the example would not show a "$" before the "100."

4. We use the term *subset* to describe the result table. This terminology hints at the fact that SQL is based on E. F. Codd's Relational Database Model. From a formal point of view this model interprets each table as a set and each SELECT statement as the definition of the subset to be displayed.

Exercises

1J. Display course number and labfee for all courses where the lab fee exceeds $100.00.

1K. Display the course names of all CIS courses.

Observe that the displayed output for all previous sample queries did not contain any duplicate rows. This can occur. Consider the next sample query.

Sample Query 1.9 Display every academic department which offers courses. (Select every row of the COURSE table. Display just the CDEPT column.)

SELECT	CDEPT
FROM	COURSE

CDEPT
___
CIS
CIS
CIS
CIS
CIS
CIS
PHIL
PHIL
PHIL
PHIL
THEO
THEO
THEO
THEO

Comments

1. This sample query does realize the objective of displaying every department which offers courses. However, because a department offers many courses, there are many duplicate rows in the displayed output. The system does not automatically remove duplicate rows from the output display. You must use the reserved word "DISTINCT" to prevent duplicate rows from being displayed. This will be described in the next sample query.

2. You should recognize when duplicate rows can possibly occur. This implies that you know some facts about the content of the COURSE table. Let us assume that our mythical college has established a reasonable policy that course numbers, course names, and course descriptions must be unique. Assuming that our sample COURSE table reflects this policy, you can be certain that duplicate rows will not be displayed under the following circumstances.

   a. The SELECT clause contains CNO, CNAME, or CDESCP (or a "SELECT *" implicitly references these columns).

   b. The WHERE clause compares the CNO, CNAME, or CDESCP columns using an equals (=) comparison operator. This implies that only one row can be selected.

   All of our previous sample queries and exercises met one of these conditions. Hence, duplicate rows never appeared in any of the previous output displays. The current example references only CDEPT. No reference is made to CNO, CNAME, or CDESCP. Hence, duplicates can and do occur in the result.

3. *General advice:* Examine each SELECT statement (prior to execution) to see if it references a "unique" column which will inhibit duplicate rows from being displayed. If this is not the case, you should anticipate duplicate rows in the output display.

Exercise

1L. Select every row. Display just the course lab fees. (Do not attempt to remove possible duplicate rows.)

DISTINCT KEYWORD

The next sample query is identical to the previous one, with the additional stipulation that the displayed output does not contain any duplicate rows. We use the keyword "DISTINCT" to achieve this objective.

Sample Query 1.10   Display every academic department which offers courses. Do not display duplicate values.

SELECT   DISTINCT   CDEPT

FROM   COURSE

CDEPT
—————
CIS
PHIL
THEO

Comments

1. *Syntax:* The keyword "DISTINCT" must directly follow "SELECT", separated by one or more spaces.

2. Only duplicate rows will be removed from the output display. In this example, the row consists of a single column. The next sample query will display multiple columns. We will see that a row is considered to be a duplicate of another row only if every column value in the first row matches every corresponding column value in the second row.

3. You are not required to remove duplicate rows. The previous sample query, by displaying the duplicate rows, indicated how many courses were offered by various academic departments. (Chapter 7 will introduce the COUNT function, which would better serve this purpose.) The use of DISTINCT is entirely contingent on the user's objective.

The next sample query selects just some rows and displays multiple columns. Such queries are less likely to produce duplicate rows. However, as the example illustrates, duplicate rows can occur.

Sample Query 1.11   For each course with a lab fee less than $100, display the academic department which offers the course and the number of awarded credits.

```
SELECT      CDEPT,  CRED

FROM        COURSE

WHERE       CLABFEE  <  100.00
```

CDEPT	CRED
CIS	3
CIS	3
CIS	3
PHIL	3
PHIL	6
THEO	3
THEO	3

Comments

1. The SELECT statement did not reference any of the "unique" columns (CNO, CNAME, CDESCP). Hence, duplicate rows can be present in the displayed result.

2. You could simply decide whether you want to see duplicate rows and then include or exclude DISTINCT according to your decision. This is an acceptable approach. However, the use of DISTINCT may force the system to do some extra work to remove the duplicate rows.

Sample Query 1.12   Same as previous sample query. However, do not display duplicate rows.

SELECT   DISTINCT CDEPT, CRED

FROM   COURSE

WHERE   CLABFEE < 100.00

CDEPT	CRED
CIS	3
PHIL	3
PHIL	6
THEO	3

Comment

Only rows which were complete duplicates of other rows were not displayed. (The reader should closely examine the results of this query as compared to the previous one.) The key concept is that DISTINCT does not refer to any individual column. It refers to the entire row.

Exercises

1M. Display the set of all course lab fees. Do not display any duplicate values.

1N. Display the credits and lab fees for all CIS courses. Allow duplicate rows to be displayed.

1O. Display the credits and lab fees for all CIS courses. Do not display any duplicate rows.

DISPLAYING CONSTANT DATA

It is possible to incorporate constant data into a column of the result table. The next sample query shows the inclusion of a character string which serves to describe the result table.

Sample Query 1.13   Display the course number and name of every course which has a lab fee over $100. Include a third column in the result table which shows "EXPENSIVE" in each row.

```
SELECT       CNO,  CNAME,  'EXPENSIVE'

FROM         COURSE

WHERE        CLABFEE  >  100
```

CNO	CNAME	EXPENSIVE
T11	SCHOLASTICISM	EXPENSIVE
T44	COMMUNISM	EXPENSIVE
P33	EXISTENTIALISM	EXPENSIVE
C66	RELATIONAL DATABASE	EXPENSIVE

Comments

1. The constant to be displayed in the result table is specified in the SELECT clause. Any constant, numeric or character, can be specified.

2. The constant is shown redundantly in each row. This is the only option SQL provides. It would probably be desirable to include "EXPENSIVE" just once as a report title for the result table. However, you would have to use the SQL/400 Query Manager Report Form facilities to achieve this objective.

3. The system will generate a default column header for the constant data. This column header is not very elegant. Chapter 10 will show you how to generate more meaningful headings.

SUMMARY

This chapter has introduced the basic structure of the SQL SELECT statement. We showed three clauses of this statement.

SELECT	column names
FROM	table name
WHERE	condition

The query is formulated by

1. Identifying the table which contains the desired data. The table name is placed in the FROM clause.
2. Identifying the columns to be displayed. The column names are placed in the SELECT clause. ("SELECT *" will display all columns.)
3. Coding a condition in the WHERE clause which specifies the row-selection criteria. The absence of a WHERE clause means that every row will be selected.

We also introduced the keyword DISTINCT, which, when placed in the SELECT clause, will inhibit the display of duplicate rows. We emphasized the semantic implications of using DISTINCT.

Summary exercises

The following exercises all pertain to the STAFF table, which has four columns. These are ENAME, ETITLE, ESALARY, and DEPT. (See App. B for a more detailed description of the STAFF table.)

1P. Display the entire STAFF table.

1Q. Display all information about any employee whose yearly salary is less than $1000.

1R. Display all information about any employee who is employed by the theology department.

1S. Display the names and titles of all staff members.

1T. Display the name and salary of any employee whose salary exceeds $1000.

1U. Display the name and title for any staff member whose name is less than "MARK" in alphabetic sequence.

1V. Display the titles of all staff members. Do not show duplicate values.

An Introduction to Query Manager

The sample queries introduced in Chap. 1 presented SELECT statements in a standard form. This standard form does not illustrate the actual screen images observed by a user who is using the SQL/400 Query Manager to enter SQL statements. The primary goal of this chapter is to introduce the reader to some of the editing and report-formatting facilities of Query Manager. After reading this chapter you will be able to use Query Manager to execute SQL statements and display the retrieved data in a simple report format.

No new SQL statements are presented in this chapter. Hence, you will not find any new sample queries. Instead, this chapter introduces a new class of statements which are properly referred to as Query Manager *options*. Most of these options are very simple to learn and use. However, there is a conceptual distinction between SQL *statements* and Query Manager options which should be understood. After introducing some basic SQL/400 options, we conclude this chapter by describing these important conceptual distinctions.

The information presented in this chapter is just enough to get you started. You will be able to use Query Manager to execute the SQL statements and exercises presented in the remaining chapters of Part 1. If you are an experienced user of the AS/400 you may wish to skim the material presented in this chapter. (If you have created the sample database described in App. B and C, you are encouraged to execute each of the sample SQL statements and Query Manager options presented in this chapter.)

Query Manager manages several components of SQL/400. These include an editor and facilities for report generation, table management, and session management. Of the variety of SQL interfaces available, Query Manager is currently the most comprehensive. In this chapter we will introduce the use of Query Manager Editor. Chapter 10 will discuss additional Query Manager facilities.

ENTERING SQL STATEMENTS

This section presents a straightforward approach to execute a SELECT statement using Query Manager which will introduce four Query Manager screens. Assume you have just accessed the Query Manager editor as described in App. A, and the system displays the "Edit Query" screen. The system is now waiting for you to enter your first SQL statement.

```
                                  Edit Query
Columns . . . : 1 70                              Query . . . :
QM . .
Type SQL Statement
      *************************** Beginning of Data ************************
' ' ' ' ' ' '
' ' ' ' ' ' '
' ' ' ' ' ' '
' ' ' ' ' ' '
' ' ' ' ' ' '
' ' ' ' ' ' '
' ' ' ' ' ' '
' ' ' ' ' ' '
      *************************** End of Data ***************************
F2=Alternate keys     F3=Exit        F4=Prompt   F5=Run report   F6=Run sample
F9=Retrieve           F15=Check syntax           F24=More keys
```

Assume you would like to execute the following SQL statement:

```
SELECT  CNO, CRED
FROM    COURSE
WHERE   CDEPT = 'CIS'
```

Simply type the entire SELECT statement as illustrated:

```
                                  Edit Query
Columns . . . : 1 70                              Query . . . :
QM . .
Type SQL Statement
      *************************** Beginning of Data ***********************
0001.00 SELECT  CNO, CRED
0002.00 FROM    COURSE
0003.00 WHERE   CDEPT = 'CIS'
' ' ' ' ' ' '
      *************************** End of Data ***************************
F2=Alternate keys     F3=Exit        F4=Prompt   F5=Run report   F6=Run sample
F9=Retrieve           F15=Check syntax           F24=More keys
```

If you choose to enter an SQL statement on multiple lines, simply type each line of the SQL statement and press the Enter or Tab key. Each time you press one of these keys, the system will position the cursor at the next line. It is not necessary to decompose an SQL statement into separate clauses as shown. It is only required that each line end with a complete word before pressing the Enter key.

After entering the SQL statement, press the F5 key to run the query. The system presents the "Run Query" screen:

```
                          Run Query
Query . . . . . . . . . : *
Library . . . . . . . :
Type choices, press Enter.
Run query mode . . . . 1              1=Interactive  2=Batch
Run sample only . . . . N             Y=Yes, N=No
Form . . . . . . . . . *SYSDFT        Name, *SYSDFT, F4 for List
Library . . . . . . . .               Name, *CURLIB, *LIBL
Output . . . . . . . . 1              1=Display, 2=Printer 3=File
                                                          Bottom
F3=Exit   F4=Prompt   F12=Cancel
```

For now, we assume the default options are acceptable. Press Enter to execute the statement. The results are presented in the "Display Report" screen.

```
                          Display Report
Query . . . . .: *                    Width . . .: 71
Form . . . . .: *SYSDFT               Column . .: 1
Control . . . .
Line ....+....1....+....2....+....3....+....4....+....5....+....6....+....7.
        CNO  CRED
        ----  ----
000001  C11    3
000002  C22    3
000003  C33    3
000004  C44    3
000005  C55    3
000006  C66    3
****** * * * * * E N D  O F  D A T A * * * * *
                                                      Bottom
F3=Exit  F12=Cancel  F19=Left  F20=Right  F21=Split
```

Temporarily ignore the information shown at the top and bottom of the screen. Observe that the result table is correctly displayed in the center of the screen. When you finish your review of the report, press the F3 key to return to the Edit Query screen. Before returning, Query Manager displays the "Exit" screen.

```
----------------------------------------------------------
|                          Exit                          |
|                                                        |
| Type choice, press Enter.                              |
|  Option . . . . . 1      1=Exit saving active data     |
|                          2=Exit without saving active data |
|                          3=Resume displayed report     |
|                                                        |
|  F12=Cancel                                            |
----------------------------------------------------------
                                                      Bottom
F3=Exit  F12=Cancel  F19=Left  F20=Right  F21=Split
```

Choose the default option of 1 and press Enter to return to the Edit Query screen. You can now modify the current query or enter a new query.

EDITING AN SQL STATEMENT

Query Manager provides some simple editing commands. We will introduce these commands next and also highlight some related options. As with the screens presented so far, function key options are identified at the bottom of the screen.

The Insert command

Assume you have just executed the previous SELECT statement, the result has been displayed, and the cursor is positioned after the last SQL line. You can request that the system insert a new line by typing an "I" over any position in the editor line number and pressing the Enter key. The system will respond by inserting a new line after the current one. Thus, the Insert command gives you the flexibility to expand your SQL statements without retyping them.

```
                               Edit Query
   Columns . . . : 1 70                           Query . . . :
   QM . .
   Type SQL Statement
       ************************* Beginning of Data *************************
   0001.00 SELECT CNO, CRED
   0002.00 FROM COURSE
   I003.00 WHERE CDEPT = 'CIS'
       *************************** End of Data ***************************

   F2=Alternate keys     F3=Exit      F4=Prompt    F5=Run report    F6=Run sample
   F9=Retrieve           F15=Check syntax          F24=More keys
```

Press Enter to execute the insert command.

```
                               Edit Query
   Columns . . . : 1 70                           Query . . . :
   QM . .
   Type SQL Statement
       ************************* Beginning of Data *************************
   0001.00 SELECT CNO, CRED
   0002.00 FROM COURSE
   0003.00 WHERE CDEPT = 'CIS'
   ' ' ' ' ' ' '
       *************************** End of Data ***************************

   F2=Alternate keys     F3=Exit      F4=Prompt    F5=Run report    F6=Run sample
   F9=Retrieve           F15=Check syntax          F24=More keys
```

The Delete command

The Delete command allows you to remove unwanted statements. Assume that you wish to remove the "WHERE" clause from your SQL statement. Simply type "D" in the first position of line three.

```
                            Edit Query
Columns . . . : 1 70                      Query . . . :
QM . .
Type SQL Statement
    ************************** Beginning of Data ***********************
0001.00 SELECT CNO, CRED
0002.00 FROM COURSE
D003.00 WHERE CDEPT = 'CIS'
' ' ' ' ' ' '
    *************************** End of Data **************************


F2=Alternate keys    F3=Exit      F4=Prompt    F5=Run report    F6=Run sample
F9=Retrieve          F15=Check syntax          F24=More keys
```

To execute the Delete command, press Enter.

```
                            Edit Query
Columns . . . : 1 70                      Query . . . :
QM . .
Type SQL Statement
    ************************** Beginning of Data ***********************
0001.00 SELECT CNO, CRED
0002.00 FROM COURSE
    *************************** End of Data **************************


F2=Alternate keys    F3=Exit      F4=Prompt    F5=Run report    F6=Run sample
F9=Retrieve          F15=Check syntax          F24=More keys
```

You can also perform a delete of a block of lines by placing "DD" on the very first and last lines of the block you wish to delete. Then press Enter.

The Copy command

The Copy command allows you to reorganize the structure of your SQL statement. Assume you entered the SQL statement in the wrong format. You could move or copy the line to the correct position by placing a "C" on the line you wish to copy and a "B" (Before) or an "A" (After) on the line you wish to copy to. The incorrect line could then be deleted.

```
                              Edit Query
Columns . . . : 1 70                          Query . . . :
QM . .
Type SQL Statement
    **************************** Beginning of Data *************************
C001.00 FROM COURSE
A002.00 SELECT CNO, CRED
    **************************** End of Data ****************************

F2=Alternate keys  F3=Exit  F4=Prompt  F5=Run report  F6=Run sample
F9=Retrieve    F15=Check syntax        F24=More keys
```

Press Enter to execute Copy command.

```
                              Edit Query
Columns . . . : 1 70                          Query . . . :
QM . .
Type SQL Statement
    **************************** Beginning of Data *********************
0001.00 FROM COURSE
0002.00 SELECT CNO, CRED
0003.00 FROM COURSE
    **************************** End of Data ****************************

F2=Alternate keys  F3=Exit  F4=Prompt  F5=Run report  F6=Run sample
F9=Retrieve    F15=Check syntax        F24=More keys
```

You can also copy a block of lines by placing "CC" on the first and last lines of the block you wish to copy. As with previous examples, specify a "B" (Before) or an "A" (After) to indicate the destination of the copied lines. Then press Enter.

SQL syntax checking

By pressing F15 you can verify the syntax of your SQL statement without executing it.

```
                              Edit Query
Columns . . . : 1 70                            Query . . . :
QM . .
Type SQL Statement
    *************************** Beginning of Data *************************
0001.00 SELECT CNO, CRED
0002.00 FROM COURSE
    *************************** End of Data ****************************

F2=Alternate keys    F3=Exit       F4=Prompt    F5=Run report    F6=Run sample
F9=Retrieve          F15=Check syntax            F24=More keys
  The SQL statement is valid.
```

This option saves the resources that are used to start the execution of a query. It should be used if you have questions about the syntax of a query, saving time and system resources.

SQL statement prompting

By pressing F4 you can invoke statement prompting. Query Manager will present a screen with the associated statement options.

```
                     Specify SELECT Statement
Type information for SELECT statement. Press F4 for a list.

FROM files . . . . . . . . .  COURSE
SELECT fields. . . . . . . .  CNO, CRED
WHERE conditions . . . . . .
GROUP BY fields. . . . . . .
HAVING conditions. . . . . .
ORDER BY fields. . . . . . .
FOR UPDATE OF fields . . . .
                                          Bottom
Type choices, press Enter.
  Number of records to optimize . . . . . . . . .
  DISTINCT records in result file . . . . . . . .   N    Y=Yes, N=No
  FOR FETCH ONLY . . . . . . . . . . . . . . . .    N    Y=Yes, N=No
  UNION with another SELECT . . . . . . . . . . .   N    Y=Yes, N=No

F3=Exit       F4=Prompt   F5=Refresh      F6=Insert line  F9=Specify subquery
F10=Copy line F12=Cancel  F14=Delete line F15=Split line  F24=More keys
```

This is a helpful option to assist you in learning SQL statements. You may also use F4 on any field for specific field choices.

Prompting in this mode is optional. However, it is possible for the System Manager to specify Prompted Query Mode as your default mode. In this case, the ability to enter free-format queries and prompt input is not optional.

DRAW command

By entering the "DRAW" command on the Query Manager statement line, Query Manager will create a generic statement to extract all fields and rows from the designated file.

```
                              Edit Query
Columns . . . : 1 70                          Query . . . :
QM . . DRAW COURSE
Type SQL Statement
    ************************* Beginning of Data *************************
0001.00
    ************************* End of Data *************************


F2=Alternate keys    F3=Exit        F4=Prompt   F5=Run report   F6=Run sample
F9=Retrieve          F15=Check syntax           F24=More keys
```

Press Enter to execute the Draw command.

```
                              Edit Query
Columns . . . : 1 70                          Query . . . :
QM . .
Type SQL Statement
    ************************* Beginning of Data *************************
0001.00
0002.00 SELECT CNO, CNAME, CDESCP, CRED, CLABFEE, CDEPT FROM COURSE
    ************************* End of Data *************************

F2=Alternate keys    F3=Exit        F4=Prompt   F5=Run report   F6=Run sample
F9=Retrieve          F15=Check syntax           F24=More keys
```

This is a helpful option to assist you in identifying columns (fields) in a table (file) and building an SQL prototype statement. Chapter 11 will discuss how to use control language commands to see the column layout.

SIMPLE REPORT FORMATTING

The previous examples display data without consideration to formatting. Query Manager provides options which can be used to display data retrieved by a SELECT statement in a traditional report. In this section we introduce some simple options to modify column titles and edit column data. In Chap. 10 we return to report formatting and describe how to produce report titles, establish control breaks, and perform summary arithmetic at control breaks. Before presenting specific commands, we make some general statements.

1. Each of the following report formatting options must be entered *before* executing the SELECT statement which retrieves the data for the report. Otherwise, Query Manager will generate a default report format.
2. Each report format is in effect as long as you specify it on the Run Query Screen form entry. *SYSDFT is the option for a system-generated report format.
3. We usually think of a report as being printed on one or more pages of paper, i.e., a hard copy. In the following discussion we use the term *report* to refer to the output display as shown on the terminal screen. In Chap. 10 we will show how to generate a hard copy which is a mirror image of the report displayed on the screen.
4. Report formats are physically independent of SQL statements. This flexibility allows you to define multiple outputs for one SQL statement.

Defining the report form

You may access the form definition screen by pressing F13 from the editor screen or by selecting "Work with Query Manager Report Forms" from the Query Manager main menu. After pressing F13 while in the editor the system will display:

```
Select Report Format
  Form . . . . . . . : *

  Type options, press Enter. Press F21 to select all.
  1=Select

  Opt     Report Format
  Edit column formatting
  Edit page heading
  Edit page footing
  Edit final text
  Edit break text
  Specify formatting options
                                             Bottom

  F3=Exit         F5=Run report  F12=Cancel  F13=Edit query  F18=Display SQL
  F21=Select all  F22=QM Statement
```

Note the report-form definitions are separate from the editor definitions. They are the same when you either run the query first or load the query from the Edit Column formatting option.

Column formatting

The "Edit Column Formatting" option has variations which serve many different purposes. We present two variations. Elements that can be modified are:

1. *Heading.* The column headings can be modified by pressing F11.

2. *Usage.* This column provides the ability to enter the type of event that will be performed on this column. Events include Omit, Aggregation, and Report Formatting. Omit provides the ability to have a column defined but excluded from the report output. Aggregation and Report Formatting will be discussed in a later chapter.

3. *Edit.* Edit codes can be entered for Character, Numeric, Date, Time, and Graphic Data.

4. *Seq.* Sequence order of the columns can be changed by changing the column sequence number.

5. *Indent.* Indentation spaces can be adjusted between the margins and columns by changing the number of characters to space. The default is two characters.

Before discussing these options, it would be helpful to reexamine the output display for Sample Query 1.1. In order to produce this "pretty" report, certain Report Formatting options (shown in the following section) had to be entered before executing the SELECT statement. What if these options had not been entered? Then the first few rows of the output display would appear as follows:

```
                              Display Report
Query . . . . .:    *                    Width . . .: 142
Form  . . . . .:    *SYSDFT              Column. . .:    1
Control . . . .
Line     ....+...1...+...2...+...3...+...4...+...5...+...6...+...7.
              CNO  CNAME                  CDESCP               CRED CLABFEE
              ---  -------------------    -------------------- ---- -------
000001   C11  INTRO TO CS             FOR ROOKIES              3 100.00
000002   C22  DATA STRUCTURES         VERY USEFUL              3  50.00
000003   C33  DISCRETE MATHEMATICS    ABSOLUTELY NECESSARY       25.00
000004   C44  DIGITAL CIRCUITS        AH HA!                   3  25.00
000005   C55  COMPUTER ARCH.          VON NEUMANN'S MACH.      3 100.00

                                                              More...

 F3=Exit   F12=Cancel   F19=Left   F20=Right   F21=Split
```

The length of each displayed row exceeds the width of the screen and is truncated on the screen. The F19 or F20 keys can be used to scroll the screen left or right. Key F21 can be used to split the screen and freeze the left columns. This allows you to view the information on the left side of the screen as you scroll the right side.

The default column width is the larger of the column name or column size definition.

The Column Format specification

This section describes the Column Formatting options specification. The modified options appear as follows:

```
                        Select Report Format
Form . . . . . . . . : *
Type options, press Enter. Press F21 to select all.
1=Select


Opt       Report Format
1         Edit column formatting
          Edit page heading
          Edit page footing
          Edit final text
          Edit break text
          Specify formatting options
                                                      Bottom


F3=Exit          F5=Run report   F12=Cancel  F13=Edit query   F18=Display SQL
F21=Select all   F22=QM Statement
```

We begin by showing the Edit Report Format options used to produce the output shown in the sample queries presented in Chap. 1. Place a "1" next to the Edit Column Formatting to display the column options.

```
                     Edit Column Formatting
Type information, press Enter.
For Usage and Edit, press F4 for list.
For Heading, press F4 for prompt.
Column     Heading            Usage    Edit    Seq   Indent    Width
1          CNO                                  1      2         3
2          CNAME                                2      2        20
3          CDESCP                               3      2        20
4          CRED                                 4      2         4
5          CLABFEE                     D2       5      2         7
6          CDEPT                                6      2         5
                                                    Bottom

F2=Alternate keys   F3=Exit      F4=Prompt    F5=Run report   F6=Insert line
F10=Copy line       F11=Edit heading          F12=Cancel      F24=More keys
```

The CNAME column-width specification is 20. This column was defined with a maximum length of 22, but none of the actual values reach this length. Therefore, we can reduce the width of this column and other columns to avoid screen truncation and not lose any data. The 20 specification saves two spaces.

The CDESCP column has a maximum length of 25. We specify 20 for the same reason as we did for CNAME.

The CLABFEE column can contain five-digit numeric values with two-digit decimal accuracy. Recall that the column was defined in the table with a width of 7 with two decimal places. If we wanted to display the data in a currency format we would enter the edit code of D2.

Figures 2.1 and 2.2 present an overview of some of the more popular Edit codes. (Other specifications for the DATE and TIME data types will be shown in Chap. 10.)

C	Character with truncate
CW	Character with width wrap
CT	Character with text wrap
D,I,J,K,L and P	Decimal notation
E	Scientific notation

Figure 2.1   Symbols used in FORMAT specifications.

EDIT CODE	Stored value	Column width*	Displayed result
C	ABC ACBDEXYZ	5	ABC ACBDE
CW	ABC ACBDEXYZ	5	ABC ACBDE (wrap) XYZ
CT	SQL FUN	4	SQL FUN
	SQL-FUN	4	SQL- FUN
DO	1099.99	6 5	$1,100 ***** (overflow)
D2	−11099.99	11 10	−$11,099.99 **********
IO	−11099.99	8	−0011100
JO	−11099.99	7	0011100
KO	−11099.99	7	−11,100
LO	−11099.99	7	−111100
E	−11099.99	10	−1.1E+004
PO	−11099.99	8	−11,100%

Figure 2.2   Sample Column Formatting specifications.

The Edit Heading

In Sample Queries 1.1 through 1.12, column names were displayed as the default column headings. A way to display an alternative column heading for a designated column is to modify the HEADING specification on the Edit Column Formatting screen. This is accomplished by pressing function key F11 to Edit Heading text. The Edit Column Formatting screen to change headings would appear as follows:

```
                        Edit Column Formatting
    Type information, press Enter.
    For Usage and Edit, press F4 for list.
    For Heading, press F4 for prompt.

    Column     Heading
    1          CNO
    2          CNAME
    3          CDESCP
    4          CRED
    5          CLABFEE
    6          CDEPT
                                                        Bottom

    F2=Alternate keys    F3=Exit      F4=Prompt    F5=Run report    F6=Insert line
    F10=Copy line    F11=Edit usage     F12=Cancel    F13=Edit query   F24=More keys
```

By pressing function key F11 you would return to the Edit Column Formatting screen.

```
                        Edit Column Formatting
    Type information, press Enter.
    For Usage and Edit, press F4 for list.
    For Heading, press F4 for prompt.

    Column     Heading              Usage    Edit    Seq    Indent    Width
    1          CNO                                    1        2        3
    2          CNAME                                  2        2        20
    3          CDESCP                                 3        2        20
    4          CRED                                   4        2        4
    5          CLABFEE                       D2       5        2        7
    6          CDEPT                                  6        2        5
                                                    Bottom

    F2=Alternate keys    F3=Exit      F4=Prompt    F5=Run report    F6=Insert line
    F10=Copy line        F11=Edit heading      F12=Cancel       F24=More keys
```

The underscore (_) is used to force the wrapping of the column heading. If we changed CLABFEE to LAB_FEE, the resulting display would place the word FEE on the line below the word LAB. Note that Query Manager will center the bottom line with the top line.

```
                                Edit Query
Columns . . . : 1 70                              Query . . . :
QM . .
Type SQL Statement
    *********************** Beginning of Data ***********************
0001.00 SELECT *
0002.00 FROM COURSE
0003.00
    *************************** End of Data ***************************

F2=Alternate keys   F3=Exit       F4=Prompt   F5=Run report   F6=Run sample
F9=Retrieve         F15=Check syntax          F24=More keys
```

Other Editor options

F6   *Run sample.*   This option will execute the SQL statement and only return the sample number of rows defined in your Query Manager profile.

F21   *System command.*   Control language commands can be entered in a window that is provided.

SUMMARY

This chapter introduced a small subset of SQL/400 Query Manager options. We saw the "tip of the iceberg." Among those options we discussed were the following:

1. Options to edit the SQL buffer: Copy, Delete, Insert, Draw

2. Options to produce report page titles and report page footers

3. Selected specifications of the Edit Column Format screen for report formatting: HEADING, EDIT, SEQUENCE, INDENT, WIDTH

We reiterate the objectives of this chapter. The first was to provide enough information so that you would be able to use the SQL/400 Query Manager to execute SQL statements and generate a readable report. A second objective was to emphasize the conceptual difference between entering SQL statements and SQL/400 options.

Summary exercise

2A. We encourage you to experiment with the commands that have been presented in this chapter.

Sorting the "Result" Table

Whenever you display more than a few rows, it is usually desirable to have the result displayed in some specific row sequence. This objective can be realized by including an ORDER BY clause in the SELECT statement. This chapter will present five sample queries which demonstrate the simplicity and flexibility of the ORDER BY clause.

Before presenting the sample queries, a simple but very important point needs to be emphasized. The process of executing a SELECT statement effectively identifies a table which constitutes the displayed output. We call this table the *result table*. Very often this result table consists of just a single column and/or a single row. Nevertheless, it is still a table. The content of the result table happens to be derived from the table specified in the FROM clause. But it is a different table. We emphasize this rather obvious point because sorting applies to the result table only. The result table is a temporary table, and it disappears when the next SQL statement is executed. The key point is that you can make no assumptions about the sequence of the underlying table referenced in the FROM clause. As stated in Chap. 1, this "permanent" table has no inherent row sequence. This is not changed by the query which contains an ORDER BY clause.

ORDER BY CLAUSE

The first sample query illustrates the ORDER BY clause to sort the result table by a single column. Note that this clause is merely appended to a standard SELECT statement.

Sample Query 3.1   Display the entire COURSE table. Sort the output display by the CLABFEE values.

```
SELECT      *

FROM        COURSE

ORDER  BY  CLABFEE
```

CNO	CNAME	CDESCP	CRED	CLABFEE	CDEPT
T33	HEDONISM	FOR THE SANE	3	.00	THEO
P44	SOLIPSISM	ME MYSELF AND I	6	.00	PHIL
C33	DISCRETE MATHEMATICS	ABSOLUTELY NECESSARY	3	.00	CIS
C44	DIGITAL CIRCUITS	AH HA!	3	.00	CIS
P22	RATIONALISM	FOR CIS MAJORS	3	50.00	PHIL
C22	DATA STRUCTURES	VERY USEFUL	3	50.00	CIS
T12	FUNDAMENTALISM	FOR THE CAREFREE	3	90.00	THEO
P11	EMPIRICISM	SEE IT-BELIEVE IT	3	100.00	PHIL
C11	INTRO TO CS	FOR ROOKIES	3	100.00	CIS
C55	COMPUTER ARCH.	VON NEUMANN'S MACH.	3	100.00	CIS
T11	SCHOLASTICISM	FOR THE PIOUS	3	150.00	THEO
T44	COMMUNISM	FOR THE GREEDY	6	200.00	THEO
P33	EXISTENTIALISM	FOR CIS MAJORS	3	200.00	PHIL
C66	RELATIONAL DATABASE	THE ONLY WAY TO GO	3	500.00	CIS

Comments

1. *Syntax:* When used, the ORDER BY clause is almost always the last clause in any SELECT statement.

2. The sort occurs in ascending sequence. This is the default sequence used by SQL/400. We could have explicitly requested an ascending sort sequence by including the ASC parameter in the ORDER BY clause. The following ORDER BY clause is equivalent to the one shown in the example.

   ```
   ORDER BY CLABFEE ASC
   ```

   The ASC parameter is rarely used in practice. Its only purpose is to enhance readability of a query by explicitly indicating an ascending sort sequence.

   It is possible to display output in a descending row sequence. The next sample query will illustrate the DESC parameter to achieve this objective.

3. The sort field, CLABFEE, is numeric. Hence the sort reflects a sequence based on mathematical value. If there were negative values in the CLABFEE column, they would have appeared before the zero and positive values.

   We can also sort on character string columns. The next sample query will illustrate sorting on a character column.

4. There are duplicate values in the CLABFEE column. We can make no assumptions about the sort sequence within matching values. Sample Query 3.3 will illustrate sorting on multiple columns to establish a second-level sort field within matching values.

5. Note that the sort column of this query is not the leftmost column. Most users typically establish the sort column as the leftmost column. This example illustrates that you can sort on any column.

6. Finally, we emphasize that sorting applies to the displayed result only. The data within the stored table remain unchanged.

Exercise

3A. Display the entire COURSE table. Sort the result by the CDEPT column in ascending sequence.

DESCENDING SORT

The next sample query demonstrates the use of the DESC parameter to produce a result which is sorted in descending sequence.

Sample Query 3.2 Select the course number, name, and credit of any course which is offered by the computer and information science department. Sort the result by course number in descending sequence.

```
SELECT      CNO, CNAME, CRED

FROM        COURSE

WHERE       CDEPT = 'CIS'

ORDER  BY  CNO  DESC
```

CNO	CNAME	CRED
C66	RELATIONAL DATABASE	3
C55	COMPUTER ARCH.	3
C44	DIGITAL CIRCUITS	3
C33	DISCRETE MATHEMATICS	3
C22	DATA STRUCTURES	3
C11	INTRO TO CS	3

Comments

1. *Syntax:* DESC follows the column name in the ORDER BY clause. One or more spaces must separate the column name and the DESC parameter. (A comma cannot be used as a separator.)

2. The sort column (CNO) contains character data. Recall that the EBCDIC codes specify the sequence for character data. Review the comments for Sample Query 1.5.

3. Within the COURSE table every CNO value is unique. Hence the row sequence was completely determined.

4. Unlike the preceding sample query, this query displays just some columns. There is a restriction which applies to SQL/400. In the SQL/400 version of SQL, the ORDER BY clause can reference only a column which is specified in the SELECT clause. For example, the following statement is *invalid* in SQL/400 because CLABFEE is not specified in the SELECT clause.

```
SELECT CNO, CNAME, CRED
FROM COURSE
WHERE CDEPT = 'CIS'
ORDER BY CLABFEE
```

Exercise

3B. Display the course name and lab fee for all courses offered by the philosophy department. Sort the result by course name in descending sequence.

SORTING ON MULTIPLE COLUMNS

Recall in Sample Query 3.1 that the sort column (CLABFEE) contained nonunique values. For this reason the row sequence was not completely determined. The next sample query illustrates that the ORDER BY clause may reference multiple columns. We will see that proper specification of multiple columns in the ORDER BY clause permits complete determination of the row sequence in any desired order.

Sample Query 3.3 Display the department identifier and name of every course. Sort the result by department identifier. Within each department, sort by course name.

```
SELECT   CDEPT,  CNAME

FROM     COURSE

ORDER BY CDEPT,  CNAME
```

CDEPT	CNAME
CIS	COMPUTER ARCH.
CIS	DATA STRUCTURES
CIS	DIGITAL CIRCUITS
CIS	DISCRETE MATHEMATICS
CIS	INTRO TO CS
CIS	RELATIONAL DATABASE
PHIL	EMPIRICISM
PHIL	RATIONALISM
PHIL	SOLIPSISM
THEO	COMMUNISM
THEO	FUNDAMENTALISM
THEO	HEDONISM
THEO	SCHOLASTICISM

Comments

1. *Terminology.* This example has two sort columns (fields). There are different ways of expressing the sort relationship between the two columns. The following statements are equivalent.

   a. CDEPT is the major sort field, and CNAME is the minor sort field.
   b. CDEPT is the primary sort field, and CNAME is the secondary sort field.
   c. CDEPT is the first-level sort field, and CNAME is the second-level sort field.
   d. The sort sequence is CNAME within CDEPT.

2. *Syntax.* The "ORDER BY" is followed by the major sort field which is followed by the minor sort field. The sort field column names must be separated by a comma.

3. Both the major and minor sorts default to ascending sequence. We can mix ascending and descending sequences within the different sort fields. (See Sample Query 3.5.)

4. Both the major and minor sort fields contain alphanumeric data. This is not necessary. (See Sample Query 3.5.)

5. There is no practical limit on the number of sort fields. The following ORDER BY clause is valid and would establish a four-level sort sequence.

```
ORDER BY CRED, CLABFEE, CDEPT, CNAME
```

Note that, as stated previously, the ORDER BY columns must also be present in the Select clause.

Exercise

3C. Display the CNAME, CNO, CRED, and CLABFEE columns (in that order) for every row in the table. Sort the displayed rows by CNO within CLABFEE. (CLABFEE is the major sort field, and CNO is the minor sort field.)

ORDER BY COLUMN-NUMBER

The ORDER BY clause can also reference a column by its relative position in the output display. This is a convenience which can save you keystroke effort. The next sample query produces an output display which is sorted by the second column.

Sample Query 3.4   Display the CNO, CLABFEE, and CRED values, in that order, for all courses. Sort the result by the second column (CLABFEE).

```
SELECT   CNO,   CLABFEE,   CRED

FROM     COURSE

ORDER   BY   2
```

CNO	CLABFEE	CRED
T33	.00	3
P44	.00	6
C33	.00	3
C44	.00	3
P22	50.00	3
C22	50.00	3
T12	90.00	3
P11	100.00	3
C11	100.00	3
C55	100.00	3
T11	150.00	3
T44	200.00	6
P33	200.00	3
C66	500.00	3

Comments

1. The use of a relative column number is not necessary in this example. The following equivalent clause will achieve the same objective.

   `ORDER BY CLABFEE`

   The use of relative column numbers is an acceptable convenience for use with one-time ad hoc queries. For statements which will be saved for future execution, it is better to explicitly name the column in the ORDER BY clause. This enhances readability and is not affected by a reordering of column names in the SELECT clause. This is especially true for SELECT statements to be embedded in application programs.

2. In future chapters we will present built-in functions and calculated columns. Display columns generated by these techniques could be referenced by their relative column position.

3. The DESC parameter can be used with relative column numbers. The following clause is valid.

   `ORDER BY 2 DESC`

Exercise

3D. Display the entire COURSE table sorted in descending sequence by the third column.

The final sample query in this chapter illustrates that all of the previously described variations of the ORDER BY clause can be incorporated within a single clause. This clause references both column numbers and names. This example is not very realistic. However, it does demonstrate the flexibility of the ORDER BY clause.

Sample Query 3.5   Display the CDEPT, CLABFEE, and CRED values, in that order, for all courses. CDEPT is the first-level sort field (ascending); CRED is the second-level sort field (descending); and CLABFEE is the third-level sort field (descending).

SELECT   CDEPT, CLABFEE, CRED

FROM   COURSE

ORDE BY CDEPT, 3 DESC, CLABFEE DESC

CDEPT	CLABFEE	CRED
CIS	500.00	3
CIS	100.00	3
CIS	100.00	3
CIS	50.00	3
CIS	.00	3
CIS	.00	3
PHIL	.00	6
PHIL	200.00	3
PHIL	100.00	3
PHIL	50.00	3
THEO	200.00	6
THEO	150.00	3
THEO	90.00	3
THEO	.00	3

Comments

1. This sample query sorts on three columns. The ORDER BY clause does the following:

   - References some columns by name (CDEPT and CLABFEE) and another by relative column number (CRED is identified as the third column).
   - Sorts one column (CDEPT) in ascending sequence and two columns (CRED and CLABFEE) in descending sequence.

2. Note that none of the displayed columns contain unique values. Hence duplicate rows can (and do) appear in the output display. Because this result is sequenced, it is easier to detect duplicate rows. Recall that duplicate rows can be removed from the displayed output by specifying DISTINCT in the SELECT clause.

Exercise

3E. Display the CDEPT, CLABFEE, and CNAME values of all three credit courses. Sort the output result. CDEPT is the first-level sort field (ascending); CLABFEE is the second-level sort field (descending); and CNAME is the third-level sort field (ascending).

SUMMARY

This chapter has expanded on the fundamental structure of the SELECT statement by including the ORDER BY clause.

```
SELECT column name(s)
FROM table name
WHERE condition
ORDER BY sort-column(s)
```

The result table can be sorted on any column(s). The ORDER BY clause can reference the column name or relative column number. The default sort sequence is ascending (ASC). A descending sequence can be established by using the DESC parameter.

We conclude with some final comments regarding the terms *sort* and *sequence*. We have casually used these terms as though they were synonymous. However, to be precise, the objective of all previous sample queries was to display the result table in some specified row sequence. The system may have to execute a sort utility to achieve this objective. Part 4 of this text will examine indexes. There we will note that the system can sometimes utilize an index to avoid execution of a sort utility. At this point you should not focus on the internal processes which the system follows to produce the output in row sequence. However, you should be aware that the ORDER BY clause usually requires the system to do more work. This could be significant if the number of selected rows is large. Therefore, you are advised to exercise judgment in use of the ORDER BY clause.

Summary exercises

The following exercises all refer to the STAFF table. The column names are ENAME, ETITLE, ESALARY, and DEPT.

3F. Display the entire STAFF table. Sort it by employee name.

3G. Display the name and salary of any employee earning less than $1000. Sort the result by salary in descending sequence.

3H. Display all information about employees who work in the theology department. Sort the result by employee title.

3I. Display the department identifier, employee name, and salary for all employees. Sort the result by salary within department.

3J. Display the department identifier, employee title, and salary for all staff members. Let department identifier be the major sort field (in ascending sequence) and salary be the minor sort field (in descending sequence).

Boolean Connectors:
AND-OR-NOT

Row selection in the previous chapters was based on a single condition. In this chapter we present the use of Boolean connectors to facilitate row selection based on multiple conditions. The first 12 sample queries illustrate the classical Boolean connectors of AND, OR, and NOT. The remaining sample queries will introduce you to the keywords IN and BETWEEN. You will learn that you can do without IN and BETWEEN because the classical operators provide the expressive power to formulate any row selection criteria. However, you will also find that IN and BETWEEN are very useful because they provide a more compact way of expressing certain row-selection criteria.

AND CONNECTOR

The first sample query illustrates the AND connector. The AND is placed between two row-selection conditions within the WHERE clause. The intent is to request the system to select an individual row only if both of the conditions are satisfied.

Sample Query 4.1   Display all information about any CIS course which has a zero lab fee.

SELECT	*
FROM	COURSE
WHERE	CLABFEE = 0
AND	CDEPT = 'CIS'

CNO	CNAME	CDESCP	CRED	CLABFEE	CDEPT
C33	DISCRETE MATHEMATICS	ABSOLUTELY NECESSARY	3	.00	CIS
C44	DIGITAL CIRCUITS	AH HA!	3	.00	CIS

Comments

1. *Logic.* The example shows two conditions which are connected by the AND Boolean connector. These two conditions are

   a. CLABFEE = 0

   b. CDEPT = 'CIS'

   Note that each of the output rows matches both conditions. Observe that the COURSE table contains additional rows which match just one or the other, but not both, of these conditions. There are philosophy and theology courses which have zero lab fees. Likewise, there are computer and information science courses with nonzero lab fees. These rows were not selected because they met only one of the two specified conditions.

2. *Syntax.* The primary requirement is that individual conditions be syntactically correct. The sample query shows the conditions written on separate lines. This is not required, but it enhances readability. Recall that a SELECT statement is free form and can be written on any number of lines. Therefore, each of the following statements is equivalent to the current example.

```
SELECT    *
FROM      COURSE
WHERE     CLABFEE = 0 AND CDEPT = 'CIS'

SELECT    *
FROM      COURSE
WHERE     CLABFEE = 0 AND
          CDEPT = 'CIS'

SELECT    *  FROM COURSE
WHERE     CLABFEE = 0 AND CDEPT = 'CIS'

SELECT    *  FROM COURSE
WHERE     CLABFEE = 0
          AND
          CDEPT = 'CIS
```

3. The order in which the conditions are specified should have no effect on the performance. The following compound WHERE conditions should execute with the same efficiency and will produce the same result.

```
WHERE CLABFEE = 0 AND CDEPT = 'CIS'
WHERE CDEPT = 'CIS' AND CLABFEE = 0
```

Exercise

4A. Display all information about three-credit courses offered by the philosophy department.

Like the previous sample query, the following example connects multiple conditions using AND. This time both of the conditions reference the same column (CLABFEE). The intention is to select rows where the CLABFEE value falls within a certain range.

Sample Query 4.2   Display all information about any course having a lab fee which is strictly between $0 and $100.

```
SELECT      *

FROM        COURSE

WHERE       CLABFEE > 0

AND         CLABFEE < 100
```

CNO	CNAME	CDESCP	CRED	CLABFEE	CDEPT
T12	FUNDAMENTALISM	FOR THE CAREFREE	3	90.00	THEO
P22	RATIONALISM	FOR CIS MAJORS	3	50.00	PHIL
C22	DATA STRUCTURES	VERY USEFUL	3	50.00	CIS

Comments

1. *Logic.* The example selected rows where the CLABFEE value was strictly greater than 0 and strictly less than 100. Note that rows with CLABFEE values of 0 and 100 were not selected.

2. *Syntax.* The column name must be specified in both conditions. The following WHERE clause is invalid and will cause an *error.*

   ```
   WHERE CLABFEE > 0 AND < 100
   ```

Exercise

4B. Display all information about any course which has a lab fee between and including $100 and $500.

MULTIPLE ANDs

It is possible to connect multiple conditions using many AND connectors. The next example illustrates four conditions which are AND-connected. In this case a given row will be selected only if it matches all four of the specified conditions.

Sample Query 4.3   Display all information about any three-credit philosophy course which has a lab fee strictly between $0 and $100.

```
SELECT      *

FROM        COURSE

WHERE       CLABFEE > 0

AND         CLABFEE < 100

AND         CDEPT = 'PHIL'

AND         CRED = 3
```

CNO	CNAME	CDESCP	CRED	CLABFEE	CDEPT
P22	RATIONALISM	FOR CIS MAJORS	3	50.00	PHIL

Comment

For all practical purposes there is no limit on the number of conditions which can be used in a WHERE clause.

Exercise

4C. Display all information about any three-credit theology course with a lab fee between and including $100 and $400.

OR CONNECTOR

Like the AND connector, the OR connector will connect multiple conditions within a WHERE clause. However, OR connectors have a different impact on the logic of the row selection process. Assuming that just two conditions are OR-connected, a given row will be selected if it matches either or both of the specified conditions. The next sample query illustrates this point.

Sample Query 4.4   Display all information about any course offered by the CIS or PHIL department.

```
SELECT      *

FROM        COURSE

WHERE       CDEPT = 'CIS'

OR          CDEPT = 'PHIL'
```

CNO	CNAME	CDESCP	CRED	CLABFEE	CDEPT
P11	EMPIRICISM	SEE IT—BELIEVE IT	3	100.00	PHIL
P22	RATIONALISM	FOR CIS MAJORS	3	50.00	PHIL
P33	EXISTENTIALISM	FOR CIS MAJORS	3	200.00	PHIL
P44	SOLIPSISM	ME MYSELF AND I	6	.00	PHIL
C11	INTRO TO CS	FOR ROOKIES	3	100.00	CIS
C22	DATA STRUCTURES	VERY USEFUL	3	50.00	CIS
C33	DISCRETE MATHEMATICS	ABSOLUTELY NECESSARY	3	.00	CIS
C44	DIGITAL CIRCUITS	AH HA!	3	.00	CIS
C55	COMPUTER ARCH.	VON NEUMANN'S MACH.	3	100.00	CIS
C66	RELATIONAL DATABASE	THE ONLY WAY TO GO	3	500.00	CIS

Comments

1. *Logic.* The OR is an "inclusive" OR. This means that a row is selected under the special case where it matches on both of the specified conditions. This cannot happen in the current example because both conditions specify a different "equals" comparison on the same CDEPT field. The next sample query will illustrate a situation where some rows will match on both conditions.

2. *Syntax.* As with the AND Boolean operator, the free format of SQL allows flexibility. The following statements are equivalent to the current sample query.

```
SELECT    *
FROM      COURSE
WHERE     CDEPT = 'CIS' OR CDEPT = 'PHIL'

SELECT    *
FROM      COURSE
WHERE     CDEPT = 'CIS' OR
          CDEPT = 'PHIL'

SELECT    * FROM COURSE
WHERE     CDEPT = 'CIS' OR CDEPT = 'PHIL'

SELECT    *
FROM      COURSE
WHERE     CDEPT = 'CIS'
          OR
          CDEPT = 'PHIL'
```

3. Both conditions refer to the same CDEPT column. However, as with the AND connector, this column must be explicitly specified in each condition. This means that the following WHERE clause is *invalid*.

```
WHERE CDEPT = 'CIS' OR 'PHIL'
```

4. The order in which the column names are specified should not affect performance. The following compound WHERE clauses should execute with the same efficiency and produce the same result.

```
WHERE CDEPT = 'PHIL' OR CDEPT = 'CIS'
WHERE CDEPT = 'CIS' OR CDEPT = 'PHIL'
```

Exercise

4D. Display all information about every course offered by the philosophy or theology department.

The next sample query illustrates a situation where it is possible for a given row to match on both conditions. This demonstrates the "inclusive" behavior of the OR connector.

Sample Query 4.5   Display all information about any CIS course or any course with a zero lab fee.

SELECT	*
FROM	COURSE
WHERE	CLABFEE = 0.00
OR	CDEPT = 'CIS'

CNO	CNAME	CDESCP	CRED	CLABFEE	CDEPT
T33	HEDONISM	FOR THE SANE	3	.00	THEO
P44	SOLIPSISM	ME MYSELF AND I	6	.00	PHIL
C11	INTRO TO CS	FOR ROOKIES	3	100.00	CIS
C22	DATA STRUCTURES	VERY USEFUL	3	50.00	CIS
C33	DISCRETE MATHEMATICS	ABSOLUTELY NECESSARY	3	.00	CIS
C44	DIGITAL CIRCUITS	AH HA!	3	.00	CIS
C55	COMPUTER ARCH.	VON NEUMANN'S MACH.	3	100.00	CIS
C66	RELATIONAL DATABASE	THE ONLY WAY TO GO	3	500.00	CIS

Comment

This SELECT statement will display any row which has a CLABFEE value of zero or a CDEPT value of "CIS". Observe that all courses having a lab fee of zero are selected, regardless of their department ID. And all CIS courses are selected, regardless of their lab fee. Also, rows which match both conditions will be selected. Note that a row which matches both conditions, like the rows with CNO values of "C33" and "C44", will occur only once in the output display.

Exercise

4E. Select all information about any course which is offered by the theology department or is worth six credits.

MULTIPLE ORs

As with the AND connector, it is possible to connect any number of conditions using multiple OR connectors. The next example illustrates four conditions which are OR-connected. In this case a row will be selected if it matches any of the four specified conditions.

Sample Query 4.6   Display all information about any course which has a lab fee equal to $50, $100, $150, or $200.

SELECT	*
FROM	COURSE
WHERE	CLABFEE = 50
OR	CLABFEE = 100
OR	CLABFEE = 150
OR	CLABFEE = 200

CNO	CNAME	CDESCP	CRED	CLABFEE	CDEPT
T11	SCHOLASTICISM	FOR THE PIOUS	3	150.00	THEO
T44	COMMUNISM	FOR THE GREEDY	6	200.00	THEO
P11	EMPIRICISM	SEE IT—BELIEVE IT	3	100.00	PHIL
P22	RATIONALISM	FOR CIS MAJORS	3	50.00	PHIL
P33	EXISTENTIALISM	FOR CIS MAJORS	3	200.00	PHIL
C11	INTRO TO CS	FOR ROOKIES	3	100.00	CIS
C22	DATA STRUCTURES	VERY USEFUL	3	50.00	CIS
C55	COMPUTER ARCH.	VON NEUMANN'S MACH.	3	100.00	CIS

Comments

1. For all practical purposes, there is no limit on the number of conditions which can be OR-connected.

2. Note that the CLABFEE column must be explicitly referenced in each of the four conditions. Sample Query 4.13 will introduce the IN operator which offers a more compact way of expressing this query.

Exercise

4F. Display all information about any course which has a lab fee in the set {0.00, 90.00, 150.00}.

NOT KEYWORD

All previous examples specified conditions which explicitly identified, in a positive sense, the rows to be selected for display. The next sample query introduces the use of the NOT keyword which allows you to indicate those rows which you do not want selected for display. When a WHERE condition identifies rows which are not to be selected, the system assumes that you want to select all the other rows.

Sample Query 4.7   Display the course name and department identifier of any course which is not offered by the CIS department.

SELECT	CNAME, CDEPT
FROM	COURSE
WHERE	NOT CDEPT = 'CIS'

CNAME	CDEPT
SCHOLASTICISM	THEO
FUNDAMENTALISM	THEO
HEDONISM	THEO
COMMUNISM	THEO
EMPIRICISM	PHIL
RATIONALISM	PHIL
EXISTENTIALISM	PHIL
SOLIPSISM	PHIL

Comments

1. *Syntax.* The NOT operator can be placed before any legitimate conditional expression. The current example has a single condition which is negated by use of NOT. The format of the WHERE condition is

   ```
   WHERE NOT (conditional expression)
   ```

   Later in this chapter we will see more complex examples where NOT is used with a WHERE clause which contains multiple conditions.

2. The following statement is equivalent to the current example. It uses the special "not equals" comparison operator ($<>$).

   ```
   SELECT    *
   FROM      COURSE
   WHERE     CDEPT <> 'CIS'
   ```

3. Avoid making the common mistake of placing the NOT before a comparison operator. The following WHERE clause is *invalid* because the NOT immediately precedes the equal sign.

   ```
   WHERE CDEPT NOT = 'CIS'
   ```

4. If you are familiar with the basics of set theory, it may be helpful to think of NOT as a keyword which identifies the complement of a subset of rows from a table. The condition (CDEPT = 'CIS') effectively identifies a subset of rows from the COURSE table. By placing a NOT before this condition, you are requesting the system to select the complement (opposite) of this subset.

Exercise

4G. Select the course number, name, and lab fee of any course with a lab fee other than $100.

The next sample query shows a WHERE clause with two conditions, each of which is negated by use of NOT, and subsequently AND-connected. We will classify this WHERE clause as "complex," because, unlike all the previous WHERE clauses, it contains two different Boolean operators (NOT and AND). Our comments on the logic of this sample query serve as a prelude to the following detailed discussion on the hierarchy of Boolean operators.

Sample Query 4.8 Display the name and department identifier of all courses with the exception of those courses offered by the CIS and PHIL departments.

SELECT	CNAME, CDEPT
FROM C	OURSE
WHERE	NOT CDEPT = 'CIS'
AND	NOT CDEPT = 'PHIL'

CNAME	CDEPT
SCHOLASTICISM	THEO
FUNDAMENTALISM	THEO
HEDONISM	THEO
COMMUNISM	THEO

Comments

1. This is the first sample query where we have utilized two different Boolean operators (NOT and AND). This raises the question of hierarchy of execution, which will be addressed on the following page. With respect to the current example, we merely note that the system evaluates the NOT before the AND. This means that the WHERE clause is the AND of two negated conditions. Therefore, the system will select any row which meets both of the negated conditions. If a row has a CDEPT value not equal to "CIS" and it is also not equal to "PHIL", it will be selected.

2. We must always be careful when we are composing queries which use multiple different Boolean operators. For example, many people would articulate the current sample query as

> Select course names and departments for courses which are not offered by the CIS or PHIL department.

This statement may be grammatically correct. However, note that using "or" in the above English-language statement may entice the careless user to code an OR into the WHERE clause. The resulting SELECT statement (shown below) appears innocuous on initial inspection. But when we consider the precise meaning we observe that it is a rather silly way of selecting every row from the COURSE table.

```
SELECT    CNAME, CDEPT
FROM      COURSE
WHERE     NOT CDEPT = 'CIS'
OR        NOT CDEPT = 'PHIL'
```

Any CIS course would be selected by the second expression (NOT CDEPT = 'PHIL'), and any PHIL course would be selected by the first expression (NOT CDEPT = 'CIS').

3. Observe that this problem and subsequent logical problems described on the following pages are only indirectly related to SQL. The primary source of such problems is the ambiguous use of natural language and a careless approach toward the semantics of the Boolean operators. This transcends not only SQL but any other structured computer programming language.

Exercise

4H. Select the course number and lab fee for any course which has a lab fee other than $100 and $200.

HIERARCHY OF BOOLEAN OPERATORS

Whenever a WHERE clause contains more than two conditions which are connected by different Boolean operators, the system must decide on the order of execution. If the WHERE clause does not contain any parentheses, the system will follow a specific sequence. This sequence is defined by a hierarchy which dictates that

NOTs are evaluated first
ANDs are evaluated next
ORs are evaluated last

If you have written programs in any other language, you will recognize that this is the same hierarchy that you most likely encountered in that language. If SQL is your first computer language, then you should pay close attention to the next four sample queries which illustrate the hierarchy of Boolean operators.

Sample Query 4.9 Display all information about any theology course which has a zero lab fee, or any course (regardless of its department and lab fee) which is worth six credits.

SELECT	*
FROM	COURSE
WHERE	CDEPT = 'THEO'
AND	CLABFEE = 0
OR	CRED = 6

CNO	CNAME	CDESCP	CRED	CLABFEE	CDEPT
T33	HEDONISM	FOR THE SANE	3	.00	THEO
T44	COMMUNISM	FOR THE GREEDY	6	200.00	THEO
P44	SOLIPSISM	ME MYSELF AND I	6	.00	PHIL

Comments

1. *Logic.* Observe the effect of the AND being evaluated before the OR. A given row will be selected if it meets either or both of the following conditions. (This is because these conditions are OR-connected.)

   a. CDEPT = 'THEO' AND CLABFEE = 0

   b. CRED = 6

   The system will examine each row of the COURSE table. If a given row has both a CDEPT value of "THEO" and a CLABFEE value of zero, it will be selected. The first row (course number of "T33") was the only row which met this condition. Furthermore, if a given row has a CRED value of 6, it will also be selected. The last two rows (course numbers "T44" and "P44") met this condition. The COURSE table does not contain any rows which match both of the above conditions. If it did, such rows would have been selected.

2. *Syntax.* We cannot arbitrarily change the order of the conditions. Consider the following statement, which is not equivalent to the sample query.

   ```
   SELECT    * FROM COURSE
   WHERE     CDEPT = 'THEO'
   AND       CRED = 6
   OR        CLABFEE = 0
   ```

   This query would select any six-credit theology course or any course with a zero lab fee (regardless of its department and credits).

3. The following two statements are equivalent to the current example. The first reorders the conditions without affecting the logic. The second makes use of parentheses which will be explained on the next page. The parentheses are superfluous, but they help readability.

   ```
   SELECT    * FROM COURSE
   WHERE     CRED = 6
   OR        CDEPT = 'THEO' AND CLABFEE = 0

   SELECT    * FROM COURSE
   WHERE     (CDEPT = 'THEO' AND CLABFEE = 0)
   OR        CRED = 6
   ```

USE OF PARENTHESES

SQL permits the use of parentheses to override the Boolean operator hierarchy. Parentheses make explicit the order of evaluation and enhance readability. The next sample query incorporates the same three conditions as the preceding sample query. This time we illustrate the use of parentheses to change the order of system evaluation. The two conditions adjacent to the OR are enclosed within parentheses. This means that they will be evaluated first. Note that the semantic meaning of this sample query is very different from the preceding one. The only syntax change, the parentheses, effectively changes the semantic meaning of the WHERE clause.

Sample Query 4.10   Display all information about theology courses which have a zero lab fee or are worth six credits.

SELECT	*
FROM	COURSE
WHERE	CDEPT = 'THEO'
AND	(CLABFEE = 0 OR CRED = 6)

CNO	CNAME	CDESCP	CRED	CLABFEE	CDEPT
T33	HEDONISM	FOR THE SANE	3	.00	THEO
T44	COMMUNISM	FOR THE GREEDY	6	200.00	THEO

Comments

1. *Logic.* Observe that the parentheses cause the OR to be evaluated before the AND. The effect is that a given row will be selected if it meets both of the following conditions.

```
CDEPT = 'THEO'
CLABFEE = 0 OR CRED = 6
```

Therefore, this example, unlike the previous, will select only theology courses. Furthermore, these theology courses must meet at least one of the conditions, CLABFEE = 0 or CRED = 6. Observe the displayed result. Note that the row for course number P44, which was present in the previous example, is absent. This is because it is not a theology course.

2. *Syntax.* The two conditions which are OR-connected within the parentheses are written on one line. This enhances readability, but it is not necessary. The following query is equivalent to the current example.

```
SELECT   * FROM COURSE
WHERE    CDEPT = 'THEO'
AND      (CLABFEE = 0
OR       CRED = 6)
```

3. If we observe that we want six-credit theology courses or zero-lab-fee theology courses, we might have written the following equivalent statement.

```
SELECT   * FROM COURSE
WHERE    (CDEPT = 'THEO' AND CRED = 6)
OR       (CDEPT = 'THEO' AND CLABFEE = 0)
```

Some individuals would find this statement to be a more explicit representation of the query objective. Note that the parentheses are not required in this statement. The default hierarchy will produce the same result.

4. *General recommendation.* Always utilize parentheses to make explicit the logic of your WHERE clause.

Exercises

4I. Select all information about any six-credit philosophy course, or any course with a lab fee which exceeds $200 (regardless of its department identifier or credits).

4J. Select all information about any three-credit course with a lab fee which is less than $100 or greater than $300.

The next sample query involves all three of the Boolean operators. Recall the hierarchy is NOT, followed by AND, followed by OR. Note that this example does not adhere to the recommendation specified on the previous page; parentheses are absent. This will force you to think about the hierarchy. Again, this is a tutorial example. In practice, you should use parentheses.

Sample Query 4.11 Display all information about all non-CIS courses or any course (regardless of department) which has a zero lab fee and is worth three credits.

```
SELECT      *

FROM        COURSE

WHERE       NOT CDEPT = 'CIS'

OR          CLABFEE = 0

AND         CRED = 3
```

CNO	CNAME	CDESCP	CRED	CLABFEE	CDEPT
T11	SCHOLASTICISM	FOR THE PIOUS	3	150.00	THEO
T12	FUNDAMENTALISM	FOR THE CAREFREE	3	90.00	THEO
T33	HEDONISM	FOR THE SANE	3	.00	THEO
T44	COMMUNISM	FOR THE GREEDY	6	200.00	THEO
P11	EMPIRICISM	SEE IT—BELIEVE IT	3	100.00	PHIL
P22	RATIONALISM	FOR CIS MAJORS	3	50.00	PHIL
P33	EXISTENTIALISM	FOR CIS MAJORS	3	200.00	PHIL
P44	SOLIPSISM	ME MYSELF AND I	6	.00	PHIL
C33	DISCRETE MATHEMATICS	ABSOLUTELY NECESSARY	3	.00	CIS
C44	DIGITAL CIRCUITS	AH HA!	3	.00	CIS

Comment

In this example, the hierarchy of operations happens to fit the objective of the sample query. However, it is better to make the logic explicit by using parentheses. The following equivalent statement does so.

```
SELECT     *
FROM       COURSE
WHERE      NOT CDEPT = 'CIS'
OR         (CLABFEE = 0 AND CRED = 3)
```

The above parentheses are superfluous. However, they emphasize that any given row (even a CIS row) will be selected if it has a zero lab fee and is worth three credits. To perhaps overdo the use of parentheses, we rewrite the statement with parentheses enclosing the first condition to emphasize that we want the system to evaluate the NOT condition first.

```
SELECT     *
FROM       COURSE
WHERE      (NOT CDEPT = 'CIS')
OR         (CLABFEE = 0 AND CRED = 3)
```

Exercise

4K. Select all information about any course with a lab fee which is not greater than $100 or any other course, regardless of its lab fee, which is offered by the theology department and is worth six credits.

The next example illustrates the use of parentheses to override the default hierarchy. In this example, the AND connector is evaluated before the NOT operator evaluated last.

Sample Query 4.12   Display all information about every row in the COURSE table except any CIS course which has a zero lab fee.

SELECT	*	
FROM	COURSE	
WHERE	NOT (CDEPT = 'CIS' AND CLABFEE = 0)	

CNO	CNAME	CDESCP	CRED	CLABFEE	CDEPT
T11	SCHOLASTICISM	FOR THE PIUS	3	150.00	THEO
T12	FUNDAMENTALISM	FOR THE CAREFREE	3	90.00	THEO
T33	HEDONISM	FOR THE SANE	3	.00	THEO
T44	COMMUNISM	FOR THE GREEDY	6	200.00	THEO
P11	EMPIRICISM	SEE IT—BELIEVE IT	3	100.00	PHIL
P22	RATIONALISM	FOR CIS MAJORS	3	50.00	PHIL
P33	EXISTENTIALISM	FOR CIS MAJORS	3	200.00	PHIL
P44	SOLIPSISM	ME MYSELF AND I	6	.00	PHIL
C11	INTRO TO CS	FOR ROOKIES	3	100.00	CIS
C22	DATA STRUCTURES	VERY USEFUL	3	50.00	CIS
C55	COMPUTER ARCH.	VON NEUMANN'S MACH.	3	100.00	CIS
C66	RELATIONAL DATABASE	THE ONLY WAY TO GO	3	500.00	CIS

Comments

1. The logic expressed in this example is straightforward. We simply write a condition to identify the rows we do not want. This is

```
CDEPT = 'CIS' AND CLABFEE = 0
```

Then we negate this condition by placing a NOT in front of the entire condition which must be enclosed by parentheses.

```
NOT (CDEPT = 'CIS' AND CLABFEE = 0)
```

2. Consider the reason the following condition without parentheses will not achieve the desired objective.

```
NOT CDEPT = 'CIS' AND CLABFEE = 0
```

The absence of parentheses means the NOT will be evaluated first, but it applies only to the first condition. This is equivalent to the following condition.

```
(NOT CDEPT = 'CIS') AND CLABFEE = 0
```

Only non-CIS rows with zero lab fees would be selected by this condition. Observe that the current sample query selected some rows for CIS courses and some rows with nonzero lab fees.

3. The sample query could have been expressed a number of other ways. The following conditions are logically equivalent to the current example.

```
(NOT CDEPT = 'CIS') OR (NOT CLABFEE = 0)
CDEPT <> 'CIS' OR CLABFEE <> 0
```

These clauses are no better than the original. We are merely illustrating logical equivalencies. To restate a point we made earlier, the issue of logic per se transcends SQL. You must be careful whenever you are writing complex queries.

Exercise

4L. Select all information about any course except three-credit philosophy courses.

IN KEYWORD

The next sample query introduces the use of IN. This provides a convenient way of asking the system to select a row if a given column contains any value in a specified set of values.

Sample Query 4.13   Display the course number, description, and credits for any course which is worth two, six, or nine credits.

SELECT	CNO, CDESCP, CRED
FROM	COURSE
WHERE	CRED IN (2, 6, 9)

CNO	CDESCP	CRED
T44	FOR THE GREEDY	6
P44	ME MYSELF AND I	6

Comments

1. *Syntax.* The set of values must be enclosed within parentheses with commas separating each value. These values can be numeric (the current example) or character. Character values must be enclosed in quotes. (See next sample query.) The values in the current example happen to be written in sequence. This helps readability, but it is not required. For all practical purposes there is no upper limit on the number of values that constitute the comparison set.

2. While the IN keyword is useful, it is also superfluous. This is because any condition using IN can be replaced with an equivalent sequence of OR conditions. The following statement is equivalent to the current example.

```
SELECT   CNO, CDESCP, CRED
FROM     COURSE
WHERE    CRED = 2
OR       CRED = 6
OR       CRED = 9
```

NOT IN

The next example illustrates use of the NOT IN phrase which, as you would expect, is the converse of IN. It will instruct the system to select a row if a given column value contains any value other than a value in a specified set of values.

Sample Query 4.14 Display the course name, description, and department identifier of any course which is not offered by the theology or computer and information science department.

```
SELECT      CNAME, CDESCP, CDEPT

FROM        COURSE

WHERE       CDEPT NOT IN ('THEO', 'CIS')
```

CNAME	CDESCP	CDEPT
EMPIRICISM	SEE IT—BELIEVE IT	PHIL
RATIONALISM	FOR CIS MAJORS	PHIL
EXISTENTIALISM	FOR CIS MAJORS	PHIL
SOLIPSISM	ME MYSELF AND I	PHIL

Comments

1. *Logic.* The NOT IN phrase, like IN, is useful but superfluous. The current example could have contained any of the following equivalent WHERE clauses.

```
WHERE NOT CDEPT = 'THEO'
AND   NOT CDEPT = 'CIS'

WHERE CDEPT <> 'THEO'
AND   CDEPT <> 'CIS'

WHERE NOT (CDEPT = 'THEO' OR CDEPT = 'CIS')
```

   It is permissible to place a NOT before a condition containing IN. The following WHERE clause is also equivalent to the current example. Notice that NOT appears before "CDEPT" instead of "IN".

```
WHERE NOT CDEPT IN ('THEO', 'CIS')
```

Using NOT IN appears to be more compact and comprehensible. This is especially true if there are a large number of values to be examined.

2. *Syntax.* Because CDEPT contains character data, the specified values, THEO and CIS, must each be enclosed within apostrophes and the system will perform a character-by-character compare.

BETWEEN KEYWORD

The next sample query illustrates the use of BETWEEN to identify a range of values. A row will be selected if a given column has a value within the specified range.

Sample Query 4.15   Display the course name and lab fee of any course with a lab fee between, and including, $100 and $200.

```
SELECT    CNAME, CLABFEE

FROM      COURSE

WHERE     CLABFEE BETWEEN 100.00 AND 200.00
```

CNAME	CLABFEE
SCHOLASTICISM	150.00
COMMUNISM	200.00
EMPIRICISM	100.00
EXISTENTIALISM	200.00
INTRO TO CS	100.00
COMPUTER ARCH.	100.00

Comments

1. Note that BETWEEN really means "between and including." The system will select rows which match the extreme values.

2. The BETWEEN keyword is also superfluous. An equivalent WHERE clause can always be written using an AND connector. The current WHERE clause could have been rewritten as

   ```
   WHERE CLABFEE >= 100.00
   AND CLABFEE <= 200.00
   ```

   Observe that the above approach required that the column name (CLABFEE) be specified in both conditional expressions. The use of the "BETWEEN ___ AND ___" phrase provides another approach which some users might find more attractive.

3. Although it may be grammatically correct to say "where lab fee is between 200 and 100," it would be silly to code the following WHERE clause.

```
WHERE CLABFEE BETWEEN 200.00 AND 100.00
```

The system would interpret this clause as the following AND-connected clause, which would always produce a "no hit" situation.

```
WHERE    CLABFEE >= 200.00
AND      CLABFEE <= 100.00
```

There is no number which is greater than 200 and less than 100. Hence, when using BETWEEN, always reference the smaller value first as the example illustrates.

Exercise

4M. Display all information about any course which has a lab fee equal to any value in the following set of values: {12.12, 50.00, 75.00, 90.00, 100.00, 500.00}

4N. Display all information about every course where the lab fee is not one of the following: {12.12, 50.00, 75.00, 90.00, 100.00, 500.00}

4O. Display the course number and lab fee for any course with a lab fee between and including $50 and $400.

NOT BETWEEN

NOT BETWEEN is used to select rows where a given column value falls outside of a specified range. The next sample query is the converse of the previous. It will display every COURSE table row which was omitted from the previous result.

Sample Query 4.16   Display the course name and lab fee of any course with a lab fee less than $100 or greater than $200.

SELECT	CNAME, CLABFEE
FROM	COURSE
WHERE	CLABFEE NOT BETWEEN 100 AND 200

CNAME	CLABFEE
FUNDAMENTALISM	90.00
HEDONISM	.00
RATIONALISM	50.00
SOLIPSISM	.00
DATA STRUCTURES	50.00
DISCRETE MATHEMATICS	.00
DIGITAL CIRCUITS	.00
RELATIONAL DATABASE	500.00

Comments

1. Note that the NOT BETWEEN will exclude extreme values from the result. This is because it is the negation of the result which would have been produced by the BETWEEN. (More formally, it yields the complement of the set identified by the BETWEEN condition.)

2. The following WHERE clause is equivalent to that of the current example.

```
WHERE CLABFEE < 100
OR    CLABFEE > 200
```

Note that the comparison operators are "strictly greater than" and "strictly less than." This is because the NOT BETWEEN clause excludes extreme values from being selected, wherewith the BETWEEN clause was inclusive of the range values.

   Also, as with any conditional expression, a NOT can precede the condition. Therefore, we could place the NOT before the column name instead of coding the NOT BETWEEN phrase. Hence the following WHERE clause is equivalent to that of the current example.

```
WHERE NOT CLABFEE BETWEEN 100 and 200
```

3. Again, the BETWEEN phrase must always reference the smaller value first. If we were to enter the following WHERE clause

```
WHERE CLABFEE NOT BETWEEN 200 AND 100
```

the system would interpret this as

```
WHERE CLABFEE < 200
OR    CLABFEE > 100
```

Every value must match this condition, which means that all rows would be retrieved. This is obviously not the query objective.

Exercise

4P. Display the course number and lab fee of any course with a lab fee which is less than $50 or greater than $400.

The next sample query shows that BETWEEN can also be used to identify a range for character string data.

Sample Query 4.17 Display the name and lab fee of any course with a course name beginning with the letter "D".

SELECT	CNAME, CLABFEE
FROM	COURSE
WHERE	CNAME BETWEEN 'D' AND 'DZZZ'

CNAME	CLABFEE
DATA STRUCTURES	50.00
DISCRETE MATHEMATICS	.00
DIGITAL CIRCUITS	.00

Comments

1. Under the realistic assumption that no course name which begins with "D" will be greater than "DZZZ", this example effectively retrieves every course with a course name beginning with the letter "D". Again, we assume that all character values stored in the database are in uppercase.

   It is important that you understand the idea of a character sequence. Note that if "DZZZ XXX" were a legitimate course name, it would not be selected by the SELECT statement because it is greater than "DZZZ".

2. The intent of this query is to have the system search for a character string pattern in the CNAME field. This pattern is a "D" followed by any string. We will see in the next chapter that the LIKE keyword provides a far more convenient way of searching for character string patterns.

Exercise

4Q. Display the course name and description for any course with a description which begins "FOR".

The last example in this chapter does not introduce any new concepts or techniques. The sole purpose is to illustrate that any of the aforementioned techniques can be used within a single SELECT statement. The only reason that this statement is longer than previous statements is because of the relative complexity of the query objective. Examine each line of code within the statement, and observe that each implements one of the SQL constructs presented earlier in this text.

Sample Query 4.18   Display the department identifier, course name, and lab fee of any three-credit CIS, THEO, or MGT course with a lab fee between, and including, $50 and $300. Sort the result by course name within department identifier sequence (ascending).

```
SELECT     CDEPT, CNAME, CLABFEE

FROM       COURSE

WHERE      CDEPT IN ('CIS', 'THEO', 'MGT')

AND        CLABFEE BETWEEN 50 AND 300

AND        CRED = 3

ORDER BY CDEPT, CNAME
```

CDEPT	CNAME	CLABFEE
CIS	COMPUTER ARCH.	100.00
CIS	DATA STRUCTURES	50.00
CIS	INTRO TO CS	100.00
THEO	FUNDAMENTALISM	90.00
THEO	SCHOLASTICISM	150.00

Exercise

4R. Display the department, course number, and description for any computer science or theology course with a lab fee which is less than $100 or greater than $400. Sort the results by course number within the department.

SUMMARY

This chapter presented the formulation of more complex WHERE clauses by use of the traditional Boolean operators. We described the syntax and behavior of AND, OR, and NOT.

WHERE cond1 AND cond2: A given row is selected only if both cond1 or cond2 or conditions are true.

WHERE cond1 OR cond2: A given row is selected if either cond1 or cond2 or both are true.

WHERE NOT cond: A given row is selected if cond is not true (is false).

When a complex WHERE clause contains more than two individual conditions, you are encouraged to use parentheses to make explicit the order of evaluation. Otherwise the traditional hierarchy of evaluation applies. This means that NOTs are evaluated first, followed by ANDs, followed by ORs.

Two other useful keywords were presented which can help in the formulation of more compact and readable code. These are BETWEEN and IN, both of which can be prefaced by NOT. These are summarized below.

WHERE col BETWEEN val1 AND val2: A given row is selected if its col value is within the range specified by val1 and val2.

WHERE col NOT BETWEEN val1 AND val2: A given row is selected if its col value falls outside the range specified by val1 and val2.

WHERE col IN (val1, val2, . . . , valn): A given row is selected if its col value equals any of the specified values.

WHERE col NOT IN (val1, val2, . . . , valn): A given row is selected if its col value does not equal all of the specified values.

Summary Exercises

The following exercises all refer to the STAFF table. The column names are ENAME, ETITLE, ESALARY, and DEPT.

4S. Display all information about any member of the philosophy or theology department.

4T. Display all information about any member of the theology department whose salary exceeds $52.

4U. Display the name of any staff member whose salary is greater than or equal to $52, but less than or equal to $1000.

4V. Display the name and title of any staff member assigned to the theology department who earns $51 or $54.

4W. Display the name and salary of any staff member whose salary equals one of the following values: 51, 53, 100, 200, 25,000.

4X. Display the names and salaries of staff members who earn less than $100 or more than $1000. Sort the result in ascending sequence by name.

4Y. Display the department identifier of every department which employs a staff member whose salary exceeds $5000. Do not show duplicate department identifiers.

5

Pattern Matching

There are times when we would like to retrieve information from rows having similar, but not necessarily equal, values in a given column. As an example, suppose we wished to display information about all introductory courses. One approach is to examine the CNAME column in the COURSE table for course names with the words "INTRODUCTION" or "INTRODUCTORY" or perhaps even "INTRO". In this case we want to select rows based on some pattern. SQL provides a method for identifying patterns. It is not necessary to specify or even know a complete column value in order to identify a row for selection.

LIKE KEYWORD

SQL allows us to provide partial information by using the keyword LIKE. The LIKE keyword is used in the WHERE clause in place of the comparison operator. The general format is

```
WHERE column-name LIKE 'pattern'
```

Column-name identifies the column to be searched for the pattern. The pattern is a character string (enclosed within apostrophes). Pattern matching applies only to character string columns.

SQL must be given some idea of where the partial string of characters is located. It could be found in the leftmost or rightmost positions, or possibly somewhere in the middle of the column. We specify the location of the character string by including special wildcard characters in the pattern. These wildcard characters are the present sign (%) and the underscore character (_). Each wildcard character will be explained in the following sample queries.

USE OF PERCENT (%) SYMBOL

The first sample query in this chapter illustrates the use of the percent sign (%) in the pattern string. This symbol is interpreted as a wildcard which can represent any character string of any length. In particular, it also can match the empty string of length zero.

The following example will search the CNAME column for character strings which have "INTRO" as the five leftmost characters. The percent sign is used to represent the remaining characters.

Sample Query 5.1   Display the course number and name of all introductory courses. (More precisely, display the CNO and CNAME values of any row which has a CNAME value beginning with "INTRO".)

```
SELECT    CNO, CNAME

FROM      COURSE

WHERE     CNAME LIKE 'INTRO%'
```

CNO	CNAME
C11	INTRO TO CS

Comments

1. The pattern string "INTRO%" contains a percent sign at the end. This means that any number of characters following "INTRO" will be considered to be a match. However, the characters "INTRO" must be found in the column as the leftmost characters. After these five characters, SQL will consider anything found in the column to meet the selection criteria.

   If the following character strings were present in the CNAME column, they would all match the pattern used in the current example.

   ```
   "INTRODUCTION TO COMPUTERS"
   "INTRO TO COMPUTERS"
   "INTRO. TO COMPUTERS"
   "INTRODUCTORY COMPUTER SCIENCE"
   "INTRODUCTION TO COMPUTERS"
   "INTRO TO INTRODUCING"
   "INTRO"
   ```

   Note that a CNAME value of "INTRO" matches the pattern. This is because the percent symbol will match on the empty string.

2. The following CNAME values would not match the "INTRO%" pattern.

   ```
   "AN INTRODUCTION TO CIS"
   "INTRO TO COMPUTERS"
   ```

   Both of these character strings contain "INTRO", but not as the leftmost five characters. The pattern for the current example requires such.

3. CNAME happens to be a variable length field. Pattern matching can also be applied to fixed-length fields like CDEPT and CNO. However, subsequent sample queries will illustrate that, unfortunately, there sometimes can be subtle differences in the pattern matching process between fixed- and variable-length fields.

Exercise

5A. Display all information about any course which has a description beginning with the string "FOR THE".

The next sample query is similar to the preceding. This time we are examining the rightmost part of a character string.

Sample Query 5.2   Display all CNAME values which end with the letters "CISM".

SELECT   CNAME

FROM   COURSE

WHERE   CNAME LIKE '%CISM'

CNAME
_____

SCHOLASTICISM
EMPIRICISM

Comments

1. The placement of the percent sign at the beginning of the pattern informed the system that the desired characters would be found in the rightmost positions of the column. Zero or more characters preceding "CISM" is considered to be a match. Again, note that because the percent symbol matches the empty string, a CNAME value of "CISM" would match the current pattern.

2. It is unlikely that a variable-length column will ever have blank characters in the rightmost position. (A database designer may define a column to be variable length just to avoid this situation.) However, it is not impossible. This can occur if the user explicitly inserts trailing blanks in the column. Therefore, it is possible for the CNAME column to contain a value like "SCHOLASTICISM". The pattern "%CISM" would not match on this value because the last four characters "ISM" do not match "CISM".

Exercise

5B. Display the course name and description of any course having a description which ends with the letter "E".

The next sample query illustrates the use of multiple percent symbols.

Sample Query 5.3   What are the names of courses which have the letters "SC" appearing anywhere in the name?

```
SELECT    CNAME

FROM      COURSE

WHERE     CNAME LIKE '%SC%'
```

CNAME
_____
SCHOLASTICISM
DISCRETE MATHEMATICS

Comments

1. The pattern will match on the string "SC" anywhere within the CNAME column. In particular, it will match these characters if they occur in the middle of the string. "DISCRETE MATHEMATICS" was such a match. Because the percent symbol matches on the empty string, the pattern also matches on strings which begin or end with "SC". Hence, "SCHOLASTICISM" was a match.

2. Any number of percent symbols can occur within a pattern string. The following will match on any CNAME value which begins with "F"; has an embedded blank, followed by "OO"; and ends with a period.

   ```
   WHERE CNAME LIKE 'F% %OO%.'
   ```

Exercise

5C. Display the course number and description of any course with a period, hyphen, or exclamation mark anywhere in its description. (*Hint:* You will need to use multiple conditions to satisfy this query.)

The next sample query involves pattern matching with a fixed-length character column (CDEPT). There is only one situation where fixed-length character strings need special consideration. This is when you want to match on the rightmost characters of the string. This is because, unlike variable-length strings, fixed-length strings often have one or more trailing blanks. Usually this occurs because the system will attach trailing blanks to any string which is smaller than the column length. Therefore, you have to construct the pattern string to account for possible trailing blanks. This is the case with the CDEPT column, which is four characters long, but can contain department identifiers which are shorter.

Sample Query 5.4   Display the department identifier of any course where the department identifier ends with "S". Do not display duplicate values.

```
SELECT    DISTINCT CDEPT
FROM      COURSE
WHERE     CDEPT LIKE '%S'
OR        CDEPT LIKE '%S '
OR        CDEPT LIKE '%S  '
OR        CDEPT LIKE 'S   '
```

CDEPT
——
CIS

Comments

1. It is important to understand the semantics of the sample query. We assume that stored trailing blanks are not really part of the department identifier. This means we would like a match on the CIS department even though the CDEPT column contains "CIS".

    The WHERE clause has four conditions which are connected with OR operators. Each condition tests for "S" in one of the four character positions of a CDEPT value.

    - CDEPT LIKE '%S' tests for "S" in the fourth position.
    - CDEPT LIKE '%S ' tests for "S" in the third position followed by a space.
    - CDEPT LIKE '%S ' tests for "S" in the second position followed by two spaces.
    - CDEPT LIKE 'S   ' tests for "S" in the first position followed by three spaces.

2. Note that the pattern "%S%" is an inadequate solution. It will account for trailing blanks; and it will match with "CIS". However, it will also select any row with *an "S" anywhere in its course name,* not necessarily the last significant (nonblank) character. This is not consistent with the query objective.

3. Note that the pattern "%S" will not work because it fails to account for the trailing blanks. The current solution is far from ideal. (Imagine if CDEPT were 50 characters long.) However, it is the best that can be realized.

Exercise

5D. Display the department identifier of any course where the department identifier ends with "IL". Do not display duplicate values.

USE OF UNDERSCORE (_) SYMBOL

Previous examples illustrated the percent sign as a wildcard symbol which could represent a substring of any length. The next sample query introduces another wildcard symbol, the underscore (_), which will always represent exactly one character position.

Sample Query 5.5   Display the course name and department identifier of any course which has the letter "H" present in the second position of its department identifier and is exactly four characters long.

SELECT	CNAME, CDEPT
FROM	COURSE
WHERE	CDEPT LIKE '_H_ _'

CNAME	CDEPT
SCHOLASTICISM	THEO
FUNDAMENTALISM	THEO
HEDONISM	THEO
COMMUNISM	THEO
EMPIRICISM	PHIL
RATIONALISM	PHIL
EXISTENTIALISM	PHIL
SOLIPSISM	PHIL

Comments

1. The difference between the percent sign and the underscore is twofold. First, the percent sign allows any number of characters to match while the underscore allows only one. Second, the percent sign is considered a match if zero characters are found. The underscore always requires exactly one character to be present.

2. The CDEPT column has a maximum length of four-character, fixed-length field. The positions of the underscore characters in the pattern permit the first, third, and fourth characters to be of any value, including blanks. The one character present in the pattern, the letter "H", must be found precisely in the second position of the column for a match to occur.

3. Because CDEPT is a fixed-length field of length four the WHERE clause would work:

```
WHERE CDEPT LIKE '_H%'
```

However, if CDEPT were a variable-length field this pattern would not be equivalent to what is shown in the example. For example, a variable-length string, "BH", would match on the pattern '_H%', but it would not match on '_H__'.

Exercise

5E. Display the course name and department identifier of any course with a three-character department identifier.

MIXING WILDCARD SYMBOLS

The next sample query illustrates the use of both of the wildcard symbols in the same pattern.

Sample Query 5.6   Display the names of courses which have a vowel as the second letter of their name.

```
SELECT    CNAME

FROM      COURSE

WHERE     CNAME LIKE '_A%'

OR        CNAME LIKE '_E%'

OR        CNAME LIKE '_I%'

OR        CNAME LIKE '_O%'

OR        CNAME LIKE '_U%'
```

CNAME
_____

FUNDAMENTALISM
HEDONISM
COMMUNISM
RATIONALISM
SOLIPSISM
DATA STRUCTURES
DISCRETE MATHEMATICS
DIGITAL CIRCUITS
COMPUTER ARCH.
RELATIONAL DATABASE

Comments

1. This example demonstrates a combination of the wildcard characters. The underscore implies that any character can appear in the first position. Each pattern is defined with a vowel in the second position, thereby identifying specific values acceptable for a match. The remaining positions of the column may be any value of any length as shown by the use of the percent sign.

2. The example showed a series of patterns, all to be tested against the same column. It might seem that there should be some shorthand method of specifying this request. Unfortunately, there is no abbreviated method available.

3. A pattern string may contain any number of wildcard symbols. For example, the following WHERE clause will match on any course name with an "E" in the second position and an "I" in the sixth position and is at least 10 characters long.

```
WHERE CNAME LIKE '_ E _ _ _ I _ _ _ _ %'
```

4. We emphasize again that you need to be careful when combining wildcard characters. You might be tempted to use the following WHERE clause to satisfy Sample Query 5.5.

```
WHERE CDEPT LIKE '_H%'
```

However, this pattern is not equivalent to '_ H _ _' because it will match on any string with an "H" in the second position which is at least two characters long. The sample query objective required a length of exactly four characters.

Exercise

5F. Display the name and description of any course where the description has "THE" in the fifth, sixth, and seventh positions, and an "A" in the tenth position.

NOT LIKE

The last sample query of this chapter illustrates the NOT LIKE phrase. As you would expect, this is used to select rows which do not conform to a specified pattern.

Sample Query 5.7   Display the names of all courses which do not have a vowel as the second letter.

```
SELECT    CNAME

FROM      COURSE

WHERE     CNAME NOT LIKE '_A%'

AND       CNAME NOT LIKE '_E%'

AND       CNAME NOT LIKE '_I%'

AND       CNAME NOT LIKE '_O%'

AND       CNAME NOT LIKE '_U%'
```

CNAME
_____
SCHOLASTICISM
EMPIRICISM
EXISTENTIALISM
INTRO TO CS

Comments

1. The NOT LIKE phrase is similar in spirit to the NOT IN and NOT BETWEEN described in the previous chapter. NOT has the effect of selecting every row which does not match the pattern string.

2. This query could have been expressed in other ways. The example shows the NOT keyword placed immediately before the LIKE keyword. However, that is not a requirement. The WHERE clause could have been formed with the NOT before the column name.

```
WHERE  NOT CNAME LIKE '_A%'
AND    NOT CNAME LIKE '_E%'
AND    NOT CNAME LIKE '_I%'
AND    NOT CNAME LIKE '_O%'
AND    NOT CNAME LIKE '_U%'
```

Another equivalent WHERE clause is

```
WHERE NOT
    (CNAME LIKE '_A%'
OR CNAME LIKE '_E%'
OR CNAME LIKE '_I%'
OR CNAME LIKE '_O%'
OR CNAME LIKE '_U%')
```

This approach simply negates the entire WHERE clause shown in Sample Query 5.6 by enclosing the conditions in parentheses and placing a NOT in front of the entire compound condition.

Exercise

5G. Display the course name and description of any course which does not end with an "E" or an "S".

SUMMARY

The WHERE clause can contain the keyword LIKE to test for a pattern in a character string. The LIKE keyword is used only to inspect columns containing character data. The general format is

```
WHERE column-name LIKE 'pattern'
```

The pattern must be enclosed in apostrophes and may contain two special wildcard characters. The percent sign (%) represents any string of any length. The underscore (_) represents exactly one character.

Summary Exercises

The following exercises all refer to the STAFF table. The column names are ENAME, ETITLE, ESALARY, and DEPT. The ENAME, ETITLE, and DEPT columns contain character string data.

5H. Display all information about any staff member whose name begins with the letters "MA".

5I. Display all information about any staff member whose title ends with the digit 1, 2, or 3.

5J. Display the name and title of any staff member who has the letter "S" occurring anywhere in both name and title.

5K. Display the department identifier of any department which has the letter "E" in the third character position. Do not display duplicate values.

5L. Display the name of any staff member whose name has the letter "I" in the fifth position. Display the result in ascending alphabetic sequence.

6

Arithmetic Expressions

This chapter presents some of the computational facilities supported by SQL. We introduce the formulation of arithmetic expressions which can be used to display columns containing calculated results. (Chapters 7 and 8 will present SQL/400's built-in functions which provide additional computational facilities.)

You will discover that it is easy to perform basic calculations with data retrieved via a SELECT statement. However, we note that SQL was not designed as a language to support complex mathematical processing. SQL is really a database language which also supports some basic computational facilities. For this reason you will find that the following sample queries illustrate relatively simple calculations.

SQL ARITHMETIC EXPRESSIONS

The ability to perform calculations on the data and derive values from existing information is useful in formulating and answering "what if" questions. This would prove beneficial to a college administrator involved with budgetary forecasting. We present a variety of "what if" sample queries which require calculations involving the CLABFEE column.

Sample Query 6.1   Suppose that we are interested in the impact of increasing the lab-fee charges for all CIS courses. What would be the lab fee for each CIS course if its lab fee were increased by $25? Display each CIS course name followed by the current lab fee and the adjusted lab fee.

```
SELECT    CNAME, CLABFEE, CLABFEE + 25

FROM      COURSE

WHERE     CDEPT = 'CIS'
```

CNAME	CLABFEE	CLABFEE+25
INTRO TO CS	100.00	125
DATA STRUCTURES	50.00	75
DISCRETE MATHEMATICS	.00	25
DIGITAL CIRCUITS	.00	25
COMPUTER ARCH.	100.00	125
RELATIONAL DATABASE	500.00	525

Comments

1. *Syntax.* The SELECT clause begins "SELECT CNAME, CLABFEE" (which produces the first two columns of the output display) followed by "CLABFEE + 25",
   which is an arithmetic expression. This arithmetic expression caused the system to
   calculate and display the third column with the desired adjusted lab-fee values.
   There are many details to be addressed regarding writing correct arithmetic
   expressions. However, for the moment, we will simply describe an arithmetic
   expression as a meaningful combination of column names, constants, and arithmetic operators. Usually, but not always, the formation of a "meaningful" arithmetic expression is quite simple.

   The following is a list of valid SELECT clauses which, in addition to containing
   column names, contain one or more arithmetic expressions. They illustrate the standard arithmetic operators of addition (+), subtraction (–), multiplication (*), and
   division (/).

   a. SELECT CNAME, 25.00 + CLABFEE

   b. SELECT CNAME, CRED * 2

   c. SELECT CLABFEE + 25, CLABFEE * 2.3

   d. SELECT CLABFEE + 100.00, CRED – 1, CNAME

   e. SELECT CLABFEE * CRED / 10

   These clauses show spaces between the arithmetic operator and the operands. This
   may improve readability, but it is not necessary.

2. *Logic.*   The calculation involved adding a constant value of 25 to the CLABFEE value for each row in the COURSE table. It is important to realize that the system performs the calculation in a temporary storage area and has no effect on the data stored in the COURSE table. The SELECT statement only displays data or data derived by some calculations. It never changes the data stored in a table.

3. *Column headings for calculated columns.*   A column which contains values produced by an expression has no predefined column name. Hence, the system uses the arithmetic expression as the column heading. The current example shows that the system produced "CLABFEE+25" as the column heading for the third column containing the results of the calculation. In addition if it is a long equation, you may see "numeric expression" as the column heading.

4. *Format of calculated values.*   Observe that the values produced by the expression "CLABFEE+25" do not contain any decimal points. The first row shows "125", not "125.00". This occurs because the system will only display a result with the decimal positions that are significant.

Sample Query 6.2   What would be the lab fee for CIS courses if lab-fee charges were reduced by $25.75?

```
SELECT    CNAME, CLABFEE, CLABFEE – 25.75

FROM      COURSE

WHERE     CDEPT = 'CIS'
```

CNAME	CLABFEE	CLABFEE–25.75
INTRO TO CS	100.00	74.25
DATA STRUCTURES	50.00	24.25
DISCRETE MATHEMATICS	.00	25.75–
DIGITAL CIRCUITS	.00	25.75–
COMPUTER ARCH.	100.00	74.25
RELATIONAL DATABASE	500.00	474.25

Comments

1. This example demonstrates the subtraction operation. There are two CIS courses which have zero lab fees. Subtracting $25.75 from these lab fees produced negative values which were accurately presented in the result. The system automatically displays any negative value with a minus sign. Note that the calculated values show the correct values with the appropriate decimal accuracy.

2. The column involved in the expression may be used in the WHERE clause. It might have been a good idea to avoid any negative lab fees derived by this example by eliminating from consideration any course with a lab fee of less than $25.75. The following statement would do so.

```
SELECT   CNAME, CLABFEE, CLABFEE – 25.75
FROM     COURSE
WHERE    CDEPT = 'CIS'
AND      CLABFEE >= 25.75
```

Sample Query 6.3   What would be the lab fee for each CIS course if its current lab fee were multiplied by 2.375?

SELECT	CNAME, CLABFEE, CLABFEE * 2.375
FROM	COURSE
WHERE	CDEPT = 'CIS'

CNAME	CLABFEE	CLABFEE*2.375
INTRO TO CS	100.00	237.50000
DATA STRUCTURES	50.00	118.75000
DISCRETE MATHEMATICS	.00	.00000
DIGITAL CIRCUITS	.00	.00000
COMPUTER ARCH.	100.00	237.50000
RELATIONAL DATABASE	500.00	1187.50000

Comments

1. This example illustrates multiplication which happens to generate some decimal results. Observe that the system will still display integer results as integers; only decimal results will be displayed with decimal accuracy. Note that the results of the computations is a five-decimal position number. This follows from the rules of basic multiplication.

2. By default, the system will not round or truncate result fields. (See Sample Query 6.5.) Obviously, these default actions often produce a less-than-desirable display. Subsequent sample queries will illustrate SQL/400 Query Manager formatting options to produce a more attractive report.

Sample Query 6.4 For each philosophy course, divide the credits in half. Display the course name, credits, and the result of dividing the credits in half.

SELECT   CNAME, CRED, CRED/2.0

FROM   COURSE

WHERE   CDEPT = 'PHIL'

CNAME	CRED	CRED/2.0
EMPIRICISM	3	1.500000000000000000000000000000
RATIONALISM	3	1.500000000000000000000000000000
EXISTENTIALISM	3	1.500000000000000000000000000000
SOLIPSISM	6	3.000000000000000000000000000000

Comment

Again, observe that the calculation produced decimal values and the default formatting rules applied. Observe that the calculation produced 31 decimal positions. Subsequent results will use the dot-dot ".." abbreviation to illustrate a repeating string of digits.

Exercises

6A. What would be the credit value for each philosophy course if its current credit value were doubled? Display each course number, current credit, and adjusted credit values.

6B. What would be the labfee of a theology course if each such course were charged $10.50 per credit? Display the course number and the adjusted lab fees of all theology courses.

6C. Assume that any course with a nonzero lab fee will have its lab fee decreased by 50 percent. Display the course number, and the current and adjusted lab fees for such courses.

All previous arithmetic expressions contained a constant. This is not always the case. Consider the next example.

Sample Query 6.5   What is the average lab fee per credit hour for courses offered by the CIS department?

SELECT   CNAME, CLABFEE / CRED

FROM   COURSE

WHERE   CDEPT = 'CIS'

CNAME	CLABFEE/CRED
INTRO TO CS	33.3333333..
DATA STRUCTURES	16.6666666..
DISCRETE MATHEMATICS	.0000000..
DIGITAL CIRCUITS	.0000000..
COMPUTER ARCH.	33.3333333..
RELATIONAL DATABASE	166.6666666..

Comments

1. *Logic.* In this example we derived information using two different column values stored in the database. (There are no constants in the expression.) The lab fee for each course was divided by the number of credits for that course to produce the calculated value, the average lab fee per credit. The system operates on a row-by-row basis. For each row selected, the CLABFEE value is divided by its corresponding CRED value.

2. *Formatting:* Note that the calculated result is not rounded, or truncated. The following query illustrates the default format.

COLUMN FORMATTING OPTIONS

In Chap. 2 we introduced the Column Formatting options to format the displayed columns. This same options can be used to format columns produced by arithmetic expressions. Simply create the definition in the Report Format. We demonstrate this facility with the following example, which formats the same calculations performed in the first four sample queries.

Sample Query 6.6   For each CIS and philosophy course, display the following calculations with the specified report formatting.

1. CLABFEE + 25: Display the result with two-digit decimal accuracy.
2. CLABFEE – 25.75: Display as an integer.
3. CLABFEE * 2.375: Display with three-digit decimal accuracy.
4. CRED/2: Display with one-digit decimal accuracy. Also, present the column heading as "HALF-CRED".

Report Format Options

CLABFEE+25	Use Edit Code L2
CLABFEE–25.75	Use Edit Code L0
CLABFEE*2.375	Use Edit Code L3
CRED/2	Use Edit Code L1
CRED/2 Heading	Change to "HALF-CRED"
CRED/2 Width	Change to 10

SELECT   CLABFEE+25, CLABFEE–25.75, CLABFEE*2.375, CRED/2.0

FROM   COURSE

WHERE   CDEPT = 'PHIL'

CLABFEE+25	CLABFEE–25.75	CLABFEE*2.375	HALF-CRED
75.00	24	118.750	1.5
225.00	174	475.000	1.5
25.00	–26	.000	3.0
125.00	74	237.500	1.5

Comments

1. Observe that the column options command operates as described in Chap. 2.
2. There are other techniques to specify format editing for calculated columns. These other techniques are appropriate when the expression is very long.

HIERARCHY OF ARITHMETIC OPERATORS

All previous arithmetic expressions contained just one arithmetic operator. It is common practice to formulate an expression which has multiple arithmetic operators. Consider the following examples where COLA, COLB, and COLC represent numeric columns in some table.

1. COLA + COLB + COLC + 100
2. COLA * COLB * 2
3. COLA + COLB – COLC

When an expression contains multiple arithmetic operators, the system must determine the sequence of operations. For the above examples it does not make any difference. For example, in item 3 the system could add COLA and COLB to produce an intermediate result which it then subtracts COLC from. Or, it could subtract COLC from COLB and then add this result to COLA. Either way, the result is the same. Using parentheses notation, we note that

```
(COLA + COLB) - COLC = COLA + (COLB - COLC)
```

This equivalence does not always occur. Consider the following examples.

4. COLA + COLB * COLC
5. COLA / COLB * COLC

The order of execution for these expressions is significant. Assume COLA = 10, COLB = 5, and COLC = 2. Then item 4 evaluates to 30 if you do the addition first and then multiply; it evaluates to 20 if you multiply first and then add. Item 5 evaluates to 4 if you divide first and then multiply; it evaluates to 1 if you multiply first and then divide. You can specify the desired sequence by use of parentheses. However, if the expression does not contain parentheses, the system will follow a standard hierarchy of arithmetic operations.

The hierarchy of arithmetic operators is defined as follows.

- Multiplication and division operations are evaluated first in a left-to-right scan of the expression.
- Then addition and subtraction operations are evaluated in a left-to-right scan of the expression.
- The order of evaluation can be changed by enclosing an expression, or part of an expression, in parentheses. Expressions within parentheses are evaluated first according to the order of the operators just mentioned. After evaluating within the parentheses, the operators outside are then evaluated.

This is the same hierarchy that applies to high school algebra and many other computer programming languages. This means that items 4 and 5 would be interpreted as

```
COLA + (COLB * COLC)
(COLA / COLB) * COLC
```

It is strongly recommended that you use parentheses to make explicit the desired order of execution. We rewrite items 1 through 5 after substituting the aforementioned values.

1. 10 + 5 + 2 + 100 evaluates to 117
2. 10 * 5 * 2 evaluates to 100
3. 10 + 5 – 2 evaluates to 13
4. 10 + 5 * 2 evaluates to 20
5. 10 / 5 * 2 evaluates to 4

You are advised to examine the following expressions to verify your understanding of the order of execution as specified by the hierarchy.

(10 + 5) * 2 evaluates to 30
10 / (5 * 2) evaluates to 1
10 + 5 * 10 + 2 evaluates to 62
(10 + 5) * (10 + 2) evaluates to 180
(10 + 5 * 10) + 2 evaluates to 62
(10 + 5) * 10 + 2 evaluates to 152

The next sample query requires writing an arithmetic expression with multiple arithmetic operators. The order of execution is significant. Parentheses are used to make this explicit.

Sample Query 6.7.1   What would be the average lab fee per credit hour for CIS courses if the lab fee were increased by $25.00?

SELECT	CNAME, CLABFEE, CRED, (CLABFEE+25)/CRED
FROM	COURSE
WHERE	CDEPT = 'CIS'

CNAME	CLABFEE	CRED	(CLABFEE+25)/CRED
INTRO TO CS	100.00	3	41.6666666..
DATA STRUCTURES	50.00	3	25.0000000..
DISCRETE MATHEMATICS	.00	3	8.33333333..
DIGITAL CIRCUITS	.00	3	8.33333333..
COMPUTER ARCH.	100.00	3	41.66666666..
RELATIONAL DATABASE	500.00	3	175.00000000..

Comment

This query required that the addition of 25 to each lab fee be performed before the division by the number of credits. We enclosed this addition operation in parentheses to ensure that it was performed first. Had we not done this, the result would have been radically different. (See the next query.)

Sample Query 6.7.2   Erroneous attempt at previous sample query. Observe what happens if you forget necessary parentheses.

SELECT   CNAME, CLABFEE, CRED, CLABFEE+25/CRED

FROM   COURSE

WHERE   CDEPT = 'CIS'

CNAME	CLABFEE	CRED	CLABFEE+25/CRED
INTRO TO CS	100.00	3	??????????..
DATA STRUCTURES	50.00	3	58.3333333..
DISCRETE MATHEMATICS	.00	3	8.33333333..
DIGITAL CIRCUITS	.00	3	8.33333333..
COMPUTER ARCH.	100.00	3	??????????..
RELATIONAL DATABASE	500.00	3	??????????..

Comment

The absence of parentheses in the expression means that the division is performed first. This is not consistent with the objective of the query. In addition, Query Manager will display '??' when it cannot determine a value because of a division by zero, invalid data, or in this case, an overflow.

Exercise

6D. For any course with a lab fee less than $200, display its course number and its adjusted lab fee which is $35 more than 150% of the current lab fee.

FLOATING-POINT NUMBERS

SQL/400 supports floating-point notation, also called *scientific notation* or *exponential notation*. Usually this notation is used to represent very large or small numbers. These are the type of numeric values used by astronomers and nuclear physicists. A business application may occasionally require such values, but usually the conventional decimal notation satisfies its requirements. Below we present a brief description of floating-point notation.

Floating-point notation represents numeric values using exponential notation with 10 as the base value. The following examples illustrate floating-point constants which can be used in SQL arithmetic expressions.

Floating-point number	Decimal equivalent
123E+06	123,000,000
1.234E+10	12,340,000,000
1.2E+20	120,000,000,000,000,000,000
123E–06	.000123
1E+00	1

You can use floating-point notation when writing arithmetic expressions. SQL/400 will normally display the calculated results in floating-point notation unless you have specified a column-edit option.

The next sample query illustrates the use of floating-point notation in arithmetic expressions and the displaying of large calculated values in floating-point notation.

Sample Query 6.8   Assume you would like to double the lab fee for the relational database course. Use a floating-point constant in an arithmetic expression to perform this calculation.

```
SELECT CNAME, CLABFEE, CLABFEE * 2E0

FROM COURSE

WHERE CNAME = 'RELATIONAL DATABASE'
```

CNAME	CLABFEE	CLABFEE*2E0
RELATIONAL DATABASE	500.00	1.00000E+003

CALCULATED CONDITIONS

All previous examples have shown arithmetic expressions placed within a SELECT clause. Arithmetic expressions can also occur in WHERE conditions. (The intent is to have the system display a given row only if it meets criteria which are to be determined by some calculation.) Such a condition is called a *calculated condition*.

Sample Query 6.9 Which CIS courses have an average lab-fee-per-credit-hour value greater than $30?

```
SELECT      CNAME, CLABFEE / CRED

FROM        COURSE

WHERE       CDEPT = 'CIS'

AND         CLABFEE / CRED > 30
```

CNAME	CLABFEE/CRED
INTRO TO CS	33.333333..
COMPUTER ARCH.	33.333333..
RELATIONAL DATABASE	166.66666...

Comments

1. The condition "CLABFEE / CRED > 30" contains an arithmetic expression "CLABFEE / CRED" which is evaluated for each row. If the result is greater than 30, the row is selected.

2. The example also specifies that the result of the evaluation of "CLABFEE / CRED" is to be displayed. This is not necessary, but it helps you verify the result.

3. An expression may appear on either side of the operator in a WHERE clause. In the present query the condition could have been expressed as

```
WHERE CDEPT = 'CIS'
AND 30 < CLABFEE / CRED
```

SUMMARY

This chapter has introduced the use of arithmetic expressions to perform basic computations with data selected from a table. These expressions have a syntax similar to algebraic expressions described in a typical high school algebra textbook.

The presence of an arithmetic expression in a SELECT clause will generate a column in the output display. We emphasize *column* because the next chapter introduces the group functions which perform calculations on the selected data to produce a row which summarizes the selected data.

The column-edit options can be used to format results produced by arithmetic expressions. You simply specify the definition on the Report Format.

Summary exercises

The following exercises refer to the STAFF table.

6E. Assume all staff members are given a hundred dollar raise. Display the name and adjusted salary of every staff member.

6F. Assume all staff members are given a 15 percent raise. Display the name, and old and new salary amounts for every staff member.

6G. Assume all salaries are decreased by one hundred dollars. Display the name and adjusted salary of every staff member whose adjusted salary is less than $25,000.

6H. Consider only staff members whose current salary is less than $25,000. Assume this group of staff members is given a thousand-dollar raise. Display their names and adjusted salaries in descending salary sequence.

2

SQL/400 Built-in Functions

SQL/400 provides a large number of built-in functions that perform many tasks you will find to be very useful. A built-in function is part of (i.e., built into) SQL. Each function has a name (e.g., SUM) which indicates the purpose of the function. Each function will also accept one or more "arguments" which the function uses as input. Typically, a column name serves as an argument. For example, SUM(CLABFEE) is a function which accepts the CLABFEE column as an argument and produces the total of all lab fees as a result.

ORGANIZATION OF CHAPTERS

SQL/400 provides three broad categories of functions. The three chapters in this part of the text correspond to each category. We describe most, but not all, functions available with the SQL/400 product.

The first category of functions is called column functions. *We present the following functions in Chap. 7.*

```
SUM
MAX
MIN
AVG
COUNT
VARIANCE
STDDEV
```

We refer to the second category of functions as scalar functions. *These functions may be characterized by the type of arguments which they take. There are functions which operate on numeric data, character data, or allow data to be converted from one data type to another. We present a number of the SQL/400 functions in Chap. 8.*

We conclude Chap. 8 with a discussion of the concatenation operator (‖), which is not really a function, but is often used in conjunction with character functions.

The third category of functions is the date functions. *Chapter 10 presents a comprehensive overview of processing date/time information in addition to describing functions which operate on date/time data. We will see that SQL/400 understands the semantics we normally associate with date/time information.*

Column Functions

Chapter 6 presented arithmetic expressions that allow you to perform computations with selected data. This chapter continues the same theme. We introduce SQL's column functions which provide additional computational facilities.

A column function is used to scan a column of selected values and perform a computation based on those values. This chapter will present sample queries which illustrate the column functions: AVG, MAX, MIN, SUM, COUNT, VARIANCE, and STDDEV.

Column functions operate on groups of rows and generate a single row for each group. At the outset we will simply consider the entire COURSE table as a single group. Sample Queries 7.1 through 7.8 will select rows from this group and then apply a column function to produce a calculated result. Thereafter, we introduce the GROUP BY clause. You will use the GROUP BY clause when you wish to decompose selected rows into multiple groups and then apply a function to each separate group.

AVG FUNCTION

The first sample query applies the AVG function to the entire COURSE table which is treated as a single group.

Sample Query 7.1 What is the average lab fee for all courses described in the COURSE table?

> SELECT   AVG(CLABFEE)
>
> FROM   COURSE

AVG(CLABFEE)
_____

110.0000 . . .

Comments

1. A column function returns a result of the same data type as the argument to which it is applied. CLABFEE is defined as a numeric value; therefore, the result is also numeric. (Note that AVG can be applied only to numeric values.)

2. The result is a calculated value. Therefore, SQL/400 must generate a column heading. By default, this heading is simply the function and argument which generated the column. Sample Query 7.7.2 will show the use of the Report Format options to override this default and generate any desired heading.

3. In this example the group processed was the entire table. This does not have to be the case. A column function could be applied to a subset of rows by using a WHERE clause to form a smaller group. See the next sample query.

MIN AND MAX FUNCTIONS

The next sample query illustrates the MIN and MAX functions which accept both numeric and character string arguments. The example applies the functions to a group which is a subset of rows from the COURSE table.

Sample Query 7.2 Consider only rows for the philosophy department. What are the lowest and highest lab fees for these courses? Also, what are the lowest and highest values in the CNO column? (In other words, if the values in the CNO column were arranged in alphabetical sequence, what would be the first and last values?)

SELECT   MIN(CLABFEE), MAX(CLABFEE), MIN(CNO), MAX(CNO)

FROM   COURSE

WHERE   CDEPT = 'PHIL'

MIN (CLABFEE)	MAX (CLABFEE)	MIN (CNO)	MAX (CNO)
.00	200.00	P11	P44

Comments

1. The present query demonstrates that column functions can be applied to a subset of the table by specifying selection criteria in a WHERE clause.

2. The WHERE clause cannot reference any of the group functions. For example, "WHERE MAX(CLABFEE) > 50" is invalid. This restriction applies only to group functions. We will see in the next chapter that this does not apply to individual functions.

3. Again, we note that a group function returns a result of the same data type as the column to which it is applied. MAX and MIN were applied to CLABFEE, a numeric column, and produced numeric results. When applied to CNO, a character string column, they generated character string results. Note that character fields are padded to the same length for comparison. SQL/400 does a binary compare and does not do a character-by-character comparison.

SUM FUNCTION

Sample Query 7.3   What is the sum of all the lab-fee values for CIS courses?

SELECT   SUM(CLABFEE)

FROM   COURSE

WHERE   CDEPT = 'CIS'

SUM(CLABFEE)
_____

    750.00

Comment

This query demonstrates the SUM column function which allows the values of a numeric column to be totaled. In this query all six rows identifying the computer and information science department courses were selected. Their lab-fee values were added together and the total presented as the result of the query.

Exercises

7A.   Display the first course name which appears in alphabetic sequence.

7B.   What is the total lab fee for courses offered by the philosophy department?

7C.   Display the average, maximum, and minimum course lab fees for those CIS courses which have nonzero lab fees.

COUNT FUNCTION

The next sample query illustrates the COUNT(*) function.

Sample Query 7.4   How many theology courses are recorded in the COURSE table?

SELECT   COUNT(*)

FROM   COURSE

WHERE   CDEPT = 'THEO'

$$\frac{COUNT(*)}{4}$$

Comments

1. COUNT(*) simply counts the number of rows which match the selection criteria. The result is always an integer.
2. COUNT(*) is different from the other column functions in that it does not consider any values within the selected rows. It merely notes the presence of a row which matches the selection criteria.

Exercise

7D. How many rows are in the COURSE table?

7E. How many course names begin with the letter "E"?

VARIANCE AND STDDEV FUNCTIONS

VARIANCE and STDDEV are somewhat specialized. Statisticians will appreciate them. Most other users will probably never use them. We illustrate these functions without explaining the underlying statistical computations.

Sample Query 7.5 Display the variance and standard deviation of all the course lab fees in the COURSE table.

SELECT   VARIANCE(CLABFEE), STDDEV(CLABFEE)

FROM   COURSE

VARIANCE(CLABFEE)	STDDEV(CLABFEE)
1.6157143E+004	1.2711075036E+002

Comment

SQL/400 supports a number of other mathematical functions such as log, sin, cosine, etc. These functions are scalar functions and will be discussed in Chap. 8.

USING COLUMN FUNCTIONS WITH ARITHMETIC EXPRESSIONS

Column functions can be used with arithmetic expressions to have the system perform more complex calculations. A function may be applied to an expression, or an expression can contain a function.

Sample Query 7.6   Display two values. The first is the sum of all lab fees assuming each has been increased by $25. The second is the result of adding $25 to the sum of all the lab fees.

SELECT	SUM(CLABFEE+25), SUM(CLABFEE)+25
FROM	COURSE

SUM(CLABFEE+25)	SUM(CLABFEE)+25
1,890.00	1,565.00

Comments

1. SUM(CLABFEE+25): An expression may serve as an argument to a built-in function. Here the expression, CLABFEE+25, is the argument of the function, SUM. The system will first evaluate the expression (increment each CLABFEE by 25) and then apply SUM to these values to determine the result.

2. SUM(CLABFEE)+25: Here an expression contains a built-in function as an operand. Note the difference between this computation and the previous one. Here the SUM was first evaluated using just CLABFEE as its argument. This intermediate result (1540) was then increased by 25 to produce the displayed result.

Exercise

7F. Assume new lab fees are to be calculated at $50 for each credit. What would be the average lab fee for courses offered by the theology department?

GROUP BY Clause

SQL provides the capability of forming smaller groups from the selected rows and then having column functions applied to each group. The column that the rows are to be grouped by is identified in the GROUP BY clause. When a GROUP BY clause is included in a query, all the selected rows are grouped by a common value within the specified column. This process is performed automatically without the need to specify actual values that may be present in the grouping column. Then the column function is applied to each group.

Sample Query 7.7   For each department which offers courses, determine the average lab fee for courses offered by the department.

SELECT   CDEPT, AVG(CLABFEE)

FROM   COURSE

GROUP BY CDEPT

CDEPT	AVG(CLABFEE)
CIS	125.00..
PHIL	87.50..
THEO	110.00..

Comments

1. The GROUP BY clause resulted in all COURSE rows being effectively reorganized in an intermediate result where the rows are grouped by the CDEPT column. This intermediate result has all rows with the same value in the CDEPT column placed in separate groups.

   In the present example all rows were arranged by common CDEPT values. After the groups were formed, the AVG function was applied to the CLABFEE values in each group. Because there are three distinct CDEPT values (CIS, PHIL, THEO), three groups were formed and three averages returned, each in a separate row.

2. Note that the SELECT clause contains a column name, CDEPT, along with a column. The CDEPT value can be displayed with the function results because of the presence of the GROUP BY CDEPT clause. This column value is a characteristic of the group. It is the same for every value in the group. Therefore, it may be displayed with the summary information produced by the function.

3. The database is not at all changed by the use of the GROUP BY clause. The rows of the table being selected from are not actually rearranged in the table.

4. *A common error:* Many users get careless and enter a statement like the following. (Presumably, the user forgot the GROUP BY clause.) This causes an *error.*

```
SELECT CDEPT, AVG(CLABFEE)
FROM   COURSE
```

Notice that the SELECT clause contains both a column name and a column function. Whenever a SELECT clause contains a column function, any other column which is not referenced by a column function must be referenced in a GROUP BY clause.

5. Recall that the ORDER BY clause can reference a column by its relative position. However, the GROUP BY clause must explicitly reference a column by its name (i.e., "GROUP BY 1" is invalid).

6. Because multiple rows are displayed, it makes sense to consider sorting the result. Note, however, that the output is already sorted by the CDEPT column. This occurred because the system will establish an internal sequence to establish the groups. Hence, the displayed sequence is somewhat of an accidental side effect of the grouping. Future versions of SQL/400 could perform the grouping operation by some other technique. Therefore, it is best to include an ORDER BY clause to explicitly indicate the desired sequence which may or may not be the same as any sort done for the purpose of grouping. See the next sample query.

The WHERE clause can be used to include or exclude certain rows from consideration *prior to* the formation of groups. The next query illustrates this point. It also explicitly specifies the sequence of the output display.

Sample Query 7.8 For each department which offers courses, determine the average lab fee of all three-credit courses offered by the department. Display the output in ascending sequence by department identifier.

SELECT   CDEPT, AVG(CLABFEE)

FROM   COURSE

WHERE   CRED = 3

GROUP BY CDEPT

ORDER BY CDEPT

CDEPT	AVG(CLABFEE)
CIS	125.0000 . . .
PHIL	166.6666 . . .
THEO	80.0000 . . .

Comments

1. The example uses a WHERE clause to select just the three-credit courses for inclusion in the groups. We emphasize that this selection applied to individual rows (not the groups) and occurred *before* the formation of the groups.

   Compare the output with that of the previous example. The average lab fee for the CIS department is unchanged because all its courses are worth three credits. However, the six-credit courses offered by the philosophy and theology departments were excluded from the groups. Hence their average lab-fee values differ from those in the previous example.

2. The ORDER BY clause established the sort sequence. Again, because this sequence corresponds to that used by the system to establish the groups, the output would be the same if we omitted the ORDER BY clause. However, it is best to include it. We reiterate a point made in Chap. 3. The ORDER BY clause is the last clause in a SELECT statement.

3. You can sort by any column in the result table. In this example, we could have sorted the result using either of the ORDER BY clauses shown in the following examples.

```
SELECT    CDEPT, AVG(CLABFEE)

FROM      COURSE

WHERE     CRED = 3

GROUP BY CDEPT

ORDER BY 1
```

```
SELECT    CDEPT, AVG(CLABFEE)

FROM      COURSE

WHERE     CRED = 3

GROUP BY CDEPT

ORDER BY 2
```

Exercises

7G. For each department which offers courses, display the department identifier followed by the total number of credits offered by the department.

7H. For each department which offers courses, display its department identifier and the number of courses it offers. Sort the result by department identifier.

7I. Do not consider six-credit courses. For each department which offers courses, display the department identifier followed by the total of the lab fees for courses offered by the department. Sort the result by the total lab fee in descending sequence.

Sometimes a particular group may consist of just one row. The next query illustrates this situation.

Sample Query 7.9   For each distinct lab-fee value, determine the total number of credits for courses having this lab-fee value. Sort the result by lab fee in descending order.

```
SELECT    CLABFEE, SUM(CRED)

FROM      COURSE

GROUP BY  CLABFEE

ORDER BY  CLABFEE DESC
```

CLABFEE	SUM(CRED)
500.00	3
200.00	9
150.00	3
100.00	9
90.00	3
50.00	6
.00	15

Comments

1. There are seven distinct CLABFEE values recorded in the COURSE table. The system formed a group corresponding to each of the seven values. The CLABFEE values of 90.00, 150.00, and 500.00 occurred only once in the table. Therefore, the system formed a group consisting of one row for each of these values. The sum of the credits for such values is what you would expect, namely, just the credit value itself.

2. The ORDER BY clause was used to establish a sort sequence different from the one done by the system for the purpose of grouping.

Sometimes the selection criteria specified in a WHERE clause will eliminate all rows from a potential group. Hence, some possible groups will never be formed and will not appear in the output.

Sample Query 7.10   For each department which offers six-credit courses, display the average lab fee of the six-credit courses.

```
SELECT    CDEPT, AVG(CLABFEE)

FROM      COURSE

WHERE     CRED = 6

GROUP  BY  CDEPT
```

CDEPT	AVG(CLABFEE)
PHIL	.0000 . . .
THEO	200.0000 . . .

Comments

1. The WHERE clause eliminated any three-credit courses from consideration. Hence, the potential group for the CIS department, which only offers three-credit courses, was not formed.

2. Note that because the philosophy and theology departments each offer just one six-credit course, the PHIL and THEO groups each contained just one row. If you wanted to know the number of rows for each group, you could apply the COUNT(*) function.

HAVING CLAUSE

The absence of a CIS group in the previous example occurred because the WHERE clause "just happened" to exclude every CIS row from the group. Sometimes we want to explicitly include just certain identifiable groups in the output display. The HAVING clause is used for this purpose. *We emphasize that the HAVING clause applies only to groups, whereas the WHERE clause applies only to individual rows.*

Sample Query 7.11   Display the department identifier and average lab fee for any department where that average exceeds $100.

```
SELECT    CDEPT, AVG(CLABFEE)

FROM      COURSE

GROUP BY CDEPT

HAVING AVG(CLABFEE) > 100
```

CDEPT	AVG(CLABFEE)
CIS	125.0000..
THEO	110.0000..

Comments

1. The purpose of the HAVING clause is to specify conditions for groups similar to the way the WHERE clause specifies conditions for rows. In row-level processing the WHERE clause identifies conditions which must be met for a row to be retrieved. Any row which does not meet the conditions will not be retrieved, and is removed from any further processing. The HAVING clause works in a similar manner but with regard to groups rather than to rows. The GROUP BY clause is used to specify how groups are formed. After the groups have been formed, a group must match the condition specified by the HAVING clause in order to be displayed. In this example, the PHIL group was formed but not displayed because its average lab fee was not greater than 100.

2. *Syntax:* The HAVING clause can only be present if the statement contains a GROUP BY clause. The HAVING clause must immediately follow the GROUP BY clause.

3. The condition specified on the HAVING clause contains a reference to the function value, AVG(CLABFEE). This is almost always the case. In the current example, the HAVING clause condition cannot reference a specific column at the row level. For example, "HAVING CLABFEE = 0" would result in an error. This occurs because the CLABFEE value is not present in the group after the AVG function has been applied. The condition can reference a value which is present only after the group has been formed.

4. As with WHERE conditions we can use NOT to exclude certain groups from the display. For example, the following HAVING clause would display those groups with an average lab fee which is less than or equal to $100.

```
HAVING NOT AVG(CLABFEE) > 100
```

The other Boolean operators, AND, OR, IN, and BETWEEN, can also be used with the HAVING clause. (See Sample Query 7.15.)

Exercises

7J. Display the department identifier and maximum lab fee for any department which offers a course where the lab fee exceeds $300.

7K. Display the department identifier and total number of credits offered by the department if that total exceeds 15.

A SELECT statement will often contain both a WHERE clause and a HAVING clause. The WHERE clause will initially select rows for inclusion into groups, and a HAVING clause will subsequently select just certain groups for display. The following query is a modification of the previous one, which excludes the theology department from consideration.

Sample Query 7.12   For every department, except the theology department, which has an average lab fee over $100, display its department identifier followed by its average lab fee.

```
SELECT    CDEPT, AVG(CLABFEE)

FROM      COURSE

WHERE     NOT CDEPT = 'THEO'

GROUP BY CDEPT

HAVING AVG(CLABFEE) > 100
```

CDEPT	AVG(CLABFEE)
CIS	125.000..

Comment

It is important that you understand the logical sequence of the operations SQL follows in response to this statement. First the WHERE clause prohibits the formation of a group for the theology department (even though its average lab fee does exceed $100). This means that the intermediate result consists of two groups corresponding to the philosophy and computer science departments. Thereafter the HAVING clause selects the CIS department for display because, unlike the philosophy department, its average lab fee exceeds $100. This process is outlined in Fig. 7.1.

COURSE Table

WHERE NOT CDEPT = 'THEO'	

CDEPT	CLABFEE
CIS	100
CIS	50
CIS	0
CIS	0
PHIL	100
PHIL	200
CIS	100
PHIL	50
CIS	500
PHIL	0

GROUP BY CDEPT

CDEPT	CLABFEE
CIS	100
CIS	50
CIS	500
CIS	100
CIS	0
CIS	0
PHIL	100
PHIL	200
PHIL	50
PHIL	0

SELECT CDEPT, AVG(CLABFEE)

CDEPT	AVG(CLABFEE)
CIS	125
PHIL	87.5

HAVING AVG(CLABFEE) > 100

CDEPT	AVG(CLABFEE)
CIS	125

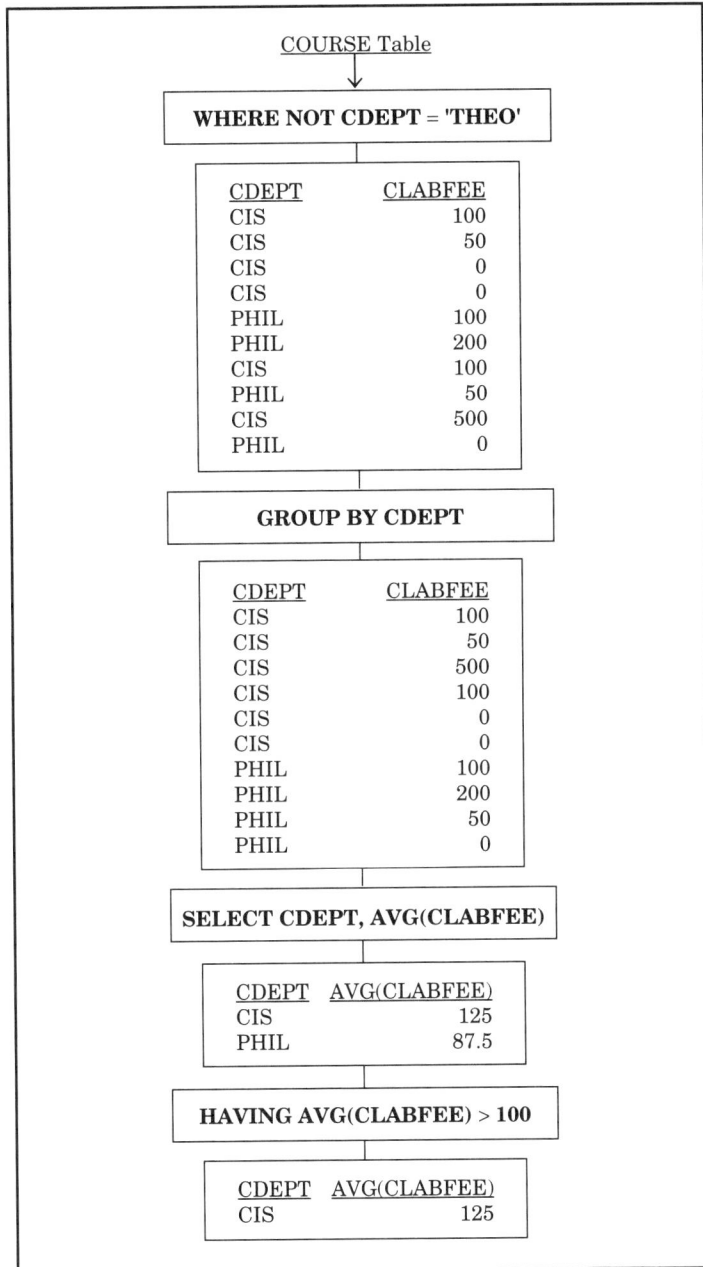

Figure 7.1 Logical sequence of operations for Sample Query 7.12.

MULTILEVEL GROUPS

It is possible to reference multiple column names in the GROUP BY clause. The intent is to specify the formation of subgroups within groups. Consider the next example.

Sample Query 7.13   We are interested in finding the average, maximum, and minimum lab-fee values for all courses offered by each department. Within each department we need to have this information broken out for each distinct credit value. Display the department identifier and credit value followed by the requested statistics.

```
SELECT   CDEPT, CRED, AVG(CLABFEE),

         MAX(CLABFEE), MIN(CLABFEE)

FROM     COURSE

GROUP BY CDEPT, CRED
```

CDEPT	CRED	AVG(CLABFEE)	MAX(CLABFEE)	MIN(CLABFEE)
CIS	3	125.0000 ...	500.00	.00
PHIL	3	116.6666 ...	200.00	50.00
PHIL	6	.0000 ...	.00	.00
THEO	3	80.0000 ...	150.00	.00
THEO	6	200.0000 ...	200.00	200.00

Comments

1. *Logic:* The sample query requested two levels of grouping to be applied. First, all courses had to be grouped by department. This was accomplished by specifying the CDEPT column in the GROUP BY clause. Second, within each of the department groups, smaller groups needed to be formed based on identical credit values. This was accomplished by specifying the CRED column after the CDEPT column in the GROUP BY clause. In the same way that we are able to specify different levels of ordering with the ORDER BY clause, we can also specify different levels of grouping with the GROUP BY clause.

2. *Syntax:* The "GROUP BY" is followed by one or more columns separated by commas. As a reminder, we observe that the SELECT clause contains some group functions and that two columns, CDEPT and CRED, are not arguments of grouping functions. This means that both columns must be referenced in the GROUP BY clause.

3. It can be observed in the output display that all of the CIS department courses have the same CRED value of 3. This is apparent because there is only a single row produced with a CDEPT value of "CIS". Remember that a group function always produces a single row for each group of records to which it is applied. In the cases of the PHIL and THEO departments, two rows were returned, indicating that these departments have courses with two different CRED values, 3 and 6.

Exercises

7L. Consider only three-credit courses. Display the department identifier and total lab fee for courses offered by each department if the total is less than or equal to $150.

7M. Do not consider courses with a lab fee over $400. Display the department identifier and maximum lab fee charged by the department if that maximum exceeds $175.

The HAVING clause can be used with multilevel grouping to select just certain groups for display.

Sample Query 7.14 Extend the previous query by retrieving the average, maximum, and minimum lab-fee values by credit within a department only for those groups which have a maximum lab fee value greater than zero.

SELECT   CDEPT, CRED, AVG(CLABFEE),

           MAX(CLABFEE), MIN(CLABFEE)

FROM   COURSE

GROUP BY CDEPT, CRED

HAVING MAX(CLABFEE) > 0

CDEPT	CRED	AVG(CLABFEE)	MAX(CLABFEE)	MIN(CLABFEE)
CIS	3	125.0000 ...	500.00	.00
PHIL	3	116.6666 ...	200.00	50.00
THEO	3	80.0000 ...	150.00	.00
THEO	6	200.0000 ...	200.00	200.00

Comment

An examination of the previous query results reveals that the HAVING clause has eliminated one row from the output display. This is the row corresponding to the six-credit philosophy group which consisted of one row having a zero lab fee. Hence the maximum lab fee of this group did not match the HAVING condition.

In Chap. 4 we observed that the WHERE clause can contain multiple conditions connected with the Boolean operators (AND, OR, NOT, IN, and BETWEEN). Likewise a HAVING clause can have multiple conditions connected by Boolean operators. Again, the only difference is that the conditions pertain to group values.

Sample Query 7.15   What is the average department lab-fee value for those departments where this average is greater than $100 and the department offers less than six courses?

```
SELECT      CDEPT, AVG(CLABFEE)

FROM        COURSE

GROUP BY CDEPT

HAVING      AVG(CLABFEE) > 100

AND         COUNT(*) < 6
```

CDEPT	AVG(CLABFEE)
THEO	110.0000 ...

Comment

This example illustrates that it is possible to specify more than one condition in a HAVING clause. Both conditions reference column functions which are applied to the groups formed by the GROUP BY clause. Both of these conditions must be met by any group if it is to be displayed because AND was used to connect the conditions. The same rules of logic and hierarchy of Boolean operators apply to the HAVING clause with multiple conditions as apply to the WHERE clause.

FINAL COMMENTS ON THE GROUP FUNCTIONS

HAVING Clause

The HAVING clause specifies a condition applied to groups which must be met in order for that group to be displayed. The HAVING condition must reflect a group-level value, something common to all rows in the group. We usually specify a group function in the HAVING clause. It is also possible, however, to specify the name of a grouping column and some condition which that column must meet for all rows in the group. Examples include statements like

```
SELECT CDEPT, CLABFEE          SELECT CDEPT, AVG(CLABFEE)
FROM   COURSE                  FROM   COURSE
GROUP BY CDEPT, CLABFEE        GROUP BY CDEPT
HAVING CLABFEE > 0            HAVING CDEPT LIKE '_H _ _'
```

These queries are acceptable to the system because the column values are common to all rows in the group. However, we note these examples produce results which can be better realized by using WHERE clauses.

Null Values

A group function might return a questionable result if it is executed with any column argument which contains null values. Because the COURSE table has no null values, the previous sample queries avoided this complexity. This topic will be discussed in detail in Chap. 14.

Limitations of Grouping

When the group functions are applied to groups, the values of the individual rows are no longer available for display. Many reports show both detail lines (corresponding to rows in the table) and summary lines (corresponding to the group statistics). For example, we might like to see the following output.

CDEPT	CLABFEE
CIS	50
CIS	100
CIS	100
CIS	500
	750

Because the group functions "compress" the individual row values, such reports cannot be directly generated by SQL. However, you can use SQL to retrieve the raw data. Then you can utilize the report formatting options of Query Manager to produce the summary line. We will present this technique in Chap. 10.

Nesting of Column Functions

Finally, we note that you cannot embed one column function within another. For example, it would seem perfectly reasonable to calculate the average lab fees for all courses on an individual department basis.

```
SELECT CDEPT, AVG(CLABFEE)
FROM COURSE
GROUP BY CDEPT
```

We might wish to follow such a request with an inquiry regarding which department had the highest of the average lab fees. However, such a request would cause an error.

```
SELECT CDEPT, MAX(AVG(CLABFEE))
FROM COURSE
GROUP BY CDEPT
```

SUMMARY

This chapter introduced SQL/400's column built-in functions. These functions operate over a group of values in a column of a table or a group of values produced by an arithmetic expression.

The GROUP BY clause was introduced. This clause forms separate groups based on some column value. When this clause is present in a SELECT statement, each group function performs its calculations on each separate group. Finally, the HAVING clause was presented. Its purpose is to identify specific groups for display. If the HAVING clause is not present, all groups are displayed.

Summary Exercises

The following exercises refer to the STAFF table. Recall that the column names are ENAME, ETITLE, ESALARY, and DEPT.

7O. Display the sum and average of all staff member salaries. Also display the largest and smallest individual salary.

7P. How many staff members are employed by the theology department?

7Q. Assume a total of $5000 is allocated for staff member raises. What is the new total salary for all staff members?

7R. For all DEPT values found in the STAFF table, display the department identifier followed by the average salary for that department.

7S. Consider only staff members whose salary exceeds $600. For each department which has such a staff member, display the department identifier followed by the total amount paid to these staff members. Sort the result by the total salary amounts.

Scalar Functions

This chapter introduces SQL/400's scalar functions. Chapter 7 presented column functions which operate on a group of values in a column. In contrast, there is no grouping with a scalar function. A scalar function only operates on one value.

There are a variety of scalar functions which support arithmetic operations, string manipulation, data conversion, date/time processing, and other miscellaneous operations. This chapter presents a sampling of the more useful functions with the exception of date/time functions which are presented in Chap. 9.

We note that many of the scalar functions are almost self-explanatory. For this reason many of the sample queries will be presented without extensive comments.

ARITHMETIC FUNCTIONS

This section describes the SQL/400 arithmetic functions. As you would expect, these functions can be applied only to numeric arguments. Figure 8.1 summarizes these functions. We only present two examples for the purposes of illustration.

"*Exp*"	Can be a valid numeric expression or column containing numeric values
ABSVAL(Exp)	Returns the absolute value
ANTILOG(Exp)	Returns the antilogarithm (Base 10)
ASIN(Exp)	Returns the arc sine, in radians
ATAN(Exp)	Returns the arc tangent in radians
ATANH(Exp)	Returns the hyperbolic arc tangent
COS(Exp)	Returns the cosine
COSH(Exp)	Returns the hyperbolic cosine
COT(Exp)	Returns the cotangent
EXP(Exp)	Returns a value that is the natural logarithm raised to the power of Exp
LN(Exp)	Returns the natural logarithm
LOG(Exp)	Returns the common logarithm Base 10 of Exp
MOD(Exp,Exp)	Returns the remainder of the division of the first Exp by the second Exp
SIN(Exp)	Returns the sine
SINH(Exp)	Returns the hyperbolic sine
SQRT(Exp)	Returns the square root
TAN(Exp)	Returns the tangent
TANH(Exp)	Returns the hyperbolic tangent

Figure 8.1 Arithmetic conversion functions.

Square Root

Sample Query 8.1   For each student display the square root of his or her I.Q.

```
SELECT    SNAME, SIQ, SQRT(SIQ)

FROM    STUDENT
```

SNAME	SIQ	SQRT (SIQ)
CURLEY DUBAY	122	1.1045E+001
MOE DUBAY	120	1.0954E+001
ROCKY BALBOA	99	9.9499E+000
LARRY DUBAY	121	1.1000E+001

Comment

Observe that the result is displayed in scientific notation. The following pages show data conversion functions that can be used to convert the results into a more traditional format.

Absolute Value

Sample Query 8.2   For each student display the absolute value between his or her I.Q. and 120.

```
SELECT    SNAME, SIQ, ABSVAL(120 – SIQ)

FROM    STUDENT
```

SNAME	SIQ	ABSVAL function
CURLEY DUBAY	122	2
MOE DUBAY	120	0
ROCKY BALBOA	99	21
LARRY DUBAY	121	1

Comment

Observe that the argument to the function is an arithmetic expression. When this occurs Query Manager will generate a column heading in a different form than that shown in earlier examples.

DATA CONVERSION FUNCTIONS

This section describes SQL/400's conversion functions. Figure 8.2 summarizes these functions.

"Exp"	Can be a valid expression or column
"P"	Precision
"S"	Scale
DECIMAL(Exp,P,S)	Returns a packed decimal value. Exp must be numeric
DIGITS(Exp)	Returns a character string representation of a numeric argument
FLOAT(Exp)	Returns a floating point value. Exp must be numeric
HEX(Exp)	Returns the hexadecimal representation of the argument
INTEGER(Exp)	Returns an integer value. Exp must be numeric
TRANSLATE(Exp)	Returns the uppercase string of the expression. Exp must be a valid character string
ZONED(Exp,P,S)	Returns a zoned decimal value. Exp must be numeric

Figure 8.2 Data conversion functions.

One of the administrative staff was assigned to determine the effect of a 5 percent raise on faculty salaries. This person decided to investigate different ways they could use scalar functions to present the results.

Sample Query 8.3.1   Show the faculty raises in decimal format.

```
SELECT   FNAME, FSALARY*1.05, DECIMAL(FSALARY*1.05,7,0)

FROM     FACULTY
```

FNAME	FSALARY*1.05	DECIMAL conversion
KATHY PEPE	36,750.00	36,750
JESSIE MARTYN	47,250.00	47,250
JOE COHN	36,750.00	36,750
AL HARTLEY	47,250.00	47,250
JULIE MARTYN	47,250.00	47,250
LISA BOBAK	37,800.00	37,800
BARB HLAVATY	36,750.00	36,750

Sample Query 8.3.2   Show the faculty raise as a character string of digits.

SELECT FNAME, FSALARY*1.05, DIGITS(FSALARY*1.05)

FROM FACULTY

FNAME	FSALARY*1.05	DIGITS conversion
KATHY PEPE	36,750.00	0367500000
JESSIE MARTYN	47,250.00	0472500000
JOE COHN	36,750.00	0367500000
AL HARTLEY	47,250.00	0472500000
JULIE MARTYN	47,250.00	0472500000
LISA BOBAK	37,800.00	0378000000
BARB HLAVATY	36,750.00	0367500000

Sample Query 8.3.3   Show the faculty raise in a floating point format.

SELECT FNAME, FSALARY*1.05, FLOAT(FSALARY*1.05)

FROM FACULTY

FNAME	FSALARY*1.05	FLOAT(FSALARY*1.05)
KATHY PEPE	36,750.00	3.675000000E+004
JESSIE MARTYN	47,250.00	4.725000000E+004
JOE COHN	36,750.00	3.675000000E+004
AL HARTLEY	47,250.00	4.725000000E+004
JULIE MARTYN	47,250.00	4.725000000E+004
LISA BOBAK	37,800.00	3.780000000E+004
BARB HLAVATY	36,750.00	3.675000000E+004

The next sample query will be of interest to those who might have some background in programming and an understanding of data types.

Sample Query 8.3.4 Show the faculty raises in hexadecimal format.

SELECT   FNAME, FSALARY*1.05, HEX(FSALARY*1.05)

FROM   FACULTY

FNAME	FSALARY*1.05	HEX(FSALARY*1.05)
KATHY PEPE	36,750.00	3675000C
JESSIE MARTYN	47,250.00	4725000C
JOE COHN	36,750.00	3675000C
AL HARTLEY	47,250.00	4725000C
JULIE MARTYN	47,250.00	4725000C
LISA BOBAK	37,800.00	3780000C
BARB HLAVATY	36,750.00	3675000C

Sample Query 8.3.5 Show the faculty raises as an integer.

SELECT   FNAME, FSALARY*1.05, INTEGER(FSALARY*1.05)

FROM   FACULTY

FNAME	FSALARY*1.05	INTEGER(FSALARY*1.05)
KATHY PEPE	36,750.00	36,750
JESSIE MARTYN	47,250.00	47,250
JOE COHN	36,750.00	36,750
AL HARTLEY	47,250.00	47,250
JULIE MARTYN	47,250.00	47,250
LISA BOBAK	37,800.00	37,800
BARB HLAVATY	36,750.00	36,750

CHARACTER FUNCTIONS

This section describes SQL/400's character functions. As you would expect, these functions can be applied only to character string arguments. Figure 8.3 summarizes most of the character string functions.

"Exp"	Can be a valid character string expression or a column containing character string values.
Length(Exp)	Length of Exp
Strip(Exp)	Removes blanks from start and end of Exp
Strip(Exp,L)	Removes leading (L) blanks from start of Exp
Strip(Exp,T)	Removes trailing (T) blanks from end of Exp
Strip(Exp,B,C)	Removes both (B) leading and trailing characters where C identifies the character to be removed
Substr(Exp,N)	Returns a substring of length N starting from the first position of Exp
Substr(Exp,N,S)	Returns a substring of length N starting at Nth position of Exp

Figure 8.3 Some character functions.

The next sample queries show examples of scalar functions which operate on character-string data. Again, there will be circumstances where the user needs to be sensitive to the differences between fixed-length and variable-length character-string columns. We note the FACULTY table has three fixed-length columns, FNO, FNAME, and FDEPT, and one variable-length column, FADDR.

Sample Query 8.4   Display the address and number of characters in the address for each faculty member.

SELECT	FADDR, LENGTH(FADDR)
FROM	FACULTY

FADDR	LENGTH (FADDR)
7 STONERIDGE RD	15
2135 EAST DR	12
BOX 1138	8
SILVER STREET	13
2135 EAST DR	12
77 LAUGHING LN	14
489 SOUTH ROAD	14

Sample Query 8.5   Display the entire faculty name, the first letter of the faculty name, and the fourth, fifth, and sixth letters of the faculty name.

SELECT	FNAME, SUBSTR(FNAME,1,1), SUBSTR(FNAME,4,3)
FROM	FACULTY

FNAME	SUBSTR function	SUBSTR function
KATHY PEPE	K	HY_
JESSIE MARTYN	J	SIE
JOE COHN	J	_CO
AL HARTLEY	A	HAR
JULIE MARTYN	J	IE_
LISA BOBAK	L	A_B
BARB HLAVATY	B	B_H

NESTING SCALAR FUNCTIONS

The next sample query demonstrates the nesting of the STRIP function within the LENGTH function. This example illustrates how to determine the number of actual characters stored in a fixed-length column.

Sample Query 8.6   Display the name and actual number of characters in the name.

```
SELECT     FNAME, LENGTH(STRIP(FNAME,T))

FROM       FACULTY
```

FNAME	LENGTH function
KATHY PEPE	10
JESSIE MARTYN	13
JOE COHN	8
AL HARTLEY	10
JULIE MARTYN	12
LISA BOBAK	10
BARB HLAVATY	12

Comment

The STRIP function is applied first to remove trailing blanks. The LENGTH function then determines the number of characters remaining in the string, i.e., the significant characters of the string.

Exercises

8A.   Display all course lab fees as integers.

8B.   Display the course number and the lab fee per credit for all courses. Present the calculated result with two decimal places.

8C.   For each philosophy course, display the last two digits of its course number, the first five characters of its name, and the fourth and fifth characters of its description.

8D.   For each course, display the length of each course name.

CONCATENATION OPERATOR (‖)

The SUBSTR function is used to extract a portion of a string, a kind of string subtraction. SQL also provides a method for putting two strings together, a kind of string addition. This operation is called "concatenation" and is specified by placing two vertical bars (‖) between the strings to be connected. We note that the concatenation operator is an operator, similar to the arithmetic operators (+, −, *, /). It is not a built-in function.

Sample Query 8.7   Display the concatenation of the FADDR and FDEPT and also the FDEPT and FADDR columns.

SELECT FADDR ‖ FDEPT, FDEPT ‖ FADDR

FROM FACULTY

FADDR ‖ FDEPT	FDEPT ‖ FADDR
7 STONERIDGE RDPHIL	PHIL7 STONERIDGE RD
2135 EAST DRTHEO	THEO2135 EAST DR
BOX 1138CIS	CIS BOX 1138
SILVER STREETCIS	CIS SILVER STREET
2135 EAST DRPHIL	PHIL2135 EAST DR
77 LAUGHING LNTHEO	THEO77 LAUGHING LN
489 SOUTH ROADCIS	CIS 489 SOUTH ROAD

Comments

1. FDEPT contains 4-byte fixed-length character strings. Observe the trailing blank after "CIS" is retained in the output of the second column.

2. Very often data are stored in separate columns which are merged in a report. For example, an employee table might have a last-name column (LAST_NAME) and a first-name column (FIRST_NAME). You could use concatenation to merge the name with an embedded blank separator as shown below. If FIRST_NAME is variable length, then

   ```
   FIRST_NAME ‖ ' ' ‖ LAST_NAME
   LAST_NAME ‖ ',' ‖ FIRST_NAME
   ```

   Otherwise, if the FIRST_NAME is a fixed-length column you would want to utilize the strip function.

   ```
   STRIP(FIRST_NAME,T) ‖ ' ' ‖ LAST_NAME
   STRIP(LAST_NAME,T) ‖ ', ' ‖ FIRST_NAME
   ```

SUMMARY

In this chapter we presented the SQL/400 scalar functions. A scalar function receives a column value or expression as an argument and returns a single value for each row on which it operates. We examined conversion, character, and arithmetic functions. The date/time functions will be discussed in Chap. 9.

It is important to note that Query Manager also provides edit functions that can substitute or enhance the output of the scalar functions.

Summary Exercises

8E. For each department which offers courses, display the department identifier and the length of the department identifier. Display each department only once.

8F. For each course having a description which is less than 15 characters, display the course number and description.

8G. Concatenate the CDESCP and CNO columns.

Processing Date and Time Information

This chapter introduces special facilities for processing data which represent date and time information. Previous chapters introduced and emphasized the differences between two major "standard" data types, numeric and character. Traditional data processing systems use some form of numeric or character data to encode date and time information. This requires the user or some application program to go through extra effort to decode this data. This approach is aggravated by the multitude of different formats for date and time information.

SQL/400 has special facilities to simplify the storage and manipulation of date and time information. Most of these facilities involve the use of special built-in functions. While these functions will reduce the effort required for programming tasks involving date and time information, the logic of such tasks can be inherently complex. For this reason, we chose to introduce only some of the more basic concepts and facilities of handling date and time information. This chapter will restrict its attention to displaying date and time information.

DATE DATA TYPE

Chapter 12 will introduce the CREATE TABLE statement where you will see how each column in a newly created table is assigned a specific data type. There you will learn that, in addition to specifying the different variations of numeric and character data, it is possible to specify that a given column can contain only date, time, or timestamp values.

SQL/400 supports a three-part DATE (year, month, day) that represents a given point in time based on the Gregorian calendar. TIME is also a three-part value (hour, minute, second) that specifies a time under a twenty-four-hour clock. TIMESTAMP is a seven-part value that designates a combined date and time based on the Gregorian calendar (year, month, day, hour, minute, second, microsecond).

We emphasize the fact that SQL/400 has its own internal representation for the date/time data types which need not concern us because this code will automatically be converted to a character-string representation when displayed. The sample queries of this chapter will describe a variety of display formats.

The availability of a data type for date information means that such information does not need to be represented as some form of numeric or character-string value. It also means that the system recognizes a column as containing date/time data and supports certain useful operations which are applicable to this data. In effect, date/time data represent a third category of data distinct from numeric and character-string data. Many of the special built-in functions introduced in this chapter can only reference columns which contain date/time data.

Because the COURSE table does not have any columns with date/time information, we introduce the REGISTRAT table. This table has a column, REG_DATE, which is declared as a DATE data type, and another column, REG_TIME, which is declared as a TIME data type.

In our mythical educational database we represent a course as a row in the COURSE table. We now assume that a student, who is identified by a student number (SNO), can register for any of these courses.

Because a department chairperson may choose to offer multiple sections of the same course, each class is identified by a combination of its course number (CNO) and a section number (SEC). Students may register for one or more classes by executing an application program which asks the student to enter his student number and the course and section numbers of the classes he wants to attend. The program will use this information to update the REGISTRAT table. It will insert one row for each class the student wants to attend.

The REGISTRAT table contains the following columns.

CNO	Course number (character string, length = 3)
SEC	Section number (character string, length = 2)
SNO	Student number (character string, length = 3)
REG_DATE	Registration date (DATE data type)
REG_TIME	Registration time (TIME data type)

This table contains a row for each class the student hopes to attend. Because some classes have a limited class size, a first-come first-served acceptance policy applies. Therefore, the application program must store the date and time of the student's registration in the table. This is the purpose of the REG_DATE and REG_TIME columns. The process by which the application program uses embedded SQL to insert rows in the REGISTRAT table is beyond the scope of this text. We assume that the program has been executed a number of times and that the REGISTRAT table now contains some number of rows that you would like to examine. The following sample queries illustrate some of the SQL facilities that you might use.

DISPLAYING DATE/TIME DATA

We stated above that date/time information has a special internal data representation. However, whenever such information is displayed, you will observe the date/time values displayed as simple character strings. This is because the system will automatically convert the internal date/time code to a character string prior to display. The first sample query will display the REG_DATE and REG_TIME values as simple character strings using the default formats.

Sample Query 9.1

Display all information in the REGISTRAT table.

```
SELECT      *

FROM        REGISTRAT
```

CNO	SEC	SNO	REG DATE	REG TIME
C11	01	800	12/15/1987	10:00:00
C11	01	325	02/04/1988	11:35:00
C11	02	150	12/17/1987	12:12:00
P33	01	100	12/23/1987	13:18:00
P33	01	800	12/23/1987	16:00:00
T11	01	100	12/23/1987	16:35:00
T11	01	150	12/15/1987	17:00:00
T11	01	800	12/15/1987	19:00:00
C11	01	111	12/26/1992	19:21:00
T33	01	325	09/19/1991	12:23:00
T33	01	100	09/19/1991	13:22:00
T33	01	150	09/19/1991	14:44:00
C66	01	200	10/02/1993	22:22:00

Comments

1. Observe the REG_DATE and REG_TIME columns. The displayed values appear as character strings formatted according to the SQL/400 Query Manager default format. Observe that the default format for REG_TIME uses a 24-hour clock notation.

2. It is possible to display date/time values using other formats. The next sample query will illustrate this facility.

3. Observe that the headings for REG_DATE and REG_TIME are wrapped because of the underscore character in the column names. (See Chap. 2.)

ALTERNATIVE DATE FORMATS: EDIT COLUMN FORMATTING FUNCTION

You are not restricted to SQL/400's default date format. The Edit Column Formatting option (one of the Query Manager options introduced in Chap. 2) can be used to display a date/time value in a variety of different formats. When the first argument is a date value, the second argument must be a valid "date format model." A number of date format models are illustrated in Fig. 9.1. The next sample query illustrates the use of Date/Time Edit Codes with the date format model ('MM/DD/YY').

Sample Query 9.2

Same as previous query. This time, show REG_DATE in the conventional MM/DD/YY format and REG_TIME in the conventional AM/PM format.

```
SELECT      *

FROM        REGISTRAT
```

CNO	SEC	SNO	REG DATE	REG TIME
C11	01	800	12/15/87	10:00 AM
C11	01	325	02/04/88	11:35 AM
C11	02	150	12/17/87	12:12 PM
P33	01	100	12/23/87	01:18 PM
P33	01	800	12/23/87	04:00 PM
T11	01	100	12/23/87	04:35 PM
T11	01	150	12/15/87	05:00 PM
T11	01	800	12/15/87	07:00 PM
C11	01	111	12/26/92	07:21 PM
T33	01	325	09/19/91	12:23 PM
T33	01	100	09/19/91	01:22 PM
T33	01	150	09/19/91	02:44 PM
C66	01	200	10/02/93	10:22 PM

Comment

Observe there is no change to the SQL SELECT statement. To change the date/time format, you must use Query Manager to specify a date/time separator on the Select Column Editing Screen as shown below. Figure 9.1 shows the Date/Time Edit Codes which can be used. The example illustrates the use of the "TDMA/" date edit code and the "TTU:" time edit code.

```
                        Edit Column Formatting

Type information, press Enter.
For Usage and Edit, press F4 for list.
For Heading, press F4 for prompt.

Column    Heading                  Usage    Edit    Seq    Indent    Width
1         CNO                                         1        2        3
2         SEC                                         2        2        3
3         SNO                                         3        2        3
4         REG_DATE                          TDMA/     4        2        8
5         REG_TIME                          TTU:      5        2        8
                                                            Bottom
F2=Alternate keys    F3=Exit   F4=Prompt   F5=Run report   F6=Insert line
F10=Copy line        F11=Edit heading      F12=Cancel      F24=More keys
```

Exercise

9A. Display the REGISTRAT table. For each REG_DATE value, show the month, day and four-digit year (e.g., 12-07-1982).

Date Formatting Edit Codes		
Edit Code	Format	Results
TDYx	YYYYxMMxDD	1987/02/29
TDMx	MMxDDxYYYY	02/29/1987
TDDx	DDxMMxYYYY	29/02/1987
TDYAx	YYxMMxDD	87/02/29
TDMAx	MMxDDxYY	02/29/87
TDDAx	DDxMMxYY	29/02/87
TTSx	HHxMMxSSx	14:42:20
TTCx	HHxMMxSS	02:42:20
TTAx	HHxMM	14:42
TTAN	HHMM	1442
TTUx	HHxMM AM/PM	02:42 PM
TSI	YYYY-MM-DD-HH.MM.SS.NNNNNN	1987-02-29-14.42.20.123456

Figure 9.1 Examples of date/time format models.

DISPLAYING CURRENT DATE/TIME INFORMATION

A typical report will usually display the date (and maybe the time) that the report was generated. In SQL/400, the "current" date or time (the date or time that the statement is executed) can be displayed by referring to CURRENT DATE or CURRENT TIME in any SELECT clause. These current values are referred to as *registers*.

Sample Query 9.3

Display the name of each theology course. Also display the current date (using the default format) in each row of the result. (Assume that the date of execution of this query is April 10, 1994.)

```
SELECT    CNAME, CURRENT DATE

FROM      COURSE

WHERE     CDEPT = 'THEO'
```

CNAME	CURRENT DATE
FUNDAMENTALISM	04/10/1994
HEDONISM	04/10/1994
COMMUNISM	04/10/1994
SCHOLASTICISM	04/10/1994

Comments

1. The syntax of the statement implies that CURRENT DATE is a column in the COURSE table. You know this is not the case. However, CURRENT DATE (or any other register) can be displayed as a column of any table.

2. This example shows the current date displayed in each row of the result table. Usually the current date is shown in a report heading. This objective can be realized by using Query Manager report formatting options. This will be demonstrated in Chap. 11.

3. SQL/400 contains two other registers, CURRENT TIME and CURRENT TIME-STAMP, which contain date/time information.

Exercise

9B. Display the current date in the "MM/DD/YYYY" format, and the current time (hours, minutes, and seconds) using conventional USA format. Also have the system append the appropriate AM or PM indicator.

COMPARING AND CALCULATING DATE VALUES

SQL/400 allows date/time values to be compared using the standard comparison operators (=, <, etc.) in a WHERE clause. Comparison is based on your intuitive semantics of chronological date/time sequence where a preceding date/time is less than (i.e., historically prior to) a subsequent date/time. For example

```
'17-MAY-78' < '07-MAR-82'
```

evaluates to "true."

SQL/400 also permits a limited kind of date/time arithmetic. The following expressions, which reference date/time values, can be specified in SQL statements. Assume "TYPE" may be DATE, TIME, or TIMESTAMP and N represents some number of date/time units (month, day, year, hour, minute, second, or microsecond).

TYPE + N	Result is a date/time
TYPE – N	Result is a date/time
TYPE1 – TYPE2	Result is a duration

You must be careful when interpreting durations. The system returns an integer which is not the number of days. The integer has the format of YYYYMMDD. We give examples below of how to interpret date durations.

$$20 = 20 \text{ days}$$

$$1155 = 11 \text{ months} + 15 \text{ days}$$

$$10214 = 1 \text{ year} + 2 \text{ months} + 14 \text{ days}$$

These concepts also apply to time durations when calculations involve the TIME and TIMESTAMP data types. Similar subtle problems of interpretations can also occur with the TIME and TIMESTAMP data types.

Sample Query 9.4

For each row in the REGISTRAT table with a REG_DATE value indicating a date after December 20, 1987, display the following. Do not display duplicate date values.

1. The REG_DATE value.

2. The date 30 days after REG_DATE. Show "Plus 30 Days" as a heading.

3. The date 30 days prior to REG_DATE. Show "Less 30 Days" as a heading.

SELECT DISTINCT REG_DATE, REG_DATE + 30 DAY,

REG_DATE – 30 DAY

FROM REGISTRAT

WHERE REG_DATE > '12/20/87'

REG DATE	PLUS 30 DAYS	LESS 30 DAYS
12/23/1987	01/22/1988	11/23/1987
02/04/1988	03/05/1988	01/05/1988
09/19/1991	10/19/1991	08/20/1991
12/26/1992	01/25/1993	11/26/1992
10/02/1993	11/01/1993	09/02/1993

Comments

Observe that the headings in the result were changed using report-formatting options of Query Manager.

CHAR FUNCTION

The CHAR function is used to reformat a date/time value. Valid formats include European (EUR), Japanese (JIS), International Standards Organization (ISO), and United States (USA). (The SQL/400 Reference Manual describes other formats.)

Sample Query 9.5

For any row in the REGISTRAT table having a REG_DATE value after 12/20/1991, display the SNO and REG_TIME values in the EUR format. Also add one hour to REG_TIME.

SELECT SNO, CHAR(REG_DATE,EUR), REG_TIME, REG_TIME+1 HOUR

FROM   REGISTRAT

WHERE   REG_DATE > '12/20/91'

SNO	CHAR conversion	REG TIME	REG TIME + 1 HOUR
111	26.12.1992	19:21:00	20:21:00
200	02.10.1993	22:22:00	23:22:00
999	02.10.1993	08:52:00	09:52:00

DATE FUNCTION

The DATE function returns a date from a value which can be a string, date, timestamp, or positive number less than 3652059. Use of a positive number will return the date which is n – 1 days past 1/1/0001. You can also use a character string formatted as "yyyyddd".

Sample Query 9.6

Display the date corresponding to the 200th day of 1993 and the date which is 3,599,999 days after 01/01/0001.

SELECT   DISTINCT DATE ('1993200'), DATE(3600000)

FROM   REGISTRAT

DATE ('1993200')	DATE (3600000)
07/19/1993	06/19/1957

Comment

Observe the significance of apostrophes to distinguish a character string from a number as an argument to the DATE function.

MORE DATE BUILT-IN FUNCTIONS

The two previous sample queries described the DATE and CHAR functions applied to date/time arguments. Figure 9.2 presents an overview of other SQL/400 functions which facilitate date/time processing.

"Exp"	Date/Time Expression
DAY(exp)	Returns an integer (1–31) of the day part of the date or timestamp
HOUR(exp)	Returns the hour part of a time, timestamp, or time-duration value
MINUTE(exp)	Returns the hour part of a time, timestamp, or time-duration value
MONTH(exp)	Returns the month part (1–12) of a date, timestamp, date or time duration value
SECOND(exp)	Returns the seconds part of a time, timestamp, time, or timestamp value
YEAR(exp)	Returns the year part of a date, timestamp, date, or timestamp duration

Figure 9.2 Date/time functions.

The next sample queries will demonstrate the use of the date/time functions presented in Fig. 9.2. We present these examples without comment as the descriptions provided in the figure should be sufficient to understand these functions. We encourage you to work through these examples to confirm your understanding of the date/time functions. Assume the current date is 12/02/93.

Sample Query 9.7

For each row in the REGISTRAT table, display the complete date followed by just the day.

SELECT	SNO, REG_DATE, DAY(REG_DATE)
FROM	REGISTRAT

SNO	REG DATE	DAY (REG DATE)
800	12/15/1987	15
325	02/04/1988	4
150	12/17/1987	17
100	12/23/1987	23
800	12/23/1987	23
100	12/23/1987	23
150	12/15/1987	15
800	12/15/1987	15
111	12/26/1992	26
325	09/19/1991	19
100	09/19/1991	19
150	09/19/1991	19
200	10/02/1993	2

Sample Query 9.8

For each row in the REGISTRAT table, display the complete time followed by just the hour for each registration.

SELECT	SNO, REG_TIME, HOUR(REG_TIME)
FROM	REGISTRAT

SNO	REG TIME	HOUR (REG TIME)
800	10:00:00	10
325	11:35:00	11
150	12:12:00	12
100	13:18:00	13
800	16:00:00	16
100	16:35:00	16
150	17:00:00	17
800	19:00:00	19
111	19:21:00	19
325	12:23:00	12
100	13:22:00	13
150	14:44:00	14
200	22:22:00	22

ADDING MONTHS AND YEARS TO A DATE

The last sample query of this chapter illustrates the distinction between two techniques for adding some number of years to a date. The first technique is to use DAY to add some multiple of 365 days to the date. The second technique is to use YEAR to add some number of years to the date. The example shows the second technique is preferred because YEAR will account for the 366 days in a leap year.

Sample Query 9.9

For each registration which occurred during 1988, display

1. The REG_DATE value
2. The date 730 days beyond the REG_DATE value
3. The date 1 year beyond the REG_DATE value

SELECT	REG_DATE, REG_DATE + (365*2) DAY, REG_DATE+1 YEAR
FROM	REGISTRAT
WHERE	YEAR(REG_DATE) = 1988

REG DATE	Date expression	REG DATE + 1 YEAR
02/04/1988	02/03/1990	02/04/1989

Comments

1. YEAR can also be used to perform subtraction of some number of years prior to a date. For example, to determine the date exactly two years prior to the current date, you would specify

    ```
    REG_DATE - 2 YEAR
    ```

2. Observe that we can add multiple durations to a date/time value

    ```
    REG_DATE + 1 YEAR + 1 DAY
    ```

SUMMARY

This chapter introduced the DATE, TIME, and TIMESTAMP data types, which are used to inform SQL/400 that we wish to store date/time information in a column. We stressed that this is different from numeric or character data. To support the processing of date/time information, a special set of built-in functions are used. We noted that SQL/400 has a default format for date values, but you can reformat these values in a variety of different ways using the CHAR function or the report-formatting options of Query Manager. Finally, we saw that chronological comparisons and arithmetic operations can be performed with date/time values.

The significance of these data types is that the system provides a consistent way of representing and processing date and time values. It is not necessary for the programmer or system designer to concoct some method of dealing with date/time values.

Summary Exercises

9C. In three separate columns, display just the hours, minutes, and seconds of the current time. Show "CURRENT HOUR," "CURRENT MINUTE," and "CURRENT SECOND" as column headings.

9D. What is the date which occurs 3 months after the registration date(s) for student 325?

9E. Display the registration date, course number, section number, and student number for each student who registered for a course after December 31, 1987.

9F. Which students registered for courses during the month of December?

3

Query Manager

Parts 1 and 2 of this book focused on the AS/400 version of SQL. Only Chap. 2 made explicit reference to Query Manager options. We reiterate the fact that Query Manager is a front-end to the SQL/400 database engine and provides a means of preparing and submitting SQL statements for execution. Furthermore, Query Manager allows you to customize the result produced by running the query with page headings, descriptive column names, etc. This part of the book explicitly covers the concepts and facilities of Query Manager.

You can skip both chapters in this part of the book if your primary objective is to learn SQL. If you choose this option, you can continue reading at Part 4 without any loss of continuity. This might be appropriate for application programmers who are learning SQL with the objective of embedding SQL statements in application programs. However, we expect that most users will want to utilize the facilities provided by Query Manager. In fact, we expect many application programmers will use Query Manager to prototype the SQL statements to be embedded in their programs.

The two major topics to be presented in this part of the text are report formatting (Chap. 10) and miscellaneous commands (Chap. 11) wh. h you will find to be quite useful.

This book teaches SQL and Query Manager. Its coverage of SQL data manipulation statements is comprehensive. Space limitations do not permit a comprehensive discussion of all Query Manager concepts and facilities. However, we believe the following chapters substantially cover the important features of Query Manager. After reading these chapters, you should be able to explore the other features described in the SQL/400 reference manuals.

ORGANIZATION OF CHAPTERS

Chapter 10 describes the Query Manager commands which allow you to display selected data in a variety of different report formats. We discuss such things as the positioning of data in a report, including page headings and footings, customizing column headings, and using control breaks to present summarized information.

Chapter 11 is an overview of a number of Query Manager commands that serve a variety of purposes. These include printing a hard copy of your report, saving Query Manager objects, creating procedures, and using parameters to generalize a query.

Report Formatting

In Chap. 2 we introduced the basic idea of using Query Manager options to format a report. There we presented the Column edit codes to format column data and headings. This chapter presents more information on this topic by introducing advanced Query Manager concepts and commands relevant to report formatting.

The basic concept in formatting reports pertains to the creation of a Query Manager Report Form. This form determines how the results of a SELECT statement will be presented to the screen or hardcopy. The objective is to provide a readable report.

Some key points to keep in mind as you use Query Manager to format SQL/400 results are:

- The report form is a separate entity. Report formatting information is not stored with the report definition.

- Creating and modifying a report form can be done either from the Query Manager SQL Editor (Function key "F13") or with the "Work with Query Manager Report Forms" (Query Manager Menu option 2).

- There are SQL reserved words that also perform data formatting (e.g., CHAR, ZONE). These work in conjunction with the report form definitions.

- Multiple report forms can be created for one SELECT statement, but only one can be used per execution of the query.

This chapter addresses the following issues.

- Creating a report form
- Controlling the order of display of columns in a report
- Establishing horizontal and vertical positioning of data
- Formatting a report with column headings, page headings, page footings, and summary information
- Using report breaks and summary functions

CREATING A REPORT FORM

Query Manager provides several options for report generation. You may create a report form via the Query Manager Main Menu option "Work with Query Manager Report Forms." This option is best suited for the changes you may wish to make to a report form that has already been created. The most logical approach is to create the report form as part of the query definition process. This is achieved by pressing F13 while you are in the SQL editor (option 1 from the Main Query Manager Menu).

Pressing F13 causes the system to display the Select Report Format Screen. The options available through this screen are:

Edit column formatting	Controls column formatting
Edit page heading	Controls the page heading output
Edit page footing	Controls the page footing output
Edit final text	Provides the ability to attach text or summary data to the end of the report
Edit break text	Defines the text that will appear at each report break
Specify formatting options	Controls global report formatting options (e.g., spacing, wrapping)

These options provide the ability to filter data presented as a result of executing the query. You do not have to define a report format unless you want to perform additional report formatting that is not supported directly via SQL/400. Query Manager will create a "run-time" format if one has not been defined.

EDIT COLUMN FORMATTING

When you enter "1" next to this option, you access the Edit Column Formatting Screen. This screen, shown on p. 185, presents the following formatting options:

Column	The original order of column selection.
Heading	The current heading for the column. By pressing F11 the default may be changed.
Usage	Defines how the column will be used and whether summary data or break levels will be established.
Edit	Provides the ability to select edit codes and separators for specific data types.
Seq	Defines the left-to-right column sequence in which the result columns will be presented. This feature allows you to change the order without changing the SELECT statement.
Indent	Indicates the number of spaces to precede the column in the display.
Width	Specifies the display width for the column data. An overflow condition occurs if this value is too small.

Comment

You may press the F1 key on any field for help, or press F4 to obtain a list of available selections.

Exercise

10A. Experiment with Edit Column Formatting using the COURSE table.

1. After executing a SELECT statement to retrieve all data from the COURSE table, change the heading of CNO to Course Number.

2. Enter a usage code of 'AVERAGE' to create a summary average for CRED.

3. Enter an edit code of 'D02' on the CLABFEE column to display a dollar sign with two-digit accuracy.

4. Execute another SELECT statement. Observe the changes in the report.

5. Return to the SQL editor by pressing F13. Remember that function key assignment is documented at the bottom of each screen.

6. Note that the Form option on the Run Query screen contains "*". This indicates that you are using a temporary report form. After running a query, a default form is used to display the report. The default form is indicated by "*SYSDFT". Save the current form as "CFORM".

7. If you encounter the message "form does not match." This means that your SQL statement and form definition are not compatible. You can correct this by either saving the query and starting over or by entering the Edit Column Format screen and pressing the function key that loads a SQL statement. This problem usually is the result of changing the SQL statement (e.g., removing a column) after a report form has been defined.

REPORT CONTROL BREAKS

In Chap. 7 we introduced the GROUP BY clause in the SELECT statement. Recall that column functions are used to perform summary arithmetic on each group. For example, consider the following SELECT statement.

Example 10.1 Display the total credits and lab fees for each department.

```
SELECT  CDEPT, SUM(CRED), SUM(CLABFEE)

FROM    COURSE

GROUP  BY CDEPT
```

CDEPT	SUM(CRED)	SUM(CLABFEE)
CIS	18	750.00
PHIL	15	350.00
THEO	15	440.00

Comment

Observe that the output display shows summary data (only) for each group of distinct CDEPT values. This statement does not display the selected rows within each group which were used to produce the summary data. What if you want to see both the raw data within each group and also the summary totals? The next example will show how to realize this objective.

Example 10.2 Execute the following SELECT statement which does not perform any calculations. This will produce just raw data. Then you can use Query Manager to format and summarize the data as shown below.

```
SELECT  CDEPT, CNAME, CRED, CLABFEE

FROM    COURSE

ORDER  BY CDEPT
```

```
                        Edit Column Formatting
Type information, press Enter.
For Usage and Edit, press F4 for list.
For Heading, press F4 for prompt.

Column    Heading          Usage    Edit   Seq   Indent   Width
1         CDEPT            Break1            1      2        5
2         CNAME                              2      2       22
3         CRED             Sum               3      2        4
4         CLABFEE          Sum      D2       5      2        7
                                                Bottom
F2=Alternate keys  F3=Exit    F4=Prompt   F5=Run report  F6=Insert line
F10=Copy line       F11=Edit heading      F12=Cancel     F24=More keys
```

CDEPT	CNAME	CRED	CLABFEE
CIS	INTRO TO CIS	3	100.00
	DATA STRUCTURES	3	50.00
	DIGITAL CIRCUITS	3	.00
	RELATIONAL DATABASE	3	500.00
	COMPUTER ARCH.	3	100.00
	DISCRETE STRUCTURES	3	.00
	*	18	750.00
PHIL	EMPIRICISM	3	100.00
	RATIONALISM	3	50.00
	SOLIPSISM	6	.00
	EXISTENTIALISM	3	200.00
	*	15	350.00

. . .

Comment

Note that to display raw data along with summary totals you would not use the GROUP BY clause. Instead, you would use a SELECT statement to retrieve the rows containing the raw data in the appropriate sequence. Then you would use Query Manager Report Form Usage options (BREAK1 and SUM) to establish a control break and perform calculations at the control break. More detail about these options will be described in the following sections.

REPORT BREAK

The Break Option defines a control break. A control break is simply a point in a report where a specified column value on one line is different from the corresponding value on the previous line. (We note that it makes sense to define a control break only on a report which is sorted by the specified column.) The Break option is used to identify a control break column. The Edit Break Text option allows you to attach break-level headings or footings.

The following example illustrates the Break Level Option. Here "Break1" is used to produce a single-level control break report.

Example 10.3

For each department, display its department identifier followed by the course name and corresponding credits for each course offered by the department. Sort the report by department identifier.

```
SELECT  CDEPT, CNAME, CRED

FROM    COURSE

ORDER   BY CDEPT
```

CDEPT	CNAME	CRED
CIS	INTRO TO CIS	3
	DATA STRUCTURES	3
	DIGITAL CIRCUITS	3
	RELATIONAL DATABASE	3
	COMPUTER ARCH.	3
	DISCRETE MATHEMATICS	3
PHIL	EMPIRICISM	3
	RATIONALISM	3
	SOLIPSISM	6
	EXISTENTIALISM	3
THEO	FUNDAMENTALISM	3
	COMMUNISM	6
	SCHOLASTICISM	3
	HEDONISM	3

COLUMN USAGE OPTIONS

The Column Usage options in the Edit Column Formatting perform a variety of report reformatting. The following options are available:

OMIT	Omit the column from the output.
AVERAGE	Display the average of the selected results.
COUNT	Display the count of selected items.
FIRST	Display the first value in the column.
LAST	Display the last value in the column.
MAXIMUM	Display the maximum column value.
MINIMUM	Display the minimum column value.
SUM	Sum the results of the selected items.
BREAK1 .. BREAK6	Set a break level for a change in column data.

Example 10.4 For each department, display its department identifier followed by the course name, credits, and lab fee for each course offered by the department. Sort the result by department identifier. Show the sum of the credit and lab fee values for each group of departments. Use the following options.

- Edit Column Formatting

```
CDEPT usage = BREAK1
CRED usage = SUM
CLABFEE usage = SUM
```

- Edit Break Footing Text

```
Text = SUM (Align Left)
```

```
SELECT  CDEPT, CNAME, CRED, CLABFEE

FROM    COURSE

ORDER   BY CDEPT
```

CDEPT	CNAME	CRED	CLABFEE
CIS	INTRO TO CIS	3	100.00
	DATA STRUCTURES	3	50.00
	DIGITAL CIRCUITS	3	.00
	RELATIONAL DATABASE	3	500.00
	COMPUTER ARCH.	3	100.00
	DISCRETE STRUCTURES	3	.00
Sum		18	750.00
PHIL	EMPIRICISM	3	100.00
	RATIONALISM	3	50.00
	SOLIPSISM	6	.00
	EXISTENTIALISM	3	200.00
Sum		15	350.00
THEO	FUNDAMENTALISM	3	90.00
	COMMUNISM	6	200.00
	SCHOLASTICISM	3	150.00
	HEDONISM	3	.00
Sum		15	440.00

Comment

There are a variety of combinations that can be used with these options. Refer to the Query Manager documentation for details.

MULTIPLE CONTROL BREAKS

The next example shows a "two-level" control break. The data are sorted on two columns and a Break option is applied to each of these columns. BREAK1 is applied to the first column and BREAK2 is applied to the second column. These options establish two distinct control breaks.

Example 10.5   For each department, display its department identifier followed by the credits, course name, and lab fee of the courses offered by the department. Sort the courses by credits within department. Establish a primary control break on department identifier and a secondary control break on credit value. No control break arithmetic is required.

```
SELECT  CDEPT, CRED, CNAME, CLABFEE

FROM    COURSE

ORDER   BY CDEPT, CRED
```

CDEPT	CRED	CNAME	CLABFEE	
CIS	3	INTRO TO CIS	100.00	
		DATA STRUCTURES	50.00	
		DIGITAL CIRCUITS	.00	
		RELATIONAL DATABASE	500.00	
		COMPUTER ARCH.	100.00	
		DISCRETE STRUCTURES	.00	*
				**
PHIL	3	EMPIRICISM	100.00	
		RATIONALISM	50.00	
		EXISTENTIALISM	200.00	*
	6	SOLIPSISM	0.00	
				*
				**
THEO	3	FUNDAMENTALISM	90.00	
		HEDONISM	0.00	
		SCHOLASTICISM	150.00	*
	6	COMMUNISM	200.00	
				*
				**

Comment

At the end of a group of BREAK1 rows, a BREAK2 also occurs generating multiple blank lines. The following Edit Column Formatting Screen shows the definition that produced the report.

```
                        Edit Column Formatting
Type information, press Enter.
For Usage and Edit, press F4 for list.
For Heading, press F4 for prompt.

Column   Heading              Usage    Edit   Seq   Indent   Width
1        CDEPT                Break1           1       2       5
2        CNAME                                 2       2       22
3        CRED                 Break2           3       2       4
4        CLABFEE                              4       2       7

                                          Bottom
F2=Alternate keys  F3=Exit   F4=Prompt   F5=Run report  F6=Insert line
F10=Copy line      F11=Edit heading      F12=Cancel     F24=More keys
```

REFORMATTING PREVIOUS QUERY OUTPUT

You may often want to execute the previous SELECT statement with different report-formatting requirements. The ability to store report formats separately from the SQL statements makes this easy to do.

Example 10.6   Assume that we had previously established a report format named "ONELVLBRK" for the previous query. This report form had a single-level control break on department identifier, skipping just one line between each group of departments. It also displayed the maximum lab-fee values for each group of departments. Given that we had saved the query with the name "CSESEC", we could execute the saved query with the "ONELVLBRK" report form by:

- Entering Query Manager
- Selecting "Work with Query Manager Queries"
- Entering a "9" Opt
- Entering "CSESEC" and pressing Enter
- Changing the form on the Run Query screen to "ONELVLBRK" and pressing Enter

CDEPT	CRED	CNAME	CLABFEE
CIS	3	INTRO TO CIS	100.00
	3	DATA STRUCTURES	50.00
	3	DIGITAL CIRCUITS	.00
	3	RELATIONAL DATABASE	500.00
	3	COMPUTER ARCH.	100.00
	3	DISCRETE STRUCTURES	.00
Max:			500.00
PHIL	3	EMPIRICISM	100.00
	3	RATIONALISM	50.00
	3	EXISTENTIALISM	200.00
	6	SOLIPSISM	.00
Max:			200.00
THEO	3	FUNDAMENTALISM	90.00
	3	SCHOLASTICISM	150.00
	3	HEDONISM	.00
	6	COMMUNISM	200.00
Max:			200.00

Comments

1. Compare the report produced in the current example with that produced in Example 10.5. The same query could be used to produce either report. The difference in these two reports is the result of the formatting and break options specified in the form.

2. Observe that the query ordered the result by multiple columns. This does not force us to use multiple break level. We can simply choose to ignore the fact that the rows are ordered.

MULTIPLE CALCULATIONS AT CONTROL BREAKS

The next example requires the specification of multiple calculations at a control break. The BREAK1 option identifies a control break for CDEPT. The usage options COUNT and SUM are used to create summary break information.

Example 10.7   Retrieve every row in the COURSE table. Display the CDEPT, CNAME, CRED, and CLABFEE values. Sort the result by CDEPT. Format the report using the following specifications.

1. Define a control break on the CDEPT column.
2. Calculate the average lab fee and determine the number of rows for each break level.
3. Use the following report formatting:
   - Edit Column Formatting

     Set CDEPT usage = BREAK1
     Set CNO usage = COUNT
     Set CLABFEE usage = AVERAGE
     Set CLABFEE edit = D2
     Set CLABFEE width = 8
   - Edit Break Text

     Specify the Create a Footing Text as "Count & Avg" (align left)
   - Edit Final Text

     Specify the Create a Final Text as "Total Courses/Count & Avg"

```
SELECT  CDEPT, CNAME, CRED, CLABFEE

FROM    COURSE

ORDER   BY CDEPT
```

CDEPT	CNAME	CRED	CLABFEE
CIS	INTRO TO CIS	3	$100.00
	DATA STRUCTURES	3	$50.00
	DIGITAL CIRCUITS	3	$.00
	RELATIONAL DATABASE	3	$500.00
	COMPUTER ARCH.	3	$100.00
	DISCRETE STRUCTURES	3	$.00
Count & Avg		6	$125.00
PHIL	EMPIRICISM	3	$100.00
	RATIONALISM	3	$50.00
	SOLIPSISM	6	$.00
	EXISTENTIALISM	3	$200.00
Count & Avg		4	$87.50
THEO	FUNDAMENTALISM	3	$90.00
	COMMUNISM	6	$200.00
	SCHOLASTICISM	3	$150.00
	HEDONISM	3	$.00
Count & Avg		4	$110.00
Total Courses/Count & Avg		14	$110.00

Comments

1. If the result shown for any column is "***" or the text was truncated, this is an indication that a format error occurred. To resolve this problem enlarge the default column size.

2. Also note that defining Heading Text displays *only* on the hardcopy report. Final (Grand Total) and Footing text will not display on the display screen.

Exercise

10B. Modify this example to include a second-level control break on the CRED column. Perform the same calculations (average) at the second control break.

DISPLAYING COLUMN VALUES AND DATES IN REPORT HEADINGS

Variable data can be displayed in report titles. The Edit Page Heading or Page Footing options of the Report Form can use special values for output. The values available are:

&N   Display the value of column N, where N is the relative position of the column in the SELECT clause.

&DATE   Display date the report was produced.

&TIME   Display time of day the report was produced.

&PAGE   Display a page counter value on each page of the report.

Example 10.8   For every row in the COURSE table, display the CNO and CLABFEE values. Sort the result by CNO within CDEPT. Format the report as follows:

1. Define a control break and break text on the CDEPT column.
2. Calculate the sum of CLABFEE values at each control break.
3. Use the following report formatting options:
   - Edit Column Formatting
     Set CDEPT usage = BREAK1
     Set CLABFEE usage = SUM
   - Edit Break Text
     Specify the Create a Heading Text as "&1 Sections:"
     Set Blank lines after = 1

SELECT CDEPT, CNO, CLABFEE

FROM   COURSE

ORDER BY CDEPT, CNO

CDEPT	CNO	CLABFEE
CIS Sections		
CIS	C11	100.00
	C22	50.00
	C33	.00
	C44	.00
	C55	100.00
	C66	500.00
		750.00
PHIL Sections		
PHIL	P11	100.00
	P22	50.00
	P33	200.00
	P44	.00
		350.00
THEO Sections		
THEO	T11	150.00
	T12	90.00
	T33	.00
	T44	200.00
		440.00
		1540.00

Comments

1. Establishing BREAK1 on the CDEPT column associates the department identifier with the &1 variable in the break text "&1 Sections:". Thus, the current value of the CDEPT column will precede "Sections:" at each control break in the report.

2. The Page Heading will contain the current date on the hardcopy report.

SAVING REPORT FORMS

Recall that a report form is stored separately from SQL Queries. A report can be saved at the time you exit Query Manager SQL Editor or when you exit the "Work with Query Manager report form" option. In addition you can use the "SAVE FORM" Query Manager command when you are in the editor.

RESULT OUTPUT DESTINATION

When you execute a Query, you can select the destination for the results as Display Screen, Printer, or File.

SUMMARY

This chapter expanded on the ideas initially presented in Chap. 2. We discussed the basic concepts of control breaks and control break arithmetic and introduced the use of system variables and user variables.

As you continue to explore the use of SQL, you will find that Query Manager provides some unique capabilities for report formatting with Report Forms which are not available through SQL. Initially it may be confusing to determine whether you should use SQL format statements or the capabilities provided by Report Forms. In general, keep the logic of the SQL statements separate from report formatting.

The use of built-in functions (SUM, MAX, etc.) can be another area of confusion. You will need to use the Report Form built-in functions in situations that require the output to display both detail and summarized results.

Over time you will start to develop the instincts to use the options appropriately. If you are not using the sample educational database, we would suggest that you limit the number of records you can select for sample data. This will prevent your experiments from negatively impacting your system's performance.

Summary Exercise

10C. Construct a single-level control break report. For each staff member, display the department, employee name, and salary, in this order. Sort the report by the DEPT value. Establish a control break at the DEPT column. Show the maximum salaries for staff in each department. Skip three lines between each department. Display a final summary total for all salaries across all departments. Show "SALARY REPORT" as a centered title at the top of the report.

More About Query Manager

This chapter concludes our discussion of Query Manager facilities and related commands by presenting a potpourri of topics which we expect you will find useful. These concepts will be more useful to the professional programmer than to users. The following topics are covered:

- Query Manager commands
- User parameters
- Procedures
- Highlighting related Control Language commands
- Error investigation

QUERY MANAGER COMMANDS

There are a variety of commands to manage query objects from within Query Manager. Commands are entered on the top line of the editor screen or by pressing F22. The available commands are:

CONNECT

Provides the ability to connect to a remote data-base for processing. This obviously assumes there is a network path to that remote database. If the IBM target machine is not an AS/400, you will need to change your naming convention to *SAA. Library or collection naming conventions will change from SQLTST/TABLE to SQLTST.TABLE.

The command has parameters for security and the ability to RESET to your local database.

DISPLAY

Applies a report form to the result produced by the most recent query. This option provides the ability to see the results of report form changes without executing the query again.

Example:
```
DISPLAY REPORT (FORM = ONELVLBRK
DISPLAY ONELVLBRK
```

DRAW

Creates a default SELECT statement for a specified table. This statement will select all the columns for the specified table.

Example:
```
DRAW COURSE
```

ERASE

Deletes a query object—Query, Form, Table, or Procedure. Provides for a CONFIRM option to allow you to verify the deletion.

Example:
```
ERASE QUERY CSESEC (CONFIRM = YES)
ERASE FORM ONELVLSEC
```

EXPORT and IMPORT

EXPORT copies the definition of a query object to an AS400 source file. (You might do this if you wished to save your query object definition in a source file. Such files could be transferred to another IBM SAA System.) IMPORT is the inverse of EXPORT. It creates a query object from the definition of an object stored in an AS/400 source file.

Example:
```
EXPORT FORM CSESEC TO CSESEC1
```

PRINT   Used to print a report or the definition of a Query, Form or Procedure.

Example:
```
PRINT REPORT (FORM=TEST
```

RUN   Executes a query or procedure. Options provide the ability to utilize the
                        active Query and/or Report Form.

Example:
```
RUN QUERY TSTQRY
```

SAVE DATA   Saves the results of the current query to a table. Note this will save the
                        data returned from the query, not the format.

Example:
```
SAVE DATA AS TEST
```

SAVE FORM   Saves the active form definition. This process creates a Report Form for
                        future use. CONFIRM is also an option.

Example:
```
SAVE FORM AS FTEST1
```

SAVE QUERY   Saves the active query definition. This command creates a Query for
                        future use.

Example:
```
SAVE QUERY AS QTEST1
```

PROCEDURES

A SQL/400 procedure allows multiple AS/400 query statements to be combined for execution. For example, the following statements can be combined into a procedure and executed with a single command to run the procedure.

```
'RUN QUERY TSTQRY'
'PRINT REPORT (FORM=TEST'
'SAVE DATA AS SQLTST.TEST'
```

These statements are entered into a source file in a specific format. (See the SQL/400 Reference Manual.) Once entered, the statements can be imported into Query Manager as a procedure. The procedure can then be RUN causing the statements in the procedure to be executed.

USER PARAMETERS

A parameter is a place holder within a query or procedure that allows a value to be specified when the query or procedure is run. An ampersand is used as the first character of a parameter name. SQL statements containing parameters can be executed interactively through Query Manager or through a Control Language program. By using parameters a query or procedure can be generalized, as illustrated in the next example.

Example 11.1   Create a query that allows the user to enter the table name from which they would like to retrieve data.

```
SELECT *

FROM &TABLE
```

System Response

When this query is executed the system will prompt the user to enter the name of a table to be substituted for &TABLE. The system will then display the results of the query executed against that table.

RELATED CONTROL LANGUAGE COMMANDS

There are a variety of commands to manage query objects from within Control Language programs. We briefly list the available commands below. Note that these are functions that are external to Query Manager. Some of these commands perform similar function to those described earlier in this chapter. The major difference is that the following commands are executed from the control language environment.

RUNQRY	Allows the execution of a query from a Control Language program or command line.
ANZQRY	Verifies the object definition as related to conversion verification.
CRTQMFORM	Create a form from a source file definition.
CRTQMQRY	Create a query from a source file definition.
DLTQMFORM	Erase a form.
DLTQMQRY	Erase a query.
DSPFFD	Display the file field description for a file. This can aid in resolving file access problems in SQL/400.
RTVQMFORM	Exports a query object definitions into a source file.
RTVQMQRY	Exports a query definitions into a source file.
STRQMPRC	Runs a query management procedure from a source file.
STRQMQRY	Runs a query from a Control Language program or command line.
WRKQMFORM	Provides a menu for form management functions.
WRKQNQRY	Provides a menu for query management functions.

ERROR INVESTIGATION

In the event that you receive an error while you are attempting to enter or execute an SQL statement, the system will display a brief error message. If you need more detailed information about this error you would do the following.

1. Position the cursor to the error message
2. Press the F1 key for Help. The system will display some more information about the problem. At this point more detail information can be obtained by pressing the F10 key.

SUMMARY

This chapter introduced some new commands and techniques which serve a variety of purposes. You will find these commands to be useful in real-world application systems as you move from a testing to a production environment. We emphasize that our examples are not comprehensive. Our objective was to make you aware of the more popular commands. Professional programmers are encouraged to read the reference manuals for more detail.

4

Data Definition and Manipulation

This part of the text introduces the SQL database definition and update statements. We could have completed our discussion of the SELECT statement prior to introducing these topics. However, many subtle points associated with complex data retrieval pertain to decisions which are made during database design and subsequently implemented using SQL's data definition and update statements. Potentially embarrassing data-retrieval errors can be avoided by understanding the key concepts of database definition and update. This is especially true for SELECT statements which must reference multiple tables or process columns which contain null values. For this reason, the fundamental concepts of data definition and update are presented in this part of the text before describing the more complex variations of the SELECT statement in Part 5.

We recommend that you scan App. B which displays all the tables in the educational database design. This is important because the remainder of the text will address issues which pertain to the relationships between multiple tables within a relational database design. In subsequent chapters we will be referring to all the tables in the educational database.

ORGANIZATION OF CHAPTERS

Chapter 12 introduces two important SQL data definition statements: CREATE TABLE and CREATE INDEX. Typically the database administrator executes these statements (among others) to initially establish the database. Unless you are able to use SQL/400 as a personal system, you will probably never have to execute either of these statements. If this is the case, you can skim over the details of syntax. However, you should understand the conceptual substance of this chapter. The CREATE TABLE statement, in addition to defining the structure of a table, can also declare certain integrity constraints.

In subsequent chapters we will see that a query which references multiple tables usually is premised on a semantic relationship corresponding to the definition of some foreign key. From a conceptual point of view, this is a very important chapter because it shows how an application design using SQL is more than just a collection of tables. We emphasize that the design is actually a semantically meaningful collection of interrelated tables which should adhere to specified integrity constraints. The semantic relationships are always the basis of a multitable query.

Chapter 13 is a comprehensive presentation of SQL's data manipulation statements: INSERT, UPDATE, and DELETE. You will find the syntax for these statements to be quite straightforward. However, these statements are potentially dangerous because erroneous execution can cause the loss of valuable data. The examples illustrate interactive execution of the statements. However, for a corporate (versus personal) database, these statements are usually embedded within application programs. Therefore, professional programmers should master the subject matter of this chapter. Those users who will not modify data can skip this chapter.

Chapter 14, which returns to the SELECT statement, is presented in this part of the text for a very important reason. Our intention is to emphasize the potential problems which can occur when a column is allowed to contain null values. If the CREATE TABLE statement does not prohibit null values, and subsequent INSERT or UPDATE statements actually store such values in a table, then special consideration must be given to the proper formulation of SELECT statements and to the interpretation of the result. The sample queries will show that the presence of null values increases the possibility of error. Therefore, both users and professional programmers should understand the content of this chapter. Hopefully it will also encourage the prohibition of null values where appropriate.

Data Definition

The primary focus of this chapter is the CREATE TABLE statement. This statement is used to establish an "empty" table. Thereafter, you can store rows in the table by executing the INSERT statement. We postpone discussion of the INSERT statement and other update statements (UPDATE and DELETE) until the next chapter.

The CREATE TABLE statement creates an "object" (the table) within the system. We will also discuss another system object, an index, which is established by executing the CREATE INDEX statement.

This chapter will present simplified versions of the CREATE TABLE and CREATE INDEX statements. For the purpose of this chapter we will use the terms TABLE and INDEX to be synonymous with PHYSICAL and LOGICAL File. SQL/400 is unique in the sense that the SQL "Engine" can access data from an SQL Collection or from a regular file written by a third-generation language (e.g., RPG, COBOL).

Database integrity is a very important issue which must be addressed when creating tables. Unfortunately, two important aspects of database integrity—entity integrity and referential integrity—are not supported by SQL/400. Fortunately, the new DB2/400 will support these features. This chapter will present a conceptual introduction to database integrity. After reading this chapter many readers will find it helpful to skip ahead and read Chap. 23 about the new integrity mechanisms found in DB2/400.

CREATE TABLE STATEMENT

We begin our discussion by presenting the CREATE TABLE statement which was used to create the COURSE table. The following comments will elaborate on the SQL keywords and related concepts.

Sample Statement 12.1   Create a table called COURSE which has six columns with the following names and descriptions.

CNO	Character string of length = 3 (nonnull).
CNAME	A variable length character string. Maximum length is 22 (nonnull).
CDESCP	A variable length character string. Maximum length is length = 25 (nonnull).
CRED	An integer (nulls allowed).
CLABFEE	A decimal value with a precision of 5 and a scale of 2 (nulls allowed).
CDEPT	Character string of length = 4 (nonnull).

```
CREATE TABLE SQLTST/COURSE

      (CNO         CHAR(3)         NOT NULL,

       CNAME       VARCHAR(22)     NOT NULL,

       CDESCP      VARCHAR(25)     NOT NULL,

       CRED        INTEGER,

       CLABFEE     DECIMAL(5,2),

       CDEPT       CHAR(4)         NOT NULL)
```

System Response

Although the CREATE TABLE statement is entered via the "Work with Query Manager Queries" function, it is not a query. Hence, there is no explicit display of data as there is with a SELECT statement. You should receive a system-generated message which states that the statement was successful.

Comments

1. The present example illustrates the general syntax of the CREATE TABLE statement. The general format of this statement is outlined in Fig. 12.1. Before addressing the details of syntax we enumerate the objectives of the CREATE TABLE statement.

2. You could also create a table (file) with any other AS/400 file creation method (e.g., DDS, IDDU) or with the Create Query Manager Table option. We note that the Create Query Manager does not provide for column constraints (e.g., NOT NULL).

Objectives of CREATE TABLE Statement

1. Establish a new table and give it a name.
2. Give a name to all the columns in the table.
3. Specify the data type of each column.
4. Specify the default column sequence.
5. Specify which columns cannot accept null values.
6. Specify integrity constraints for tables.

The following pages elaborate on each of these six points.

```
CREATE TABLE [library/]name-of-table

(column1-name    data-type    [column-constraint],
 column2-name    data-type    [column-constraint],
                     .
                     .
                     .
 columnN-name    data-type    [column-constraint])
─────────────────────────────────────────────────
column-constraint may be:

   ▪ NOT NULL WITH DEFAULT
   ▪ NOT NULL
   ▪ NULL
```

Figure 12.1 CREATE TABLE statement.

Table names.   The name of a table may be from 1 to 10 characters long. It may include letters, numbers, or the special characters, dollar sign ($), number (#) and at (@). In addition the underscore (_) can be used in positions 2 to 10. The name of the library/table is specified immediately after "CREATE TABLE." The present example shows "SQLTST/COURSE" as the library/table name.

The CREATE TABLE statement and previous SELECT statements referenced this table as "COURSE." However, "COURSE" is not the complete name. This is because the AS/400 is a multiuser system and it is possible for different users to specify "COURSE" in individual CREATE TABLE statements used to create different tables. To handle this situation, the system will use the specified library to organize the storage of tables. For this reason only one table named "COURSE" can exist in a given library. Therefore, the library must be specified when a table is created.

Another key point about the CREATE TABLE statement is your security access. In order to execute the CREATE TABLE statement, your Query Manager Profile must indicate that you are authorized to use the CREATE reserve word. This is controlled by the system manager via your Query Manager profile.

Column names. Column names are formulated according to the same syntax rules as table names. Column names must be unique within a given table but it is possible to have the same column name specified within multiple tables. For example, both the COURSE table and the REGISTRAT table contain a column named "CNO". There is no ambiguity when a SELECT statement refers to CNO because the FROM clause indicates the appropriate table.

Chapter 15 will introduce the join operation which references multiple tables in the same SELECT statement. If two tables have a column with the same name, then these column names must be qualified by specifying a table name as a prefix. For example, you would specify "COURSE.CNO" to reference the CNO column of the COURSE table and "REGISTRAT.CNO" to reference the CNO column of the REGISTRAT table. Chapter 15 will present sample queries where table name qualification of columns is required.

Data types. The data type of each column is specified after the column name. We have seen that the type of data in a column can affect how conditions are formulated in a WHERE clause. For example, we saw that character strings, unlike numeric constants, must be enclosed in apostrophes. Serious consideration should be given to the choice of data type. We shall present an overview of available data types below.

Default column sequence. The example shows the column definitions specified in a certain order. CNO is defined first, CNAME second, etc. This order establishes the default left-to-right column sequence to be displayed when a SELECT statement uses an asterisk to indicate the display of all columns (SELECT * FROM . . .).

NULL values. The next chapter will present examples of the INSERT statement, where values are not specified for some columns. When a row is inserted into a table and a column value is not specified, the system interprets the missing information as a special "null" value. This value is interpreted as "value unknown."

There are circumstances where null values may be unreasonable. For example, CNO serves as a unique identifier ("primary key") for a course. Also, it is academic policy that every course must be assigned a name and description and be sponsored by some academic department. For these reasons the NOT NULL clause is entered with the CNO, CNAME, CDESCP, and CDEPT column definitions. In effect, specifying NOT NULL helps maintain database integrity. The presence of this clause will instruct the system to reject any update to the COURSE table which would produce a null value in any of these columns.

The CRED and CLABFEE columns will accept null values. We could have specified the NULL keyword, however this is the default. We caution the reader that the presence of null values may be confusing and requires that greater attention be given to query formulation. (These issues will be discussed in Chap. 14.) Attaching NOT NULL to a column definition can eliminate these potential problems. It is strongly suggested that NOT NULL be specified wherever appropriate.

Another option exists pertaining to NULL values, NOT NULL WITH DEFAULT. This is similar to NOT NULL because it prevents NULL values from occurring in a column. However, it does not require that an actual value be specified during an insert operation. Instead the omission of a column value means that the system will automatically supply an appropriate default value.

Database integrity constraints. A database contains data which models real-world "entities" (e.g., student, faculty, course) and "relationships" between the entities (e.g., faculty advise students). The notion of entity gives rise to the issue of "entity integrity." And the notion of relationship gives rise to the issue of "referential integrity." In a relational database entity integrity is usually enforced with the specification of a PRIMARY KEY clause in a CREATE TABLE statement. Referential integrity is enforced with the specification of a FOREIGN KEY clause. Unfortunately, SQL/400 does not support these clauses. (Fortunately, DB2/400 does!) Following, we present a conceptual overview of primary and foreign keys. (The precise syntax for DB2/400 users will be described in Chap. 23.)

Primary key.   It is recommended, but not required, that every table have some column or group of columns specified as the primary key of the table. The primary key is a value which should always be (1) nonnull and (2) unique. It is this value that uniquely identifies a row in the table.

Foreign key.   Foreign keys, like primary keys, enhance database integrity. In the previous discussion of null values we noted that school policy requires that each course be sponsored by some academic department. This means that NOT NULL should be specified for the CDEPT column. However, the NOT NULL clause only keeps null values out of the CDEPT column. It would not prohibit any "garbage" character string values like "WXYZ" or "PSYC" from being stored in this column. A more desirable objective is to restrict CDEPT values to those found in the DEPT column of the DEPARTMENT table. This is the function of a foreign key.

A foreign key is a column or group of columns where each column value equals some primary key value in a related table. For the COURSE table we would like the CDEPT column to be a foreign key which references the DEPARTMENT table because any value in the CDEPT column must equal some existing primary key value in the DEPARTMENT table.

Because SQL/400 does not recognize primary keys and foreign keys, the associated constraints must be enforced by techniques which are implemented by the database administrator and/or application programmers.

SQL/400 DATA TYPES

SQL/400 supports a variety of data types. These fall into one of three categories: (1) character string data, (2) numeric data, and (3) date/time data. We describe each category and its associated data types below.

Character String Data

The different character string data types are enumerated in Fig. 12.2. Each string data type represents alphanumeric characters using EBCDIC codes.

You will find the greatest use for the CHAR data type which is specified for character strings. Earlier in the text, we classified data with the more general terms *character data* and *numeric data*. The CHAR data type is used to define a column which contains character data. We can use any of the string functions and perform comparisons on this data type.

Date/Time Data

Character and numeric data types are found in traditional high-level programming languages (e.g., RPG, COBOL, FORTRAN). Programmers often use one of the traditional data types to encode a value which represents a date or a time. However, SQL has a "primitive" date/time data type, which can help avoid the complexity of the encoding process and can be used as arguments to the date/time functions presented in Chap. 10. Values are stored in a special internal format (not described here) which can be converted to or from a variety of display formats. These data types simplify the storing of chronological information which can be operated on for comparisons and computations.

Name	Description
CHAR(n)	Character strings represented EBCDIC. n is in the range of 1 to 32766.
VARCHAR(n)	Variable-length character strings represented in EBCDIC. n is in the range of 1 to 32740.
DATE	Dates can range from 1/1/0001 A.D. to 12/31/9999 A.D.
TIME	A three-part value of a 24-hour clock (hours, minutes, seconds).
TIMESTAMP	A seven-part value (year, month, day, hour, minute, second, and microsecond). The range follows that of DATE and TIME with the addition of microseconds.

Figure 12.2 SQL character and date data types.

Numeric Data

Numeric data types are defined for data items which will be used in arithmetic operations. Figure 12.3 presents the numeric data types.

Name	Description
SMALLINT	An integer between −32768 and +32767.
INTEGER	An integer between −2147483638 and +2147483637. Also called INT.
FLOAT(n)	A single-precision floating point number where n = 1 to 24. Also called REAL.
FLOAT(n)	A double-precision floating point number where n = 1 to 25. Also called DOUBLE PRECISION.
DECIMAL	A zoned-decimal or packed-decimal number with an implied decimal point. The number has a 31-digit precision. Also called DEC or NUMERIC.

Figure 12.3 SQL numeric data types.

Exercises

12A. Examine the CREATE TABLE statements for the educational database shown in App. C.

12B. Create a table called JUNK. It has three columns:

  C1:   Character string of length = 10 (nonnull)
  C2:   An integer (nulls allowed)
  C3:   A decimal value with a precision of 7 and a scale of 2 (nonnull)

ENTITY INTEGRITY AND REFERENTIAL INTEGRITY

The purpose of this section is to elaborate on the concepts of entity and referential integrity. The identification of primary and foreign keys occurs during database design when the semantic issues of entities, relationships, and database integrity are explicitly considered. A comprehensive discussion of database design is beyond the scope of this text. This is a very complex topic which requires attention to many issues which transcend SQL. But it is impossible to present the CREATE TABLE or CREATE INDEX statements without touching on design issues. The following discussion offers some insight into the notions of entity and referential integrity.

Entity Integrity

A row in a table usually corresponds to an instance of an entity type which the database is modeling. An entity may be described as any identifiable object. For example, the COURSE table represents a type of entity, *course,* and each row in the COURSE table corresponds to a particular course offered by the college. Because each real-world course entity is uniquely identifiable, it is desirable that each corresponding row in the COURSE table also be uniquely identifiable by some column or group of columns. This is the purpose of defining a primary key. Consider the ambiguity which occurs when a table contains two or more rows which cannot be distinguished from each other. There would be a loss of entity integrity because the one-to-one correspondence between a real-world course entity and its corresponding row would be destroyed. By identifying CNO as the primary key we would state that a course number can always be used to uniquely identify a course. Also, there are circumstances where the proper formulation of an SQL statement requires that the WHERE condition select only one row. If you write the statement such that multiple rows are actually selected, an error will occur. (This is an especially important consideration when embedding SQL statements in an application program.)

Sometimes it is necessary to specify more than one column value in order to uniquely identify a row in a table. For example, because multiple sections of a course may be offered during a given semester, the CLASS table can have multiple rows with the same CNO value. For this reason, a composite primary key would be required to include the CNO and SEC columns.

Occasionally you will find that you have more than one choice for a primary key. For example, assume it is school policy that every course has a unique name. Then you could choose either CNO or CNAME as the primary key. But only one primary key is specified. How would you choose? A choice of CNO could be based on the fact that the school established course numbers for the purpose of uniquely identifying courses. However, choosing CNAME would not be wrong. And it would even be a better choice if there were significantly more queries which selected rows based on CNAME values than CNO values. This is because you enforce uniqueness on a column by creating a unique index on that column. The same index will help the system perform more efficient retrieval of rows. We will return to this issue in our discussion of the CREATE INDEX statement.

Referential Integrity

We have indicated that the CDEPT column in the COURSE table serves as a foreign key which references the DEPARTMENT table. We continue with this example to introduce terminology relevant to referential integrity.

Parent table.   A table which would be referenced by some foreign key. DEPARTMENT is a parent table because it is referenced by the CDEPT foreign key. A primary key, such as DEPT in DEPARTMENT, must be specified for the parent table. This is because any nonnull foreign key (CDEPT) value must be equal to some existing primary key (DEPT) value. We say that a foreign key references the parent table. It does so by identifying some primary key value in the parent table.

Dependent table.   A table which contains a foreign key. COURSE, which contains CDEPT as a foreign key, is a dependent table. It is dependent on DEPARTMENT, the parent table. The academic policy requiring every course to be sponsored by some department means that courses are dependent on departments. At the database level this means every dependent (COURSE) row is dependent on some parent (DEPARTMENT) row. A dependent row cannot contain a foreign key (CDEPT) value unless that value exists as some primary key (DEPT) value in the parent table. Many people refer to a dependent table as a "child" table.

Descendant table.   It is possible for a table which is dependent on one table to be the parent of another table. For example, assume it is school policy that every class correspond to some course. This means that every CNO value in the CLASS table must equal some existing CNO value in the COURSE table. Therefore, CNO in the CLASS table would be defined as a foreign key referencing COURSE. [In this example the foreign key (CNO) would be part of the primary key (CNO,SEC) for CLASS. This will occur often in practice.] This relationship means that COURSE becomes a parent table for CLASS in addition to being a dependent for DEPARTMENT. It also means that CLASS is dependent on COURSE, which is in turn dependent on DEPARTMENT. Under this circumstance we say that CLASS is a descendant of DEPARTMENT.

Figure 12.4 illustrates the notions of parent, dependent, and descendent table relationships.

Independent table. A table without any foreign keys. The STAFF table is an example of an independent table. (Note that the DEPT column in the STAFF table will contain department identifier values. However, this column would not be specified as a foreign key because it may contain values not found in the primary key column of the DEPARTMENT table.)

A table may have multiple parent and/or dependent tables. Consider the REGIS-TRAT table originally introduced in Chap. 10. The key of this table is a composition of three columns (CNO,SEC,SNO). To ensure referential integrity we would specify two foreign keys in this table. The compound foreign key (CNO,SEC) would reference the CLASS table. The SNO foreign key would reference the student table. Hence, REGISTRAT is dependent on two tables, CLASS and STUDENT. Also, assume that all students must major in a subject corresponding to some existing academic department. This means the CREATE TABLE statement for STUDENT would specify SMAJ as a foreign key referencing DEPARTMENT. Hence, DEPARTMENT is the parent of two tables, COURSE and STUDENT. Figure 12.5 reflects this expanded view of the design.

Cycle. Foreign keys can be defined such that a cyclic relationship is established. Assume it is school policy that each faculty member is assigned to some academic department. Then the FDEPT column in the FACULTY table would be specified as a foreign key referencing DEPARTMENT. (DEPARTMENT is the parent table and FACULTY is the dependent table.) Also assume that the chairperson of each academic department is some faculty member. Then the DCHFNO value in the DEPARTMENT is specified as a foreign key referencing FACULTY. (Here, FACULTY is the parent table and DEPARTMENT is the dependent table.) Figure 12.6 illustrates this relationship.

Sometimes a cycle involves more than two tables. TABLE1 could be the parent of TABLE2, which could be the parent of TABLE3, which could be the parent of TABLE1. In general, a cycle is formed if the descendant of any table becomes the parent of that table. In effect, every table in a cyclic relationship becomes the descendant of itself.

Self-referencing cycle. It is possible for a table to be the parent and dependent of itself. In other words, the table contains a foreign key which references itself. For example, assume that some courses have at most one prerequisite course which students must take before registering for a class on the course. We could denote the prerequisite course in the COURSE table by altering this table to include a new column, PCNO, which contains the course number of the prerequisite course. Then the PCNO column would be a foreign key referencing COURSE. Figure 12.7 illustrates this relationship. This self-referencing cycle is sometimes called a *recursive* relationship.

The data type and length of each component of a foreign key must be the same as the primary key. This is true for all the previous examples. But a foreign key, unlike a primary key, may be allowed to contain null values. (Thus, it is not necessary to specify NOT NULL for a foreign key column. The business rules reflected in the database design determine whether nulls are allowed.) For example, there are many introductory courses which do not have a prerequisite course. Rows for such courses could have a null value in the PCNO column. Another example is the SMAJ column in the STUDENT table. If we assume that some students do not have to declare a major, then corresponding SMAJ values could be null.

Thus far only the structural aspect of referential integrity has been considered. We now outline some of the processing rules which impose reasonable constraints on data manipulation statements which reference primary and/or foreign key values. These statements (INSERT, UPDATE, and DELETE) will be described in the next chapter. When executing these statements you should verify that the update operation does not violate any of the integrity constraints.

Insert of primary key. The primary key value should be unique. If it is not, the insert should be rejected.

Insert of foreign key. Any nonnull foreign key should equal some existing primary key in the parent table. If it does not, the insert should be rejected.

Update of primary key. Updating the primary key should be rejected if there exists any dependent rows referencing the current primary key value.

Update of foreign key. The new foreign key should equal some existing primary key in the referenced table (or be null, if allowed). Otherwise, the update should be rejected.

Delete of primary key. Do not delete a row if its primary key value is referenced by any foreign key value. (You could delete the corresponding foreign key rows and then retry the deletion of the primary key row.)

Delete of foreign key. No restrictions (unless the foreign key is part of a primary key or some other foreign key where other restrictions apply.)

Again, we emphasize that this discussion was largely conceptual because SQL/400 does not provide direct support for primary and foreign keys.

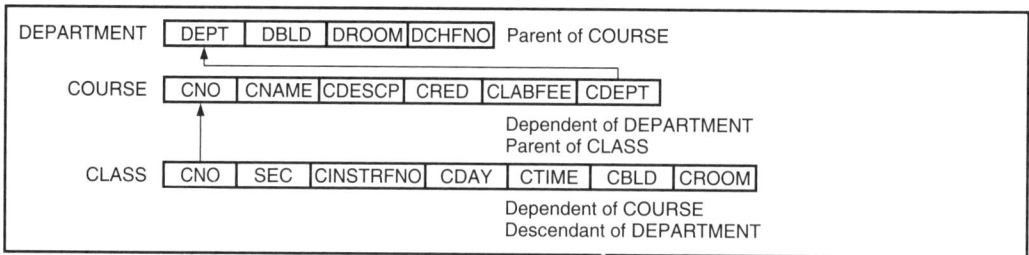

Figure 12.4 Parent, dependent, and descendant tables.

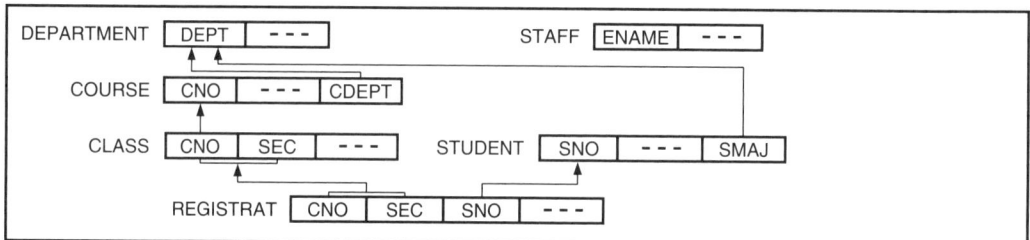

Figure 12.5 Expanded view of database design.

Figure 12.6 A cycle.

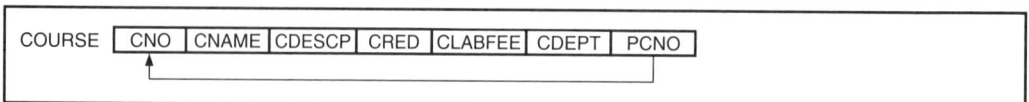

Figure 12.7 Self-referencing cycle.

CREATE INDEX STATEMENT

The CREATE INDEX statement is used to create a database object called an index. Before introducing the CREATE INDEX statement, we present the fundamental objectives and concepts of database indexes. (In terms of traditional AS/400 objects, an index is a logical file.)

What Is an Index?

An index is an internal structure which the system can use to find one or more rows in a table. Figure 12.8 presents the general idea of an index. In effect, a database index is conceptually similar to an index found at the end of this or any other textbook. In the same way that a reader of a book would refer to an index to determine the page locations of a specified topic, a database system would read an index to determine the disk locations of rows selected by a SQL query. Simply put, the presence of an index can help the system process some queries in a more efficient manner.

A database index is created for a column or group of columns. Figure 12.8 shows an index (XCNAME) for the CNAME values found in the COURSE table. Observe that the index, unlike the COURSE table, represents the CNAME values in sequence. Also, the index is small relative to the size of the table. Therefore, it is probably easier for the system to search the index to locate a row with a given CNAME value than to scan the entire table in search of that value. For example, the XCNAME index might be helpful to the system when it executes the following SELECT statement.

```
SELECT   *
FROM     COURSE
WHERE    CNAME = 'EXISTENTIALISM'
```

Because the WHERE clause references CNAME, the system would consider using the XCNAME index. Now consider the following statement.

```
SELECT   *
FROM     COURSE
WHERE    CDESCP = 'FOR THE GREEDY'
```

The XCNAME index is of little use when searching for CDESCP values. Therefore, the system would probably not reference it. Of course, we might consider creating an index on CDESCP values.

There are many complex issues pertaining to database indexes. Some of these issues will be introduced below. However, we first present an example of the CREATE INDEX statement which is used to create the CNAME index.

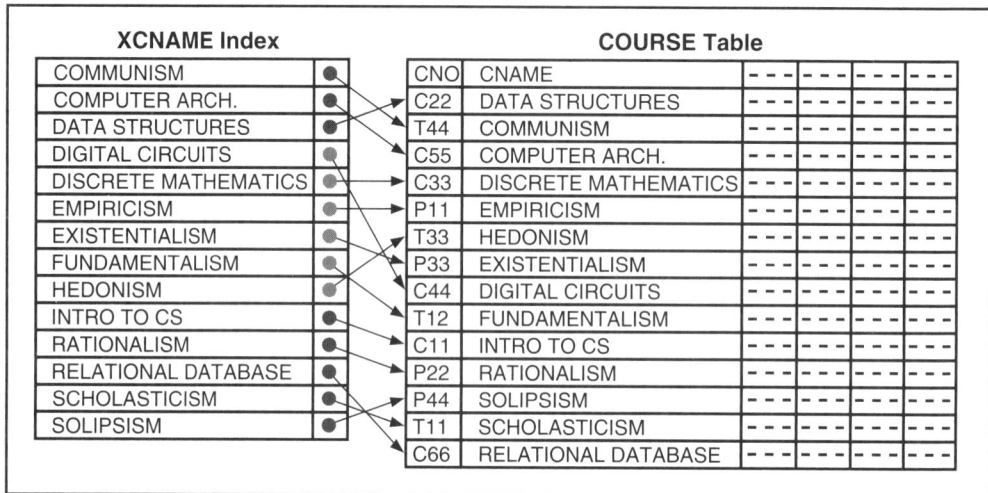

Figure 12.8 Index (XCNAME) based on CNAME column in COURSE table.

Sample Statement 12.2   Create an index on the CNAME column of the COURSE table. Call this index XCNAME.

CREATE INDEX SQLTST/XCNAME

ON SQLTST/COURSE (CNAME)

System Response

Like the CREATE TABLE statement, the CREATE INDEX statement is not a query and, hence, there is no output display. Instead the system returns a diagnostic which (presumably) indicates the successful creation of the XCNAME index. This index will be conceptually like that shown in Fig. 12.8. Its actual internal structure is considerably more complex.

Comments

1. *Syntax.*   A simplified version of the general syntax is

   ```
   CREATE INDEX index-name
   ON table-name (column-name)
   ```

   An index is given a name (XCNAME in our example) according to the same rules as apply to table names. The ON clause must reference a valid table name. The column name must be enclosed within parentheses and must identify a valid column name within the specified table. Like the CREATE TABLE statement, you must specify the library which is to hold the index.

2. In this example the COURSE table already has rows stored in it. The system will scan this table to obtain the CNAME values and corresponding row locations to construct the index. In practice it is better to issue the CREATE INDEX statement before any rows are actually inserted into the table. However, the index can be created at any time.

3. Once the index is created, the system will automatically maintain it. For example, if you issue an INSERT statement to place a new row in the COURSE table, the system will automatically determine the CNAME value and location of the new row and place a new entry in the XCNAME index. Simply put, once you create the index, the system does the rest.

Do Indexes Force a Change to the SELECT Statement?

There is absolutely no change to the coding of a SELECT statement due to the presence of an index. The SELECT statements for all previous sample queries would remain the same. This means that many users of the system can remain ignorant of the presence or absence of any database indexes.

Whenever a SELECT statement is submitted by a user, the system uses a special internal module, the "optimizer," to analyze the statement to determine if using an index would be beneficial. If it is, the system will consider using the index. If it is not, the system simply scans the table to search for the desired rows.

The use of an optimizer to determine the most efficient access path means that SQL/400 possesses the desirable characteristic of physical data independence. The system manager can modify internal data structures without forcing changes to previously written applications. In particular, indexes can be created and dropped without affecting the validity of any existing or future SELECT statements.

What Are the Advantages of Indexes?

The system can use an index to enhance machine efficiency in a number of circumstances. Some of these are described below.

1. *Direct access to a specified row.*   Assume an index is defined on the appropriate column. The previous discussion illustrated direct access to rows in the COURSE table. This would avoid the need to scan the entire table, which would be costly for a large table.

2. *Sorting.*   Note that Fig. 12.8 showed the CNAME values in sequence. This means that the system can use the XCNAME index to retrieve the COURSE rows in CNAME sequence. If an index is not established on an appropriate column, the system must execute an internal sort routine which can be costly, especially for a large number of rows. The optimizer may consider using an index whenever the SELECT statement contains any of the following keywords or clauses: ORDER BY, DISTINCT, GROUP BY, or UNION.

3. *Join operation.*   The join operation is presented in Chap. 15. Here we merely state that the join operation can be costly, and indexes can facilitate this process.

How Many Indexes Can Be Created?

Any number of indexes can be created for a given table. However, there is a cost associated with each index which may offset its advantages.

What Are the Disadvantages of Indexes?

There are two cost factors associated with database indexes which prohibit their unlimited use.

1. *Disk space used by the index.* An index, although it is smaller than the table, can occupy a considerable amount of disk storage. A table with many rows means that the index will have many entries. This means a large index is created. And, if the table has many indexes, it could cause the total disk space used by all the indexes to exceed the size of the table itself.

2. *Update costs.* While indexes expedite the retrieval process, they penalize the update process. Whenever a new row is inserted into or deleted from a table, the system must make the corresponding change to the indexes. If, for example, a table has five indexes, then an insert or delete operation forces an update to the five indexes. This could severely impact response time.

COMPOSITE INDEXES AND UNIQUE INDEXES

The CREATE INDEX statement provides other advantages in addition to those specified above. By including special keywords in the statement (to be described below), either of the following special type indexes can be created.

1. *Composite index.* An index can be created on a combination of column names. A simple example of such an index is a CNO-SEC composite index for the CLASS table. Note that a composite index is just a single index where the key is composed of data found in multiple columns. Also note that the order of the index components is significant. For example, the CNO-SEC index is different from the SEC-CNO index.

2. *Unique index.* A unique index is an index which cannot contain any duplicate values. The presence of a unique index causes the system to reject any update to the table which will result in duplicate values in the column(s) specified by the index. *A unique index should be created for the primary key column(s).* Although only one primary key can be specified for a table, any number of unique indexes can be specified for a table. For example, if you wanted the system to enforce uniqueness on CNAME values, you could have included the keyword "UNIQUE" in the CREATE INDEX statement shown in Sample Statement 12.2.

These types of indexes are not mutually exclusive. It is possible for a single index to have both of the above characteristics.

Figure 12.8 illustrated an index on the CNAME column. We observed that the CNAME values in the index are sorted. To be precise, the values are sorted in an ascending (ASC) sequence. When you create an index, it is possible to specify a descending (DESC) sequence. This could help when a SELECT statement contains the following clause:

```
ORDER BY CNAME DESC
```

Figure 12.9 shows a more general syntax of the CREATE INDEX statement which can be used to establish the above special types of indexes. This figure shows the syntax and keywords necessary to establish a compound or unique index, or to specify the sequence of index values.

CREATE [UNIQUE] INDEX library/index-name
ON library/table-name
  (column1-name [ASC/DESC,]
  column2-name [ASC/DESC,]
     . . .
  columnN-name [ASC/DESC])

Figure 12.9 CREATE INDEX statement.

GUIDELINES FOR CREATING INDEXES

Choosing the right set of indexes is a challenging task. In fact, choosing the optimal set of indexes for a large design is practically impossible. In the absence of performance information (e.g., frequency of retrieval or update), the best you can do is to follow some established guidelines.

- Create a unique index on the primary key.
- Create an index on each foreign key.
- Create an index on any column(s) which will be frequently referenced in a WHERE clause or an ORDER BY clause.

Sample Statement 12.3   Create a unique composite index for the CLASS table shown in Fig. 12.4. The composite key is based on the CNO and SEC columns.

CREATE   UNIQUE INDEX SQLTST/XCNOSEC

ON SQLTST/CLASS (CNO, SEC)

Comments

1. The keyword "UNIQUE" is specified prior to "INDEX." This causes the system to reject any update which would cause multiple rows to have the same CNO-SEC combination.

2. This index is a composite index because it is defined for more than one column (CNO, SEC). Note that the order specified is significant.

3. The sequence of each component of the composite key can be designated as ascending (ASC) or descending (DESC). The ON clause could have been written as

```
ON CLASS (CNO ASC, SEC ASC)
```

Exercise

12C. Create a unique index for the SNO "primary key" of the STUDENT table.

DROP STATEMENT

All of the aforementioned database objects can be removed from the system by the DROP statement. This statement is the inverse of the CREATE statement. It is executed whenever the created object no longer serves any purpose in the application environment. We illustrate this statement with two examples.

Sample Statement 12.4   Remove the XCNOSEC index.

```
DROP INDEX SQLTST/XCNOSEC
```

System Response

The system will produce some message which should confirm that the specified statement was successful.

Comments

1. The XCNOSEC index is based on the CLASS table. Note that the DROP statement does not need to specify the table name.

2. Again we note that the CLASS table still exists and any queries against this table will still work. The system optimizer will simply choose an access path which does not rely on the dropped index.

Sample Statement 12.5   Drop the COURSE table. (Do not actually execute this statement if you are testing the examples shown in this text.)

```
DROP TABLE SQLTST/COURSE
```

System Response

The system would display a message which confirms that the statement was successful.

Comments

1. Execution of the DROP TABLE statement not only deletes all rows present from the table, it removes the very table/file from the system. This means that a subsequent attempt to insert rows into the table would fail. The DELETE statement (described in the next chapter) is used to delete any or all rows in a table without removing the table definition. Obviously, the DROP TABLE statement is potentially dangerous, which is why we advised you not to actually execute the above statement. If you did, you would have to go through the effort of recreating the COURSE table and inserting its rows.

2. Whenever a table is dropped, any indexes based on the table are also automatically dropped. If the COURSE table were dropped, the system would drop the previously described XCNAME index.

3. SQL does not have any statement which can be used to remove specified columns from a table (i.e., there is no "drop column" statement). To realize this objective a new table must be created with just the desired columns. Chapter 13 will show a variation of the INSERT statement which can be used to copy data from selected columns in the original table to the new table.

SUMMARY

This chapter has introduced some of SQL/400's most useful data definition statements, as follows.

CREATE TABLE	To create a new table
CREATE INDEX	To create an index on an existing table
DROP INDEX	To remove an index
DROP TABLE	To remove a table

In a production environment, where the database contains corporate data, these statements would only be executed by the system manager. The system manager would also execute other SQL statements not covered in this text because such statements would reference specific physical objects other than tables or indexes. However, some users and programmers may have permission to create tables for personal data or testing purposes. This chapter has covered the above data definition statements in enough detail to realize these objectives.

Summary Exercise

12D. Create a table called CISCOURSE. It should have four columns called CISCNO, CISCNAME, CISCRED, and CISCLABFEE which, respectively, have the same attributes as the CNO, CNAME, CRED, and CLABFEE columns in the COURSE table. Also create a unique index for the "primary key" (CNO).

13

Data Manipulation

The previous chapter introduced the CREATE TABLE statement which is used to create an empty table. We now turn our attention to SQL's data manipulation statements which are used to store rows in a table and subsequently modify these rows. These are the INSERT, UPDATE, and DELETE statements.

The INSERT statement is used to store rows in a table. This statement could be used to store rows into an empty table or a table which already contains some number of rows. Thereafter, if you wish to change the contents of any existing rows, you must use the UPDATE statement. The DELETE statement is used to remove one or more rows from the table. In this chapter we will discuss each of these statements. Again we emphasize that execution of these statements is potentially dangerous because errors could cause the loss of valuable data. If you are running the sample statements on a sample database, double-check each statement before execution.

THE INSERT STATEMENT

There are two forms of the INSERT statement. The first allows for exactly one row to be inserted into a table. In this form, data which currently do not exist in the database may be inserted into a table. The second form allows data from multiple rows already existing in some table to be inserted into another table. Both forms are shown in Fig. 13.1. We introduce the first form of the INSERT statement by illustrating the addition of a new row into the COURSE table.

Sample Statement 13.1   Assume the CIS department offers a new course with the name "INTRODUCTION TO SQL". The course number is "C77". This course is worth three credits, and its lab fee is $150.00. The course description is "GOOD STUFF!". Insert a new row into the COURSE table corresponding to this course.

```
INSERT   INTO COURSE
VALUES   ('C77', 'INTRODUCTION TO SQL',
         'GOOD STUFF!', 3, 150.00, 'CIS')
```

System Response

The system will display a message which indicates that the system either (1) successfully inserted the new row, or (2) rejected the insert operation due to an error (e.g., syntax, NOT NULL violation, unique value violation). Assuming that the insert operation is successful, you can further verify the presence of the new row by executing the following SELECT statement.

```
SELECT * FROM COURSE WHERE CNO = 'C77'
```

The system should display the following.

CNO	CNAME	CDESCP	CRED	CLABFEE	CDEPT
C77	INTRODUCTION TO SQL	GOOD STUFF!	3	150	CIS

Comments

1. *Syntax.* INSERT Clause. The name of the table, COURSE, immediately follows "INSERT INTO". The table name must correspond to some previously created table.

2. *Syntax.* VALUES Clause. The VALUES keyword is followed by a pair of parentheses enclosing the values to be placed in the fields of the newly inserted row. The example shows that the values are specified in the COURSE table's default left-to-right column sequence. Each value must comply with the data type of the corresponding column. Apostrophes must be used to enclose character string and date/time values. Numeric values must not be enclosed within apostrophes. Each value must be separated by a comma, which may or may not be followed by one or more spaces.

3. Recall that the relational model makes no assumptions about the ordering of rows within a table. This simplifies the insertion process because it is not necessary (in fact, it is not possible) to specify where the row actually gets placed in the table. Recall that the ORDER BY clause can be used in a SELECT statement to display rows in any desired sequence.

4. The previous chapter described the concept of entity integrity. If we assume that there is a unique index on the CNO column, then an error message indicating the violation of an integrity constraint could occur if the CNO value in the new row equals some existing CNO value.

Format 1:
INSERT INTO name-of-table [(col1, col2, . . . , colN)]
VALUES (value1, value2, . . . , valueN)

Format 2:
INSERT INTO name-of-table [(col1, col2, . . . , colN)]
subselect-statement

Figure 13.1 SQL INSERT statement.

5. What if a certain value is unknown? For example, determination of a course lab fee may require further financial analysis, but it still may be necessary to insert a row for a new course. Sample Statement 13.3 will illustrate the use of the NULL keyword to handle this situation.

6. You must have permission (recognized by the system) to insert rows into the table. If you created the table, then you automatically have permission to insert rows into it. Otherwise, you must obtain INSERT privileges from the creator of the table. The process of granting privileges is described in Chap. 20.

7. The current example does not explicitly specify the column names. Therefore, the VALUES clause must contain values for all columns specified in the default left-to-right column sequence. This requires that you know the data type and position of every column in the table. The next example will illustrate a variation of the INSERT statement which allows you to relate a value to a column by explicitly referencing the name of the column.

8. *Inserting date/time values.*   You need to be careful when inserting date/time information. If you are inserting a date using SQL/400's default date format, then you only need to enclose the date within apostrophes. You can also specify date and time registers. The following examples illustrate these points.

```
INSERT INTO REGISTRAT VALUES
('T33', '01', '325', '08/19/81')

INSERT INTO REGISTRAT VALUES
('T11', '01', '325', CURRENT DATE)
```

Sample Statement 13.2   Same as previous example. This time specify the column names in the INSERT statement.

INSERT INTO COURSE

  (CNO, CNAME, CDESCP, CRED, CLABFEE, CDEPT)

VALUES ('C77', 'INTRODUCTION TO SQL',

       'GOOD STUFF!', 3, 150.00, 'CIS')

System Response

Same as the previous example.

Comment

The specification of the column names requires extra typing. However, it forces you to confirm your understanding of the columns in the table. The specification of column names also allows for some flexibility. The column names may be specified in any left-to-right sequence as long as the values in the VALUES clause match the same sequence. The following INSERT statements would produce the same result.

```
INSERT   INTO COURSE
         (CNAME, CNO, CDESCP, CRED, CLABFEE, CDEPT)
VALUES   ('INTRODUCTION TO SQL', 'C77',
         'GOOD STUFF!', 3, 150.00, 'CIS')

INSERT   INTO COURSE
         (CRED, CNAME, CDEPT, CDESCP, CLABFEE, CNO)
VALUES   (3, 'INTRODUCTION TO SQL', 'CIS',
         'GOOD STUFF!', 150.00, 'C77')
```

Using this variation of INSERT eliminates the need to know the actual left-to-right sequence of the columns. However, it is still necessary to know the data types of the columns.

INSERTING ROWS WITH UNKNOWN VALUES

The previous INSERT statements specified values for all columns. However, there may be circumstances where some data values are unknown, yet you would still like to insert the row using just the known values. The next two examples illustrate techniques where only some column values are entered for a row. The column for any unknown value will be set to the null value.

Sample Statement 13.3   Insert a row into the COURSE table with the following information. (Assume the course description, credit, and lab-fee values are unknown.)

- Course number: C78
- Course name: EMBEDDED SQL
- Department: CIS

INSERT INTO COURSE VALUES

('C78', 'EMBEDDED SQL', ' ', NULL, NULL, 'CIS')

Comments

1. This example does not specify column names. Therefore, the VALUES clause should provide a value for all columns in the proper left-to-right sequence. (The absence of explicit column names is the same as naming all the columns.) Because the CRED and CLABFEE values are unknown, their values are specified by using the keyword NULL. The CDESCP value is also unknown, but NULL cannot be specified because NOT NULL was declared in its definition. For this reason, a space (or some other default character) must be specified. Specifying NULL for a column defined with the "NOT NULL" parameter would cause an error.

2. NULL can be used for any data type, not just numeric values as in this example. Also, observe that NULL is not enclosed by apostrophes.

The next example illustrates another technique for inserting a row with just some known values.

Sample Statement 13.4   Perform the same insert as in the previous example, but explicitly identify the columns for which you are providing information.

INSERT INTO COURSE (CNO, CNAME, CDEPT, CDESCP)

VALUES ('C78', 'EMBEDDED SQL', 'CIS', ' ')

Comments

1. This example specifies the column names and corresponding values of just those columns where the values are known. When column names are explicitly identified, it is not necessary to use the NULL keyword. This is because any unspecified column will be set to a null value, provided that the column has not been defined as NOT NULL. In this case the CRED and CLABFEE values are set to null.

2. Again, note that the system will not let a column value default to the null value for any column which was defined as NOT NULL. For this reason the CDESCP column must receive a value.

Exercises

13A. Insert a row into the STAFF table with the following values.
```
ENAME: ALAN
ETITLE: LAB ASSIST
ESALARY: 3000
DEPT: CIS
```

13B. Insert a row into the STAFF table with the following values. (The ETITLE and ESALARY values are unknown.)
```
ENAME: GEORGE
DEPT: CIS
```

The previous examples illustrated the first format of the INSERT statement which is used to insert exactly one row into a table. The next sample statement illustrates the second format of the INSERT statement which can be used to extract information from one or more rows in a table and use that information to insert one or more rows into another table.

The next sample statement assumes that the CISCOURSE table has been created. (See Exercise 12D.) This table contains columns CISCNO, CISCNAME, CISCRED, and CISCLABFEE, which have the same respective definitions as the CNO, CNAME, CRED, and CLABFEE columns in the COURSE table.

Sample Statement 13.5   Copy the course number, course name, credits, and lab fee for all CIS courses from the COURSE table into the CISCOURSE table.

```
INSERT   INTO  CISCOURSE

         SELECT    CNO, CNAME, CRED, CLABFEE

         FROM      COURSE

         WHERE     CDEPT = 'CIS'
```

Comments

1. *Syntax.* Like previous examples, this example begins with an INSERT clause ("INSERT INTO CISCOURSE"). Unlike previous examples, it does not have a VALUES clause. Instead, the INSERT clause is followed by a "good old SELECT statement" which conforms to the syntax rules presented earlier in this text. Considered in isolation, this SELECT statement is

```
SELECT  CNO, CNAME, CRED, CLABFEE
FROM    COURSE
WHERE   CDEPT = 'CIS'
```

A SELECT statement which follows an INSERT clause is called a "subselect" or a "subquery." (Chapters 16 and 18 will examine subqueries placed within other SELECT statements.)

   The sequence in which the rows are to be inserted cannot be specified. This means that the ORDER BY clause cannot be used in the subselect.

2. *Behavior.* The subquery behaves like previous queries. It extracts the CNO, CNAME, CRED, and CLABFEE columns for rows corresponding to the CIS department. However, this time it does not display the selected rows. Instead, the system inserts copies of these rows into the CISCOURSE table. The columns of rows selected by the subselect must be data-type-compatible with the columns of the CISCOURSE table. Observe that the left-to-right column sequence of the subselect is the same as the columns of the CISCOURSE table. The data types of corresponding columns are the same. If these conditions are not met, the system will reject the insert.

3. This example did not explicitly name the columns of the receiving table. The following INSERT statement is equivalent to the current example.

```
INSERT INTO CISCOURSE
      (CISCNO, CISCNAME, CISCRED, CISCLABFEE)
      SELECT   CNO, CNAME, CRED, CLABFEE
      FROM     COURSE
      WHERE    CDEPT = 'CIS'
```

THE UPDATE STATEMENT

The UPDATE statement can be used to change any value in a table. It will contain a SET clause to identify the columns to be changed. The UPDATE statement may include a WHERE clause to identify the rows to be modified. The next sample statement simply changes one value in one row. Sample Statement 13.7 will illustrate how to change many row and column values by executing a single UPDATE statement.

Sample Statement 13.6   Change the lab fee for the course with course number "C77" to $175.00.

UPDATE COURSE

SET CLABFEE = 175

WHERE CNO = 'C77'

System Response

The system will display a message which indicates either (1) a successful statement, or (2) failure of the update operation due to an error. (Assuming that the update operation is successful, you can further verify the change by displaying the COURSE table.)

Comments

1. The keyword "UPDATE" is followed by the name of the table (COURSE) to be changed.

2. The SET clause, which follows the UPDATE clause, specifies the column(s) to be changed. "SET CLABFEE = 175" means CLABFEE will be set to 175 in the row(s) identified by the WHERE clause. The previous CLABFEE value is lost. It is overlaid by the value of 175. All other column values remain unchanged.

3. The WHERE clause, which follows the SET clause, identifies the row(s) to be changed. Knowing that CNO is the primary key (and presumably has a unique index) gives us assurance that only the C77 row will be changed.

The previous example simply changed one value in a table. Figure 13.2 outlines the general syntax of the UPDATE statement which shows that the SET clause can reference many columns and the WHERE clause can specify any search condition. Both the SET and WHERE clauses are described below.

SET Clause

The SET clause identifies each column to be changed and specifies the value to be used in making the change. This value can be an expression which is evaluated. The expression can also be a simple constant value, the NULL keyword, or it may involve a subselect. More than one column can be changed in a single UPDATE statement by ending the first expression with a comma and following it with another column and expression.

WHERE Clause

The WHERE clause identifies the row(s) to be changed. The changes made by the SET clause will apply only to the rows which match the condition specified by the WHERE clause. If the WHERE clause identifies multiple rows, then all such rows are updated. The WHERE clause is coded just like a WHERE clause in the SELECT statement. Its syntax is the same and can contain any of the Boolean operators. The WHERE clause can also contain a subselect statement (See Sample Statement 13.8).

The WHERE clause is optional. *However, we emphasize that the absence of a WHERE clause will cause every row in the table to be changed.* For example, if we wanted to change all CISCRED values to 9, we would execute

```
UPDATE  CISCOURSE
SET     CISCRED = 9
```

This behavior parallels that of the SELECT statement. The absence of a WHERE clause means that all rows are selected for display. The UPDATE statement without a WHERE clause is used to make a global change to every row in the table.

```
UPDATE name-of-table
   SET  name-of-column-1 = expression-1,
        name-of-column-2 = expression-2,
                    .
                    .
                    .
        name-of-column-n = expression-n
   [WHERE search-condition]
```

Figure 13.2 SQL UPDATE statement.

The next example illustrates the set-level processing of SQL which allows many rows to be updated by execution of a single UPDATE statement.

Sample Statement 13.7 Make the following changes to any course with a course number beginning with "C7".

- Set the credit value equal to 6
- Increase the lab fee by 10 percent
- Change the description to "THE LANGUAGE OF SQL/400"

```
UPDATE  COURSE

SET       CRED = 6,

          CLABFEE = CLABFEE * 1.10,

          CDESCP = 'THE LANGUAGE OF SQL/400'

WHERE CNO LIKE 'C7%'
```

Comments

1. Previous examples inserted two rows into the COURSE table with course numbers C77 and C78. These are the only courses which match the WHERE condition. Hence, two rows will be changed by the UPDATE statement.

2. This example changes three columns in each target row. All changes are expressed in a single SET clause. Each expression except the final expression is terminated by a comma. If the comma is omitted, an error occurs.

   Both the CRED and CDESCP columns are assigned new values in the same manner as in the previous example. The new value assigned to the CLABFEE column is based on the value presently existing in the column. The result of the calculation replaces the existing value.

The next example uses a subselect to obtain the new value to be used in the update operation.

Sample Statement 13.8 The WHERE clause can contain a subselect. The following example will change the credits for any course having a lab fee greater than the smallest salary recorded in the STAFF table.

UPDATE CISCOURSE

SET CRED = 4

WHERE CLABFEE ›

      (SELECT MIN(ESALARY)

      FROM STAFF)

Comment

There are a number of issues pertaining to subselect statements. These will be described in detail in Chap. 16.

Exercise

13C. Update the ESALARY value for any staff member assigned to the CIS department. The new salary for all such individuals is $4000.

THE DELETE STATEMENT

The DELETE statement is used to remove an entire row or group of rows from a table. You cannot delete a column or just part of a row.

Sample Statement 13.9   Delete all rows from the COURSE table which have a course number beginning with "C7". (Remove the two rows previously inserted into the COURSE table.)

DELETE

FROM COURSE

WHERE CNO LIKE 'C7%'

System Response

The system responds with a message which either (1) confirms successful statement, or (2) rejects the deletion due to an error.

Comments

1. Given the current status of the COURSE table, the WHERE clause identifies the C77 and C78 courses for deletion. After deletion of these rows, the contents of the COURSE table becomes the same as it was prior to the execution of the data manipulation examples shown in this chapter.

2. The general format of the DELETE statement is shown in Fig. 13.3. The syntax is simple, but you should be careful to accurately specify the correct rows for deletion.

3. The DELETE keyword identifies the operation. The FROM clause is followed by the name of the target table.

The WHERE clause is used to identify the row(s) to be deleted. The search condition has the same structure as that of the SELECT and UPDATE statements. (It can also reference a subselect.) The WHERE clause can be used to identify many rows and is therefore subject to the same accuracy considerations. (The previous example illustrated the set-level processing capabilities of the DELETE by selecting multiple rows for deletion.) Therefore, we again recommend caution in the coding of the WHERE clause to avoid the erroneous deletion of rows. If you want to delete just one row, make certain the WHERE clause identifies the row by the "primary key" or some other column which has a unique index defined for it.

4. The WHERE clause is optional. *However, we emphasize that failure to include it will cause every row in the table to be deleted.* For example, the following statement will delete every row in the CISCOURSE table.

```
DELETE
FROM CISCOURSE
```

Because the WHERE clause is omitted, all rows are deleted from the table. The table will still exist, but will not contain any rows. A subsequent reference to the CISCOURSE table in a SELECT statement would not cause an error, but would not return any rows.

Exercise

13D. Delete all rows in the STAFF table corresponding to employees assigned to the CIS Department.

```
DELETE
FROM name-of-table
[WHERE search-condition]
```

Figure 13.3 SQL DELETE statement.

SUMMARY

In this chapter we introduced the data manipulation statements of SQL which allow

- The insertion of new rows into a table using the INSERT statement
- The modification of data in existing rows of a table using the UPDATE statement
- The deletion of existing rows from a table using the DELETE statement

These statements may be executed in the interactive environment as demonstrated in this chapter. However, operations which affect the content of the database will usually be performed from within an application program using embedded SQL to ensure greater control and reduce the change of error.

Summary Exercises

13E. Create a table called EXPENSIVE with the columns EXPCNO, EXPCNAME, EXPCLABFEE, and EXPDEPT, which, respectively, have the same data types and lengths as the CNO, CNAME, CLABFEE, and CDEPT columns in the COURSE table. Then, for every COURSE table row with a CLABFEE value over $100, copy the COURSE table information into the corresponding columns of the EXPENSIVE table.

13F. Update the EXPENSIVE table by subtracting $50 from the EXPCLABFEE column if its current value exceeds $400.

13G. Delete all rows in the EXPENSIVE table which correspond to courses offered by the theology department.

13H. Insert a new row into the EXPENSIVE table. The EXPCNO value is "X99", and the EXPDEPT value is "XXX". The EXPCNAME and EXPCLABFEE values are unknown.

13I. Change every EXPCNAME value in the EXPENSIVE table to "JUNK".

13J. Delete all rows from the EXPENSIVE table.

13K. Drop the EXPENSIVE table.

Processing Null Values

When we first encountered the STAFF table we observed that the DEPT value for the row describing Da Vinci contained a null value. This value implies that Da Vinci's department is unknown. All the previous sample queries and exercises involving the STAFF table were designed to avoid any potential problems which can result from the presence of null values. This chapter will describe these potential problems and present techniques for handling such problems.

In Chap. 12 we emphasized that the creator of a table should consider using the NOT NULL option to prohibit any database operation from storing null values in a specified column. However, there are circumstances when values are unknown. For example, a genealogist might be unable to determine family background if records do not exist. Such information is undetermined and must be recorded as "unknown." Chapter 13 described how the INSERT statement allows a column to be assigned or default to a null value. Unless the designer uses the traditional default approach of using a specific value, typically blank or zero, to represent an unknown value, null values may be present in database tables. When this occurs, the results produced by a SELECT statement may not be what you expect. This is because of the semantic subtleties associated with unknown values. This chapter presents sample queries which illustrate the behavior of the SELECT statement when it encounters null values. You may think that this behavior is unnecessarily complex and may conclude, as others have, that null values are just not worth the trouble. However, null values can occur in SQL/400 tables. Therefore, you should understand how to code SELECT statements which process them correctly.

NULLTAB TABLE

To present sample queries on this topic we digress from our educational database design and introduce a special table which contains a spectrum of null values (displayed by "–"). The table's name is NULLTAB, and its content is shown in Fig. 14.1. In particular, note that NULLTAB has some rows where every value is null. This is most unusual, but is nonetheless valid.

PKEY	COLA	COLB	COLC
1	10	20	5
2	30	30	5
3	160	–	10
4	–	170	5
5	–	–	10
6	10	40	5
7	30	60	5
8	–	–	–
–	–	–	–
–	–	–	–
–	–	–	–

Figure 14.1 NULLTAB table.

CALCULATING WITH NULL VALUES

Assume you were asked to add 10 to the winning number of tomorrow's Connecticut Million-Dollar Lottery. Unfortunately, today you cannot guarantee to calculate the correct answer. Because the calculation involves at least one unknown value, the result of the calculation is unknown. SQL applies this logic when evaluating an arithmetic expression involving an unknown value. The result is a null value.

Sample Query 14.1   Calculate the sum and the difference of the COLA and COLB values in NULLTAB.

SELECT   PKEY, COLA, COLB, COLA+COLB, COLA–COLB

FROM   NULLTAB

PKEY	COLA	COLB	COLA+COLB	COLA–COLB
1	10	20	30	10–
2	30	30	60	0
3	160	–	–	–
4	–	170	–	–
5	–	–	–	–
6	10	40	50	30–
7	30	60	90	30–
8	–	–	–	–
–	–	–	–	–
–	–	–	–	–
–	–	–	–	–

Comments

1. This example shows that any arithmetic expression will produce a null value if one or more of its operands is a null value.

2. A null value is shown as a hyphen preceded by spaces.

3. Observe that the COLA – COLB calculation resulted in negative amounts for the rows with PKEY values of 1, 6, and 7. Do not confuse the minus sign shown for these values with the hyphen indicating null elsewhere in the result. A column cannot have a known value and a null value. "30–" is a negative 30.

Sample Query 14.2   Find the sum, average, maximum, and minimum values of COLA in NULLTAB.

SELECT   SUM(COLA), AVG(COLA), MAX(COLA), MIN(COLA)

FROM   NULLTAB

SUM(COLA)	AVG(COLA)	MAX(COLA)	MIN(COLA)
240	48.00..	160	10

Comments

1. This example shows that group functions ignore nulls in their calculation. These functions do not simply treat an unknown value as zero. If this were the case, the average of column COLA would be 240/10 = 24.00. Instead, the AVG function only used the five known values to determine the result, 240/5 = 48.00.

2. We stress the apparent lack of symmetry in the way SQL handles nulls. For group functions, it ignores the null values and produces a nonnull result based on the present known values. But, as Sample Query 14.1 illustrates, the presence of a null value causes an arithmetic expression to evaluate to null.

3. What if all values passed to a column function are null? Then the result of the function is also null.

We did not include the COUNT function in the previous example because its behavior is different from the other column functions. This is because the COUNT(*) function counts the number of rows selected. Unlike the other column functions, it does not examine the actual values, which may or may not be null, that are stored in the rows.

Sample Query 14.3   How many rows does NULLTAB have?

```
SELECT  COUNT(*)

FROM    NULLTAB
```

COUNT(*)
———————
     11

Comment

The result (11) is reasonable once we realize that the COUNT(*) function simply counts the number of selected rows. It does not consider whether any of the selected rows contain null values. In particular, a row consisting of all null values is still included in the count.

We stated above that null values are potentially dangerous. The next Sample Query demonstrates that the previous reasonable behavior of arithmetic expressions and built-in functions may generate confusing results when processing null values.

Sample Query 14.4   Calculate the average of COLA two ways. Apply (1) the AVG function and (2) SUM and COUNT functions.

SELECT   SUM(COLA), COUNT(*),

           SUM(COLA)/COUNT(*), AVG(COLA)

FROM   NULLTAB

SUM(COLA)	COUNT(*)	SUM(COLA)/COUNT(*)	AVG(COLA)
240.00	11	21.8	48.00..

Comment

Note the difference in the averages. The third column was calculated as 240.00/11. The fourth column was calculated as 240.00/5. Which is correct? Regardless of how you answer this question, the example shows subtleties of null values.

Sample Query 14.5 Calculate the overall total of the values found in COLA and COLB. Use two approaches: (1) find the sum of COLA, then the sum of COLB, then add the results; (2) for each row, add the COLA and COLB values, then summarize these row totals.

```
SELECT  SUM(COLA)+SUM(COLB), SUM(COLA+COLB)

FROM    NULLTAB
```

NUMERIC EXPRESSION	SUM(COLA+COLB)
560	230

Comment

Note the different results to two apparently equivalent mathematical expressions. In effect they are only equivalent when all the COLA and COLB values are known. Review Sample Queries 14.1 and 14.2 to confirm your understanding of this example.

COMPARING WITH NULL VALUES

Assume you have $10 in your pocket and you pass a complete stranger on the street. If you were asked to compare your $10 to the presumably unknown amount the stranger has, the result would be unknown. Again, SQL applies the same reasonable logic. When it does a comparison involving at least one null value, the result is null. And again, we will see that this reasonable behavior has potential pitfalls.

Sample Query 14.6   Display all rows from NULLTAB where the COLA value equals the COLB value.

```
SELECT    *

FROM      NULLTAB

WHERE     COLA = COLB
```

PKEY	COLA	COLB	COLC
2	30	30	5

Comments

This query returned only one row. Consider why the WHERE clause resulted in a "no hit" for the other 10 rows.

1. Rows corresponding to PKEY values of 1, 6, and 7 have known COLA and COLB values which are not equal to each other. Hence it is clear why they are not selected.

2. Rows corresponding to PKEY values of 3 and 4 have one null value in either COLA or COLB. Because one value is unknown, the comparison results in a "no hit," and hence these rows are not selected. Note this is the case even though one of the unknown (null) values could possibly be equal to the known value. SQL only selects a row when it is certain that the WHERE condition evaluates to true.

3. Rows corresponding to PKEY values of 5, 8, and null have null values in both COLA and COLB. These rows are not selected. *SQL does not consider two null values to be equal to each other.* This is analogous to trying to deduce whether two complete strangers have the same amount of money in their pockets. The answer is "unknown," not "true." Again, SQL only selects a row when it is certain that the WHERE condition evaluates to true. To emphasize the point, this means that SQL does not consider "null = null" to be true. (Likewise, "null <> null" is not considered to be true.)

4. The example uses the equals comparison operator. The same logic applies to the other comparison operators. A greater than (>), less-than (<), etc., comparison results in "unknown" if any operand is null.

Exercises

14A. Refer to the FACULTY table for this exercise. Display the average number of dependents and the total number of dependents for all faculty members together with the number of faculty members.

14B. Assume that each faculty member was awarded a $250.00 tuition credit for each dependent. What would be the total remuneration for each faculty member if this amount were added to his or her salary? In other words, display the total of the salary and $250.00 for each dependent for all faculty members. (Consider Sample Query 14.4 when reviewing your solution.)

14C. Display any row in NULLTAB where the COLA value is not equal to the COLB value. (If you execute this query, observe that only three rows are selected for this display. These correspond to PKEY values 1, 6, and 7. Because Sample Query 14.6 selected only one row, and there are 11 rows in NULLTAB, it might seem that this exercise should produce 10 rows. Why not? See the following sample queries for a discussion of this point.)

The next two examples together show the potential problems with WHERE clauses involving null values.

Sample Query 14.7.1   How many staff members are assigned to the theology department?

SELECT COUNT(*) FROM STAFF

WHERE   DEPT = 'THEO'

COUNT(*)
───────────
    4

Comment

This query selected the four rows corresponding to Matthew, Mark, Luke, and John.

Sample Query 14.7.2   How many staff members are not assigned to the theology department?

SELECT COUNT(*) FROM STAFF

WHERE   DEPT <> 'THEO'

COUNT(*)
───────────
    4

Comment

This query selected the four rows corresponding to Dick Nix, Hank Kiss, Euclid, and Archimedes.

The previous two queries show four members assigned to the theology department and four members not assigned to the theology department. Can we deduce that we have a total of eight staff members? No! There are nine rows in the STAFF table. Neither of the above queries had a match on the row corresponding to Da Vinci, whose DEPT value is null. In particular, Sample Query 14.7.1 did not select Da Vinci's row because SQL could not conclude that Da Vinci is assigned to the theology department. Likewise, Sample Query 14.7.2 did not select Da Vinci's row because SQL concludes that he could be assigned to the theology department. The WHERE clause in both sample queries evaluates to "unknown" when considering Da Vinci's row. Again, SQL will select only those rows which evaluate to "true."

These sample queries illustrate the potential danger associated with using a WHERE clause to test for the presence or absence of a given value when a null value can occur. Sample Query 14.12 will introduce the use of "IS NULL" as a means of testing for the presence of a null value. Then, if we assume that a null DEPT value can be interpreted as "not assigned to any department, including the theology department," Sample Query 14.7.2 could be expressed as

```
SELECT   COUNT (*)
FROM     STAFF
WHERE    DEPT <> 'THEO'
OR       DEPT IS NULL
```

The result of executing this statement is 5. Most users would consider this to be a better answer than 4. However, the choice of which answer is "correct" depends on how you interpret the query objective.

THREE-VALUE LOGIC

Traditional database systems and traditional computing languages which manipulate them are based on a system of two-value logic. This simply means that any comparison will always result in a "true" or "false" conclusion. The source of the potential confusion in the aforementioned problems lies in the fact that null values force the introduction of a three-value logic system where a comparison reduces to a "true," "false," or "unknown" result. A three-value logic system is more complex and requires greater attention in entering SELECT statements and interpreting the results of a query.

In Chap. 4 we presented the Boolean operators (AND, OR, NOT) in the context of the traditional two-value logic. Figure 14.2 summarizes the behavior of these operators in a three-value logic system. We do not explain the details of each comparison except to note that the evaluations of "true" (T), "false" (F), and "unknown" (U) are consistent with the notions of AND, OR, and NOT as described earlier. The AND of two conditions only evaluates to "true" if both conditions are "true." The OR of two conditions evaluates to "true" if either or both of the conditions are "true." The NOT of a "true" condition is "false" and vice versa. The NOT of an "unknown" condition is "unknown."

Logic of NOT:	condition		T	F	U
	NOT condition		F	T	U

Logic of AND:	AND		T	F	U
	T		T	F	U
	F		F	F	F
	U		U	F	U

Logic of OR:	OR		T	F	U
	T		T	T	T
	F		T	F	U
	U		T	U	U

Figure 14.2 Boolean operators in a three-value logic system.

Sample Query 14.8   Display any row from NULLTAB where COLA is equal to COLB, or where COLA is greater than COLC.

```
SELECT     *

FROM       NULLTAB

WHERE      COLA = COLB

OR         COLA > COLC
```

PKEY	COLA	COLB	COLC
2	30	30	5
1	10	20	5
7	30	60	5
6	10	40	5
3	160	–	10

Comment

You should work through the logic of this query to confirm your understanding of the three-way logic.

SORTING NULL VALUES

We begin by noting that the system will place null values at the high end of the sort sequence. The next Sample Query illustrates this point.

Sample Query 14.9   Display all rows of NULLTAB in ascending sequence by COLA.

```
SELECT PKEY, COLA

FROM   NULLTAB

ORDER BY COLA
```

PKEY	COLA
1	10
6	10
2	30
7	30
3	160
4	–
5	–
8	–
–	–
–	–

Comments

1. Null values appear at the bottom of the output display because they sort higher than any known value.

2. This raises another subtle semantic issue. Earlier we emphasized that a comparison involving a null value evaluates to "unknown." However, sorting a collection of values involves comparing them, and, if the system doesn't know a value (because it's null), how does it know where to put it in sequence? This is an apparent contradiction. It is resolved by noting that the displayed row must go somewhere. SQL/400 decides to put it at the high end of the sequence. This is an arbitrary decision.

SQL also treats null values like known values when it does internal sorting for the sake of removing duplicate values or forming groups. The next two examples illustrate this point.

Sample Query 14.10   Display COLA of NULLTAB. Do not display duplicate values.

```
SELECT  DISTINCT COLA
FROM    NULLTAB
```

COLA
——
    10
    30
   160
    –

Comment

We emphasize that DISTINCT considers null values equal to each other. Hence only one null value is shown in the result.

Exercise

14D. Display the name, faculty number, and number of dependents for all faculty members. Arrange the result in descending sequence by the number of dependents.

Sample Query 14.11   Using the NULLTAB table, form groups of COLC values and display the sum of the COLA values for each group.

SELECT COLC, SUM(COLA)

FROM   NULLTAB

GROUP BY COLC

COLC	SUM(COLA)
5	80
10	160
–	–

Comment

We emphasize that SQL treats null values as equal for the purpose of grouping. Hence only one group is formed for the nulls found in COLC. The sum of the COLA values shown in SUM(COLA) for this group is null because all the corresponding COLA values are null and the sum of null values is null.

Exercise

14E. Display the average salary of faculty members who have the same number of dependents.

SUMMARY OF PROBLEMS WITH NULL VALUES

The previous examples presented a number of situations where an unsophisticated user could easily misinterpret the contents of an output display. The general source of the problem is the more complex semantics of a three-value logic. So again we encounter complexity which transcends SQL. To briefly consider the semantics, note that the "null value" is not really a "value" since its purpose is to designate the absence of a value. Sometimes, when performing calculations and comparisons, SQL behaves in a way which is consistent with this "absence of a value" concept. Under other circumstances, for example, when you use ORDER BY, DISTINCT, and GROUP BY features, SQL ends up treating nulls as though they were values.

AVOIDING THE COMPLEXITY OF NULL VALUES

The easiest way to avoid the complexity described above is to simply keep nulls out of the database by using the NOT NULL option for every column of every table in the database. Many database designers adopt this approach. However, others say that this is just sweeping the problem under the carpet. The real world presents situations where data are unknown, and our database should reflect this reality. In this case, nulls should be allowed to appear in some columns of some tables. The remaining examples present some SQL techniques for handling null values when they are necessary.

IS NULL

It is possible to explicitly test for the presence of a null value in a row by using "IS NULL" in a WHERE clause.

Sample Query 14.12   Display any row in NULLTAB which has a null value in COLA.

```
SELECT  *

FROM    NULLTAB

WHERE   COLA IS NULL
```

PKEY	COLA	COLB	COLC
4	–	170	5
5	–	–	10
8	–	–	–
–	–	–	–
–	–	–	–
–	–	–	–

Comments

1. Only those rows with a null value in COLA are displayed.

2. You cannot use an equal sign with the NULL predicate. (That is, "WHERE COLA = NULL" does not make any sense. You must specify "IS NULL".)

Exercise

14F. Display the names, number of dependents, and department numbers of all faculty members for whom it is not known whether they have any dependents.

IS NOT NULL

The NOT keyword can be used with the NULL predicate. The "IS NOT NULL" phrase is probably more useful than "IS NULL" because it allows you to bypass some of the aforementioned problems by explicitly excluding null values from consideration. The next sample query is a modification of Sample Query 14.5, where null values caused two different summary totals to be displayed.

Sample Query 14.13 Calculate the overall total of the values found in COLA and COLB. Use two approaches: (1) find the sum of COLA, then the sum of COLB, then add the results; (2) for each row, add the COLA and COLB values, then summarize these row totals. Exclude those rows which have null values in COLA or COLB.

```
SELECT   SUM(COLA+COLB), SUM(COLA)+SUM(COLB)
FROM     NULLTAB
WHERE    COLA IS NOT NULL
AND      COLB IS NOT NULL
```

SUM(COLA+COLB)	NUMERIC EXPRESSION
230	230

Comments

1. The WHERE clause eliminated any rows having a null value in COLA or COLB. Hence only five rows were selected and both expressions resulted in the same result.

2. The not equal operator cannot be used with the NULL predicate. Do not specify "WHERE COLA <> NULL".

VALUE BUILT-IN FUNCTION

The previous examples showed the null value displayed as a hyphen (-). It is possible to substitute a more meaningful value for a null value in an output display. This is the purpose of the VALUE function.

Sample Query 14.14   Display NULLTAB as described below.

1. Display COLC. Substitute 999 for any null values.
2. Display COLB. Substitute the value of COLC whenever the COLB value is null.
3. Display COLA. Whenever COLA is null substitute the COLB value. If COLB is also null, substitute the COLC value.

```
SELECT  PKEY, VALUE(COLC, 999),

        VALUE(COLB, COLC),

        VALUE(COLA, COLB, COLC)

FROM NULLTAB
```

PKEY	COLC	COLB	COLA
1	5	20	30
2	5	30	60
3	10	10	160
4	5	170	170
5	10	10	10
6	5	40	10
7	5	60	30
8	999	–	–
–	999	–	–
–	999	–	–
–	999	–	–

Comments

1. You are advised to examine the NULLTAB table to verify the value substitutions shown in the output display.

2. The first argument of the VALUE function is a column or an expression which could possibly evaluate to null. The second argument is a (presumably nonnull) value to be substituted in the output display whenever the first argument is actually null. For example, if we specified VALUE(COLA, 0), the system would display 0 instead of the standard null value symbol whenever COLA was null.

3. The VALUE function can have more than two arguments. This handles the case where the second argument is also null by substituting the value of the third argument. If the third argument is also null, but a fourth argument is present, it substitutes the value of the fourth argument, and so on. The standard null symbol is displayed only if all arguments evaluate to null. The primary restriction on the arguments is that they must have comparable data types.

4. The NULLTAB table contains all numeric values. Hence, all the substituted values were numeric. The other data types (character strings, date, time) can be used as well in the VALUE function. For example, if the CDESCP column in the COURSE table could contain nulls, we could specify VALUE(CDESCP, 'DESCRIPTION UNKNOWN'). The character string "DESCRIPTION UNKNOWN" would be displayed whenever CDESCP is null.

5. Sometimes a built-in function evaluates to null. For example, applying the SUM function to a column of null values produces a null result. Assume the sum of some COLX could be null. Then you could specify VALUE(SUM(COLX),0) to display a 0 whenever the sum is actually null.

SUMMARY

This chapter introduced null values. We examined the complexities of dealing with a three-value logic system incorporating the notion of an unknown value. The following major points were discussed:

1. A null "value" does not represent 0 or spaces, but indicates that the value is not known. This results in a three-value logic system. We note that the null value is essentially typeless, and, hence, can represent "unknown value" for any data type.

2. Because we do not have any knowledge about unknown values, two such values can be said to be neither equal nor unequal. The same approach to handling null values is used by SQL/400. This means that one null value is neither equal nor unequal to another. A special syntax is used to examine a column for null values. Rather than using "=" as the comparison operator, we must use "IS NULL" and in the negative sense, "IS NOT NULL".

3. Null values affect the results of computations in both calculated expressions and group built-in functions. Null values do not participate in these operations and therefore may distort the results if you are not aware of their presence.

4. The VALUE scalar function is used to prevent null values from appearing in a query result. It allows you to specify an alternative value to replace a null value in the result table.

5. Null values sort higher than any other value when the system is required to order the result.

Summary Exercises

14G. Display the name and department of any staff member who is not assigned to a known department.

14H. For each department, display its department identifier and the number of all staff members in the department.

5

Accessing Multiple Tables

In this part of the text we return to the task of data retrieval. The following chapters complete our exhaustive examination of the SELECT statement. As you progress through these chapters you will notice a shift in perspective. The logical considerations for most examples presented in Part 1 of the text were relatively simple. Our primary focus was on the syntax of the SELECT statement. In this part of the text you will find it easy to learn the new syntactical constructs. However, the sample queries and exercises become more complex because you will be required to give more thought to the logical dimension of the query objective. The complexity of these examples will pertain to the "conceptual navigation" required when multiple tables need to be referenced.

ORGANIZATION OF CHAPTERS

Chapter 15 presents the "inner join" operation, which is probably the most important topic covered in this part of the book. The inner join operation is the most useful technique for referencing multiple tables. Many of the sample queries presented in subsequent chapters can also be solved using the inner join operation.

Chapter 16 introduces subqueries. Most of the sample queries and exercises presented in this chapter can be solved using the inner join operation.

Chapter 17 introduces the union (UNION) operation. This simple operation is very useful. Many reasonable queries could not be expressed if the UNION keyword were missing from SQL. This topic is covered before correlated subqueries because some of the more interesting correlated subquery examples also utilize the union operation.

Chapter 18 presents correlated subqueries. These subqueries are important because, unlike those described in Chap. 16, they allow us to solve certain problems which could not be solved using the inner join operation. The logic of correlated subqueries is different from that of the subqueries presented earlier. This is our rationale for discussing them in a separate chapter. This chapter also introduces the "outer join" operation.

Join Operation

This chapter introduces the join operation, which allows a single SELECT statement to reference multiple tables. The join operation allows a query to specify the merging of columns from two or more tables by matching values found in columns from each table. The precise definition of this "merging" and "matching" will be described below. We begin by presenting three queries which could utilize the join operation. This is followed by a detailed explanation of the join operation and a number of sample queries which demonstrate its use.

To be precise, this chapter describes the "inner join" operation, which is usually referred to as the "join" operation. However, the (inner) join is different from an "outer join," which will be described in Chap. 18.

Query 1. For every employee who is assigned to some existing department, select that person's name, title, salary, and department identifier, along with the department building, room location, and department chairperson faculty number.

This query requires that the system display the following:

1. All columns from the STAFF table

2. All columns from the DEPARTMENT table (with the possible exception of the DEPT column because each value would be identical to the DEPT column from the STAFF table)

This query is based on the fact that some of the DEPT values in the STAFF table match the DEPT values in the DEPARTMENT table. Note this query is phrased to exclude Archimedes and Euclid, who are assigned to nonexistent departments; and Da Vinci, whose department assignment is unknown.

Query 2. For every course with a lab fee over $175, display the course name and lab fee, along with the faculty number of the chairperson responsible for the course.

This query requires that the system display the following:

1. CNAME and CLABFEE from the COURSE table

2. DCHFNO from the DEPARTMENT table

This query presumes that every CDEPT value in the COURSE table matches some DEPT value in the DEPARTMENT table.

Observe that neither of the above queries could be satisfied using the previously described SQL techniques. A join operation is necessary because the result of each query contains data from more than one table. However, there are other reasons for using the join operation. For example, we might want to display columns from one table, but specify row selection criteria relative to some other table. Consider the third query.

Query 3. Display the name and title of every staff member who is known to work in the humanities building.

This query displays the ENAME and ETITLE columns, which are both found in the STAFF table. However, the system must examine the DEPARTMENT table to determine which departments are located in the humanities building. Only staff members assigned to these departments will be selected. (Again, the query is phrased to exclude Archimedes, Euclid, and Da Vinci, whose DEPT values do not match any DEPT value in the DEPARTMENT table.)

You could satisfy this query with your current knowledge of SQL. However, the process would be awkward because you must execute two independent SELECT statements. The first statement would determine which departments are located in the humanities building. This is

```
SELECT   DEPT
FROM     DEPARTMENT
WHERE    DBLD = 'HU'
```

The output would identify the "THEO" and "PHIL" values. You would then use this information to construct the following SELECT statement.

```
SELECT   ENAME, ETITLE
FROM     STAFF
WHERE    DEPT = 'THEO'
OR       DEPT = 'PHIL'
```

While this approach will work, it is not desirable for a couple of reasons. The first is that the user must memorize or write down the intermediate result (THEO and PHIL). This requires some effort, especially if the intermediate result is large. A second reason why this approach is undesirable is machine inefficiency. The execution of two separate SELECT statements is usually more costly than executing a single equivalent statement.

Each of the previous queries can be satisfied by issuing a single SELECT statement which implements a join operation. The following pages explain the important concepts pertaining to the join operation. After you understand these concepts, the sample queries will demonstrate that the SQL syntax for expressing the join operation is relatively straightforward.

JOINING TWO TABLES

From a conceptual point of view, the join of two tables is the concatenation of rows from the two tables where values from a column in the first table match values from a column in the second table. The result of the join operation is a new table which has a row for each match which occurred between the original two tables. The original tables remain unchanged. This is best illustrated by an example.

Figure 15.1 shows two tables, TABLE1 and TABLE2, which will be joined to form a third table, shown in Fig. 15.2. The first step is to specify the *join column* (match column) for each table. Column C3 of TABLE1 and column CA of TABLE2 are specified as the join columns. This means that whenever the C3 value of a row in TABLE1 is equal to the CA value of a row in TABLE2, a new row is established in the resulting join table. This row is formed by concatenating the rows where the match occurred. We make the following observations about the join result.

- In TABLE1, the rows with C3 values of 45, 55, and 15 did not match any values in column CA of TABLE2. Hence, they do not appear in the join result.

- Likewise, in TABLE2, the rows with CA values of 35, 65, and 75 did not match any values in column C3 of TABLE1. Hence, they do not appear in the join result.

- There was one match on the value 10. This produced the first row of the join result.

TABLE1			Join Columns	TABLE2	
C1	C2	**C3**	← ─┴─ →	**CA**	CB
A	AAA	10		35	R
B	BBB	45		10	S
C	CCC	55		65	T
D	DDD	20		20	U
E	EEE	20		90	V
F	FFF	90		90	W
G	GGG	15		75	X
H	HHH	90		90	Y
				35	Z

Figure 15.1 Tables to be joined.

- Both of the TABLE1 rows with a C3 value of 20 matched the CA value of 20 in TABLE2. These two matches produced the second and third rows in the join result.
- In TABLE1 there are two rows with a C3 value of 90. Each of these two rows matched the three rows in TABLE2 with CA values of 90. This is a total of six matches for the value of 90. It produced the last six rows of the join result.

Observe that neither of the join columns, CA and C3, is a primary key or a foreign key. Usually a foreign key in one table and its corresponding primary key in another table are specified as the join columns. However, as the example shows, this is not necessary. That is, the system is not restricted to the semantics of foreign key relationships. Any columns with comparable data types can be specified as join columns.

Subsequent sample queries will illustrate the syntax of a SELECT statement which implements a join operation. These will show both tables referenced in the FROM clause and the join columns specified in the WHERE clause. The SELECT statement to produce the join result of Fig. 15.2 is

```
SELECT    *
FROM      TABLE1, TABLE2
WHERE     C3 = CA
```

We will postpone further discussion of syntax until the presentation of this chapter's sample queries. For the moment we return to the more important conceptual considerations.

C1	C2	C3	CA	CB
A	AAA	10	10	S
D	DDD	20	20	U
E	EEE	20	20	U
F	FFF	90	90	V
F	FFF	90	90	W
F	FFF	90	90	Y
H	HHH	90	90	V
H	HHH	90	90	W
H	HHH	90	90	Y

MATCHING
COLUMNS

Figure 15.2 Join result.

To reiterate a previously mentioned point, it is necessary to specify the join columns. We could have joined TABLE1 and TABLE2 on *any* two columns. For example, we could have requested the system to join the tables by matching columns C1 and CB. In this case, no matches would occur, and the result would be an empty table. In most realistic situations, we join tables only by matching columns which contain values based on some common set of values. For example, in the COURSE, DEPARTMENT, and STAFF tables of our sample database, we will be matching those columns which contain department identifier values.

Observe that two extreme results can occur when joining any two tables.

1. *"Empty-Table" result.* This is the case mentioned above where no matches occur.

2. *"Worst-Case" result.* This occurs when every column of the first table matches every column of the second table. Figure 15.3 illustrates this situation. TABLE3 is joined with TABLE4 on columns C2 and CB. Every "X" value in column C2 matches every "X" value in column CB. Because TABLE3 has three rows and TABLE4 has four rows, the join result has 3 * 4 = 12 rows. This is the largest number of rows which could be generated. We call this the "worst case" because it takes more computer time to process a large join result than a small one.

TABLE3

C1	C2
1	X
2	X
3	X

TABLE4

CA	CB
9	X
8	X
7	X
6	X

Join Result

C1	C2	CA	CB
1	X	9	X
1	X	8	X
1	X	7	X
1	X	6	X
2	X	9	X
2	X	8	X
2	X	7	X
2	X	6	X
3	X	9	X
3	X	8	X
3	X	7	X
3	X	6	X

MATCHING COLUMNS

Figure 15.3 "Worst-case" join.

NULLS IN THE JOIN COLUMNS

The preceding examples referenced tables which did not contain null values. Recall that null means "value unknown." Therefore, a null cannot match with any other value; it does not even match another null value. Figure 15.4 shows TABLE1A and TABLE2A. These tables are similar to TABLE1 and TABLE2 except that nulls have replaced some values. The result of joining TABLE1A and TABLE2A on columns C3 and CA is shown in Fig. 15.5. We make the following observations.

- The nonnull values matched (or didn't match) in the same way as occurred in the join of the original TABLE1 and TABLE2.

- The null values in the join columns did not match with any other values. In particular, note that the null values in the last row of each table did not match with each other.

- The only null value which appears in the join result is the null which is present in column CB. This is not a join column; hence, it is treated like any other data value.

A final comment before turning to the sample queries. The term "match" is not very precise. In this chapter it means "equal to." From a formal point of view, the join operation described thus far is called "inner equijoin." This is the most common join operation used in practice. The SQL language allows for other types of joins where the join condition can include any of the comparison operators. These other join operations will be introduced in Sample Query 15.13.

TABLE1A

C1	C2	**C3**
A	AAA	10
B	BBB	45
C	CCC	55
D	DDD	20
E	EEE	20
F	FFF	90
G	GGG	15
H	HHH	—

Join Columns

TABLE2A

CA	CB
35	R
10	—
65	T
20	U
90	V
90	W
75	X
90	Y
—	Z

Figure 15.4 Nulls in join columns.

C1	C2	C3	CA	CB
A	AAA	10	10	—
D	DDD	20	20	U
E	EEE	20	20	U
F	FFF	90	90	V
F	FFF	90	90	W
F	FFF	90	90	Y

MATCHING COLUMNS

Figure 15.5 Join of TABLE1A and TABLE2A.

JOIN STAFF AND DEPARTMENT TABLES

The first sample query involving a join operation will join the STAFF and DEPARTMENT tables. The semantic relationship which justifies this join is the "employee works in department" relationship. The match is based on join columns which happen to have the same name (DEPT). Although this query itself is not very realistic, it serves the purpose of illustrating a pure equijoin.

Sample Query 15.1   For all staff members assigned to existing departments, select all information about the staff members and their respective departments.

```
SELECT    *

FROM      STAFF, DEPARTMENT

WHERE     STAFF.DEPT = DEPARTMENT.DEPT
```

ENAME	ETITLE	ESALARY	DEPT	DEPT	DBLD	DROOM	DCHFNO
HANK KISS	JESTER	25000	PHIL	PHIL	HU	100	60
DICK NIX	CROOK	25001	PHIL	PHIL	HU	100	60
MATTHEW	EVANGLIST1	51	THEO	THEO	HU	200	10
MARK	EVANGLIST2	52	THEO	THEO	HU	200	10
LUKE	EVANGLIST3	53	THEO	THEO	HU	200	10
JOHN	EVANGLIST4	54	THEO	THEO	HU	200	10

Comments

1. *Logic.* Confirm your understanding of the join operation by observing that both DEPT columns in the result table have equal values. Also note that certain STAFF and DEPARTMENT rows do not appear in the join result. STAFF rows corresponding to EUCLID, ARCHIMEDES, and DA VINCI did not match on DEPT values; likewise, the MGT row from the DEPARTMENT table is absent for the same reason.

2. *Syntax*

a. **FROM** clause: The logic of the query requires that data be extracted from two tables. Therefore, both tables are referenced in the FROM clause. The table names must be separated by a comma. The table names can be specified in any order. A complex query could involve more than two tables. The general rule is simple: If the query references any column of a table in either the SELECT or the WHERE clause, the name of the table must be included in the FROM clause. (See Sample Query 15.9 which illustrates the join of three tables.)

b. **WHERE** clause: The join columns are specified in the WHERE clause. The match is effected by specifying that the two join columns are equal. Our sample query illustrates

```
WHERE STAFF.DEPT = DEPARTMENT.DEPT
```

This condition is called a "join condition." Note that the column names are qualified. Qualification is required in this statement because both the join columns have the same name (DEPT). An error would occur if the join column names were not qualified.

c. **SELECT** clause: "SELECT *" means the same as in previous queries. In this example, the system will display all columns in the join result. Since the FROM clause references STAFF before DEPARTMENT, the columns of the STAFF table are displayed first (to the left of the DEPARTMENT table columns).

Observe that the result displays both DEPT columns which have the same values. In practice, we would not display redundant columns. We would identify just those columns we want displayed. See the next sample query.

DISPLAYING A SUBSET OF THE JOIN RESULT

We rarely want to see all rows and columns of a join result. For example, the previous equijoin result showed duplicate DEPT columns which are completely redundant. Usually our intention is to display only some of the row and column data present in the join result. This objective is achieved by applying previously described row and column selection techniques to the intermediate table produced as the result of the join operation. The next sample query shows that the syntax is the same as with previous queries that referenced just one table. The only difference is conceptual. The row and column selection criteria apply to the intermediate table produced as a result of the join operation.

Sample Query 15.2   Display the name, salary, department identifier, and building and room location for every staff member assigned to an existing department whose yearly salary exceeds $1000.

```
SELECT    ENAME, ESALARY, STAFF.DEPT,
          DBLD, DROOM
FROM      STAFF, DEPARTMENT
WHERE     STAFF.DEPT = DEPARTMENT.DEPT
AND       ESALARY > 1000
```

ENAME	ESALARY	DEPT	DBLD	DROOM
HANK KISS	25000	PHIL	HU	100
DICK NIX	25001	PHIL	HU	100

Comments

1. *Logic.* Any query which involves a join requires that the user really understand the meaning of the data items. This is especially true of the relationships between the tables as reflected by the join columns. Consider the following semantic assumptions implicit in the SQL code for the current sample query.

   - Staff members always work in the same building and room where their department is located. (Is it possible for a staff member to work in a building other than the department's location?) We must confirm that department location and staff work location are the same thing.

   - We are not interested in information about staff members who are not assigned to existing departments. Rows corresponding to these staff members are "flushed out" by the join operation.

   These issues are logical. They transcend the SQL language. They must be addressed by the database administrator during the process of database analysis and design. This is beyond the scope of this text. However, it is mandatory that users properly interpret the meaning of the data and relationships implicit in the database design.

   The current sample query illustrates that there are potential pitfalls even with a simple database. Throughout the remainder of this text we will assume that the semantics of the sample queries are correct. This is necessary to focus on the SQL code and to avoid a long digression into issues of database analysis and design.

2. *Syntax*

   a. The FROM clause and join condition are identical to the previous sample query. This is

   ```
   FROM STAFF, DEPARTMENT
   WHERE STAFF.DEPT = DEPARTMENT.DEPT
   ```

b. As mentioned above, there is no syntax change just because we are working with an intermediate join result.

- We want only some rows. These rows correspond to staff members whose salary exceeds $1000. This implies that another condition should be appended to the join condition. This is

```
AND ESALARY > 1000
```

- We want only some columns. These are explicitly named in the SELECT clause. Columns from different tables can be specified because the columns are selected from the join result. Thus, we have

```
SELECT ENAME, ESALARY, STAFF.DEPT, DBLD, DROOM
```

Qualification of the DEPT column is necessary. We may understand that both DEPT columns in the join result are identical, but the system does not. If DEPT is not qualified, an error will occur. Either table name may be used as the qualifier. The following SELECT clause will produce the same result.

```
SELECT ENAME, ESALARY, DEPARTMENT.DEPT, DBLD, DROOM
```

3. *Physical efficiency.* Earlier we identified the "worst-case" situation where all the join columns match each other. When we consider that we usually want just some subset of rows and columns from the join result, it seems that the system could incur the cost of generating a large intermediate join result. This is not necessarily the case. SQL/400 has an internal software module called an "optimizer" which can usually avoid this effort. In fact, the "AND ESALARY > 1000" clause will help the optimizer. From a user's point of view, only two comments are necessary.

a. Don't worry about efficiency. That is the job of the optimizer. It is intelligent enough to avoid the unnecessary generation of a large intermediate join result. SQL performance tuning is beyond the scope of this book.

b. Even though the system may not actually generate the full intermediate join result, it may be helpful for you to think that it does.

4. *Mental steps.* There are three basic steps which you can follow when you need to reference multiple tables.

   a. *Join the tables.* Determine the tables to be joined and their respective join columns. Then construct the FROM clause and the join condition. In the current example, this leads to

   ```
   FROM STAFF, DEPARTMENT
   WHERE STAFF.DEPT = DEPARTMENT.DEPT
   ```

   b. *Specify the desired columns.* Construct the SELECT clause which identifies the columns that you want displayed. Don't forget any necessary qualification. In the current example, this yields

   ```
   SELECT ENAME, ESALARY, STAFF.DEPT, DBLD, DROOM
   ```

   c. *Specify the desired rows.* Use the AND connector to append other selection criteria to extract the desired rows from the join result. In the current example, this is

   ```
   AND ESALARY > 1000
   ```

   These pieces of code are put together in the standard order of

   ```
   SELECT---------
   FROM   ---------
   WHERE  ---------
   AND    ---------
   ```

   You are encouraged to apply these mental steps to future workshop exercises.

JOIN BASED ON PRIMARY KEY AND FOREIGN KEY VALUES

We remind the reader that the concepts of primary key and foreign keys are not supported in the current release (V2.2) of SQL/400. However, it is often the case that the database administrator will use some other application programming technique to enforce the concept of entity and referential integrity. This means that the concepts of primary key and foreign key are applicable (and very important!) even though the current version of SQL/400 does not *directly* support these concepts.

The next sample query joins the COURSE and DEPARTMENT tables. The semantic relationship which justifies this join is the "course is offered by department" relationship. This example reflects a typical situation where the join operation matches the *foreign key* of the referencing table (CDEPT in COURSE) with the *primary key* of the referenced table (DEPT in DEPARTMENT). The notion of referential integrity tells us that *because every CDEPT value will be equal to some DEPT value, we can expect every row of the COURSE table to be present in the intermediate join result.*

Sample Query 15.3   For every course with a lab fee over $175, display the course name, lab fee, and faculty number of the chairperson responsible for the course. Display the output by course name in ascending sequence.

```
SELECT    CNAME, CLABFEE, DCHFNO

FROM      COURSE, DEPARTMENT

WHERE     CDEPT = DEPT

AND       CLABFEE > 175

ORDER BY CNAME
```

CNAME	CLABFEE	DCHFNO
COMMUNISM	200.00	10
EXISTENTIALISM	200.00	60
RELATIONAL DATABASE	500.00	80

Comments

1. The course name and lab fee are stored in the COURSE table, and the chairperson's faculty number is stored in the DEPARTMENT table. The join columns are CDEPT in the COURSE table and the DEPT column in the DEPARTMENT table. Hence, the example shows

```
FROM  COURSE, DEPARTMENT
WHERE CDEPT = DEPT
```

Note that, unlike the previous two examples, qualification of column names is unnecessary. The join columns have distinct names, so there is no possible ambiguity. We could have used qualified names for the purpose of documentation. Then the WHERE clause would be

```
WHERE COURSE.CDEPT = DEPARTMENT.DEPT
```

2. Unlike previous sample queries, neither of the two join columns, CDEPT and DEPT, is referenced in the SELECT clause. It is not necessary to display join columns.

3. Sorting the result implies use of the ORDER BY clause. Any column(s) from either table which appears in the SELECT clause can be specified. All the variations of the ORDER BY clause, described in Chap. 3, apply.

The next sample query displays columns from just one table (STAFF). This is not unusual. The purpose of the join is to permit row selection based on information found in a second table (DEPARTMENT).

Sample Query 15.4   Display the name and title of every staff member who works in the humanities building.

SELECT	ENAME, ETITLE
FROM	STAFF, DEPARTMENT
WHERE	STAFF.DEPT = DEPARTMENT.DEPT
AND	DBLD = 'HU'

ENAME	ETITLE
HANK KISS	JESTER
DICK NIX	CROOK
MATTHEW	EVANGLIST1
MARK	EVANGLIST2
LUKE	EVANGLIST3
JOHN	EVANGLIST4

Comments

1. Observe that both of the displayed columns are located in the STAFF table. The join operation is necessary to determine which departments are located in the humanities building.

2. Sample Query 16.8 will illustrate an alternative solution to this problem. It will show a "nested subquery" solution which can be applied only because all the displayed columns come from a single table. This point will be emphasized in Chap. 16 when we introduce nested subqueries.

Recall that displaying just some columns of a table can produce an output display with duplicate rows. (The DISTINCT keyword was used to remove this duplication.) The next example shows that duplicate rows can occur in a result produced by a join operation.

Sample Query 15.5   Where can I find an evangelist? More precisely, display the building and room of any academic department which employs a staff member whose title begins with "EVANGLIST".

SELECT   DBLD, DROOM

FROM   DEPARTMENT, STAFF

WHERE   DEPARTMENT.DEPT = STAFF.DEPT

AND   ETITLE LIKE 'EVANGLIST_'

DBLD	DROOM
HU	200
HU	200
HU	200
HU	200

Comment

Because all four evangelists reside in the same room of the same building, the output display contains four duplicate rows. Duplicate rows can be removed from the output display by including DISTINCT in the SELECT clause. We rewrite the SELECT statement including the DISTINCT keyword.

```
SELECT   DISTINCT DBLD, DROOM
FROM     DEPARTMENT, STAFF
WHERE    DEPARTMENT.DEPT = STAFF.DEPT
AND      ETITLE LIKE 'EVANGLIST_'
```

Exercises

15A. Display the equijoin of the COURSE and DEPARTMENT tables where the join operation matches the CDEPT values in COURSE with the DEPT values in DEPARTMENT.

15B. The "natural join" of the two tables is the same as the equijoin except that one of the duplicate columns present in the equijoin is not displayed. Modify the previous exercise so that it produces the natural join of the COURSE and DEPARTMENT tables based on the CDEPT and DEPT columns. (You can display either the CDEPT column or the DEPT column from the join result, but not both columns.)

15C. For each course with a lab fee over $100, display the course name and its lab fee along with the faculty number of the chairperson of the department which offers the course.

15D. Display the course number and name of any course which is offered by a department chaired by the person having the faculty number of 60. Display the output result in descending sequence by course number.

15E. Display the name and salary of any staff member assigned to a department which is located in the science building.

15F. For any staff member who is assigned to an existing department and whose salary exceeds $200, display the building and room location of the staff member. The output should not display any duplicate rows.

Previous sample queries illustrated the use of familiar techniques to display a given row-column subset of a join result. We also saw that the DISTINCT keyword and ORDER BY clause apply. In fact, there do not exist any special display restrictions specific to a join result. You can treat a join result like any other table. In particular, you can perform calculations with a join result. The next three sample queries illustrate some of the computational techniques originally presented in Chaps. 6 and 7. This time the techniques are applied to intermediate join results.

Sample Query 15.6 What is the total salary of staff members who work in room 100 of the humanities building?

SELECT	SUM (ESALARY)
FROM	DEPARTMENT, STAFF
WHERE	DEPARTMENT.DEPT = STAFF.DEPT
AND	DBLD = 'HU'
AND	DROOM = '100'

SUM(ESALARY)
_____
     50001

Comments

1. There is really nothing new in this example. The FROM and WHERE clauses identify the join operation and row selection criteria. The SUM function is then applied to the ESALARY column. As usual, a group built-in function compresses the displayed output to a single row.

2. All the SQL built-in functions described in Part 2 of this text apply. The function arguments may be any of the columns in the intermediate join result.

The next sample query joins the COURSE and STAFF tables. The semantic relationship which justifies this join is the "employee works in the department which offers the course" relationship. The join columns are CDEPT and DEPT, both of which contain department identifier values.

Note that the semantics of this relationship are more complex than the previously described "employee works in department" and "course is offered by department" relationships. This is because courses and employees are only indirectly related via the aforementioned direct relationships with a department. Proper understanding of the next sample query requires that you comprehend these relationships and further assumptions specified below.

Assume that any staff member employed by an existing department is available and qualified to serve as tutor for any course offered by the department. Staff members not assigned to existing departments are not required to tutor. If a given department does not offer courses or does not have any staff members assigned to it, then that department does not offer tutoring services. Some of the following sample queries are based on these assumptions.

Sample Query 15.7   Display the name and salary for every staff member who has tutoring responsibilities, along with the course number and credits of any course he can tutor. Also, display the ratio of salary to credits for each staff member and course combination. Sort the output by course number within staff member name.

```
SELECT    ENAME, ESALARY, CNO, CRED, ESALARY/CRED

FROM      STAFF, COURSE

WHERE     DEPT = CDEPT

ORDER BY ENAME, CNO
```

ENAME	ESALARY	CNO	CRED	ESALARY/CRED
DICK NIX	25,001.00	P11	3	8333.66666
DICK NIX	25,001.00	P22	3	8333.66666
DICK NIX	25,001.00	P33	3	8333.66666
DICK NIX	25,001.00	P44	6	4166.83333
HANK KISS	25,000.00	P11	3	8333.33333
HANK KISS	25,000.00	P22	3	8333.33333
HANK KISS	25,000.00	P33	3	8333.33333
HANK KISS	25,000.00	P44	6	4166.66666
JOHN	54.00	T11	3	18.00000
JOHN	54.00	T12	3	18.00000
JOHN	54.00	T33	3	18.00000
JOHN	54.00	T44	6	9.00000
LUKE	53.00	T11	3	17.66666
LUKE	53.00	T12	3	17.66666
LUKE	53.00	T33	3	17.66666
LUKE	53.00	T44	6	8.83333
MARK	52.00	T11	3	17.33333
MARK	52.00	T12	3	17.33333
MARK	52.00	T33	3	17.33333
MARK	52.00	T44	6	8.66666
MATTHEW	51.00	T11	3	17.00000
MATTHEW	51.00	T12	3	17.00000
MATTHEW	51.00	T33	3	17.00000
MATTHEW	51.00	T44	6	8.50000

Comments

1. This example illustrates the generation of a column containing calculated values. This is the rightmost column produced by dividing ESALARY by CRED. The fact that these two columns come from different tables is incidental. They are both present in the intermediate join result and hence can be referenced in the expression to calculate the ratio.

2. The column showing the calculated result is processed and displayed according to the rules for arithmetic expressions presented in Chap. 6.

The next sample query demonstrates grouping within the context of a join operation.

Sample Query 15.8 For every department which offers tutoring services, display the department identifier along with the average lab fee of the courses it offers and the average salary of staff members who can tutor such courses. Sort the output by department identifier.

SELECT   DEPT, AVG(CLABFEE), AVG(ESALARY)

FROM   STAFF, COURSE

WHERE   DEPT = CDEPT

GROUP BY DEPT

ORDER BY DEPT

DEPT	AVG(CLABFEE)	AVG(ESALARY)
PHIL	87.50000	25000.5000
THEO	110.00000	52.5000

Comments

1. Again, there is nothing new in this example. The example merely demonstrates the GROUP BY clause with values present in an intermediate join result. All previously specified rules pertaining to grouping must apply. (See Chap. 7.)

2. The summary output of this example confirms our earlier observations regarding the content of the sample tables. Only the philosophy and theology departments offer courses and have staff members assigned to them. Hence, only these departments appear in the output display.

Exercises

15G. Display the smallest and largest lab fees associated with any course offered by a department located in the science building.

15H. What is the total number of staff members assigned to departments which are described in the DEPARTMENT table?

15I. Assume a staff member can tutor any course offered by his department. If the lab fee for a course he tutors exceeds his salary by at least $52, then display the staff member's name and salary along with the course lab fee and the difference between the lab fee and the salary.

15J. For each department which employs staff members, display the department identifier followed by the total staff salary and average staff salary for the department.

15K. For those courses which have staff members available as tutors, display the course name followed by the number of available tutors for the course.

15L. Display the department identifier of any department described in the DEPARTMENT table which employs at least three staff members.

15M. For each department described in the DEPARTMENT table which employs at least one staff member, display the department identifier followed by the number of staff members assigned to the department.

JOIN OF THREE TABLES

The next sample query requires the join of three tables. Again, we rely on the previous assumptions about staff members tutoring courses offered by their departments.

Sample Query 15.9   For any course which has a staff member available to tutor students, display its number, the names and titles of the staff members who can serve as a tutor for the course, and their respective building and room locations. Sort the output by staff member name within course number.

SELECT   CNO, ENAME, ETITLE, DBLD, DROOM

FROM   COURSE, STAFF, DEPARTMENT

WHERE   CDEPT = STAFF.DEPT

AND   CDEPT = DEPARTMENT.DEPT

ORDER BY CNO, ENAME

CNO	ENAME	ETITLE	DBLD	DROOM
P11	DICK NIX	CROOK	HU	100
P11	HANK KISS	JESTER	HU	100
P22	DICK NIX	CROOK	HU	100
P22	HANK KISS	JESTER	HU	100
P33	DICK NIX	CROOK	HU	100
P33	HANK KISS	JESTER	HU	100
P44	DICK NIX	CROOK	HU	100
P44	HANK KISS	JESTER	HU	100
T11	JOHN	EVANGLIST4	HU	200
T11	LUKE	EVANGLIST3	HU	200
T11	MARK	EVANGLIST2	HU	200
T11	MATTHEW	EVANGLIST1	HU	200
T12	JOHN	EVANGLIST4	HU	200
T12	LUKE	EVANGLIST3	HU	200
T12	MARK	EVANGLIST2	HU	200
T12	MATTHEW	EVANGLIST1	HU	200
T33	JOHN	EVANGLIST4	HU	200
T33	LUKE	EVANGLIST3	HU	200
T33	MARK	EVANGLIST2	HU	200
T33	MATTHEW	EVANGLIST1	HU	200
T44	JOHN	EVANGLIST4	HU	200
T44	LUKE	EVANGLIST3	HU	200
T44	MARK	EVANGLIST2	HU	200
T44	MATTHEW	EVANGLIST1	HU	200

Comments

1. It is necessary to display CNO (from the COURSE table), ENAME and ETITLE (from the STAFF table), and DBLD and DROOM (from the DEPARTMENT table). This requires the join of three tables based on columns containing the department identifiers.

2. A join of three tables requires two join conditions. The COURSE and STAFF tables are joined by

   ```
   WHERE CDEPT = STAFF.DEPT
   ```

   and the COURSE and DEPARTMENT tables are joined by

   ```
   AND CDEPT = DEPARTMENT.DEPT
   ```

3. The system behaves as follows.

   a. It joins two tables to establish an intermediate join result. If the first two tables are the COURSE and STAFF tables, COURSE rows corresponding to the CIS courses, and STAFF rows for staff with "ENG", "MATH" and null values in the DEPT column will not match. They will not be part of the intermediate join result. Hence, they will not appear in the final result.

   b. If the next join operation is based on the condition "CDEPT = DEPARTMENT. DEPT", the system will join the DEPARTMENT table with the previous intermediate result (not just the COURSE table as the code might indicate). Here the row for the MGT department will not match any value in the intermediate result. Hence it will not appear in the final result.

   Item *a* above stated, "If the first two tables are the COURSE and STAFF tables . . ." We said "If" because the system may, for reasons of efficiency, initially choose to join the COURSE and DEPARTMENT tables or the STAFF and DEPARTMENT tables to establish an intermediate join result. Then it would join the third table to the intermediate result. The result would be the same.

CROSS PRODUCT

The next example has a FROM clause which refers to two tables, but there is no WHERE clause specifying a join condition. Usually someone writes such a statement by accident. They intend to perform a regular join operation, but forget to include the join condition. Then they are surprised by the large number of rows displayed. What they get is known as the "cross product" or the "Cartesian product" where every row of the first table is paired with every row of the second table. This occurs because the join condition, which restricts the join result to matching values, is not present.

Sample Query 15.10   Form the cross product of the STAFF table and the DEPARTMENT table.

SELECT *

FROM STAFF, DEPARTMENT

Comments

1. Observe that the columns of the STAFF table are displayed to the left of the columns of the DEPARTMENT table. This is because "STAFF" was referenced before "DEPARTMENT" in the FROM clause. The following statement would result in the DEPARTMENT columns being displayed to the left of STAFF columns.

   ```
   SELECT *
   FROM STAFF,DEPARTMENT
   ```

2. The cross product coincides with the "worst-case" join situation described earlier. The number of rows generated could be very large. For example, if two tables each had one thousand rows, their cross product would have one million rows. As indicated above, users rarely need a cross product.

3. Null values will be displayed as "-".

ENAME	ETITLE	ESALARY	DEPT	DEPT	DBLD	DROOM	DCHFNO
HANK KISS	JESTER	25000.00	PHIL	THEO	HU	200	10
DICK NIX	CROOK	25001.00	PHIL	THEO	HU	200	10
MATTHEW	EVANGLIST1	51.00	THEO	THEO	HU	200	10
MARK	EVANGLIST2	52.00	THEO	THEO	HU	200	10
LUKE	EVANGLIST3	53.00	THEO	THEO	HU	200	10
JOHN	EVANGLIST4	54.00	THEO	THEO	HU	200	10
DA VINCI	LAB ASSIST	500.00	—	THEO	HU	200	10
EUCLID	LAB ASSIST	1000.00	MATH	THEO	HU	200	10
ARCHIMEDES	LAB ASSIST	200.00	ENG	THEO	HU	200	10
HANK KISS	JESTER	25000.00	PHIL	MGT	SC	100	—
DICK NIX	CROOK	25001.00	PHIL	MGT	SC	100	—
MATTHEW	EVANGLIST1	51.00	THEO	MGT	SC	100	—
MARK	EVANGLIST2	52.00	THEO	MGT	SC	100	—
LUKE	EVANGLIST3	53.00	THEO	MGT	SC	100	—
JOHN	EVANGLIST4	54.00	THEO	MGT	SC	100	—
DA VINCI	LAB ASSIST	500.00	—	MGT	HU	100	—
EUCLID	LAB ASSIST	1000.00	MATH	MGT	HU	100	—
ARCHIMEDES	LAB ASSIST	200.00	ENG	MGT	HU	100	—
HANK KISS	JESTER	25000.00	PHIL	CIS	SC	300	80
DICK NIX	CROOK	25001.00	PHIL	CIS	SC	300	80
MATTHEW	EVANGLIST1	51.00	THEO	CIS	SC	300	80
MARK	EVANGLIST2	52.00	THEO	CIS	SC	300	80
LUKE	EVANGLIST3	53.00	THEO	CIS	SC	300	80
JOHN	EVANGLIST4	54.00	THEO	CIS	SC	300	80
DA VINCI	LAB ASSIST	500.00	—	CIS	SC	300	80
EUCLID	LAB ASSIST	1000.00	MATH	CIS	SC	300	80
ARCHIMEDES	LAB ASSIST	200.00	ENG	CIS	SC	300	80
HANK KISS	JESTER	25000.00	PHIL	PHIL	HU	100	60
DICK NIX	CROOK	25001.00	PHIL	PHIL	HU	100	60
MATTHEW	EVANGLIST1	51.00	THEO	PHIL	HU	100	60
MARK	EVANGLIST2	52.00	THEO	PHIL	HU	100	60
LUKE	EVANGLIST3	53.00	THEO	PHIL	HU	100	60
JOHN	EVANGLIST4	54.00	THEO	PHIL	HU	100	60
DA VINCI	LAB ASSIST	500.00	—	PHIL	HU	100	60
EUCLID	LAB ASSIST	1000.00	MATH	PHIL	HU	100	60
ARCHIMEDES	LAB ASSIST	200.00	ENG	PHIL	HU	100	60

JOINING A TABLE WITH ITSELF

All previous join operations involved two or more *different* tables. The next example illustrates that a table can be joined with itself. The SQL technique involves the use of a "table alias" for a table name. In this case, we assign the STAFF table two distinct aliases, which allows us to think of and reference this single table as two distinct tables. An alias is assigned to a table by placing it after the table name in the FROM clause. The following example assigns two aliases, ST1 and ST2, to the STAFF table. Then all reference to columns of the conceptually distinct STAFF tables is done by using the alias names for qualification.

The solution to this sample query is intentionally incomplete. There is a considerable amount of redundant information in the output. Our intention is to show the matching of values which occurs when a table is joined with itself. Sample Query 15.12 will present a more precise solution which does not display redundant information.

Sample Query 15.11   For each department referenced in the STAFF table, we would like to form a committee composed of two staff members from the department. For each possible pair of staff members, display the department identifier followed by the names of two staff members. The result should contain a row for every possible pair of staff members.

SELECT   ST1.DEPT, ST1.ENAME, ST2.ENAME

FROM   STAFF ST1, STAFF ST2

WHERE   ST1.DEPT = ST2.DEPT

DEPT	ENAME	ENAME
ENG	ARCHIMEDES	ARCHIMEDES
MATH	EUCLID	EUCLID
PHIL	DICK NIX	DICK NIX
PHIL	DICK NIX	HANK KISS
PHIL	HANK KISS	DICK NIX
PHIL	HANK KISS	HANK KISS
THEO	JOHN	JOHN
THEO	JOHN	LUKE
THEO	JOHN	MARK
THEO	JOHN	MATTHEW
THEO	LUKE	JOHN
THEO	LUKE	LUKE
THEO	LUKE	MARK
THEO	LUKE	MATTHEW
THEO	MARK	JOHN
THEO	MARK	LUKE
THEO	MARK	MARK
THEO	MARK	MATTHEW
THEO	MATTHEW	JOHN
THEO	MATTHEW	LUKE
THEO	MATTHEW	MARK
THEO	MATTHEW	MATTHEW

Comments

1. *Syntax.*   A table alias is placed after the table name in the FROM clause. One or more spaces must separate the table name from its alias. (Note that a comma should not be used to separate a table name from its alias. The separator comma follows the alias.)

   A *table alias* is sometimes called a *correlation variable.* We will have more to say about correlation variables in Chap. 18.

2. *Logic.* After defining aliases in the FROM clause, we can conceptually operate under the assumption that there are two distinct tables with the names of ST1 and ST2, both of which happen to have the same data as the STAFF table. (The system does not actually make two copies of the STAFF table. Our discussion of correlation variables in Chap. 18 will provide more insight into the actual process.) The WHERE clause specifies a join condition which joins the ST1 and ST2 "tables" by matching each of their DEPT columns.

Observe the duplication of information present in the result. This is less than desirable. Because every staff member's name and department identifier is in both ST1 and ST2, each row in ST1 matches with its corresponding row in ST2. Therefore, every staff member appears on the same committee with himself. In particular, ARCHIMEDES, who is the only staff member with "ENG" as a department identifier, can be on a committee with only himself. (Likewise for EUCLID.) Also, if MARK is in the same department as JOHN, then JOHN is in the same department as MARK. This means that the result table will show two rows for each match of different staff members assigned to the same department. The joining of a table with itself produces these matches. The solution to the next sample query presents a trick to eliminate these undesirable rows from the result.

Sample Query 15.12   Refine the previous sample query. For each department identifier referenced at least twice in the STAFF table, display a row for each possible combination of *distinct* staff member names. The row should contain the department identifier followed by staff member names.

SELECT	ST1.DEPT, ST1.ENAME, ST2.ENAME
FROM	STAFF ST1, STAFF ST2
WHERE	ST1.DEPT = ST2.DEPT
AND	ST1.ENAME < ST2.ENAME

DEPT	ENAME	ENAME
PHIL	DICK NIX	HANK KISS
THEO	JOHN	LUKE
THEO	JOHN	MARK
THEO	JOHN	MATTHEW
THEO	LUKE	MARK
THEO	LUKE	MATTHEW
THEO	MARK	MATTHEW

Comment

The additional condition (ST1.ENAME < ST2.ENAME) removes redundant rows from the output. It also prohibits any staff member with a unique department identifier (e.g., ENG or MATH) from appearing in the result. Because this clause compares two columns from (conceptually) different tables, it could be considered as defining a second join condition where the comparison operator is "less than" instead of "equals" as in previous examples. This leads us into a discussion of the more general concept of *theta join,* which is described in the following sample queries.

THETA-JOIN

SQL permits a join condition to be formulated with any of the standard comparison operators. The term *theta-join* is used to indicate this more general capability where *theta* represents a given comparison operator. The next sample query illustrates use of the "less-than" operator to define the join condition.

Sample Query 15.13   Assume we would like to compare the salary of every staff member with every course lab fee. Whenever the salary is less than the lab fee, display the staff member name and salary followed by the corresponding course name and lab fee.

```
SELECT    ENAME, ESALARY, CNAME, CLABFEE

FROM      COURSE, STAFF

WHERE     ESALARY < CLABFEE
```

Comments

1. *Syntax.*   The syntax is consistent with all previous rules pertaining to the syntax of a join operation. The FROM clause identifies the names of the tables, and a WHERE clause specifies the join condition. The join condition can use any of the comparison operators. This example used the "<" operator.

2. *Logic.*   The process is similar to previous join examples. The only difference in this example is that comparison is based on the "less than" operator. Examination of each row in the output shows the ESALARY value is less than the corresponding CLABFEE value. The definition of what we mean by a "match" has to be expanded to incorporate all the comparison operations.

3. Equijoin is just a special case of the theta-join where theta represents the "equals" operator. Because equijoin has greatest application, the term *join* usually implies *equijoin*. However, to be precise, *join* in the general sense is really *theta-join* and therefore encompasses all the comparison operators.

ENAME	ESALARY	CNAME	CLABFEE
MATTHEW	51.00	SCHOLASTICISM	150.00
MATTHEW	51.00	FUNDAMENTALISM	90.00
MATTHEW	51.00	COMMUNISM	200.00
MATTHEW	51.00	EMPIRICISM	100.00
MATTHEW	51.00	EXISTENTIALISM	200.00
MATTHEW	51.00	INTRO TO CS	100.00
MATTHEW	51.00	COMPUTER ARCH.	100.00
MATTHEW	51.00	RELATIONAL DATABASE	500.00
MARK	52.00	SCHOLASTICISM	150.00
MARK	52.00	FUNDAMENTALISM	90.00
MARK	52.00	COMMUNISM	200.00
MARK	52.00	EMPIRICISM	100.00
MARK	52.00	EXISTENTIALISM	200.00
MARK	52.00	INTRO TO CS	100.00
MARK	52.00	COMPUTER ARCH.	100.00
MARK	52.00	RELATIONAL DATABASE	500.00
LUKE	53.00	SCHOLASTICISM	150.00
LUKE	53.00	FUNDAMENTALISM	90.00
LUKE	53.00	COMMUNISM	200.00
LUKE	53.00	EMPIRICISM	100.00
LUKE	53.00	EXISTENTIALISM	200.00
LUKE	53.00	INTRO TO CS	100.00
LUKE	53.00	COMPUTER ARCH.	100.00
LUKE	53.00	RELATIONAL DATABASE	500.00
JOHN	54.00	SCHOLASTICISM	150.00
JOHN	54.00	FUNDAMENTALISM	90.00
JOHN	54.00	COMMUNISM	200.00
JOHN	54.00	EMPIRICISM	100.00
JOHN	54.00	EXISTENTIALISM	200.00
JOHN	54.00	INTRO TO CS	100.00
JOHN	54.00	COMPUTER ARCH.	100.00
JOHN	54.00	RELATIONAL DATABASE	500.00
ARCHIMEDES	200.00	RELATIONAL DATABASE	500.00

MULTIPLE JOIN CONDITIONS

It is possible to facilitate a join operation where multiple columns from each table are matched to determine the join result. All that is required is the specification of multiple join conditions. Consider the next example, which is a refinement of the previous example.

Sample Query 15.14 We want to compare the salary of every staff member with the lab fee of every course offered by their respective departments. Whenever a staff member has a salary which is less than the lab fee of a course offered by his department, display the department identifier, followed by the staff member name and salary, and the corresponding course name and lab fee.

```
SELECT   DEPT, ENAME, ESALARY, CNAME, CLABFEE

FROM     STAFF, COURSE

WHERE    ESALARY < CLABFEE

AND      DEPT = CDEPT
```

DEPT	ENAME	ESALARY	CNAME	CLABFEE
THEO	MATTHEW	51.00	SCHOLASTICISM	150.00
THEO	MARK	52.00	SCHOLASTICISM	150.00
THEO	LUKE	53.00	SCHOLASTICISM	150.00
THEO	JOHN	54.00	SCHOLASTICISM	150.00
THEO	MATTHEW	51.00	FUNDAMENTALISM	90.00
THEO	MARK	52.00	FUNDAMENTALISM	90.00
THEO	LUKE	53.00	FUNDAMENTALISM	90.00
THEO	JOHN	54.00	FUNDAMENTALISM	90.00
THEO	MATTHEW	51.00	COMMUNISM	200.00
THEO	MARK	52.00	COMMUNISM	200.00
THEO	LUKE	53.00	COMMUNISM	200.00
THEO	JOHN	54.00	COMMUNISM	200.00

The final sample query in this chapter utilizes the techniques introduced in the previous four sample queries. It joins a table with itself based on a comparison of multiple join conditions.

Sample Query 15.15   Assume the dean is considering moving the administrative office of the management department. The intention is to combine its administrative facilities with those of another department which is located in the same building (which is unknown to the dean). To evaluate all possible options, display all information about the management department followed by all information about any other department which is located in the same building.

SELECT   *

FROM   DEPARTMENT D1, DEPARTMENT D2

WHERE   D1.DBLD = D2.DBLD

AND   D1.DEPT <> D2.DEPT

AND   D1.DEPT = 'MGT'

DEPT	DBLD	DROOM	DCHFNO	DEPT	DBLD	DROOM	DCHFNO
MGT	SC	100	—	CIS	SC	300	80

Comment

Again, we have not introduced any new SQL techniques. Previous techniques were applied to solve this problem. Any complexity pertains to the logical dimension of the query. This is dealt with in the WHERE clause as explained below.

1. "D1.DBLD = D2.DBLD" satisfies the requirement that the two departments be located in the same building.

2. "D1.DEPT = 'MGT' " indicates that we are specifically concerned with the management department.

3. "D1.DEPT <> D2.DEPT" eliminates any nonsense combinations where a department matches itself.

SUMMARY

The basic structure of a SELECT statement which joins two or more tables is essentially the same as one which references just one table. For two tables this is

```
SELECT    col1, col2, col3, ...
FROM      table1, table2
WHERE     table1.joincol1 = table2.joincol2
AND       (other row selection conditions)
ORDER BY  (any columns)
```

The logic of a join condition is another matter. You must understand the relationship between the tables as reflected in the join columns. Sometimes the database design can simplify the situation. For example, every CDEPT value in the COURSE table matches some DEPT value in the DEPARTMENT table. Also, there were no null values in the CDEPT column. Therefore, every COURSE row will be present in a join of these two tables. There is no chance of an undetected COURSE row missing from an output display. Desired rows are explicitly selected (or undesired rows explicitly rejected) by coding conditions in the SELECT statement. It is possible for a designer to establish this simplified situation by (1) using the NOT NULL option for the CDEPT column when creating the COURSE table, and (2) editing all INSERT and UPDATE commands for the COURSE table to verify that CDEPT values match some existing DEPT value in the DEPARTMENT table. In SQL/400, this second step usually involves the writing of an application program using embedded SQL. In DB2/400, the automatic support for referential integrity will simplify this task.

Very often the application environment does not permit the designer to incorporate the above procedures. We mirrored this complexity in the STAFF and DEPARTMENT tables. Some departments might not have chairpersons, staff, or courses. Some staff members might not have department assignments or might be assigned to nonexisting departments. This creates a situation where the join of the DEPARTMENT and STAFF tables causes "no match" situations, which remove certain rows from the join result. The key point is that users of SQL must be sensitive to this situation. Otherwise, incorrect output displays could be generated. Once again we emphasize that this issue transcends SQL. *Simply, users must understand the semantic structure of their database.*

Summary Exercises

15N. Display the faculty number of any faculty member who chairs a department which offers six-credit courses.

15O. Display the course number, name, and section of every class which is offered on a Monday.

15P. Display the course number and name of every course that student 800 is registered for.

15Q. Display all information about any scheduled class which has a lab fee less than $100 and is not offered on a Friday.

15R. Display the student number and date of registration from all students who registered for at least one course offered by the theology department.

15S. How many students are registered for all sections of the EXISTENTIALISM course?

15T. How many students have registered for classes offered by the philosophy department?

15U. Display the name and number of every faculty member who teaches a class which meets on a Monday or a Friday. Do not display duplicate rows.

The following exercises are more of a challenge. They require that you use techniques presented toward the end of this chapter.

15V. Display the name of any faculty member who chairs a department which offers a six-credit course.

15Wa. Produce a class list for the first section of the EXISTENTIALISM course. Display the course number, section number, course name, and faculty number of the instructor followed by the student number of every student registered for the class.

15Wb. Modify the previous "class list" query. For each student, display the student's name followed by the student's number.

15Wc. Make another modification to the "class list" query. Display the faculty name instead of faculty number.

15X. This is a "paper and pencil" exercise. Verify that any of the following join sequences involving three tables will produce the same result.

    a. Join the COURSE and STAFF tables to get an intermediate result. Then join this with the DEPARTMENT table.

    b. Join the COURSE and DEPARTMENT tables to get an intermediate result. Then join this with the STAFF table.

    c. Join the STAFF and DEPARTMENT tables to get an intermediate result. Then join this with the COURSE table.

15Y. Display the cross product of the COURSE and FACULTY tables.

15Z*a.* Display the department identifiers of each pair of departments which are located in the same building.

15Z*b.* Compare the salaries for each pair of staff members. Whenever the salary of the first staff member exceeds the salary of the second staff member by more than $1000, display the name and salary of both staff members followed by the difference in salaries.

15Z*c.* Modify the previous "salary comparison" query. Compare only the salaries of staff members who have the same department identifier value specified in the STAFF.DEPT column.

15Z*d.* Make another modification to the "salary comparison" query. This time, compare just the salaries of staff members who are assigned to existing departments which are located in the humanities building.

Subqueries

This chapter introduces the technique of nesting a SELECT statement within another SELECT statement. Figure 16.1 shows the basic structure of a SELECT statement which contains another SELECT statement nested within it. The nested SELECT statement is called a "subquery," a "subselect," or an "inner SELECT." For discussion purposes we will refer to the first SELECT as the "main query" or the "outer SELECT." Most of the sample queries presented in this chapter can be solved using the join operation. However, the use of a subquery is often considered to provide a simpler solution. There are some circumstances where the use of a subquery becomes necessary. Chapter 18, which describes correlated subqueries, will present examples of such queries.

BACKGROUND

We first examine a deceptively simple query, which cannot be conveniently expressed in a single SELECT statement given the SQL techniques described thus far.

Query 1. Display the course number and name of the course(s) with the highest lab fee.

Recall that it is easy to display the highest lab fee. This is achieved by executing the following statement

```
SELECT   MAX(CLABFEE)
FROM     COURSE
```

The system would return 500.00, which enables us to enter the following statement.

```
SELECT   CNO, CNAME
FROM     COURSE
WHERE    CLABFEE = 500.00
```

While this procedure will work, it requires the execution of two independent SELECT statements. This is less than desirable for the same reasons specified earlier in our discussion of the join operation. (See preliminary discussion in Chap. 15.)

Recall that the following statement will *not* work.

```
SELECT   CNO, CNAME, MAX(CLABFEE)
FROM     COURSE
```

Because the SELECT clause contains a group function, MAX(CLABFEE), the other columns, CNO and CNAME, must be referenced in a GROUP BY clause.

The basic problem is that we do not know what the largest CLABFEE value is. Essentially, we want to construct a WHERE clause for an unknown value. This represents a class of queries where a subquery can be used to determine the unknown value.

A second reason to use a subquery is to avoid explicit coding of a join operation for a query which requires examination of multiple tables, but displays only columns from a single table. The following query illustrates this situation.

Query 2. Display the name and title of every staff member who works in the humanities building.

Sample Query 15.4 presented a solution to this query by joining the DEPARTMENT and STAFF tables. This was as follows.

```
SELECT    ENAME, ETITLE
FROM      STAFF, DEPARTMENT
WHERE     STAFF.DEPT = DEPARTMENT.DEPT
AND       DBLD = 'HU'
```

Because all the displayed columns, ENAME and ETITLE, are in a single table, the STAFF table, it is possible to code a subquery solution to this problem. Sample Query 16.8 will illustrate this solution. Many users will prefer the subquery solution because it circumvents some of the logical complexities associated with the join operation.

The sample queries presented in this chapter employ subquery solutions to a variety of problems. The first seven sample queries present subqueries which produce a single value. The remaining sample queries illustrate subqueries which can produce multiple values. You will see that you must be aware of whether a subquery can produce more than a single value.

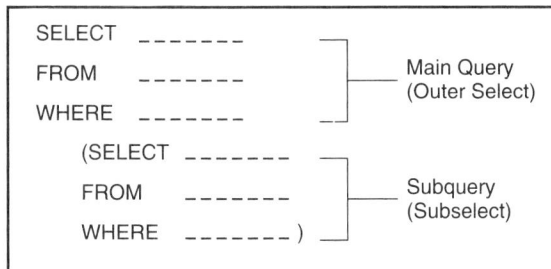

Figure 16.1 Subquery SELECT statement.

SUBQUERY: WHERE CLAUSE EXAMINES AN UNDETERMINED VALUE

The first seven sample queries in this chapter have a WHERE clause which compares a column to a single unknown value. This unknown value is resolved by a nested subquery. After the subquery is evaluated, its result is returned to the WHERE clause of the main query which is then evaluated to determine which rows should be selected for display.

Sample Query 16.1 Display the course number and name of the course(s) with the highest lab fee.

```
SELECT    CNO, CNAME
FROM      COURSE
WHERE     CLABFEE =
          (SELECT  MAX (CLABFEE)
          FROM     COURSE)
```

CNO	CNAME
C66	RELATIONAL DATABASE

Comments

1. *Logic.*   The system will execute the subquery first. In this case it will find the maximum lab fee value of 500.00 and substitute this value in the WHERE clause of the main query. The main query then becomes

```
SELECT    CNO, CNAME
FROM      COURSE
WHERE     CLABFEE = 500.00
```

The main query is then executed and the result is displayed. Note that the sub-query result of 500.00 is not displayed. It is just substituted in the WHERE clause of the main query. If you also wanted to display the maximum lab-fee value, you would reference CLABFEE in the main query SELECT clause. The entire statement would be

```
SELECT   CNO, CNAME, CLABFEE
FROM     COURSE
WHERE    CLABFEE =
         (SELECT MAX(CLABFEE)
         FROM    COURSE)
```

2. *Syntax:*   The subquery must be enclosed within parentheses.

The WHERE clause in the main query has an equals sign. Effectively, it is stating "where the CLABFEE is equal to some value" (not "values"). Because the WHERE clause is written to compare the CLABFEE with a single value, the subquery must be coded such that only a single value is returned by the subquery. In the current example the subquery returns the maximum lab-fee value, which is a single value (500.00). Note that this would be the case even if multiple COURSE rows contained the same maximum value.

Both the main query and the subquery happen to reference the COURSE table. This is not necessary. (See Sample Query 16.7.)

As with all previous SQL statements, the format is free-form. Indentation is arbitrary.

Exercise

16A. Display the course number, name, and department of the course(s) with the smallest lab fee.

SUBQUERY CONTAINS A WHERE CLAUSE

To further influence the result of the main query, the subquery could contain a WHERE clause to exclude certain rows. A subquery can contain any valid WHERE clause.

Sample Query 16.2   Display the course number, name, and lab fee of the course(s) with the smallest nonzero lab fee.

```
SELECT    CNO, CNAME, CLABFEE

FROM      COURSE

WHERE     CLABFEE =

          (SELECT    MIN(CLABFEE)

          FROM       COURSE

          WHERE      NOT CLABFEE = 0)
```

CNO	CNAME	CLABFEE
C22	DATA STRUCTURES	50.00
P22	RATIONALISM	50.00

Comments

1. *Logic.*   The WHERE clause in the subquery will exclude zero as a minimum value. Assuming there are no negative lab-fee values, the subquery will return the smallest positive lab-fee value to the WHERE clause of the main query. The main query will select rows based on this value. The output will display this value after the course number and name of any courses which have this lab-fee value.

   This WHERE clause is simple. It has only one condition. In general, the WHERE clause can include any number of conditions connected with Boolean operators.

2. The subquery WHERE clause could have been written as

   ```
   WHERE CLABFEE > 0
   ```

   This would eliminate any concern about possible negative lab-fee values.

3. *Syntax.*   No special syntax requirements exist. The subquery is a standard SELECT statement enclosed with parentheses.

Exercises

16B. Assume you know that the highest lab fee is 500.00. Write a SELECT statement which will display the course number, name, department, and lab fee of the course(s) having the second-highest lab fee.

16C. Assume that you know the lowest lab fee is 0. Write a SELECT statement which will display the course number, name, department, and lab fee of the course(s) having the second-lowest lab fee.

The next sample query includes the same WHERE clause in both the main query and the subquery. The logic of the query forces us to code it this way. Once again we see that, although SQL is simple, the logic of a query can be subtle.

Sample Query 16.3   Display the course number and name of the philosophy course(s) with the highest lab fee.

```
SELECT    CNO, CNAME
FROM      COURSE
WHERE     CDEPT = 'PHIL'
AND       CLABFEE =
          (SELECT    MAX(CLABFEE)
          FROM       COURSE
          WHERE      CDEPT = 'PHIL')
```

CNO	CNAME
P33	EXISTENTIALISM

Comments

1. *Logic.*   The subquery determines the maximum lab fee for any philosophy course. This value ($200.00) is substituted in the WHERE clause of the main query. Thus, the statement reduces to

```
SELECT    CNO, CNAME, CLABFEE
FROM      COURSE
WHERE     CDEPT = 'PHIL'
AND       CLABFEE = 200.00
```

Both the main query and the subquery must contain the same condition (WHERE CDEPT = 'PHIL') in order to restrict the displayed courses to those offered by the philosophy department. This might appear to be redundant, but it is not. Consider the effect of excluding this condition in either case.

```
SELECT    CNO, CNAME, CLABFEE
FROM      COURSE
WHERE     CLABFEE =
          (SELECT   MAX(CLABFEE)
           FROM     COURSE
           WHERE    CDEPT = 'PHIL')
```

This statement displays all courses with a $200.00 lab-fee value. In particular, it would display the row for the "T44" theology course. This is not consistent with the objective to display only philosophy courses. The following statement is also incorrect, but for a different reason.

```
SELECT    CNO, CNAME
FROM      COURSE
WHERE     CDEPT = 'PHIL'
AND       CLABFEE =
          (SELECT   MAX(CLABFEE)
           FROM     COURSE)
```

This statement results in a "no hit" because the subquery evaluates to $500.00 and the main query determines that no philosophy courses have a lab fee equal to this value.

2. *Syntax.*   The subquery is simply another condition which is AND-connected to the main query WHERE clause. Subqueries do not need to be written last. The following statement is valid.

```
SELECT    CNO, CNAME, CLABFEE
FROM      COURSE
WHERE     CLABFEE =
          (SELECT   MAX(CLABFEE)
           FROM     COURSE
           WHERE    CDEPT = 'PHIL')
AND       CDEPT = 'PHIL'
```

Exercise

16D. Display the course number, name, department, and lab fee of the six-credit course(s) with the most expensive lab fee.

The logic of the preceding sample query required the same WHERE clause to be included in both the main query and subquery. This is not always the case. You need to be very sensitive to the objective of the query and the logic to achieve the objective. Again, this is an issue which transcends the relatively simple syntax rules of SQL (or that of any other computer language). The next two sample queries demonstrate this point. They have different objectives, but they are sufficiently similar that ambiguity can occur unless the objectives are precisely articulated and understood.

Sample Query 16.4   Display the course number and name of any non-CIS course with the smallest lab fee of all courses. (This is the smallest lab fee recorded in the COURSE table, including rows for CIS courses.)

```
SELECT    CNO, CNAME

FROM      COURSE

WHERE     NOT CDEPT = 'CIS'

AND       CLABFEE =

          (SELECT MIN(CLABFEE)

          FROM COURSE)
```

CNO	CNAME
T33	HEDONISM
P44	SOLIPSISM

Comment

The sample query examines courses offered by every department, including CIS, to determine the minimal CLABFEE value. However, because of the WHERE clause in the main query, the output will not contain any CIS courses with this minimal lab fee. Note the difference between this example and Sample Query 16.5, which has a WHERE clause in both the main query and subquery.

Sample Query 16.5 Do not consider CIS courses. Display the course number and name of the course(s) with the smallest lab fee.

```
SELECT    CNO, CNAME
FROM      COURSE
WHERE     NOT CDEPT = 'CIS'
AND       CLABFEE =
          (SELECT    MIN(CLABFEE)
           FROM      COURSE
           WHERE     NOT CDEPT = 'CIS')
```

CNO	CNAME
T33	HEDONISM
P44	SOLIPSISM

Comment

This result is the same as the previous query. However, it is important to note that this is just a coincidence. It happened because the current contents of the COURSE table has CIS rows and non-CIS rows with the same minimal CLABFEE value of zero.

Assume that the COURSE table was updated such that courses T33 and P44 have lab-fee values of $5.00. This means that neither the philosophy nor the theology department had any courses with zero lab fees. Under this circumstance, the difference between the two preceding queries would be observable in the displayed results. Sample Query 16.4 would result in a "no hit" situation because none of the non-CIS courses have the minimal lab fee of zero. However, Sample Query 16.5 would display the same two rows for courses T33 and P44.

All previous subquery examples showed the WHERE clause of the main query with an "equals" comparison operator. In practice, any of the other comparison operators (<, >, <=, >=, <>) can be used. The next sample query uses the "less than" operator in comparing the intermediate result produced by the subquery.

Sample Query 16.6   Display the course number, name, and lab fee of any course with a lab fee which is less than the overall average lab fee.

```
SELECT    CNO, CNAME, CLABFEE

FROM      COURSE

WHERE     CLABFEE <

          (SELECT    AVG(CLABFEE)

          FROM       COURSE)
```

CNO	CNAME	CLABFEE
T12	FUNDAMENTALISM	90.00
C11	INTRO TO CS	100.00
T33	HEDONISM	.00
C22	DATA STRUCTURES	50.00
C33	DISCRETE MATHEMATICS	.00
C44	DIGITAL CIRCUITS	.00
C55	COMPUTER ARCH.	100.00
P22	RATIONALISM	50.00
P44	SOLIPSISM	.00
P11	EMPIRICISM	100.00

Comments

1. The WHERE clause of the main query contains a "less than" comparison operator. Any valid comparison operator is permitted.

2. The subquery references the AVG built-in function. Like the previous subqueries, this returns a single value which is used as the comparison value in the WHERE clause of the main query. Because the average lab-fee value is $110.00, the main query reduces to

```
SELECT   CNO, CNAME, CLABFEE
FROM     COURSE
WHERE    CLABFEE < 110.00
```

Exercise

16E. Display the course number, name, and lab fee of any course with a lab fee which is less than the average lab fee of courses offered by the theology department.

16F. Display all information about any course with a lab fee which exceeds the maximum lab fee for any theology or philosophy course.

All the preceding examples illustrated subqueries which reference the same table as the main query. Although this is common, it is not a requirement. In the next example, the main query and subquery reference different tables.

To understand the basis of this query, we assume that it may be poor policy to have the lab fee of any course greater than or equal to the salary of any staff member. The goal is to determine which courses, if any, have such lab fees.

Sample Query 16.7 Display the course number, name, and lab fee of any course which has a lab fee greater than or equal to the salary of any staff member.

```
SELECT   CNO, CNAME, CLABFEE

FROM     COURSE

WHERE    CLABFEE >=

         (SELECT   MIN(ESALARY)

         FROM      STAFF)
```

CNO	CNAME	CLABFEE
T12	FUNDAMENTALISM	90.00
C11	INTRO TO CS	100.00
T44	COMMUNISM	200.00
C55	COMPUTER ARCH.	100.00
C66	RELATIONAL DATABASE	500.00
T11	SCHOLASTICISM	150.00
P33	EXISTENTIALISM	200.00
P11	EMPIRICISM	100.00

Comments

1. The logic determines the lowest salary paid to any staff member, and then which courses, if any, have lab fees greater than or equal to this amount.

2. The main query references the COURSE table and the subquery references the STAFF table. The subquery returns the minimum salary which, as a legitimate numeric value, can be compared to lab-fee values in the main query. Because the minimum ESALARY value is 51, the main query reduces to

```
SELECT   CNO, CNAME, CLABFEE
FROM     COURSE
WHERE    CLABFEE >= 51
```

3. There exists an alternative solution to this problem. See Sample Query 15.13 for a discussion of the "theta-join."

Exercises

16G. Display the employee name and salary of any staff member whose salary is less than or equal to the maximum course lab fee.

16H. Display all information about any CIS course with a lab fee which is less than the average salary of staff members assigned to the theology department.

SUBQUERY: WHERE CLAUSE EXAMINES MULTIPLE UNKNOWN VALUES

All previous subquery examples and workshop exercises involved a subquery which returned a single value. The value was substituted in the WHERE clause of the main query. This basic format is

```
WHERE column comparison-operator single-value
```

Subsequent sample queries will illustrate subqueries which return multiple values to be referenced by the main query. In place of a single comparison operator, the WHERE clause uses the IN keyword.

```
WHERE column IN set-of-values
```

Allowing the subquery to return multiple values extends the use of the subquery technique to a broader class of problems. It also permits alternative SQL solutions to some problems which could be solved using the join operation.

Sample Query 16.8   Display the name and title of every staff member who works in the humanities building. (Same as Sample Query 15.4.)

```
SELECT   ENAME, ETITLE
FROM     STAFF
WHERE    DEPT IN
         (SELECT   DEPT
          FROM     DEPARTMENT
          WHERE    DBLD = 'HU')
```

ENAME	ETITLE
HANK KISS	JESTER
DICK NIX	CROOK
MATTHEW	EVANGLIST1
JOHN	EVANGLIST4
LUKE	EVANGLIST3
MARK	EVANGLIST2

Comments

1. The logic of this sample query is to have the subquery examine the DEPARTMENT table to determine which departments are located in the humanities building. Then the main query will examine the STAFF table to determine the name and title of staff members who work in those departments.

2. The subquery will return the department identifiers for the two departments located in the humanities building. These are "THEO" and "PHIL." These values will be substituted into the WHERE clause of the main query as follows:

```
SELECT   ENAME, ETITLE
FROM     STAFF
WHERE    DEPT IN ('THEO', 'PHIL')
```

3. Note that, unlike previous subqueries, multiple values are returned as an intermediate result. For this reason, the main query WHERE clause must use the IN keyword. If the WHERE clause contained an equals sign, an error would result. This is because, after substitution of the subquery values, the clause would be WHERE DEPT = ('THEO', 'PHIL'). This is invalid because the comparison operators can be applied only to a single value.

4. This same problem was solved using the join technique in Sample Query 15.4. The reason the subquery technique can be applied is that all the displayed columns come from a single table (STAFF). This is the only table referenced in the main query.

   Many users find the subquery approach easier to understand than the join technique. This is a matter of personal preference from a logical problem-solving point of view.

Exercise

16I. Display the department name and the chairperson faculty number for all departments responsible for a six-credit course.

It was noted in our previous discussion of the join operation that sometimes many matches could occur and duplicate rows could be displayed. Sample Query 15.5 was such a case where the same row was displayed four times. You were instructed to use the DISTINCT keyword to avoid this duplication. The following shows a subquery solution to the same sample query. However, note that this solution does not contain DISTINCT, yet duplicate rows are not displayed. Our comments will address this point.

Sample Query 16.9   Where can I find an evangelist? Display the building and room of any academic department which employs a staff member whose title begins with the character string "EVANGLIST".

SELECT   DBLD, DROOM

FROM   DEPARTMENT

WHERE   DEPT IN

    (SELECT   DEPT

    FROM   STAFF

    WHERE   ETITLE LIKE 'EVANGLIST%')

DBLD	DROOM
HU	200

Comments

1. Why were duplicate rows not displayed? Consider the intermediate result returned by the subquery. If it were executed as an independent query, it would display the following table.

    THEO
    THEO
    THEO
    THEO

This table is interpreted by the system as a "set" of four department values. These same values are substituted into the WHERE clause of the main query, which would be evaluated as

```
SELECT  DBLD, DROOM
FROM    DEPARTMENT
WHERE   DEPT IN ('THEO', 'THEO', 'THEO', 'THEO')
```

Execution of the above statement would display the same single row shown for the subquery solution. The precise explanation involves recognition of the fact that a mathematical set does not contain duplicate elements. SQL would interpret the four occurrences of "THEO" as one value. Hence, the main query effectively becomes

```
SELECT  DBLD, DROOM
FROM    DEPARTMENT
WHERE   DEPT IN ('THEO')
```

2. The following solution makes the logic explicit by using DISTINCT in the subquery.

```
SELECT  DBLD, DROOM
FROM    DEPARTMENT
WHERE   DEPT IN
  (SELECT DISTINCT DEPT
    FROM  STAFF
    WHERE ETITLE LIKE 'EVANGLIST%')
```

The use of DISTINCT in a subquery is always superfluous. However, this is not the case with the main query. The next sample query describes a situation where DISTINCT must be present in the main query SELECT clause.

The next sample query uses DISTINCT in the main query. This is necessary if we assume that a faculty member could be the chairperson of more than one academic department.

Sample Query 16.10   Display the faculty number of any faculty member who serves as chairperson of any department which offers a six-credit course. Do not display duplicate values.

```
SELECT   DISTINCT DCHFNO

FROM     DEPARTMENT

WHERE    DEPT IN

         (SELECT   CDEPT

         FROM      COURSE

         WHERE     CRED = 6)
```

DCHFNO
_____
10
60

Comments

1. In this example, the subquery returns the CDEPT values of rows in the COURSE table which have a CRED value of 6. Only two rows match this condition. Their CDEPT values are "THEO" and "PHIL". Hence, the main query is evaluated as

   ```
   SELECT   DISTINCT DCHFNO
   FROM     DEPARTMENT
   WHERE    DEPT IN ('THEO', 'PHIL')
   ```

2. Conceptually speaking, DCHFNO is a foreign key to the faculty table. Unlike primary keys we can not assume that a foreign key is unique. Examination of the current contents of the DEPARTMENT table reveals that DCHFNO values are unique. (At this point, it just happens to be the case that no faculty member is serving as chairperson for more than one department.) Hence, the displayed results would have been the same if you omitted DISTINCT in the main query. It is important to note that this is a matter of luck. Because school policy permits a faculty member to chair multiple departments, it is possible for the same DCHFNO value to occur in multiple rows of the DEPARTMENT table. It is poor show to write SQL code which is correct only under special conditions. Therefore, DISTINCT should be included in the main query SELECT clause.

3. This query displayed faculty numbers. What if you wanted to display faculty names? Note that faculty names are not stored in the DEPARTMENT table. This problem can be solved by nesting the current example within another SELECT statement. Try to code this query before examining the next sample query, which describes the solution in detail.

Exercise

16J. Display the course number, section number, and building of any class which is offered in the same building where staff member Dick Nix works.

SECOND LEVEL OF NESTING

The next sample query is an extension of the previous query. This extension requires that we nest the previous SELECT statement, which already contains a subquery, within another SELECT statement. This leads to multiple levels of nesting of SELECT statements. We will see that there is nothing new to learn relative to syntax. However, the logic of the query becomes slightly more complex.

Sample Query 16.11   Display the faculty number and name of any faculty member who serves as chairperson of any department which offers a six-credit course.

```
SELECT    DISTINCT FNO, FNAME
FROM      FACULTY
WHERE     FNO IN
          (SELECT    DCHFNO
           FROM      DEPARTMENT
           WHERE     DEPT IN
                     (SELECT    CDEPT
                      FROM      COURSE
                      WHERE     CRED = 6))
```

FNO	FNAME
10	JULIE MARTYN
60	FRANK MARTYN

Comments

1. The system will execute the innermost subquery first. In this example it will return the department identifiers of all six-credit courses. The COURSE table has two such courses. One is offered by the theology department, and the other is offered by the philosophy department. Hence the query reduces to

```
SELECT    DISTINCT FNO, FNAME
FROM      FACULTY
WHERE     FNO IN
          (SELECT   DCHFNO
          FROM      DEPARTMENT
          WHERE     DEPT IN ('THEO', 'PHIL'))
```

This intermediate result still contains a subquery which requires evaluation. This subquery will examine the DEPARTMENT table and return the faculty numbers of chairpersons of the theology and philosophy departments. These values are 10 and 60, respectively. The query is now reduced to

```
SELECT    DISTINCT FNO, FNAME
FROM      FACULTY
WHERE     FNO IN (10, 60)
```

2. Conceptually speaking, FNO is the primary key of the faculty table. Thus, the use of DISTINCT in the main query is unnecessary because FNO values are unique within the FACULTY table. From a logical point of view, it is simpler to always use DISTINCT to avoid displaying duplicate rows.

3. Note that if a single department offered multiple six-credit courses, or if any faculty member was chairperson of multiple departments where each department offered at least one six-credit course, duplicate values would have been produced by the subqueries. Recall that DISTINCT is always superfluous in a subquery. (See Sample Query 16.9 for discussion.)

4. This query could have been expressed as a three-way join operation.

```
SELECT    FNO, FNAME
FROM      FACULTY, DEPARTMENT, COURSE
WHERE     FNO = DCHFNO
AND       DEPT = CDEPT
AND       CRED = 6
```

USING NOT IN WITH SUBQUERIES

The intermediate result generated by a subquery can be compared using NOT IN. The next example illustrates this fact. The logic is simple enough. However, there is a subtle circumstance which occurs with this example that can lead to an erroneous interpretation of the result. Try to detect this circumstance prior to reading the comments.

Sample Query 16.12   Display the name, title, and department identifier of every staff member with a department identifier not found in the DEPARTMENT table.

```
SELECT    ENAME, ETITLE, DEPT

FROM      STAFF

WHERE     DEPT NOT IN

          (SELECT DEPT

          FROM DEPARTMENT)
```

ENAME	ETITLE	DEPT
EUCLID	LAB ASSIST	MATH
ARCHIMEDES	LAB ASSIST	ENG

Comments

1. The subquery produces the set of DEPT values found in the DEPARTMENT table. These are "THEO", "PHIL", "CIS", and "MGT". Hence, the main query reduces to

```
SELECT    ENAME, ETITLE
FROM      STAFF
WHERE     DEPT NOT IN ('THEO', 'PHIL', 'CIS', 'MGT')
```

2. Note that "DA VINCI" does not occur in the output. This is the subtle circumstance which needs to be recognized. DA VINCI has a null DEPT value. It cannot evaluate to "true" on any comparison. Hence, it is not selected for display. Sample Query 16.5 will show a solution which includes DA VINCI.

Exercise

16K. Display the name and department of any faculty member who is not teaching a class.

SUBQUERY WITHIN HAVING CLAUSE

The next sample query illustrates the use of a subquery to generate an intermediate result for subsequent comparison within a HAVING clause. Other than the fact that the subquery is located within a HAVING clause, there is really nothing new to learn.

Sample Query 16.13   For every department which offers courses, display the department identifier and the average lab fee of courses offered by the department if that average is less than the overall average lab fee for all courses.

```
SELECT    CDEPT, AVG(CLABFEE)

FROM      COURSE

GROUP     BY CDEPT

HAVING    AVG(CLABFEE) <

          (SELECT AVG(CLABFEE)

          FROM   COURSE)
```

CDEPT	AVG(CLABFEE)
PHIL	87.500 . . .

Comment

Because we want to display the average lab fee by department, it is necessary to establish groups using the GROUP BY clause. Because we only want to display those groups where the average is less than the overall average, a HAVING clause is required to compare the group averages to the overall average. A subquery is necessary to calculate this overall average. The subquery will determine that the overall average is 110. The main query is then evaluated as

```
SELECT   CDEPT, AVG(CLABFEE)
FROM     COURSE
GROUP BY CDEPT
HAVING AVG(CLABFEE) < 110
```

The next sample query includes many of the aforementioned subquery techniques and includes an ORDER BY clause to sort the final displayed result. Note, however, that the SQL statement is longer than previous examples because of the complexity of the query. No new concepts are introduced.

Sample Query 16.14   For all departments recorded in the DEPARTMENT table which employ staff members, display the department identifier and the average salary of staff members in the department if that average is less than the largest lab fee recorded in the COURSE table. Sort the displayed result by department identifier.

SELECT   STAFF.DEPT, AVG(ESALARY)

FROM   STAFF, DEPARTMENT

WHERE   STAFF.DEPT = DEPARTMENT.DEPT

GROUP BY STAFF.DEPT

HAVING AVG (ESALARY) <

    (SELECT MAX(CLABFEE) FROM COURSE)

ORDER BY STAFF.DEPT

DEPT	AVG(ESALARY)
THEO	52.500 . . .

Comment

The query is processed as follows. The STAFF and DEPARTMENT tables are joined as prescribed by the condition in the WHERE clause. Only PHIL and THEO rows match. From these rows, logical groups are formed on the basis of a common DEPT value. The system then acts upon these logical groups to summarize the average salary for the comparison in the HAVING clause. (Each group is then represented by a single row containing the DEPT value together with the average salary of all staff members associated with that department.)

The subquery in the HAVING clause is evaluated to return the highest lab-fee value of any course recorded in the COURSE table (500). This value is compared with each average salary value in the summarized group records. If the average salary for a group is less than 500, the summary record for the group is selected for display.

The final step is to satisfy the ORDER BY clause and sequence the result by ascending DEPT values.

ANY AND ALL

The keywords ANY and ALL can be used with WHERE conditions which reference subqueries. Before discussing these keywords, we emphasize two facts.

1. Given a query which can be solved using ANY or ALL, it is always possible to specify an alternative SQL solution which does not contain these keywords.

2. Under certain circumstances, it is easy to misinterpret the logical behavior of statements containing ANY or ALL.

For these reasons, some authorities have argued that ANY and ALL should not be part of the SQL language. However, this is wishful thinking. They are part of SQL. Hence, we discuss them with the preliminary recommendation that you should understand these keywords, but should also restrict your use of such.

We need to review an important point prior to discussing the use of ANY and ALL. When a subquery is executed, it can return one or more values. Sample Queries 16.8 through 16.12 were coded such that the subquery could produce multiple values. These queries used the IN keyword. Sample Queries 16.2 through 16.7 were coded so that the subquery always produced a single value. Therefore, the WHERE condition in the main query used the standard comparison operators (=, <, >, <>) when evaluating the subquery result. The following sample queries use the standard comparison operators in conjunction with ANY and ALL to evaluate an intermediate result produced by a subquery which can return multiple values.

The following sample query introduces the ANY keyword. The ANY keyword can be used with any of the standard comparison operators when the subquery can return one or many values. When ANY is used in a comparison, the condition evaluates to "true" if the expression is true for any of the values returned by the subquery.

Sample Query 16.16   Display the name and title of any staff member employed by an existing academic department.

SELECT   ENAME, ETITLE

FROM   STAFF

WHERE   DEPT = ANY

          (SELECT   DEPT

          FROM   DEPARTMENT)

ENAME	ETITLE
HANK KISS	JESTER
DICK NIX	CROOK
MATTHEW	EVANGLIST1
JOHN	EVANGLIST4
LUKE	EVANGLIST3
MARK	EVANGLIST2

Comments

1. The subquery returns the name of existing departments: "CIS", "PHIL", "THEO", and "MGT". Hence, the query reduces to

```
SELECT   ENAME, ETITLE
FROM     STAFF
WHERE    DEPT = ANY ('CIS','PHIL','THEO','MGT')
```

Only staff members with a DEPT value "equal to any" of the values returned by the subquery appear in the output display.

2. An alternative solution to the sample query is

```
SELECT   ENAME, ETITLE
FROM     STAFF
WHERE    DEPT IN (SELECT DEPT FROM DEPARTMENT)
```

The only difference is that "IN" has replaced "= ANY" in the WHERE clause. In effect, "IN" and "= ANY" are synonymous.

3. Another solution involves use of the join operation.

```
SELECT   ENAME, ETITLE
FROM     STAFF, DEPARTMENT
WHERE    STAFF.DEPT = DEPARTMENT.DEPT
```

The ALL keyword, like ANY, can be used with any of the standard comparison operators when a subquery can return multiple values. When ALL is used, the condition evaluates to "true" if the expression is true for all of the values returned by the subquery.

Sample Query 16.17   Display the course number, name, and lab fee of any course having a lab fee less than all the salaries of staff members.

```
SELECT    CNO, CNAME, CLABFEE

FROM      COURSE

WHERE     CLABFEE < ALL

          (SELECT   ESALARY

           FROM     STAFF)
```

CNO	CNAME	CLABFEE
T33	HEDONISM	.00
C22	DATA STRUCTURES	50.00
C33	DISCRETE MATHEMATICS	.00
C44	DIGITAL CIRCUITS	.00
P22	RATIONALISM	50.00
P44	SOLIPSISM	.00

Comments

1. The subquery returns every ESALARY value in the STAFF table. If a course has a CLABFEE value "less than all" of these ESALARY values, then its number, name, and lab fee appear in the output.

2. Note that if a CLABFEE value is less than all the ESALARY values, then it is less than the smallest ESALARY value. This observation motivates the following alternative solution.

```
SELECT    CNO, CNAME, CLABFEE
FROM      COURSE
WHERE     CLABFEE < (SELECT MIN(ESALARY) FROM STAFF)
```

Sample Query 16.18   Display the name and salary of any staff member whose salary is greater than or equal to all the course lab fees.

SELECT   ENAME, ESALARY

FROM   STAFF

WHERE   ESALARY >= ALL

      (SELECT   CLABFEE

      FROM   COURSE)

ENAME	ESALARY
HANK KISS	25000
DICK NIX	25001
DA VINCI	500
EUCLID	1000

Comments

1. The subquery returns every CLABFEE value in the COURSE table. If a staff member has a lab-fee value "greater than or equal to all" of these values, then that person's name and salary appear in result.

2. Note that if an ESALARY value is greater than or equal to all the CLABFEE values, then it is greater than or equal to the largest CLABFEE value. This observation motivates the following alternative solution.

```
SELECT  ENAME, ESALARY
FROM    STAFF
WHERE   ESALARY = (SELECT MAX(CLABFEE) FROM COURSE)
```

3. We stated that all of the comparison operators can be used with ALL. Regardless of the operator, an alternative solution can be specified which is usually more direct. This especially applies to "= ALL", which can evaluate to "true" only if the subquery returns just one value which equals the comparison field value.

LOGIC OF ANY AND ALL

The following comments pertain to the logical behavior of ANY and ALL when used with certain comparison operators.

1. "= ANY" is equivalent to "IN". (But do not jump to the erroneous conclusion that "<> ANY" means the same thing as "NOT IN". See comment 4 below.)

2. "<> ANY" has little application. Consider the following examples.

   a. WHERE COLX <> ANY (2,4,6)
   This condition is always true. Even if the COLX value appears in the set of values, it will not be equal to some other value which is also in the set.

   b. WHERE COLX <> ANY (4)

   This condition is the same as WHERE COLX <> 4.

3. "= ALL" has little application. Consider the following examples.

   a. WHERE COLX = ALL (2,4,6)
   This condition is always false because COLX will always contain only a single value and, therefore, cannot match all of the values in the set.

   b. WHERE COLX = ALL (4)
   This condition is the same as WHERE COLX = 4.

4. "<> ALL" means the same thing as "NOT IN". (It is good mental exercise to think this through. It may be helpful to reexamine the previous discussion on NOT IN in Sample Query 4.14.)

These comments reinforce the position that use of ANY and ALL should be restricted. Alternative solutions were presented to each sample query which used these keywords. From a formal point of view, both ANY and ALL are superfluous.

Exercises

16L. Display the name and number of dependents for faculty members who have as many dependents as the number of credits offered for any course. Give two solutions. The first should use the ANY keyword. The second should not.

The final sample query of this chapter illustrates the use of ALL within the context of a problem which requires grouping for the purpose of performing calculations.

Sample Query 16.19   Display the department identifier and average lab fee of the academic department(s) having the highest average course lab fee.

```
SELECT    CDEPT, AVG(CLABFEE)

FROM      COURSE

GROUP BY CDEPT

HAVING AVG(CLABFEE) >= ALL

    (SELECT AVG(CLABFEE)

    FROM COURSE

    GROUP BY CDEPT)
```

CDEPT	AVG(CLABFEE)
CIS	125

Comments

1. The intermediate result produced by the subquery is a set of three values ($87.50, $110.00, $125.00) corresponding to the average lab fees of the PHIL, THEO, and CIS departments. ALL is necessary because the subquery returns multiple values. Thus, the main query is reduced to:

```
SELECT    CDEPT, AVG(CLABFEE)
FROM      COURSE
GROUP BY CDEPT
HAVING AVG(CLABFEE) >= ALL (87.50, 110.00, 125.00)
```

2. Note that the objective of the query is to determine the average lab fee for each department and then display the maximum of these averages. SQL does not provide a tidy way to express this. (Recall that SQL does not permit the nesting of group functions.) The use of ALL was necessary because of the grouping and computational aspects of this problem.

SUMMARY

This chapter has introduced the use of a subquery to generate an intermediate result for comparison purposes within a WHERE or HAVING clause. You must use this technique when you want to compare a field with an unknown value. The subquery was also illustrated as an alternative to coding a join operation when the desired displayed results all come from one table.

A subquery is simply another SELECT statement which is most often used to produce a single column result which is compatible with the comparison operation to be performed within the WHERE or HAVING clause of another SELECT statement.

We noted one significant restriction in the coding of a subquery. The subquery itself cannot contain an ORDER BY clause. Sorting applies only to the result table. The ORDER BY clause must be the last clause in the entire statement.

This chapter introduced the fundamental subquery techniques which are used most often. Chapter 18 will continue our discussion of subqueries by presenting alternatives to some of the techniques shown in this chapter and introducing some new keywords and techniques which can be applied to more challenging problems.

Summary Exercises

16M. Display the course number and name for every course that student 800 is registered for.

16N. Display all information about any scheduled class which has a lab fee less than $100 and is not offered on a Friday.

16O. Display the student number and date of registration for all students who are registered for at least one course offered by a department located in the science (SC) building.

16P. Assume that you do not know the highest lab fee. Write a SELECT statement which will display the course number, name, department, and lab fee of the course(s) having the second-highest lab fee.

16Q. Display the name and number of dependents for faculty members who have fewer dependents than the number of credits offered for all courses.

UNION Operation

This chapter describes a simple but very useful feature of SQL, the union operation. The purpose of the union operation is introduced by means of a simple example. Assume you were asked to display the names of all faculty and staff members. This simple request could be satisfied by executing two separate SELECT statements.

1. Display all the faculty names.

```
SELECT    FNAME
FROM      FACULTY
```

2. Display all the staff member names.

```
SELECT    ENAME
FROM      STAFF
```

These are two *separate* SELECT statements which are executed independently of each other and which generate two *separate* result tables. This approach is not satisfactory if we want all the faculty and staff member names to be merged into a single result table. The union operation must be used to achieve this objective.

UNION KEYWORD

The union operation allows execution of multiple SELECT statements as a single statement. The result of each statement is merged into and subsequently displayed as a single result table.

Sample Query 17.1   Display the names of all faculty and staff members (in a single result table).

SELECT FNAME

FROM   FACULTY

UNION

SELECT ENAME

FROM   STAFF

FNAME
_____

AL HARTLEY
ARCHIMEDES
BARB HLAVATY
DA VINCI
DICK NIX
EUCLID
FRANK MARTYN
HANK KISS
JOE COHN
JOHN
JULIE MARTYN
KATHY PEPE
LISA BOBAK
LUKE
MARK
MATTHEW

Comments

1. *Syntax.*   The UNION keyword is placed between the two SELECT statements separated by one or more spaces. As with other SQL statements, the format is free-form and can be written on any number of lines.

    A single query may contain more than one union operation. Sample Query 17.5 will demonstrate this point.

2. *Logic.*   The UNION keyword tells the system to execute each SELECT statement and then merge the intermediate results into a single result table.

    a. *Question.*   What if duplicate rows occur in the intermediate results?

    b. *Answer.*   Duplicate rows selected by individual SELECT statements are not displayed. This is because the UNION keyword corresponds to the union operation as defined in classical set theory. This theory defines the union of two sets as the set of all values taken from both sets. Because a mathematical set must contain distinct values, the result of the union operation, which is a set, will not contain duplicate values. For example, given set $A = \{2,4,6,8\}$ and set $B = \{1,4,5,6\}$, the union of sets A and B is $\{1,2,4,5,6,8\}$. Observe that the values common to both sets, 4 and 6, occur only once in the union result. The same principle applies to the formation of a result table, which is the union of two or more intermediate tables generated by independent SELECT statements. We emphasize that duplicate rows are not displayed, even though the DISTINCT keyword is not specified in either SELECT statement.

    Notice that all the FNAME values in the FACULTY table are distinct from all ENAME values in the STAFF table. Hence, in this example it just so happens that duplicate rows do not occur in the intermediate results.

3. We cannot arbitrarily form the union of any two SELECT statements. The intermediate tables produced by the individual SELECT statements must be "union-compatible." This means that

   a. Each intermediate result table must have the same number of columns.

   b. Corresponding columns must have comparable data types. If a given column contains numeric, character, date, or time data, then its corresponding column must respectively contain numeric, character, date, or time data.

   In the current example each SELECT statement produces a table with just one column. The first contains FNAME values which are defined as character. The second contains ENAME values which are also defined as character.

4. Observe that the corresponding column names in the SELECT statements do not need to be identical. However, only one such name can occur as the column heading for the displayed result. The system will use the first SELECT statement to determine the column headings for the output display. Hence the output column heading shows FNAME. Because the column values actually represent both faculty and staff names, it is recommended that you use the Report Formatting Option to change the heading to a more representative title (e.g., "EMPLOYEE NAME").

5. It is not possible by mere examination of the output display to determine which rows were selected from which table. Sample Query 17.5 will illustrate a technique to realize this objective.

6. Observe that the result is sorted even though the ORDER BY clause is not specified. This is because the system will order the output using an internal sort to facilitate the identification of duplicate rows. However, this implicit sort should not be relied on. Future releases of SQL/400 may take a different approach to removing duplicates. The only sure way to specify order is with the ORDER BY clause.

The next example illustrates a situation where the union operation causes duplicate rows to be removed from the displayed result.

Sample Query 17.2   Display every department identifier referenced in the STAFF and FACULTY tables.

SELECT DEPT

FROM STAFF

UNION

SELECT FDEPT

FROM FACULTY

DEPT
___

CIS
ENG
MATH
PHIL
THEO
—

Comments

1. This example illustrates how the union operation removes duplicate rows from the intermediate results. For example, THEO occurs many times in both the FACULTY and STAFF tables, but it appears only once in the output display. Also, multiple null values are considered duplicates so that only one null value appears in the output.

2. Again note that an internal sort was done to facilitate the removal of duplicate rows. The null value appears at the high end of the sequence. The next example will show use of the ORDER BY clause, which should be used to specify a desired row sequence.

Exercise

17A. Display the salaries of all staff and faculty as a single result table.

The next example illustrates union-compatible SELECT statements which display multiple columns. The SELECT statements contain WHERE clauses, and the result is sorted in a specified row sequence.

Sample Query 17.3   Display the name, department identifier, and title (in that order) of all staff members assigned to the theology department. Include the name, department identifier, and address (in that order) of all faculty members assigned to that department. Sort the output by name in descending sequence.

```
SELECT  ENAME, DEPT, ETITLE

FROM    STAFF

WHERE   DEPT = 'THEO'

UNION

SELECT  FNAME, FDEPT, FADDR

FROM    FACULTY

WHERE   FDEPT = 'THEO'

ORDER BY 1 DESC
```

ENAME	DEPT	ETITLE
MATTHEW	THEO	EVANGLIST1
MARK	THEO	EVANGLIST2
LUKE	THEO	EVANGLIST3
LISA BOBAK	THEO	77 LAUGHING LANE
JOHN	THEO	EVANGLIST4
JESSIE MARTYN	THEO	2135 EASTON DRIVE

Comments

1. The SELECT statements fit the definition of "union-compatible" even though the content of the third column, which is a mixture of titles and addresses, is probably confusing. The point is that the system has no insight into the fact that the ETITLE and FADDR columns contain semantically different kinds of data.

2. Both WHERE clauses happen to identify columns containing the same type of data (department identifiers). This is typical, but it is not necessary. In general, each individual SELECT statement may contain any valid WHERE clause.

3. Special rules apply to the ORDER by clause when used with the union operation.

   a. The ORDER BY clause can appear only once, and (with the exception of the OPTIMIZE FOR n ROWS clause) the ORDER BY clause must be the last clause of the entire statement.

   b. The ORDER BY clause must reference a column by its relative column number, not by a column name.

Exercise

17B. Display the department identifier, number of credits, and the description of all philosophy courses together with the department identifier, number of dependents, and the address of each faculty member from that same department.

UNION ALL

Assume our mythical college had a policy which prohibited anyone from simultaneously holding both a faculty and a staff appointment. If we know that employee names (i.e., FNAME and ENAME values) are unique, we can conclude that any union operation involving these values would not encounter duplicate rows. Under these circumstances, effort on the part of the system to remove duplicate rows is unnecessary. This situation occurred in Sample Query 17.1. It did not require a sorted result, and there were no duplicate rows to be removed, but the system still performed the sort. In such circumstances the use of UNION ALL is appropriate. The next sample query illustrates UNION ALL, which behaves like UNION with the exception that duplicate rows are not removed from the output display. This means the system will not initiate an internal sort for this purpose.

Sample Query 17.4   Display every department identifier referenced in the STAFF and FACULTY tables. Show duplicate department identifier values.

```
SELECT  DEPT FROM STAFF

UNION   ALL

SELECT  FDEPT FROM FACULTY
```

DEPT
___

THEO
THEO
THEO
PHIL
PHIL
THEO
MATH
ENG
—
THEO
PHIL
CIS
THEO
PHIL
CIS
CIS

Comments

1. Compare this result with that shown in Sample Query 17.2 which uses UNION instead of UNION ALL. The output for this example displays duplicate rows which are not sorted. UNION ALL simply combines the intermediate result tables into a single table.

2. The output presents some idea of how many employees are assigned to the different departments. Assume that you would like to apply grouping with the COUNT function to the above result table. Unfortunately, this cannot be done. A general restriction on the use of both UNION and UNION ALL is that the column built-in functions cannot be applied to the final result table as a whole. SQL simply has no way to express this process. All arithmetic must be coded within individual SELECT statements. The intermediate results can contain calculated values (see the next sample query), but calculations cannot be applied to the final result table. You must use the host system report generation facilities to achieve this objective.

3. The real advantage of UNION ALL occurs when it is impossible for duplicate values to occur in any of the intermediate result tables. This was the case with Sample Query 17.1 and is the same for the next sample query. It becomes the user's responsibility to deduce this fact. Then you should use UNION ALL instead of UNION. This can lead to a significant savings in computing time.

In the last sample query demonstrating UNION ALL, the individual SELECT statements associate constant data with the computed values. This provides a means of attaching identification labels to rows displayed in the final result.

Sample Query 17.5   Assume the second character of a course's CNO value represents the level of the course. Lower-level courses have a "1" or "2". Intermediate-level courses have a "3" or "4". Upper-level courses have a "5" or "6". Calculate the average lab fee for each of the three levels of courses. Also, tag a self-identifying label to each row.

```
SELECT    'LOWER', AVG(CLABFEE)

FROM      COURSE

WHERE     CNO LIKE '_1%'

OR        CNO LIKE '_2%'

UNION ALL

SELECT    'INTERMEDIATE', AVG(CLABFEE)

FROM      COURSE

WHERE     CNO LIKE '_3%'

OR        CNO LIKE '_4%'

UNION ALL

SELECT    'UPPER', AVG(CLABFEE)

FROM      COURSE

WHERE     CNO LIKE '_5%'

OR        CNO LIKE '_6%'
```

LOWER	AVG(CLABFEE)
LOWER	90.000000
INTERMEDIATE	66.666666
UPPER	300.000000

Comments

1. Observe that the output does not indicate a sort of the final result table. If we had used the UNION keyword, the same rows would have been displayed, but the row sequence would be different.

2. The specification of a constant identifier in each SELECT statement is most helpful in this example. The preceding examples did not include any self-identifying constants, but such constants would have made the output more readable.

3. Unlike the previous sample queries, the individual SELECT statements in this example refer to the same table (COURSE) and utilize a group function (AVG). In effect, the three individual SELECT statements perform a calculation with rows from the COURSE table to produce three summary rows which are subsequently merged into the final result by UNION ALL.

   This example shows the utility of the union operation. Note that it allows for a type of grouping which cannot be done with the GROUP BY clause. The GROUP BY clause will form a group for each individual value found in a specified column. The current example illustrates the formation of groups where each group corresponds to a set of multiple values.

SUMMARY

This chapter presented the UNION keyword which allows for the union of different sets of rows selected by individual SELECT statements. The specification of UNION will cause the system to sort all selected rows as a means of detecting and removing duplicate rows. Because this involves some performance costs, and because there may be circumstances where the removal of duplicate rows is unnecessary or undesirable, SQL provides the UNION ALL feature which simply merges all the intermediate tables without examining for or removing duplicate rows.

It is possible to use both UNION and UNION ALL in the same statement. In this case, you have to consider the order of evaluation. The system will perform the evaluation in a left-to-right sequence. (Visually, this a top-to-bottom sequence.) It simply performs whatever union operation it first encounters. Parentheses can be used to override this default sequence.

We conclude this chapter by listing constraints associated with the UNION and UNION ALL keywords. Some of these have been specified in the previous examples, while others are mentioned for the first time.

1. All intermediate result tables produced by the SELECT statements must be union-compatible. This means that they have the same number of columns and each corresponding column has a comparable data type. Whenever a given column is union-compatible with its corresponding column, but the two columns do not have the exact same SQL data type, the data type conversion rules specified in Chap. 7 apply. For example, a column specified as SMALLINT is union-compatible with a DECIMAL column. When they are merged by the union operation the result is displayed as a DECIMAL column.

2. The ORDER BY clause may be specified only once. If used, it must be placed after the last SELECT statement. Furthermore, it must reference the sort column(s) by relative column number(s).

3. It is not possible to apply any of the group functions to the final result table which is produced by the union operation.

4. A SELECT statement may contain a subquery. However, the subquery itself may not contain UNION or UNION ALL.

5. Views (to be described in Chap. 19) may not be defined with UNION or UNION ALL.

A final comment: the union operation is a very important and powerful feature of SQL. This is evidenced by the fact that every example presented in this chapter required the union operation and could not have been expressed using just those SQL facilities described earlier in this text.

Summary Exercises

17C. Display the lab-fee value and number of credits for each CIS course together with a label of "COURSE". Also display rows which contain the salary and number of dependents for each faculty member from the CIS department. Identify the faculty rows with a tag of "FACULTY".

17D. Display the course name, department identifier, and the lab-fee value for all courses with a lab-fee value that is at least $200.00. Append a label of "EXPENSIVE" on each row retrieved. Display the columns for those courses with a lab-fee value of $50.00 or less. Append to these rows the label of "CHEAP". Display all of the rows in a single result.

17E. Display all of the salaries of staff and faculty members. Do not remove any duplicate values from the result.

Correlated Subqueries

This chapter expands on the subquery concept by introducing a variation known as a "correlated subquery." This is an important and powerful feature which allows you to solve certain data-retrieval problems which cannot be solved by the techniques described previously. There are significant differences between correlated subqueries and the subqueries introduced in Chap. 16. These differences introduce a new level of complexity which motivates the placement of this topic in a separate chapter.

As indicated above, correlated subqueries are relatively complex compared to the other concepts and keywords of SQL described in the previous chapters. It is possible that many users will never have to utilize correlated subqueries. However, there are many important problems that can only be solved using correlated subqueries. Therefore we consider this chapter to be an important chapter and encourage professional programmers to master the concepts presented. End users who will be executing relatively simple queries may want to skip ahead to Chap. 19. The concepts and techniques described in the remaining chapters of this book are relatively straightforward and easy to learn.

PRELIMINARY COMMENTS

Before presenting correlated subquery problems and their solutions, it is important to make three preliminary observations about the subquery examples presented in Chap. 16. These observations are made to emphasize the unique features of correlated subqueries.

Observation 1

This first observation is the most important because it applies to all correlated subqueries.

Previous examples presented subqueries which were self-contained. This is an informal term to describe the fact that the subquery constitutes a valid SELECT statement and could be independently executed if it were detached from the main query. For example, consider the following SELECT statement, which displays information about any course with a lab fee equal to the maximum lab fee of all theology courses.

```
SELECT   CDEPT, CNO, CNAME, CLABFEE
FROM     COURSE
WHERE    CLABFEE =
             (SELECT MAX(CLABFEE)
             FROM COURSE
             WHERE CDEPT = 'THEO')
```

The subquery, considered as an independent statement, is

```
SELECT   MAX(CLABFEE)
FROM     COURSE
WHERE    CDEPT = 'THEO'
```

This statement could be executed to return a result of $200.00. All previous subquery examples demonstrated this self-contained property. We emphasize this point because the correlated subqueries presented in this chapter do not have this property. *Trying to execute any correlated subquery as an independent, self-contained query will cause an error.* This is because the SELECT statement of a correlated subquery will contain a variable (a correlation variable) which references the outer query.

Observation 2

The second observation is that SQL/400 will execute a self-contained subquery just once. In the above example, the single execution of the subquery returned a value ($200.00). This result is used to reformulate the outer query as

```
SELECT  CDEPT
FROM    COURSE
WHERE   CLABFEE = 200.00
```

Even though the COURSE table contains 14 rows, the self-contained subquery is executed just once. This behavior differs from a correlated subquery which will (at least conceptually) be executed many times. This means that you will not be able to conceptualize the solution as a one-time execution of the subquery to obtain an intermediate result, followed by a one-time substitution of the result to reformulate the outer query as shown above. For correlated subqueries, each execution of the subquery may produce a different result which leads to a different reformulation of the outer query.

Observation 3

The third observation pertains to syntax. None of the previously described self-contained subqueries contained a correlation variable. Correlation variables are usually used to reference values specified by the outer query. (This is why the subquery is not self-contained.) We will see that a correlation variable can be explicitly specified in the FROM clause or, in some cases, implicitly specified by simple reference in the subquery. The following sample queries will illustrate both explicit and implicit specification of correlation variables.

The first sample query of this chapter shows a correlated subquery containing "CX" as the correlation variable. Correlation variables are sometimes referred to as *correlation names* or *range variables*. We choose to use the term *correlation variable*.

We introduce the first sample query and its solution as the basis of a detail discussion on the special logic of correlated subqueries.

Sample Query 18.1   For each department which offers courses, display the department's identifier followed by the number, name, and lab fee of the department-sponsored course having the largest lab fee.

SELECT   CDEPT, CNO, CNAME, CLABFEE

FROM   COURSE CX

WHERE   CLABFEE =

          (SELECT MAX(CLABFEE)

          FROM COURSE

          WHERE CDEPT = CX.CDEPT)

CDEPT	CNO	CNAME	CLABFEE
THEO	T44	COMMUNISM	200.00
CIS	C66	RELATIONAL DATABASE	500.00
PHIL	P33	EXISTENTIALISM	200.00

Comments

1. *Syntax.*   The FROM clause in the main query contains

   ```
   FROM COURSE CX
   ```

   The presence of CX after COURSE means that CX is defined as a correlation variable for the COURSE table. There must be one or more spaces between the table name and the corresponding correlated variable name. (Do not use a comma as a separator. If you do, the system will incorrectly interpret CX as the name of another table.)

Assuming the correlation variable CX has been defined in the outer SELECT statement, it can then be referenced in a subquery. In the current example, we see

```
WHERE CDEPT = CX.CDEPT
```

We will describe the function of CX.CDEPT below. For the moment we ask you to consider just the subquery in isolation and note that it is not self-contained.

```
SELECT   MAX(CLABFEE)
FROM     COURSE
WHERE    CDEPT = CX.CDEPT
```

Independent execution of this statement would result in an error because the system has no knowledge of CX.CDEPT. However, it is valid as a correlated subquery where CX has been specified as a correlation variable in the FROM clause of an outer SELECT statement.

2. *Logic.* It is absolutely imperative that you understand the logic of this sample query in order to understand the purpose of the correlation variable. It is helpful to distinguish the objective of this example from the query mentioned in our preliminary comments which illustrated a self-contained subquery. That query used a subselect to determine that the maximum lab-fee value for any theology course was $200.00. Then the system compared the CLABFEE value in every row to $200.00. If the CLABFEE value equaled $200.00, it was selected for display. The key point is that every row, regardless of its CDEPT value, had its CLABFEE value compared to $200.00. This value remained constant throughout the execution of the statement.

The current sample query is quite different because the system needs to *compare the CLABFEE value in each row to the maximum CLABFEE value for the department identified by the CDEPT value in the row under consideration. This CDEPT value may vary from row to row. Hence, the maximum CLABFEE will usually vary from row to row.*

In effect, for each row in the COURSE table, the system must

- Examine the CDEPT value of the row.

- Execute the subquery to determine the maximum CLABFEE value for that department.

- Compare the CLABFEE value of the row under consideration to see if it equals the value returned by the subquery. If it is equal to that value, the row is selected for display.

This is the essence of a correlated subquery. The execution of the subquery must be correlated with a particular value (CDEPT in this case) which will vary from row to row. Hence, the subquery must be executed for each row in the table. It also means that the system must keep track of the particular row being processed. This is the precise purpose of a correlation variable. It serves as a pointer to the row being considered for selection. These concepts will be illustrated below.

Because the COURSE table has 14 rows, the system will (at least conceptually) execute the subquery 14 times. On each execution the system will use CX to point to a row. In order to illustrate the overall process, we need to assume that the system encounters the COURSE table rows in some sequence. Assume the first four rows of this sequence are

CNO	CNAME	CDESCP	CRED	CLABFEE	CDEPT
T11	SCHOLASTICISM	FOR THE PIOUS	3	150.00	THEO
P33	EXISTENTIALISM	FOR CIS MAJORS	3	200.00	PHIL
C11	INTO TO CS	FOR ROOKIES	3	100.00	CIS
T12	FUNDAMENTALISM	FOR THE CAREFREE	3	90.00	THEO
.	.	.	.	.	.
.	.	.	.	.	.

We describe the system logic for processing the first four rows.

a. The system examines the first row shown below.

T11	SCHOLASTICISM	FOR THE PIOUS	3	150.00	THEO

This means that the correlation variable CX will initially point to this row. Hence, the CDEPT value of this row (THEO) is substituted for CX.CDEPT in the subquery. Thus, the subquery is evaluated as

```
SELECT   MAX(CLABFEE)
FROM     COURSE
WHERE    CDEPT = 'THEO'
```

Execution of this query returns a value of $200.00. After substitution of this intermediate result, the main query is evaluated as

```
SELECT   CDEPT, CNO, CNAME, CLABFEE
FROM     COURSE CX
WHERE    CLABFEE = 200.00
```

This query is effectively asking whether the current row under consideration (i.e., the row pointed to by CX, the T11 row) has a CLABFEE value of $200.00. It does not. Hence, this row is not selected and does not appear in the output display.

We emphasize that this behavior is considerably different from other main query SELECT statements which scanned the entire table and selected all rows which matched the selection criteria. *This main query SELECT statement, which has a CX in its FROM clause, is only asking if the current row, the one referenced by the correlation variable, has a CLABFEE value of $200.00.* The same logic will be described for the next two rows.

b. Next, the system examines the second row shown below.

P33	EXISTENTIALISM	FOR CIS MAJORS	3	200.00	PHIL

The CDEPT value of "PHIL" is substituted for CX.CDEPT in the subquery. Thus, the subquery is evaluated as

```
SELECT    MAX(CLABFEE)
FROM      COURSE
WHERE     CDEPT = 'PHIL'
```

Execution of this query returns a value of $200.00. Then the main query is evaluated as

```
SELECT    CDEPT, CNO, CNAME, CLABFEE
FROM      COURSE CX
WHERE     CLABFEE = 200.00
```

This statement is only asking if the current row (P33) has a CLABFEE value of $200.00. It does, so it appears in the output.

c. The system then examines the third row shown below.

C11	INTRO TO CS	FOR ROOKIES	3	100.00	CIS

Its CDEPT value of "CIS" is substituted for CX.CDEPT in the subquery. Thus, the subquery is evaluated as

```
SELECT    MAX(CLABFEE)
FROM      COURSE
WHERE     CDEPT = 'CIS'
```

Execution of this query returns a value of $500.00. Then the main query is evaluated as

```
SELECT    CDEPT, CNO, CNAME, CLABFEE
FROM      COURSE CX
WHERE     CLABFEE = 500.00
```

This statement is asking if the current row (C11) has a CLABFEE value of $500.00. It does not. Hence it does not appear in the output.

d. The system then examines the fourth row shown below.

T12	FUNDAMENTALISM	FOR THE CAREFREE	3	90.00	THEO

Its CDEPT value of "THEO" is substituted for CX.CDEPT in the subquery. Thus, the subquery is at least conceptually evaluated as

```
SELECT    MAX(CLABFEE)
FROM      COURSE
WHERE     CDEPT = 'THEO'
```

You may observe that the system previously calculated the maximum lab fee for the THEO department. It could have saved this value in temporary storage for future reference within this query. For our purposes, from a conceptual point of view, it is of no concern as to whether or not the system (1) actually recalculates this maximum value, or (2) has retained and reuses this temporary value from the processing of the first row (T11).

In either case evaluation of the subquery returns a value of $150.00. Then the main query is evaluated as

```
SELECT    CDEPT, CNO, CNAME, CLABFEE
FROM      COURSE CX
WHERE     CLABFEE = 150.00
```

This statement is asking if the current row (T12) has a CLABFEE value of $150.00. It does not. Hence it does not appear in the output.

The same process continues for the remaining 10 rows. Each time the subquery determines the maximum departmental lab-fee value for the department corresponding to the CDEPT value for the row. If the CLABFEE value equals this maximum, then the row is selected for display.

3. *Efficiency.*   The execution of a correlated subquery for each row in a table will obviously use more computer time than the single execution of a self-contained subquery. This is especially true if the table has a large number of rows. However, for some problems, like the current example, there is no alternative way of expressing the query in a single SELECT statement.

4. The current example shows the *explicit declaration* of the CX correlation variable by specifying it in the main query FROM clause. There are circumstances where a correlation variable can be *implicitly* declared. The next sample query will show the implicit declaration of a correlation variable.

   The explicit declaration of a correlation variable is necessary in the current example because the main query and subquery both reference the same table. If CX were omitted, the statement would be *incorrectly* written as

```
SELECT CDEPT, CNO, CNAME, CLABFEE
FROM   COURSE
WHERE  CLABFEE =
          (SELECT MAX(CLABFEE)
           FROM   COURSE
           WHERE  CDEPT = CDEPT)
```

Note the subquery WHERE clause, "WHERE CDEPT = CDEPT", specifies a condition which is always true and hence meaningless in this context.

Exercise

18A. Display the name, department identifier, and salary for those faculty members who have a salary which is greater than the average faculty salary for their department.

The next sample query illustrates a correlated subquery which utilizes, but does not explicitly declare, a correlation variable.

Sample Query 18.2   For each department which offers courses, display the department identifier, number, name, and lab fee of any department-sponsored course having a lab fee which exceeds the salary of the highest-paid staff member employed by that department.

SELECT   CDEPT, CNO, CNAME, CLABFEE

FROM   COURSE

WHERE   CLABFEE >

          (SELECT MAX(ESALARY)

          FROM STAFF

          WHERE DEPT = COURSE.CDEPT)

CDEPT	CNO	CNAME	CLABFEE
THEO	T12	FUNDAMENTALISM	90.00
THEO	T44	COMMUNISM	200.00
THEO	T11	SCHOLASTICISM	150.00

Comments

1. *Logic.*   The logic of this query requires a correlated query because we want to compare the lab fee for each course with the maximum salary of a staff member employed by the same department which offers the course. The department is identified by the CDEPT value, which changes from row to row. Hence the need for a correlated subquery.

2. *Syntax.*   As a self-contained statement the WHERE clause in the subquery is invalid because COURSE.CDEPT does not refer to a column in the STAFF table. However, this SELECT statement is meaningful as a subquery within an outer query which contains a "FROM COURSE" clause. Then, the system will interpret the subquery as a correlated subquery with COURSE.CDEPT as an implicitly declared correlation variable.

The explicit definition of a correlation variable (similar to CX in the previous example) is unnecessary because the main query and subquery reference different tables in their FROM clauses. However, it enhances readability and, therefore, it is better to explicitly define correlation variables whenever you need to write a correlated subquery. The current example is rewritten using C as a correlation variable.

```
SELECT    CDEPT, CNO, CNAME, CLABFEE
FROM      COURSE C
WHERE     CLABFEE >
                (SELECT MAX(ESALARY)
                 FROM    STAFF
                 WHERE   DEPT = C.CDEPT)
```

It is common practice to define a correlation variable for all tables, including those identified in the FROM clause of the subquery. The following equivalent statement includes S as a correlation variable for STAFF.

```
SELECT    CDEPT, CNO, CNAME, CLABFEE
FROM      COURSE C
WHERE     CLABFEE >
                (SELECT MAX(ESALARY)
                 FROM    STAFF S
                 WHERE   S.DEPT = C.CDEPT)
```

3. If a subquery refers to a column (CDEPT) which is not in a table referenced by the subquery FROM clause (FROM STAFF), then the system assumes that the subquery is a correlated subquery.

```
SELECT    CDEPT, CNO, CNAME, CLABFEE
FROM      COURSE
WHERE     CLABFEE >
                (SELECT MAX(ESALARY)
                 FROM    STAFF
                 WHERE   DEPT = CDEPT)
```

Exercise

18B. Display the name and department identifier for those faculty members who have a number of dependents greater than the average number of credits for courses offered by their department.

EXISTS KEYWORD

In previous subquery examples the main query WHERE clause was used to perform an explicit comparison with the value returned by the subquery. Sometimes the logic of the problem implies that an explicit comparison is unnecessary. Instead, a subquery is used only to determine if there are any rows in a table which match some condition. In this case, the main query can use the EXISTS keyword to test whether any match on the condition occurred.

Sample Query 18.3   Display the name and title of any staff member assigned to an existing department. More precisely, display the ENAME and ETITLE values in those STAFF table rows which have a DEPT value equal to any DEPT value in the DEPARTMENT table.

```
SELECT    ENAME, ETITLE
FROM      STAFF
WHERE     EXISTS
    (SELECT    *
     FROM      DEPARTMENT
     WHERE     DEPARTMENT.DEPT = STAFF.DEPT)
```

ENAME	ETITLE
HANK KISS	JESTER
DICK NIX	CROOK
MATTHEW	EVANGLIST1
MARK	EVANGLIST2
LUKE	EVANGLIST3
JOHN	EVANGLIST4

Comments

1. *Logic.*   The subquery is a correlated subquery where STAFF.DEPT is an implicitly defined correlation variable in the subquery. Therefore, the system will execute the subquery for each row in the STAFF table. Assume that the first STAFF table row encountered corresponds to "LUKE" which has a DEPT value of "THEO". Then the subquery (for the "LUKE" row) reduces to

```
SELECT    *
FROM      DEPARTMENT
WHERE     DEPARTMENT.DEPT = 'THEO'
```

This statement results in a "hit" because there are at least one row in the DEPARTMENT table with a DEPT value of "THEO". This means that the EXISTS test of the main query results in a "true" condition and the "LUKE" row is selected for display.

   Next assume that the second STAFF table row corresponds to "EUCLID", which has a DEPT value of "MATH". Then the subquery reduces to

```
SELECT    *
FROM      DEPARTMENT
WHERE     DEPARTMENT.DEPT = 'MATH'
```

This statement results in a "no hit" because there are no rows in the DEPARTMENT table with a DEPT value of "MATH". This means that the main query EXISTS test results in a "false" condition; hence the "EUCLID" row is not selected. Likewise, the row corresponding to "ARCHIMEDES" is not selected because its CDEPT value ("ENG") does not exist in the DEPARTMENT table. The "DA VINCI" row is not selected because its DEPT value is null. (Note that the "DA VINCI" row would not be selected even if a null value did exist in the DEPT column of DEPARTMENT. This is because the "null = null" compare results in "unknown," and cannot be considered "true.")

2. *Syntax.*   The subquery SELECT clause contains an asterisk even though column names could be specified. An asterisk is usually specified in the subquery when the main query performs an EXISTS test because the system does not return values from the subquery; rather, it confirms existence based on the test.

3. The query could have been satisfied by equivalent SELECT statements without using EXISTS. The following statements would produce the same result.

```
SELECT    ENAME, ETITLE
FROM      STAFF, DEPARTMENT
WHERE     STAFF.DEPT = DEPARTMENT.DEPT

SELECT    ENAME, ETITLE
FROM      STAFF
WHERE     DEPT IN
             (SELECT  DEPT
              FROM     DEPARTMENT)
```

However, there are problems which can be solved only by using the EXISTS keyword; you should recognize that EXISTS is an important keyword in the SQL language and understand its behavior. See Sample Query 18.8.

Exercise

18C. Display the name and department identifier of any faculty member assigned to a department which offers a six-credit course. (For this exercise, write three SELECT statements which will satisfy the query. The first statement should be a correlated subquery which utilizes the EXISTS keyword. The second statement should be a self-contained subquery. The third statement should represent a join operation.)

The next example demonstrates the use of EXISTS with a correlated subquery where the correlation variables are explicitly specified.

Sample Query 18.4   Display the course number, name, and lab fee of any course where there exists some staff member whose salary is less than that lab fee.

```
SELECT    CNO, CNAME, CLABFEE

FROM      COURSE C

WHERE     EXISTS

    (SELECT    *

    FROM       STAFF S

    WHERE      S.ESALARY < C.CLABFEE)
```

CNO	CNAME	CLABFEE
T12	FUNDAMENTALISM	90.00
C11	INTRO TO CS	100.00
T44	COMMUNISM	200.00
C55	COMPUTER ARCH.	100.00
C66	RELATIONAL DATABASE	500.00
T11	SCHOLASTICISM	150.00
P33	EXISTENTIALISM	200.00
P11	EMPIRICISM	100.00

Comment

For each row in the COURSE table, the subquery determines if any row in the STAFF table has an ESALARY value less than the CLABFEE value of the COURSE row. If such a row exists in the STAFF table, then the COURSE row is selected.

Exercise

18D. Rewrite the current sample query using (1) a self-contained subquery, and (2) a join operation.

NOT EXISTS

A correlated subquery can be formulated using NOT EXISTS, which, as you would expect, tests for a "does not exist" condition. It will select precisely those rows which would not be selected by the EXISTS condition. In fact, you will probably find that NOT EXISTS is more useful than EXISTS.

Sample Query 18.5   Display the name, title, and department identifier of any staff member who is not assigned to an existing department. More precisely, display the ENAME, ETITLE, and DEPT values of any row in the STAFF table with a DEPT value which does not match any value in the DEPT column of the DEPARTMENT table.

SELECT   ENAME, ETITLE, DEPT

FROM   STAFF

WHERE   NOT EXISTS

      (SELECT   *

      FROM   DEPARTMENT

      WHERE   DEPARTMENT.DEPT = STAFF.DEPT)

ENAME	ETITLE	DEPT
DA VINCI	LAB ASSIST	—
EUCLID	LAB ASSIST	MATH
ARCHIMEDES	LAB ASSIST	ENG

Comments

1. The subquery is identical to that of Sample Query 18.3. Here the main query will select just those rows where a "no hit" occurs in the subquery.

2. Observe that the "DA VINCI" row, which has a null DEPT value, is shown in the output display. When the main query was considering the "DA VINCI" row for selection, the subquery did not select any rows because it is impossible for the STAFF.DEPT value, which is null, to equal any DEPARTMENT.DEPT, including another null value. This "no hit" situation in the subquery means that the "DA VINCI" row (or any other STAFF row with a null DEPT value) will be selected under the NOT EXISTS condition.

We emphasize this point to note that, while EXISTS may be logically equivalent to IN, NOT EXISTS is not logically equivalent to NOT IN. The presence of NULL values is the cause of this subtle problem. In particular the following statement is not equivalent to the current example.

```
SELECT    ENAME, ETITLE, DEPT
FROM      STAFF
WHERE     DEPT NOT IN
    (SELECT DEPT
    FROM    DEPARTMENT)
```

This statement will not select the "DA VINCI" row because it has a null DEPT value. In effect, this difference in behavior means that EXISTS always operates on a two-value logic unlike the other SQL operators, which operate on a three-value logic.

It is possible to write a SELECT statement which is equivalent to the current example, but you must explicitly test for null values.

```
SELECT    ENAME, ETITLE
FROM      STAFF
WHERE     DEPT NOT IN
    (SELECT DEPT
    FROM    DEPARTMENT)
OR DEPT IS NULL
```

3. The correlation variable STAFF.DEPT is implicitly specified in the subquery. There is no possible ambiguity because the main query and subquery reference different tables in their FROM clauses.

Exercise

18E. Display the name and department identifier of any faculty member in a department which does not offer a six-credit course. Specify two SELECT statements which will satisfy the query. The first statement should be a correlated subquery which utilizes the NOT EXISTS keywords. The second statement can use any other technique.

The next sample query uses NOT EXISTS with a correlated subquery. Correlation variables are explicitly specified because the main query and subquery both reference the same table.

Sample Query 18.6   Display the course number, name, and lab fee of any course which has a unique lab fee. This is a lab fee which does not equal the lab fee of any other course.

```
SELECT    CNO, CNAME, CLABFEE

FROM      COURSE C1

WHERE     NOT EXISTS

          (SELECT    *

          FROM       COURSE C2

          WHERE      C1.CLABFEE = C2.CLABFEE

          AND        C1.CNO <> C2.CNO)
```

CNO	CNAME	CLABFEE
T12	FUNDAMENTALISM	90.00
C66	RELATIONAL DATABASE	500.00
T11	SCHOLASTICISM	150.00

Comments

1. The correlated variable C1 is necessary. C2 is not necessary, but its use makes the statement more readable.

2. Each row in the COURSE table is considered for selection with C1 serving as the correlation variable for referencing these rows. The corresponding course number and lab-fee values are substituted for C1.CNO and C1.CLABFEE for each execution of the subquery. If the subquery results in a "no hit," the row under consideration (the one pointed to by C1) is selected.

CORRELATION VARIABLES WITHOUT SUBQUERIES

It is possible to utilize correlation variables in SELECT statements which do not contain a subquery. Sample Queries 15.11 and 15.12 illustrated the joining of a table with itself. The SELECT statement for 15.12 is shown below.

```
SELECT    ST1.DEPT, ST1.ENAME, ST2.ENAME
FROM      STAFF ST1, STAFF ST2
WHERE     ST1.DEPT = ST2.DEPT
AND       ST1.ENAME < ST2.ENAME
```

Recall ST1 and ST2 were effectively two names to the same table. In fact, ST1 and ST2 are correlation variables. The system will use ST1 as a pointer to a given row. It will then execute the statement substituting that row's DEPT value for ST1.DEPT and that row's ENAME value for ST1.ENAME. Likewise, it will do the same for ST2. If the WHERE condition is true after substituting the corresponding values referenced by ST1 and ST2, the ST1.DEPT, ST1.ENAME, and ST2.ENAME values are displayed. Both ST1 and ST2 range over the entire STAFF table to compare every possible pair of rows.

This discussion provides insight into an alternative, but less elegant, solution to Sample Query 18.6.

```
SELECT    CNO, CNAME, CLABFEE
FROM      COURSE
WHERE     CNO NOT IN
             (SELECT CA.CNO
              FROM    COURSE CA, COURSE CB
              WHERE   CA.CLABFEE = CB.CLABFEE
              AND     CA.CNO <> CB.NO)
```

Observe that the subquery is self-contained; it is *not correlated with the main query*. However, the subquery does use correlation variables, CA and CB, to implement the join of the COURSE table with itself.

OUTER JOIN

In Chap. 15 we emphasized that the result of joining two tables will only contain rows where a match occurred on the join condition. The expression *inner join* is a more precise label for this kind of join operation. This distinguishes it from a different kind of join operation, called the *outer join*. Because nonmatching rows will be excluded from the final result of an inner join, there is the potential for a loss of information. The result of an outer-join operation, however, will contain the same rows as an inner-join operation plus a row corresponding to each row from the original tables which did not match on the join condition.

There are three variations of the outer-join operation. Figure 18.1 illustrates each variation of an outer equijoin of TABLE1 and TABLE2 using columns C2 and CA as the join columns.

Full Outer Join

The result of a full outer join is shown in table FULLOJ of Fig. 18.1. Note that the first three rows of FULLOJ correspond to the inner equijoin of TABLE1 and TABLE2. The fourth and fifth rows correspond to rows in TABLE1 (the "left" table) which did not match in the compare operation. The last row of table FULLOJ corresponds to the row in TABLE2 (the "right" table) which did not match. The "no match" rows from the left table have null values appended to the right. And the "no match" rows from the right table have null values appended to the left. Obviously the terms *left* and *right* are relative. We could visualize TABLE1 as the right table and TABLE2 as the left table.

Left Outer Join

The LEFTOJ outer join result in Fig. 18.1 is the *left outer join* of TABLE 1 and TABLE2. This result excludes the "no match" rows of TABLE2, the right table, from the result of FULLOJ. It includes the "no match" rows of only TABLE1, the left table. In practice you will find greater application for the left outer-join operation than the full outer-join operation.

Right Outer Join

The RIGHTOJ outer join result in Fig. 18.1 is the *right outer join* of TABLE1 and TABLE2. This result excludes the "no match" rows of TABLE1, the left table, from the result of FULLOJ. It includes the "no match" rows of only TABLE2, the right table. Because left and right are relative terms, there is no difference in principle between the left and right outer joins. It is simply a matter of which table you visualize as the left table.

TABLE1				TABLE2	
C1	C2			CA	CB
A	10			10	S
B	45			20	U
C	45			35	Z
D	20				
E	20				

C1	C2	CA	CB	
A	10	10	S	⎤
D	20	20	U	⎬ Inner join rows
E	20	20	U	⎦
B	45	—	—	⎤ Nonmatching rows
C	45	—	—	⎦ from TABLE1
—	—	35	Z	— Nonmatching row from TABLE2

FULLOJ

C1	C2	CA	CB	
A	10	10	S	⎤
D	20	20	U	⎬ Inner-join rows
E	20	20	U	⎦
B	45	—	—	⎤ Nonmatching rows
C	45	—	—	⎦ from (left) TABLE1

LEFTOJ

C1	C2	CA	CB	
A	10	10	S	⎤
D	20	20	U	⎬ Inner-join rows
E	20	20	U	⎦
—	—	35	Z	— Nonmatching row from (right) TABLE2

RIGHTOJ

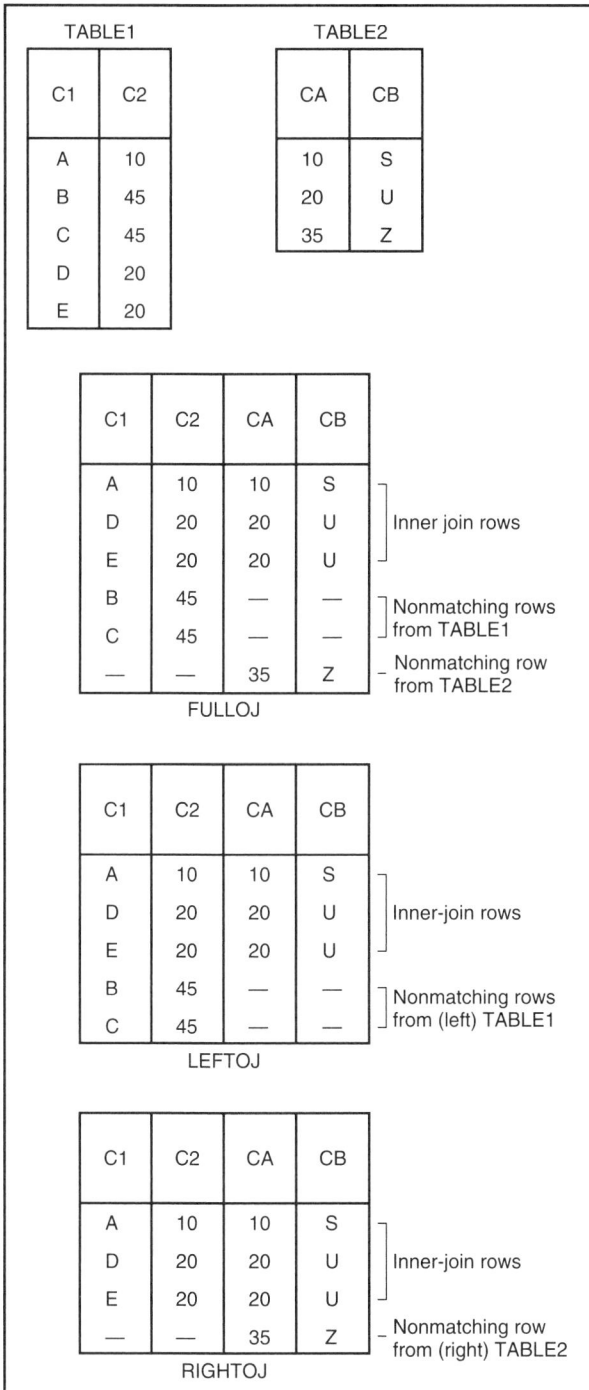

Figure 18.1 Outer-join operations.

LEFT OUTER JOIN

You may find the outer join very useful. Unfortunately, SQL/400 does *not directly* support this operation. Therefore, we now show a "do it yourself" approach to achieve the same results using a correlated subquery.

Sample Query 18.7   For every staff member recorded in the STAFF table, display his or her name, title, salary, and department identifier along with all information about the department to which he or she is assigned (i.e., department identifier, building, room, and faculty number of the department chairperson). If the staff member is not assigned to an existing department, or if the assignment is unknown (null), display blanks for department information.

```
SELECT    *

FROM      STAFF, DEPARTMENT

WHERE     STAFF.DEPT = DEPARTMENT.DEPT

UNION     ALL

SELECT    ENAME, ETITLE, ESALARY,

          STAFF.DEPT, ' ',' ',' ',' '

FROM      STAFF

WHERE     NOT EXISTS

    (SELECT    *

     FROM      DEPARTMENT

     WHERE     DEPARTMENT.DEPT = STAFF.DEPT)
```

ENAME	ETITLE	ESALARY	DEPT	DEPT	DBLD	DROOM	DCHFNO
DICK NIX	CROOK	25001	PHIL	PHIL	HU	100	60
HANK KISS	JESTER	25000	PHIL	PHIL	HU	100	60
JOHN	EVANGLIST4	54	THEO	THEO	HU	200	10
LUKE	EVANGLIST3	53	THEO	THEO	HU	200	10
MARK	EVANGLIST2	52	THEO	THEO	HU	200	10
MATTHEW	EVANGLIST1	51	THEO	THEO	HU	200	10
EUCLID	LAB ASSIST	1000	MATH				
ARCHIMEDES	LAB ASSIST	200	ENG				
DA VINCI	LAB ASSIST	500	—				

Comments

1. The sample query formed a left outer join using UNION ALL to merge two SELECT statements (Why do we use UNION ALL versus UNION? See comment 3 of Sample Query 17.4). The first SELECT statement generates those rows which correspond to the conventional (inner) equijoin of DEPARTMENT and STAFF along the DEPT columns. The second SELECT statement generates those rows which correspond to the "no match" rows from the STAFF table. These rows pertain to those employees who are not assigned to an existing department. This second SELECT uses NOT EXISTS in conjunction with a correlated subquery.

2. The example shows blanks instead of null values appended to the "no match" rows. What if you wanted to display null values instead of blanks? This cannot be done. Although it seems reasonable, the following SELECT clause is invalid. The NULL keyword cannot be used in the SELECT clause.

    ```
    SELECT ENAME, ETITLE, ESALARY, DEPT, NULL, NULL, NULL, NULL
    ```

3. We could form a full outer join of the STAFF and DEPARTMENT tables along the DEPT columns by appending the following code to the current example.

    ```
    UNION ALL
    SELECT '', '', 0, '', DEPARTMENT.DEPT, DBLD, DROOM, DCHFNO
    FROM DEPARTMENT
    WHERE NOT EXISTS
            (SELECT  *
            FROM    STAFF
            WHERE   STAFF.DEPT = DEPARTMENT.DEPT)
    ```

    Note that zero, or any other numeric value, instead of blanks must be displayed in the ESALARY column. This is necessary for reasons of union compatibility.

4. Recall that SQL permits an inner-join condition to be formulated with any of the standard comparison operators. The term *theta-join* is used to indicate this more general capability where *theta* represents a given comparison operator. The same operators may be used with an outer join. Hence, a more general term which describes an outer join is *outer theta-join*.

"FOR ALL"

The final sample query of this chapter illustrates the formulation of a SELECT statement which embodies the notion of "for all the values in a column, there exists . . ." SQL has no keyword which directly supports "for all." However, it is possible to write an equivalent statement using NOT EXISTS twice. This is effectively a double negative, which is poor grammar but logically correct. In fact, it is the only way to express "for all" within SQL.

The complexity of the following example occurs for two reasons. The first is that SQL is far from a perfect language. In this case, the absence of a "for all" operator means that the query must be reformulated into an equivalent, but far less concise, expression of the problem. The second reason is that five different tables need to be referenced in order to satisfy the query objective. This means that you must have a good understanding of the semantic relationships reflected in the database design. Finally, the authors felt that it would be "good for the soul" to conclude this chapter with a problem which is deceptively nasty. This is a problem which is simple to articulate in everyday English, but can be considered a real challenge.

Sample Query 18.8   Are there any students who are taking a course from every department which offers courses? If so, display the name of each student.

To put it another way:

> Display the name of any student who has registered for at least one class in a course offered by each department which offers courses.

Or, to put it yet another way, using the double-negative articulation of the problem:

> Display the name of any student where there does not exist a department (which offers courses) such that there does not exist a class on a course offered by that department where the student has registered for a class offered by that department.

```
SELECT    SNAME
FROM      STUDENT S
WHERE     NOT EXISTS
          (SELECT  *
          FROM      DEPARTMENT D
          WHERE    D.DEPT IN
                   (SELECT CDEPT FROM COURSE)
          AND NOT EXISTS
                   (SELECT *
                   FROM      REGISTRAT R, CLASS CL, COURSE C
                   WHERE    R.CNO = CL.CNO
                   AND       R.SEC = CL.SEC
                   AND       CL.CNO = C.CNO
                   AND       C.CDEPT = D.DEPT
                   AND       R.SNO = S.SNO))
```

SNAME

MOE DUBAY
ROCKY BALBOA

Comments

In the following comments we refer to the *second-level* and *third-level* queries. These references are correlated with the indentation used in the sample query.

1. *Syntax.*   The example shows a second-level subquery which contains two other third-level subqueries. (Nesting of subqueries was introduced in Sample Query 16.11.) The key difference here is that the second-level subquery and one of the third-level subqueries are correlated subqueries. This is no more than an extension of the idea of a correlated subquery to a lower-level subquery.

2. *Logic.* In this example the top-level SELECT statement of the main query references the STUDENT table. This means that the system will examine each row in the STUDENT table to determine if any rows are selected by the second-level SELECT statement. If no rows are selected, then the corresponding SNAME value is displayed.

   Assume the system encounters a row corresponding to a student who matches the selection criteria (i.e., the student has registered for at least one course offered by each of the departments which offer courses (THEO, PHIL, and CIS). If this student has a SNO value "800", then the second-level SELECT statement, after making the substitution for S.SNO, reduces to

```
SELECT   *
FROM     DEPARTMENT D
WHERE    D.DEPT IN (SELECT CDEPT FROM COURSE)
AND      NOT EXISTS
         (SELECT  *
         FROM     REGISTRAT R, CLASS CL, COURSE C
         WHERE    R.CNO = CL.CNO
         AND      R.SEC = CL.SEC
         AND      CL.CNO = C.CNO
         AND      C.CDEPT = D.DEPT
         AND      R.SNO = '800')
```

For the moment consider this statement as an independent SELECT statement. The first subquery, "SELECT CDEPT FROM COURSE", is a self-contained subquery which selects the department identifiers of those departments which offer courses. We can replace this subquery with the CDEPT values found in the COURSE table. This statement then becomes

```
SELECT   *
FROM     DEPARTMENT D
WHERE    D.DEPT IN ('CIS', 'PHIL', 'THEO')
AND      NOT EXISTS
         (SELECT  *
         FROM     REGISTRATION R, CLASS CL, COURSE C
         WHERE    R.CNO = CL.CNO
         AND      R.SEC = CL.SEC
         AND      CL.CNO = C.CNO
         AND      C.CDEPT = D.DEPT
         AND      R.SNO = '800')
```

This statement contains the second correlated subquery which causes the system to examine each row of the DEPARTMENT table to determine if any rows are selected by the low-level subquery. If none are selected, and the department identifier is "CIS", "PHIL", or "THEO", the corresponding DEPARTMENT row is selected. Assume the system encounters the CIS department row. Then the bottom-level subquery reduces to

```
SELECT    *
FROM      REGISTRATION R, CLASS CL, COURSE C
WHERE     R.CNO = CL.CNO
AND       R.SEC = CL.SEC
AND       CL.CNO = C.CNO
AND       C.CDEPT = 'CIS'
AND       R.SNO = '800'
```

The statement is a three-way join of the REGISTRATION, CLASS, and COURSE tables. (Sample Query 15.9 originally introduced a three-way join.) The objective of this statement is to determine if the student identified by SNO value "800" has registered for any class offered by the CIS department. Assume there is a "hit" on this condition.

Returning to the second-level SELECT statement, a "hit" on student 800 registering for a CIS course means that the NOT EXISTS condition evaluates to false and hence the row for the CIS department is not selected. For the same reason, the DEPARTMENT rows for the theology and philosophy departments are not selected. Finally, the row for the management department is not selected because the "MGT" identifier is not in the set ("CIS", "PHIL", "THEO"). This means that none of the four DEPARTMENT rows is selected by the second-level subquery. We have a "no hit" for the second-level subquery.

Returning to the top-level SELECT statement, the NOT EXISTS condition is met because none of the DEPARTMENT rows were selected. Hence, the STUDENT row for student number 800 is selected and the SNAME value (ROCKY BALBOA) is displayed.

The same process begins all over again for the next STUDENT row encountered by the system. The SNO value is held constant during the iteration over the four DEPARTMENT rows indicated by the second-level subquery. The bottom-level correlated subquery then determines if the student registered for a course offered by the department. You are encouraged to work through the example for a student who did not register for a course offered by some department which offers courses. A "no hit" on the bottom-level correlated subquery means that the second-level NOT EXISTS condition is true for some department, which in turn means that the top-level NOT EXISTS condition is not met. Hence, the name of this student would not be displayed.

3. We could have simplified the innermost subquery in our example to

```
SELECT   *
FROM     DEPARTMENT D
WHERE    D.DEPT IN ('CIS', 'PHIL', 'THEO')
AND      NOT EXISTS
         (SELECT  *
         FROM     REGISTRATION R, COURSE C
         WHERE    R.CNO = C.CNO
         AND      C.CDEPT = D.DEPT
         AND      R.SNO = S.SNO)
```

This simplification is only possible if we have assurance that Referential Integrity constraints are enforced. In our example this means that every registration will refer to an existing class which in turn refers to an existing course. Hence there would be no need for our example to reference the CLASS Table.

SUMMARY

This chapter introduced the notion of a correlated subquery, a subselect which relates back to, and is dependent on, a higher-level SELECT statement. The reference is made through a correlation variable. The concept of existence testing was introduced through the EXISTS keyword. We saw that the "for all" operation could be implemented by double specification of NOT EXISTS. Finally, it was demonstrated that the outer-join operation could also be implemented through the use of correlated subqueries and EXISTS. All told, this chapter revealed some very important aspects of relational database which are supported (albeit not directly) in SQL.

Summary Exercises

18F. Display the course name, department identifier, and lab fee for each course which has the largest lab fee of all courses in that department.

18G. Display a list for each department of all classes offered by the department. The list contains department identifier and department building and room location, followed by course number and name of courses offered by the department, followed by section number and day of any classes on those courses. If a department does not offer any courses, or a course has no class offerings, display spaces in the respective positions.

6

More about SQL/400

The previous parts of this text introduced the data definition, data retrieval, and data manipulation statements of SQL. Part 6 will introduce another dimension of SQL by presenting statements which facilitate the management of your data. In particular, we focus on those techniques which allow you to share your data with other users of the system. This topic involves the notion of creating views and granting privileges. We also consider the idea of a database transaction as it relates to database integrity and recovery. We include in our discussion of these topics the notion of a data dictionary in the context of a collection. You will find the SQL statements presented in these chapters to be useful, powerful, and easy to learn.

ORGANIZATION OF CHAPTERS

Chapter 19 presents a comprehensive discussion of the CREATE VIEW statement. This statement permits you to define a view which is essentially a "virtual" table. A view generally corresponds to the notion of "local view" which is applicable within most multiuser database systems.

Chapter 20 introduces some of the key ideas behind database security. This is not a comprehensive discussion of the topic. Instead, we present a programmer/user (versus database administrator) perspective by introducing those variations of the GRANT and REVOKE statements which are relevant to this audience.

Chapter 21 presents an overview of collections, the SQL/400 counterpart of a data dictionary. A data dictionary contains data about data, sometimes referred to as "metadata." This chapter will help you determine information about tables you or other users have created, the columns in these tables, the views based on these tables, etc.

Chapter 22 introduces the transaction concept by presenting the COMMIT and ROLLBACK statements. This is an important chapter for programmers who will write application programs which update tables. Most users can skip this chapter. However, those users who intend to execute interactive update operations (a questionable practice) should read this chapter because of its relevance to database integrity and recovery.

The View Concept

Most database management systems provide some facility which allows for the definition of a "local view" of the database. "Local view" is a generic expression corresponding to some subset of the database which a particular user or group of users can display and/or update. A local view is usually defined by the system manager and then made available to a user. Because a local view is usually defined for a specific purpose, a given file/table may have many local views defined on it. SQL/400 supports the local-view concept through the CREATE VIEW statement. Execution of this statement will create an "SQL view" which is similar but not identical to the local-view concept.

Some AS/400 users may be familiar with the creation of a nonkeyed logical file with Data Definition Specifications (DDS). Within the context of Relational Databases, the view mechanism is similar in spirit to the DDS logical File.

The local view approach serves at least three purposes.

1. *Security.*   Using views prevents accidental or intentional retrieval or modification of data which are not within the defined local view. The following chapter will illustrate how views are used as a security feature.

2. *Simplicity.*   The user can disregard all data which are not within his or her local view. In fact, the user might be unaware of any other data in the database.

3. *Correctness.*   Because a local view is usually much smaller than the entire database, the user's view is simplified and a possibility source of error is reduced.

Below we describe an SQL view and then relate it to the local view concept.

The CREATE VIEW statement is used to define the content of a table which, in AS/400 community, is sometimes called a *logical file/table*. We say *table* because the user perceives and manipulates an SQL view in the same manner as a "good old table." To introduce some SQL terminology, we use the phrase *base table* to designate any table created by a CREATE TABLE statement. All the educational database tables in this book (COURSE, STAFF, DEPARTMENT, etc.) are base tables. The CREATE VIEW statement is used to establish an SQL view which is defined on some base table. An SQL view can be thought of as a window into some subset of a base table. Figure 19.1 illustrates this perspective of an SQL view. Later we will see that the CREATE VIEW statement provides more power and flexibility than the window analogy implies.

Once an SQL view is established you can execute a SELECT statement which references the view. The system will associate the SQL view with a base table and then extract and display the data from the base table.

This chapter will introduce the details of the CREATE VIEW statement. We will see that an SQL view is perceived as exactly one (virtual) table. To relate an SQL view to the generic notion of a local view, note that a user might have a local view which consists of multiple tables. Some of these tables might be base tables, and others might be SQL views. We will also see that the CREATE VIEW statement defines only the content of the virtual table. It does not specify which user can access a view, nor does it specify what operations may be performed against the view. The next chapter will present the GRANT statement which serves these purposes. There we will see that the local view concept is usually implemented by utilization of both the CREATE VIEW and GRANT statements. For the remainder of this chapter the term *view* implies an SQL view.

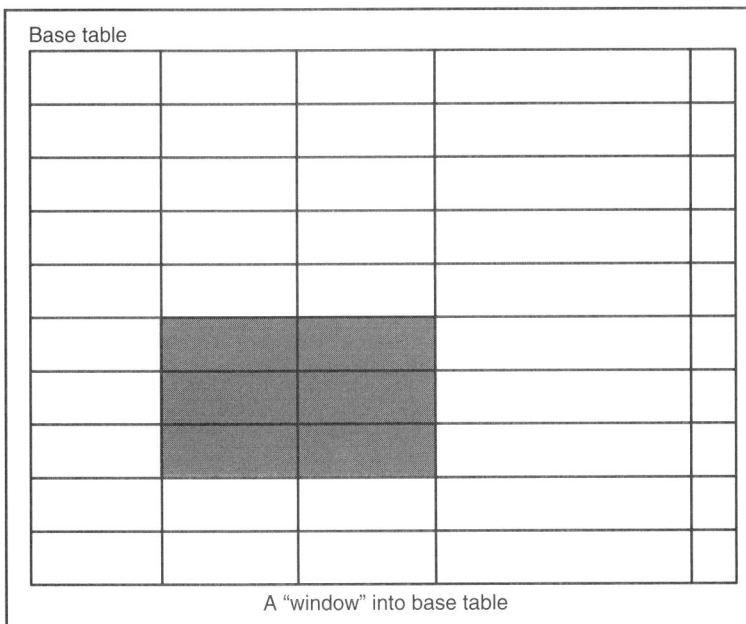

Figure 19.1 View concept.

CREATE VIEW STATEMENT

The first example draws upon the aforementioned window analogy for a view by creating a view which corresponds to a subset of columns and of rows from the COURSE table.

Sample Statement 19.1   Create a view (a virtual table) called CISC which contains just the rows corresponding to courses offered by the CIS department. The view should contain all of the columns from the COURSE table with the exception of the CDEPT column. The left-to-right column sequence of the view should be CNAME, CNO, CRED, CLABFEE, CDESCP.

```
CREATE   VIEW CISC AS
         SELECT    CNAME, CNO,
                   CRED, CLABFEE, CDESCP
         FROM      COURSE
         WHERE     CDEPT = 'CIS'
```

System Response

Like all previous CREATE statements, the system should display a message confirming the successful creation of the object.

Comments

1. The name of the view, CISC, immediately follows the CREATE VIEW keywords. View names are formulated according to the same rules that apply to table names.

2. A discussion of the internal representation of a view is beyond the scope of this book. However, the creation of a view of the COURSE table does not create a static replica of COURSE table. Subsequent changes to the COURSE table will be reflected in related view tables.

3. The keyword AS follows the view name. The definition of the view follows the AS keyword. Observe that this definition is simply a "good old" SELECT statement (This means that there is very little new syntax to learn). In this example it is

   ```
   SELECT   CNAME, CNO, CRED, CLABFEE, CDESCP
   FROM     COURSE
   WHERE    CDEPT = 'CIS'
   ```

   If we were to directly execute this SELECT statement, the result would correspond to the content of the desired view definition.

4. In this example the view inherited the names of its columns from the COURSE table. Sample Statement 19.4 will demonstrate a version of the CREATE VIEW statement which allows the assignment of different column names.

PROCESSING VIEWS

We can usually manipulate views just as we have done with base tables throughout this text. However, there are some important exceptions which will be described as we progress through the examples. In general, you will find that many views can be treated exactly like base tables, so much so that a view is often referred to simply as a *table* instead of *virtual table*.

Sample Query 19.2   Display the entire CISC table.

```
SELECT   *

FROM     CISC
```

CNAME	CNO	CRED	CLABFEE	CDESCP
INTRO TO CS	C11	3	100.00	FOR ROOKIES
DATA STRUCTURES	C22	3	50.00	VERY USEFUL
DISCRETE MATHEMATICS	C33	3	.00	ABSOLUTELY NECESSARY
DIGITAL CIRCUITS	C44	3	.00	AH HA!
COMPUTER ARCH.	C55	3	100.00	VON NEUMANN'S MACH.
RELATIONAL DATABASE	C66	3	500.00	THE ONLY WAY TO GO

Comment

The syntax of the SELECT statement (and all other SQL data manipulation statements) remains unchanged. In this example we see that the view name is referenced in the FROM clause.

Exercise

19A. Create a view called FPAYROLL which contains all rows of the FACULTY table. The view is to contain just the FNAME, FSALARY, FHIRE_DATE, and FNUM_DEP columns. Issue a SELECT statement against this view and examine the results.

Sample Query 19.3 For any row in the CISC table with a lab fee greater than or equal to $100, display its name followed by its lab fee. Sort the result by course name in ascending sequence.

SELECT   CNAME, CLABFEE

FROM   CISC

WHERE   CLABFEE >= 100

ORDER BY CNAME

CNAME	CLABFEE
COMPUTER ARCH.	100.00
INTRO TO CS	100.00
RELATIONAL DATABASE	500.00

Comments

1. Again observe that the view is referenced like a base table. In the current sample query, a WHERE clause and an ORDER BY clause were used to select specific rows from the view and to display them in a specific row sequence.

2. This query could have been satisfied by executing the following (more complex) statement which directly refers to the base table.

```
SELECT    CNAME, CLABFEE
FROM      COURSE
WHERE     CDEPT = 'CIS'
AND       CLABFEE >= 100
ORDER BY CNAME
```

This statement presumes that the user is aware of both the existence and content of the COURSE table. In many situations the database administrator allows the user to access only a view.

SPECIFYING COLUMN NAMES FOR A VIEW

The column names in the CISC view were inherited from the COURSE table. The next example illustrates a method for explicitly naming the columns of a view and then referencing them in a SELECT statement.

Sample Statement 19.4   Create a view called VEXPCOURSE which corresponds to rows from the COURSE table where the lab fee exceeds $150. The columns of the view correspond to CNO, CNAME, and CLABFEE. Their respective names in the view are CNUMBER, COURSE_NAME, and EXPENSIVE_LABFEE.

CREATE VIEW VEXPCOURSE

(CNUMBER, CRSE_NAME, EXP_LABFEE)

AS   SELECT   CNO, CNAME, CLABFEE

    FROM   COURSE

    WHERE   CLABFEE > 150

System Response

Like all previous CREATE statements, the system should display a message confirming the successful creation of the object.

Comments

1. In the CREATE VIEW statement, the column names of the view are specified after the view name. Note that they are enclosed within parentheses and separated by commas.

2. We chose to begin the view name with the letter *V* to serve as a reminder that this table is really a view. This is a useful convention, but it is not necessary.

Sample Query 19.5 Display the course name and lab-fee values from the VEXPCOURSE table. Display the result in course-name sequence.

```
SELECT    CRSE_NAME, EXP_LABFEE

FROM      VEXPCOURSE

ORDER BY CRSE_NAME
```

CRSE_NAME	EXP_LABFEE
COMMUNISM	200
EXISTENTIALISM	200
RELATIONAL DATABASE	500

Comment

The SELECT statement must reference the column names as defined in the view. These names appear as column headings in the displayed result. Whenever a VIEW is defined with explicit column names, only those names may be referenced in a SELECT statement. For example, you must use CRSE_NAME, not CNAME, to refer to course names.

Exercise

19B. Create a view called FPAYROLL2 on the FACULTY table. The view is to contain the FNAME, FSALARY, and FHIRE_DATE columns from the FACULTY table. The corresponding column names in the FPAYROLL2 view should be called F2N, F2S, and F2H. Issue a SELECT statement against this view and examine the result.

RULES FOR CREATE VIEW

Figure 19.2 outlines the general format of the CREATE VIEW statement. We address the issues of specification of column names and the formulation of a valid SELECT statement.

As Sample Statement 19.1 indicated, the designation of specific column names may be optional. If you do not specify the column names, the view inherits its column names from the base table. Sample Statement 19.4 illustrated a situation where the columns of VEXPCOURSE were assigned names different from the underlying base table. Observe that we could allow the columns of VEXPCOURSE to inherit the column names from the COURSE table. Sometimes the creator of a view is required to specify column names. Sample Statement 19.6 will present a situation where the view contains a column of derived values. In such cases it is necessary to explicitly specify column names because the values in a column do not directly correspond to any predefined (base table) column and, hence, cannot inherit a name.

"Almost any" SELECT statement is permitted as a view definition. There are three restrictions. *UNION ALL, UNION, and ORDER BY cannot be included in the SELECT statement.* The ORDER BY is reasonable when you consider that the relational model dictates that a base table or a view should not have any predefined sequence. The ORDER BY clause may be attached to the SELECT statement which retrieves data from the view.

Aside from these restrictions, any valid SELECT statement can serve as a view definition. The FROM clause may even specify a view, which means that it is possible to define a view on top of a view. See Sample Statement 19.10.

This approach of using a SELECT statement to define a view is simple, powerful, and conceptually elegant. In all previous examples the direct execution of a SELECT statement was interpreted by the system as the definition of a subset of the database to be retrieved for display. (This perspective is consistent with the theory of a relational database which defines the database structure as a collection of sets and the query language as a notation which defines a subset to be retrieved.) In the context of CREATE VIEW, a SELECT statement constitutes the definition of a subset (i.e., a window) which is a view into a base table.

There are no restrictions when you formulate a SELECT statement which references a view. However, there are a number of restrictions which apply to updating views. These will be described at the end of the chapter.

The following pages will show sample statements which define views which represent a statistical summary and a join operation. The techniques illustrated in these views are extremely useful because they allow information to be synthesized from one or more tables and presented to the user as a single (presumably simpler) table.

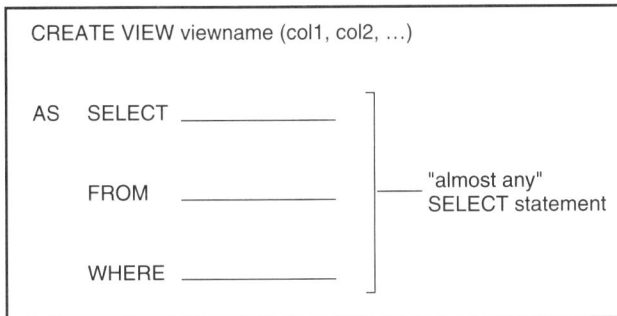

CREATE VIEW viewname (col1, col2, ...)

AS   SELECT _____ ⎤

                                              ⎥____ "almost any"
         FROM   _____   SELECT statement

         WHERE _____ ⎦

Figure 19.2 CREATE VIEW statement.

VIEW DEFINED AS A STATISTICAL SUMMARY

The next example shows that we can create a view with columns containing summary data derived from a base table.

Sample Statement 19.6   Create a view called VCSTAT which has one row for each department which offers courses. The columns are the department identifier followed by the sum and the average lab-fee values for each department.

```
CREATE  VIEW VCSTAT

        (CDEPT,  SUM_FEE, AVG_FEE) AS

        SELECT  CDEPT, SUM(CLABFEE), AVG(CLABFEE)

        FROM    COURSE

        GROUP  BY  CDEPT
```

System Response

Like all previous CREATE statements, the system should display a message confirming the successful creation of the object.

Comments

1. The SELECT clause contains group functions which perform the required calculations for each department group. The derived results effectively become the values of the second and third columns of the view.

2. The example shows that the column names of the view are explicitly named. This is necessary because view columns which contain derived data do not directly correspond to, and hence cannot inherit the names of, any base table columns.

3. Recall that the GROUP BY clause will cause the system to sort by the grouping field. This sorting is incidental to the grouping process. You should explicitly use the ORDER BY clause if you want the result to be sorted. However, we did not include an ORDER BY clause in the definition of VCSTAT because the ORDER BY clause is not permitted in the definition of any view.

4. This view cannot be updated because it contains derived data. To be precise the system will not permit update operations on any view which is defined with a GROUP BY clause or a built-in function.

Sample Query 19.7 Display the average lab fee for courses offered by the philosophy and theology departments. Sort the result by average lab fee in descending sequence.

```
SELECT    CDEPT, AVG_FEE

FROM      VCSTAT

WHERE     CDEPT = 'PHIL'

OR        CDEPT = 'THEO'

ORDER BY AVG_FEE DESC
```

CDEPT	AVG_CLABFEE
THEO	110.000..
PHIL	87.500..

Comment

The following SELECT statement is invalid (even though some systems allow it). AS/400 would reject this statement because AVG_FEE really contains the result produced by a column function. In SQL/400, column functions cannot be used in a WHERE clause.

```
SELECT  CDEPT, AVG_FEE
FROM    VCSTAT
WHERE   AVG_FEE < 100
```

VIEW DEFINED AS JOIN OF TABLES

In Chap. 15 we described the subtle logical issues associated with the join operation. We noted that the SQL syntax was easy but the logic of the join could be misunderstood by the user. The database administrator can help unsophisticated SQL users avoid the potential problems of the join operation by creating a view which is a join of some tables. Then the user would perceive the tables as a single table. Such a user could then utilize just those techniques described in Parts 1 through 3 of this text. This approach involves extra effort by the database administrator. However, it simplifies the user's task and removes a potential source of error. The next example illustrates the creation of such a view.

Sample Statement 19.8   Create a view called VCSD which is the join of the COURSE, STAFF, and DEPARTMENT tables on the columns containing the department identifier values. VCSD should contain all the columns from these base tables with the exception of the department identifiers, which will be equal to each other and, therefore, should occur only once in the view.

```
CREATE   VIEW VCSD AS
         SELECT     CNO, CNAME, CDESCP, CRED, CLABFEE,
                    DEPARTMENT.DEPT, DBLD, DROOM,
                    DCHFNO, ENAME, ETITLE, ESALARY
         FROM       COURSE, STAFF, DEPARTMENT
         WHERE      CDEPT = STAFF.DEPT
         AND        CDEPT = DEPARTMENT.DEPT
```

System Response

Like all previous CREATE statements, the system should display a message confirming the successful creation of the object.

Comments

1. Recall that certain rows from the STAFF table and the DEPARTMENT table will not appear in the join result. The creator of this view should be aware of this fact and verify that it is acceptable within the context of the application environment. This would be the case for the following sample query where we make the same semantic assumptions specified in Chap. 15. Namely, a staff member can tutor any course offered by his department; the staff member is also located in the same building and room as is specified for his department in the DEPARTMENT table.

2. Because DEPT is a column in both the STAFF and DEPARTMENT tables, the SELECT statement must qualify the column names. The view inherited the column name DEPT from the DEPARTMENT.DEPT column, which contains the department identifiers. It does not inherit the qualifier (DEPARTMENT). The complete column name in the view becomes VCSD.DEPT. The SELECT statement in the view definition could have referenced STAFF.DEPT instead of DEPARTMENT.DEPT, in which case the view column would still inherit the same name (VCSD.DEPT).

   The content of the view would be the same if the SELECT clause referenced CDEPT, in which case the view would have inherited the name of CDEPT (really VCSD.CDEPT). We could have explicitly named the view columns using the technique shown in Sample Statement 19.4.

3. If we wanted to include all base table columns in the view, especially the three identical columns containing the department identifier values, then we would have to code the department identifier column names such that they are unique. Furthermore, we must explicitly name the view columns because inheritance would imply that two columns would be named DEPT, which is invalid. For example, the SELECT clause in the CREATE VIEW statement could be written as

```
CREATE VIEW
VCSD2 (CNO, CNAME, CDESCP, CRED, CLABFEE, CDEPT, DDEPT, DBLD, DROOM,
DCHFNO, SDEPT, ENAME, ETITLE, ESALARY)
    AS
SELECT CNO, CNAME, CDESCP, CRED, CLABFEE, CDEPT,
DEPARTMENT.DEPT, DBLD, DROOM, DCHFNO,
STAFF.DEPT, ENAME, ETITLE, ESALARY
FROM    COURSE, STAFF, DEPARTMENT
WHERE   CDEPT = STAFF.DEPT
AND     CDEPT = DEPARTMENT.DEPT
```

In this view, the three columns containing the department identifiers are named CDEPT, DDEPT, and SDEPT. Also note that the SELECT statement had to explicitly reference the name of every column in all three tables. A common error is the writing of a SELECT clause with an asterisk (SELECT * FROM ...). This would cause an error whenever the same column name is used in multiple tables. Such is the case with DEPT in the current example.

Sample Query 19.9   For any staff member who can tutor philosophy courses, display his name, the name of the course he can tutor, and his building and room location. Sort the result by staff member name.

SELECT	ENAME, CNAME, DBLD, DROOM
FROM	VCSD
WHERE	DEPT = 'PHIL'
ORDER	BY ENAME

ENAME	CNAME	DBLD	DROOM
DICK NIX	EMPIRICISM	HU	100
DICK NIX	RATIONALISM	HU	100
DICK NIX	EXISTENTIALISM	HU	100
DICK NIX	SOLIPSISM	HU	100
HANK KISS	SOLIPSISM	HU	100
HANK KISS	EXISTENTIALISM	HU	100
HANK KISS	RATIONALISM	HU	100
HANK KISS	EMPIRICISM	HU	100

Comment

This query is comparatively simple. The user extracts all the data from one (virtual) table instead of constructing a complex query using the join operation. The complexity of constructing the VCSD view has been passed onto the database administrator (where it belongs).

VIEW DEFINED ON ANOTHER VIEW

The SELECT statement which defines a view can itself reference another view. The next example creates a view based on the CISC view which is, in turn, based on the COURSE base table. (See Sample Statement 19.1.)

Sample Statement 19.10   Create a view called VCHEAPCISC, which contains rows for CIS courses with a cheap lab fee. These are CIS courses with a lab fee less than $100. The view should contain just the CNAME and CLABFEE columns and inherit those column names.

```
CREATE    VIEW VCHEAPCISC AS

          SELECT    CNAME, CLABFEE

          FROM      CISC

          WHERE     CLABFEE < 100
```

System Response

Like all previous CREATE statements, the system should display a message confirming the successful creation of the object.

Comments

1. All the data required for the VCHEAPCISC view are found in the CISC view. It may be the case that the user does not have access to the COURSE table, but does have access to CISC. Hence, the FROM clause in the SELECT statement references CISC.

2. *Restrictions.*   Obviously, the previous restriction on view definition applies. (No ORDER BY clause is allowed.)

3. Can we define another view on the VCHEAPCISC view? (Can we base a view on a view on a view, etc.?) Yes. There is no arbitrary limit on the number of views dependent on other views.

Sample Query 19.11   Display the entire VCHEAPCISC table.

```
SELECT   *

FROM     VCHEAPCISC
```

CNAME	CLABFEE
DATA STRUCTURES	50.00
DISCRETE MATHEMATICS	.00
DIGITAL CIRCUITS	.00

Comments

1. Observe that only CIS department courses appear in the result. This is because the underlying view, CISC, allows access to only CIS courses.

2. The lab fee values are all less than $100, as prescribed in the definition of VCHEAPCISC.

Exercises

19C. Create a view of the FACULTY table, called VFSAL, which presents the highest and lowest salaries of faculty members by department. The columns in the view will have the names of DEPARTMENT, HIGHEST_SALARY, and LOWEST_SALARY. Issue a SELECT statement against this view and examine the results.

19D. Create a view on the view FPAYROLL which presents the average faculty salary and average number of dependents. Call the view FAVERAGES and use the column names FAVG_SAL and FAVGNUMDEP. Issue a SELECT statement against this view and examine the results.

VIEW UPDATE RESTRICTIONS

Sometimes it is possible to execute INSERT, UPDATE, and DELETE statements which reference a view. When allowed, the updates against the view are automatically applied to the underlying base table. However, there are some restrictions to these operations which are contingent on the view definition. In general, you can operate under the following assumption: "If it makes sense to update a view, and you have been granted permission to update the view, then you can (probably) update it."

Example 1.   Consider the CISC table (view) defined in Sample Statement 19.1. The content of this view, shown in Sample Query 19.2, is essentially a "mirror image" of the CIS rows in the COURSE table excluding the CDEPT column. Now consider each of the following two update operations as applied to CISC.

```
DELETE FROM CISC WHERE CNO = 'C66'
```

This statement would be allowed. The WHERE clause identifies the CISC row(s) to be deleted. The corresponding row(s) would be deleted in the COURSE table. The above statement "makes sense" and SQL/400 would apply the delete operation to the underlying base table.

```
UPDATE CISC SET CLABFEE = 25 WHERE CLABFEE = 0
```

This statement would be allowed. The WHERE clause identifies the CISC row(s) to be updated. The corresponding row(s) would be updated in the COURSE table. The above statement makes sense and SQL/400 would apply the update operation to the underlying base table.

Example 2. Consider the VCSTAT view defined in Sample Statement 19.6. This view is not a mirror image of some rows and columns in the underlying base table. The rows in VCSTAT are compressed by the SUM and AVG functions. Also the GROUP BY operation has effectively resequenced the rows. INSERT, UPDATE, and DELETE operations against VCSTAT just don't make sense and will *not* work. How would you apply them to COURSE? Accordingly, SQL/400 would reject any attempt at modifying VCSTAT.

Example 3. Consider the VCSD view defined in Sample Statement 19.8. This definition of this view contains a join operation. During a join operation some rows match with many other rows, producing duplicate data in the view table. This occurred in VCSD (see Sample Query 19.9). VCSD is not a mirror image of an underlying base table. This is an example of a view utilizing multiple tables which *prohibit* the use of an INSERT, DELETE or UPDATE.

These examples show that some reasonable update operations can be applied to mirror-image views. Other views cannot be updated. This is true. But our notion of "mirror image" is just a conceptual analogy which corresponds to the precise rules specified in the SQL/400 reference manual, which states that

1. You can DELETE rows in a base table through a view if the view definition references just one table (e.g., no join operation) and does not contain GROUP BY, DISTINCT, or any group function.

2. You can UPDATE rows in a base table through a view if the view definition observes the above restrictions and, furthermore, does not update a column defined with an expression.

3. You can INSERT rows into a base table through a view if the view definition observes both the above restrictions and, furthermore, the view does not exclude any of the NOT NULL columns from the base table.

We conclude our discussion of view update by mentioning that these rules are imperfect because there are circumstances where it does make sense to update a view but SQL/400 prohibits the update operation. We invite you to find an example of such a circumstance. We note that all relational DBMS products have some imperfections pertaining to the view-update process. This is because the view-update problem is still an open area of database research.

DROP VIEW STATEMENT

This chapter illustrated the creation of five views (CISC, VEXPCOURSE, VCSTAT, VCSD, and VCHEAPCISC). The DROP VIEW statement is very simple and can be used to remove the view from the database. The next example demonstrates its use.

Sample Statement 19.12   Drop the VCSTAT table from the database. More precisely, drop the VCSTAT view.

```
DROP VIEW VCSTAT
```

System Response

The system will display a message confirming that VCSTAT has been dropped.

The next example drops a view on which another view is based. When this occurs, all views dependent on the dropped view are also dropped.

Sample Statement 19.13   Drop the CISC "table" from the database. More precisely, drop the CISC view.

```
DROP VIEW CISC
```

Comment

This statement drops both CISC and VCHEAPCISC, a view which is dependent on CISC.

The DROP TABLE statement will cause all views which are dependent on the base table to be dropped. Hence, dropping the COURSE table would cause all the views created by the sample statements illustrated in this chapter to be dropped.

Exercises

19E. Drop the view VFSAL which was created in Exercise 19C. Issue a SELECT statement against this view and notice the system response.

19F. Drop the view FPAYROLL. Issue a SELECT statement against the view FAVERAGES, which was based on the FPAYROLL view.

SUMMARY

We conclude this chapter by noting that the CREATE VIEW statement is quite simple because it utilizes the SELECT statement as a vehicle for defining a view. The only potential problems pertain to the restrictions for defining and updating views.

Summary Exercises

19G. Create a view called VTHEOSTAFF based on the STAFF table. It is to reflect the ENAME, ESALARY, and ETITLE information for all staff members assigned to the THEO department.

19H. Create a view which represents the average salary of all staff members assigned to each department. The view will be called VAVG_STAFF and will have the column names of DEPT and AVG_SALARY.

19I. Create a view based on the VTHEOSTAFF view which represents the total of the salaries for all staff members in the THEO department.

19J. Create a view which reflects the join of the FACULTY, COURSE, and CLASS tables. The view is to represent the name of the faculty member teaching the class and the name of the course for all courses for which there are class offerings. Use the column names of INSTR and COURSE_NME. The view will be called VINSTR.

19K. Drop the VTHEOSTAFF view.

19L. Can you issue an UPDATE statement against the VCSD view created in Sample Statement 19.8?

Database Security

Database security is a broad topic which can be examined from the systems administrator, database administrator, professional programmer, or casual user point of view. SQL/400 has a comprehensive authorization subsystem which allows for the protection of any database object from illegitimate access or manipulation. The general scheme involves identification of: (1) who the user is, (2) what object is referenced, and (3) what processes can be executed against the specified object. This chapter will examine the authorization scheme from the programmer-user point of view. SQL/400 supports the GRANT and REVOKE statements which are used to grant and subsequently retract database privileges.

The following sample statements assume that the database administrator has granted you permission to create tables. We assume that you previously executed the CREATE TABLE statement to create the COURSE table. SQL/400 then recognizes you as the creator of this table. As creator of the COURSE table, you automatically have all privileges (to be described below) on this table. Also, with the exception of the system manager known as QSECOFR, no other users have any privileges on the COURSE table until you grant them such privileges. The following examples illustrate how you can use the GRANT statement to pass privileges to other users.

SQL/400 object security and access is implemented in multiple levels. For Query Manager users it involves Query Manager Profiles, SQL/400 security (GRANT, REVOKE), and AS/400 object security. GRANT and REVOKE use system commands (GRTOBJAUT, RVKOBJAUT) to set security for SQL objects. These system commands can also be used directly against SQL objects. Note that System Catalog Tables can only be secured with system security commands.

THE GRANT STATEMENT

The general syntax of the GRANT statement is described below. Note that the execution of a single statement allows for the granting of many privileges on an object to many users.

```
GRANT    privilege-1, privilege-2, ...
ON       object
TO       username-1, username-2, ...
```

We describe each of the above parameters within the context of table privileges.

Object.   The object may be a base table or a view.

Privileges.   The following privileges pertain to base tables or views.

- ALL
- DELETE
- INDEX
- INSERT
- SELECT
- UPDATE

   The granting of a particular privilege means that the user who is granted the privilege can execute the corresponding statement against the specified object. The SELECT, INSERT, UPDATE, and DELETE privileges can be granted on a base table or a view. The INDEX privilege can only be granted on a base table. The SELECT, INSERT, and DELETE privileges pertain to entire rows of a base table or view.

   Granting UPDATE privileges allows the user to update any column in the base table or view. You can also grant all the above privileges by specifying selecting the ALL privilege.

Username.   Your username is typically the same sign-on identifier used to access the AS/400. There is a special username, PUBLIC, which can be specified when you wish to grant a privilege to all users.

GRANTING PRIVILEGES ON A BASE TABLE

Sample Statement 20.1   You would like to give MOE permission to display your COURSE table. You do not want him to be able to perform any other operations involving this table. More precisely, you would like to grant SELECT privileges on COURSE to MOE.

```
GRANT   SELECT
ON      COURSE
TO      MOE
```

System Response

The system displays a message which confirms the granting of the privilege.

Comments

1. The general syntax of the GRANT statement is rather straightforward as described on the previous page.

2. MOE (really the person with the username of MOE) can now issue any valid SELECT statement referencing your COURSE table. He can display all columns of all rows.

3. Query Manager users should note that MOE should also have the access to the SQL command which is controlled by the Query Manager Profiles.

GRANTING PRIVILEGES ON A VIEW

Sample Statement 20.2   Allow LARRY and CURLEY to display just those rows from the COURSE table corresponding to courses offered by the CIS department. Also allow them to delete any row corresponding to a CIS course. Assume you have already created the CISC view as described in Sample Statement 19.1.

GRANT   SELECT, DELETE

ON   CISC

TO   LARRY, CURLEY

System Response

The system displays a message which confirms the granting of the privileges.

Comments

1. This example illustrates the general approach to database security for application data. Typically, the database administrator creates base tables. Then the DBA grants access on certain tables to certain views so they can do the least amount of damage. This is done by:

    a. Creating a view which limits the user's access to some subset of rows and/or columns in a base table.

    b. Granting some, usually not all, privileges on views to individual users.

    This scheme provides a simple but powerful and flexible approach to database security.

2. LARRY and CURLEY can now issue SELECT and DELETE statements against CISC. They cannot issue any statement against the COURSE table.

3. LARRY and CURLEY cannot grant their newly received privileges to other users. (This capability should be supported in DB2/400 which will support the WITH GRANT OPTION clause.)

THE REVOKE STATEMENT

Any granted privilege can subsequently be revoked by executing the REVOKE statement. The syntax is similar to the GRANT statement, but it has the opposite effect. The general syntax is

```
REVOKE   privilege-1, privilege-2, ...
ON       object
FROM     username-1, username-2, ...
```

The following example demonstrates this statement.

Sample Statement 20.3 CURLEY has abused his update privilege on CISC. Revoke his UPDATE privileges but allow him to retain his SELECT privilege.

REVOKE   UPDATE

ON   CISC

FROM   CURLEY

Comments

1. After you execute this statement, the system will reject any UPDATE statement issued by CURLEY which references CISC.

2. You can revoke all privileges on an object by using the ALL keyword. (REVOKE ALL ON ...)

REFERENCING ANOTHER USER'S TABLE

Assume that you have been granted privileges on a table or view created by another user. Under these circumstances you must reference the table or view by its complete name. This means that you must include the library or collection as a prefix to the table name, or add the library to your library list. Otherwise, the system will assume your current library list, resulting in an error because you are not the creator of the table or view.

Sample Statement 20.4   In Sample Statement 20.1 we granted SELECT privileges on COURSE to MOE. Assume that the COURSE table resides in the SQLTST library. What statement must MOE execute in order to display the COURSE table?

SELECT *

FROM   SQLTST/COURSE

CNO	CNAME	CDESCP	CRED	CLABFEE	CDEPT
T11	SCHOLASTICISM	FOR THE PIOUS	3	150.00	THEO
T12	FUNDAMENTALISM	FOR THE CAREFREE	3	90.00	THEO
T33	HEDONISM	FOR THE SANE	3	.00	THEO
T44	COMMUNISM	FOR THE GREEDY	6	200.00	THEO
P11	EMPIRICISM	SEE IT-BELIEVE IT	3	100.00	PHIL
P22	RATIONALISM	FOR CIS MAJORS	3	50.00	PHIL
P33	EXISTENTIALISM	FOR CIS MAJORS	3	200.00	PHIL
P44	SOLIPSISM	ME MYSELF AND I	6	.00	PHIL
C11	INTRO TO CS	FOR ROOKIES	3	100.00	CIS
C22	DATA STRUCTURES	VERY USEFUL	3	50.00	CIS
C33	DISCRETE MATHEMATICS	ABSOLUTELY NECESSARY	3	.00	CIS
C44	DIGITAL CIRCUITS	AH HA!	3	.00	CIS
C55	COMPUTER ARCH.	VON NEUMANN'S MACH.	3	100.00	CIS
C66	RELATIONAL DATABASE	THE ONLY WAY TO GO	3	500.00	CIS

SUMMARY

In this chapter we introduced the notion of database security through the SQL GRANT and REVOKE statements. The AS/400 has a very rich implementation of security options, the details of which are far beyond the scope of this book. This chapter has attempted to provide some basic background so that you are aware of the impact of authority settings when you attempt to access a table or view.

You can use the DSPOBJAUT system command to determine which privileges have been granted to you. The system level security options are related to SQL/400 as follows.

SQL option	Object			Data			
	Opr	Mgt	Exist	Read	Add	Update	Delete
Delete	X						X
Index		X					
Insert	X				X		
Select	X			X			
Update	X					X	
All	X	X		X	X	X	X

Data authorities relate to what can be done to data contained within an object (file/table). The Object authorities relate to what can be done to an object. For example:

Operational (Opr) specifies whether you may look at an object and access data as allowed by Data authorities.

Management (Mgt) specifies whether you have the ability to specify authority, move or rename the object, and add members if the object is a database file.

We conclude this chapter with a final word of warning. The default Object authority for a SQL object created with Query Manager is controlled by the Query Manager Profiles. The standard default is *ALL for the table owner and *Change for PUBLIC, which gives all users full data access to your table. You may wish to modify these defaults.

Summary Exercises

20A. Grant SELECT and INSERT privileges on the STAFF table to CURLEY.

20B. Grant all privileges on the DEPARTMENT table to PUBLIC. Revoke all privileges granted to PUBLIC on the DEPARTMENT table.

Exploring SQL/400 Collections

In previous chapters we assumed that you wished to use SQL statements to display and update data stored in preexisting "native" AS/400 files. This same data appeared as a set of files to RPG and COBOL users, or, as a set of tables to SQL/400 users. Under this scenario, collections were not necessary.

In this chapter, we assume that you are not interested in preexisting AS/400 files. Instead, we assume that you are implementing a new system and you wish to operate entirely within the "SQL/400 world." As illustrated in previous chapters, you will execute CREATE statements to define your database. Then you will use SELECT, INSERT, UPDATE, and DELETE statements to manipulate your database. However, in this scenario, you will define one or more collections *before* you create any database tables, views, or indexes.

A collection is really an AS/400 library which will contain specified tables, views, and indexes. In this respect, a collection is similar to any "good old" AS/400 library. However, creating a collection provides some additional services. One such service is the creation and automatic maintenance of a data dictionary catalogue for SQL/400 users. A strong argument can be made that a data dictionary is a critical component of any relational DBMS. For this reason we believe that you should give serious consideration to creating collections before you create any tables, indexes, or views.

In this chapter we will describe:

- How to create a collection
- How to create tables, views, and indexes within a collection
- How to utilize the data dictionary

CREATING A COLLECTION

Sample Statement 21.1   Create a collection called SQLTEST.

CREATE COLLECTION SQLTEST

System Response

The system should display a message which confirms that the collection has been created.

Comments

1. Because a new collection is really a new AS/400 library, we assume that the collection name, SQLTEST, is not already in use as the name of some other previously defined library. Subsequent CREATE statements will create database objects (files) in the new collection (library).

2. The CREATE COLLECTION statement will automatically create the following objects within the collection.

   a. *Data dictionary.*   A set of tables that will describe the tables, columns, views, and indexes to be created within the collection.

   b. *Catalog.*   A series of tables (which are really views) based upon the data dictionary tables. Some of these views will be described below. This chapter will present sample queries which examine these catalog tables.

   c. *Journals.*   Files that keep track of changes to application tables. These files, which are used for transaction processing, will be discussed in the next chapter.

   Because the CREATE COLLECTION statement creates these objects, it might take a few minutes to complete.

3. Most users will not have authority to execute the CREATE COLLECTION statement. You may have to ask your system administrator to execute this statement for you.

CATALOG TABLES

The following tables (really views) are created when you create a collection. You can examine these tables using a SELECT statement. The information stored in these tables describes any tables, views, and indexes which are created within a collection. We briefly summarize the catalog tables.

SYSTABLES	Contains one row for every table and view in the collection.
SYSCOLUMNS	Contains one row for each column of every table and view in the collection.
SYSINDEXES	Contains one row for every index in the collection.
SYSKEYS	Contains one row for each column of every index in the collection.
SYSVIEWS	Contains one or more rows for each view in the collection.
SYSVIEWDEP	Records the dependencies of views.
SYSPACKAGE	Contains one row for each package in the collection (packages pertain to embedded SQL which is beyond the scope of this text.)

Sample Queries 21.5 through 21.10 will identify and display selected columns from some of these tables. You are encouraged to examine your SQL/400 reference manual for a more detailed description of the information contained within these tables.

CREATING OBJECTS WITHIN A COLLECTION

After a collection has been created, you can place database objects in the collection using the CREATE TABLE, CREATE VIEW, and CREATE INDEX statements. The names of the objects are specified using the "dot notation." The following sample statements illustrate this notation with different CREATE statements.

Sample Statement 21.2   Create the COURSE table in the SQLTEST collection.

```
CREATE  TABLE  SQLTEST.COURSE
    (CNO      CHAR (3)        NOT NULL,
    CNAME     VARCHAR (22)    NOT NULL,
    CDESCP    VARCHAR (25)    NOT NULL,
    CRED      INTEGER,
    CLABFEE   DECIMAL (5,2),
    CDEPT     CHAR (4)        NOT NULL)
```

System Response

The system should display a message which confirms that the table has been created.

Comments

1. The name of the table, SQLTEST.COURSE, illustrates the dot notation. This notation requires that the collection name precede the table name with a period (.) as a separator.

2. When you wish to use the dot notation in Query Manager, your user profile naming convention *must* be set to SAA.

3. Finally, note that your default QM Library or Library List must include the name of the collection.

The use of the dot notation is optional for the CREATE TABLE, CREATE VIEW, and CREATE INDEX statements if the appropriate name is specified for the default QM Library.

Sample Statement 21.3   Assume SQLTEST is the default QM Library. Create a view on the COURSE table in this library.

```
CREATE  VIEW VCOURSE AS

SELECT  CNO, CNAME, CDESCP

FROM    COURSE
```

System Response

The system should display a message which confirms that the view has been created.

Comment

Observe that neither the view name (VCOURSE) nor the table name (COURSE) uses the dot notation to explicitly reference the SQLTEST collection. However, the view was created in SQLTEST and the dictionary was updated because SQLTEST was specified as the default QM library.

Sample Statement 21.4   Again, assume SQLTEST is the default QM Library. Create a unique index on the COURSE table in this library.

```
CREATE UNIQUE INDEX XCOURSE

ON SQLTEST.COURSE (CNO)
```

System Response

The system should display a message which confirms that the index has been created.

Comment

This example explicitly used the dot notation to reference the SQLTEST collection even though it was not necessary.

EXPLORING THE CATALOG

The following sample queries illustrate use of the SELECT statement to explore the catalog tables introduced in Sample Statement 21.1. We assume that the COURSE table, VCOURSE view, and XCOURSE index have been created in the SQLTEST collection. We also assume that other tables, views, and indexes have also been created in this collection.

Sample Query 21.5   Assume the default library is SQLTEST. Display the names of all tables in this collection.

```
SELECT  NAME

FROM    SYSTABLES

WHERE   TYPE = 'T'
```

FILE NAME
_____

COURSE
FACULTY
STAFF
DEPARTMENT
REGISTRAT
CLASS
STUDENT
etc.

Comments

1. The SELECT clause references the NAME and TYPE columns in SYSTABLES. However, Query Manager will often display a column heading (e.g., FILE NAME) which does not exactly match the column name.

2. In addition to application tables (e.g., COURSE, STAFF), SYSTABLES also contains rows (not shown above) which describe dictionary tables and catalog views. This means that the catalog is self-descriptive.

3. Examination of the displayed result illustrates there are at least seven tables in SQLTEST. The WHERE clause identified rows where the TYPE column contained "T" corresponding to "Table." This condition excluded those rows which describe objects other than tables.

4. SYSTABLES also contains other columns which are described in the SQL/400 reference manual.

Sample Query 21.6 What if you forgot the names and data types of the columns in the COURSE table? You could examine SYSCOLUMNS to display this information.

```
SELECT  NAME, COLTYPE

FROM    SQLTEST.SYSCOLUMNS

WHERE   TBNAME = 'COURSE'
```

FIELD NAME	DATA TYPE
CNO	CHAR
CNAME	VARCHAR
CDESCP	VARCHAR
CRED	INTEGER
CLABFEE	NUMERIC
CDEPT	CHAR

Comment

Again, note that Query Manager displays column headings which do not exactly correspond with the column names.

Sample Query 21.7 Examine SYSVIEWS. Display the name and definition of every view in SQLTEST which has a name which begins with "V".

```
SELECT  NAME, TEXT

FROM    SYSVIEWS

WHERE   NAME LIKE 'V%'
```

FILE NAME	SQL CREATE TEXT
VCOURSE	CREATE VIEW VCOURSE AS SELECT CNO, CNAME, CDESCP FROM SQLTEST/COURSE
VSIX	CREATE VIEW VSIX AS SELECT CNO FROM SQLTEST/COURSE WHERE CRED = 6

Comment

Note that the view text contains a reference to the COURSE table using the "slash notation."

Sample Query 21.8   What table does the VCOURSE view depend upon?

```
SELECT  BNAME
FROM    SYSVIEWDEP
WHERE   DNAME = 'VCOURSE'
```

BNAME
_____
COURSE

Comment

The results of the query show that the VCOURSE view was defined over the table COURSE.

Sample Query 21.9   What is the name of any index defined on the COURSE table?

```
SELECT  NAME
FROM    SYSINDEXES
WHERE   TBNAME = 'COURSE'
```

NAME
_____
XCOURSE

Comment

The result shows that there is only one index defined for the COURSE table. However, we do not know what specific column(s) it is defined on. This information is stored in the SYSKEYS table.

Sample Query 21.10   What column is referenced by the XCOURSE index.

```
SELECT  COLNAME

FROM    SYSKEYS

WHERE   IXNAME = 'XCOURSE'
```

FIELD NAME
CNO

Comment

We can now deduce that the XCOURSE index is defined on the CNO column. Naturally, it would have been better to have initially created a more meaningful name for the index (e.g., XCNO).

SUMMARY

This chapter introduced collections. We introduced the data dictionary which is a useful feature provided by a collection. We remind you that the dictionary is self-descriptive. SYSTABLES contains the names of every table in the collection, including the dictionary tables.

Summary Exercises

21A. Display the names of the dictionary tables which begin with "SYS".

21B. Display the table and corresponding column names of the "SYS" dictionary tables.

22

Commitment Control

Chapter 13 introduced the INSERT, UPDATE, and DELETE statements. For most production information systems these statements are usually, but not always, placed within application programs. However, there are occasions when these statements will be executed within an interactive environment. When this is necessary, the user should follow procedures which ensure database integrity. An important consideration within this context is the specification of database transactions. This chapter introduces the concept of a transaction and two new SQL statements, COMMIT and ROLLBACK. In the AS/400 community the term "commitment control" is often used instead of "transaction processing." We will use both terms interchangeably.

Before we describe transaction processing, we note that transaction processing within Query Manager requires that your tables be stored in collections. This is because the system utilizes the journal files mentioned in Sample Statement 21.1. You cannot execute the COMMIT and ROLLBACK statements when processing "native" files with Query Manager.

PRELIMINARY EXAMPLE

The first example does not introduce any new SQL reserved words, but it does illustrate the objectives of transaction processing. For this example, assume the COURSE table contains a row for a course with a CNO value of "XXX". Also assume there are classes on this course described in the CLASS table and there are student registrations for these classes in the REGISTRAT table.

Sample Statement 22.1   Assume course "XXX" has been dropped from the curriculum. Hence its row must be removed from the COURSE table. Furthermore, all class offerings for this course must be removed from the CLASS table. Registrations for those classes must be removed from the REGISTRAT table.

```
DELETE

FROM REGISTRAT

WHERE CNO = 'XXX'


DELETE

FROM CLASS

WHERE CNO = 'XXX'


DELETE

FROM COURSE

WHERE CNO = 'XXX'
```

System Response

The system should display a message after each DELETE statement which confirms that the rows have been deleted.

Comment

The example shows three independent DELETE statements. However, from the user's viewpoint, these changes constitute a single "logical unit of work" equivalent to the deletion of all rows from all tables which reference the course with the CNO value of "XXX". This logical unit of work is called a database *transaction*. This single transaction requires the execution of multiple DELETE statements because multiple tables need to be changed. The next example will illustrate how to bundle the set of DELETE statements to form a single transaction.

Why is it necessary to define the three DELETE statements as a single transaction just because the user sees this as a single logical unit of work? Assuming that each DELETE statement is correct, why not simply execute each statement? In other words, why bundle? The answer to this question lies in recognition of events which are beyond the control of the SQL user.

Computer systems "go down." This can happen in the middle of a terminal session when you are executing any of the three DELETE statements. What is the status of the database if the computer goes down at some time just before, during, or after you have issued the second DELETE statement? If this happens, you cannot be sure if the updates to the CLASS table actually occurred. (In fact, you cannot even be sure that the changes for the first DELETE statement were written to the disk before the problem occurred.) You could verify the status by displaying the tables. However, this usually is not practical, especially if the tables are large.

What we want is an all-or-nothing situation. Either all the rows in all three tables containing a CNO value of "XXX" have been deleted or none of them have. If all rows which reference "XXX" are deleted, we have realized our objective. If none are deleted, we have to start all over again. This requires some extra effort, but it is the necessary cost of database integrity. This all-or-nothing situation is exactly what a transaction provides.

DEFINING A TRANSACTION

In the previous example we observed that the three separate DELETE statements are logically related. It would be unacceptable if only the first one or two statements, but not the third, executed successfully. How is the system able to ensure that if only some of the statements execute successfully that their effect will be canceled? The answer is that the system will consider the initial changes as "tentative" until the completion of the transaction occurs. If a problem is encountered prior to the successful completion of all statements in the transaction, then the tentative changes will be undone. Obviously, the system must be informed of which SQL statements constitute the transaction. In other words, we must define the boundaries of each transaction. This is done by specifying *synchronization points*.

Synchronization points, often called *sync points,* define the scope of a database transaction. A sync point is usually established at the beginning of each terminal session or application program. Thereafter, the user or programmer can use the COMMIT and ROLLBACK statements to specify other sync points. These statements establish the end of a previous transaction and the beginning of a new transaction. Under normal circumstances, a transaction is concluded by executing the following.

- A COMMIT statement which informs the system that all changes made within the transaction are acceptable and that they should be applied to the database.

- A ROLLBACK statement which informs the system that an unacceptable situation has been encountered and that any changes made since the start of the transaction are to be voided.

If the computer system goes down in the middle of a transaction (before you can issue either a COMMIT or ROLLBACK statement), any changes to the database specified within that transaction are automatically undone. This is because SQL/400 has a recovery subsystem which will automatically issue a ROLLBACK statement for all transactions which were pending when the problem occurred. Of course, this means that you have to reissue those update statements which were undone.

The COMMIT and ROLLBACK statements will be illustrated in the next two sample statements.

COMMIT STATEMENT

The function of the COMMIT statement is to terminate a transaction and cause any update operations to be applied to the database and thus made permanent.

Sample Statement 22.2   Assume course "XXX" has been dropped from the curriculum. Remove all references to this course from the COURSE, CLASS, and REGISTRAT tables. Bundle the changes into a single transaction to be committed after successful execution of all DELETE statements.

```
DELETE
FROM REGISTRAT
WHERE CNO = 'XXX'


DELETE
FROM CLASS
WHERE CNO = 'XXX'


DELETE
FROM COURSE
WHERE CNO = 'XXX'


COMMIT
```

System Response

The system should display a message after each DELETE statement which confirms that the rows have been deleted. It should also issue a message indicating successful completion of the COMMIT operation.

Comments

1. The COMMIT statement caused the delete operations to become permanent. All three tables were updated to reflect the removal of the rows with a CNO value of "XXX."

2. With transaction processing, the system uses a "locking" technique to insure that two users do not access the same record at the same time. The system will attach a lock to a row when it accesses that row on behalf of a user. This lock effectively prohibits another user from accessing the same row until the first user completes a transaction (i.e., performs a commit or rollback). This is necessary to provide database integrity.

3. SQL/400 supports four levels of transaction control. These levels are specified in the profile for Query Manager users. Each level provides a greater level of row/record locking.

NONE	Commitment Control is not active. This is a potential integrity problem if multiple users are accessing the same data.
CHG	*Change* specifies that rows that were updated, inserted, or deleted will be locked until a COMMIT or ROLLBACK is executed. It is possible for two users to simultaneously read the same row. This likewise has potential problems in the event that one of the users updates the row after reading it.
CS	*Cursor Stability* specifies that rows that were updated, inserted, or deleted will be locked until a COMMIT or ROLLBACK is executed. In addition locks are placed on all rows identified by the WHERE clause in a SELECT statement. Each lock stays in effect until you scroll beyond the selected rows.
ALL	*All* rows that were read, updated, inserted, or deleted will be locked until a COMMIT or ROLLBACK is executed.

ROLLBACK STATEMENT

The following example illustrates the use of the ROLLBACK statement to undo changes made to the COURSE table.

Sample Statement 22.3   Assume you were told that all classes for course number "C11" were canceled and, therefore, you should delete all rows which reference this course in the CLASS and REGISTRAT tables. After you enter the DELETE statements (but before you commit them), you decide to undo them because you feel that this action should be confirmed by the CIS department chairperson.

```
DELETE
FROM REGISTRAT
WHERE CNO = 'C11'


DELETE
FROM CLASS
WHERE CNO = 'C11'


ROLLBACK
```

System Response

The system should display a message after each DELETE statement which confirms that the rows have been tentatively deleted. It should also issue a message indicating that completion of the ROLLBACK operation was successful, meaning that the tentative deletions were not applied to the table.

Comment

If you displayed the REGISTRAT table after executing the first DELETE statement but before executing the second DELETE statement, you would observe that the C11 rows were deleted. If you examined the CLASS table after executing the second DELETE statement you would observe that the C11 rows were deleted. Finally, after executing the ROLLBACK statement, displaying the rows from other tables would again show the presence of the C11 rows.

DATABASE RECOVERY

The ROLLBACK statement allows you to undo any uncommitted changes to the database. But what if you discover update errors after they have been committed? You could execute further update statements to make corrections. But this is potentially dangerous, especially if the changes are complex. This could lead to a loss of database integrity. It is safer to undo the committed changes. The undoing of committed changes requires the intervention of the DBA who would execute special system utility programs to restore the database to a previous state. An examination of SQL/400's recovery system is beyond the scope of this text. However, because the recovery subsystem is based on the transaction concept, it is important that users define their logical units of work and establish transactions via proper utilization of the COMMIT and ROLLBACK statements.

SUMMARY

This chapter introduced two new SQL statements, COMMIT and ROLLBACK, which allow the definition of a logical unit of work called a *transaction*. The effect of these two statements is to mark the end of one transaction and the beginning of another, thus establishing what is called a *sync point*. The COMMIT statement causes all pending database changes (those which occurred after the last sync point) to be committed. The ROLLBACK statement causes the pending changes to be undone. The effect is just as if the update statements had never been executed.

We conclude by noting two default actions on the part of the system.

1. Some SQL statements automatically cause an implicit commit. These include the CREATE and DROP statements.

2. The user must issue a COMMIT before exiting an interactive session or the system will perform a ROLLBACK on the noncommitted transactions.

3. Care should be used when using commitment control in an interactive environment, as careless use could delay other users from accessing information.

Summary Exercise

22A. Check your profile. Make sure Commitment Control is not set to NONE. Delete all CIS rows from the COURSE table. Display the table to verify their (tentative) removal. Now issue the ROLLBACK statement. Again, display the COURSE table and observe that the tentative changes have been undone; the CIS rows are back in the table.

7

DB2/400:
SQL/400 Joins the DB2 Family

This part presents an overview of the significant database enhancements anticipated in OS/400 version 3. This new version OS/400 will contain an integrated database management system called DB2/400. This enhancement can be perceived as a revision and a renaming of the SQL/400 database system. The new DB2 label places this product in the same family as IBM's major DBMS product, DB2, which runs in a mainframe MVS environment. We note that, unlike SQL/400, DB2/400 is integrated with and is actually a part of the OS/400 system.

The technical evolution that this change represents is significant. The additions and changes enhance the database implementation with functional compatibilities that represent "main stream" industry implementations provided by other IBM products (e.g., DB2/MVS, DB2/6000, DB2/2) and non-IBM products (e.g., ORACLE, SYBASE, INFORMIX, INGRES). It is important to note that the SQL/400 statements described in Parts 1–6 will still work as described. The changes will be "under the hood" and should not seriously impact SQL users and application programmers. However, you will find some of the new features to be very useful.

Previous chapters have prepared you to understand and exploit these new features. As with any product announcement the final release may differ to some degree from the initial descriptions. The primary goal of this part of the book is to provide a conceptual understanding of the anticipated changes and their impact on the use of SQL in the AS/400 world.

There are a number of major enhancements. This part is organized into three chapters with each chapter devoted to one of the following topics.

- *Database Integrity in DB2/400 (Chap. 23)*
- *DB2/400 in a Client-Server Environment (Chap. 24)*
- *DB2/400 Application Programming Interfaces (Chap. 25)*

Database Integrity in DB2/400

Chapter 12 introduced the concepts of entity integrity and referential integrity. (We encourage you to review this chapter prior to reading this section.) We noted that the current version of SQL/400 does not directly support these notions. A major, perhaps the most significant, feature of DB2/400 is direct (declarative) support for entity integrity and referential integrity.

It can be argued that without automatic support for database integrity, the SQL/400 product is really no more than a query language used within a decision support system. The integrity mechanism (along with other features) means that the use of SQL with DB2/400 will become a true production database management system.

This chapter will review the ideas of entity and referential integrity and describe how these features are implemented in DB2/400.

DECLARATIVE ENTITY INTEGRITY

DB2/400 allows the specification of the PRIMARY KEY clause in the CREATE TABLE statement. This allows you to identify a column (or group of columns) as the primary key of a table. This approach to specifying a primary key is called *declarative* because it is explicitly specified in the CREATE TABLE statement rather than a do-it-yourself approach by the creation of a unique index.

DECLARATIVE REFERENTIAL INTEGRITY

Chapter 12 introduced the ideas related to the concepts of referential integrity. In a nutshell, referential integrity provides for the creation of constraints related to the relationship between parent and child tables. DB2/400 allows the specification of the FOREIGN KEY clause in the CREATE TABLE statement. This allows you to identify a column (or group of columns) as a foreign key. This approach is called "declarative" because it is explicitly specified in the CREATE TABLE statement rather than a do-it-yourself approach by using edit programs or triggers (to be described in Chapter 25). There are a number of constraints applicable to the notion of referential integrity. Before discussing these constraints we present a simple example.

Sample Statement 23.1 Create the same COURSE table shown in Sample Statement 12.1. This time specify CNO as the primary key and CDEPT as a foreign key referencing the DEPARTMENT table.

```
CREATE TABLE SQLTST/COURSE

      (CNO       CHAR(3)        NOT NULL,

      CNAME      VARCHAR(22)    NOT NULL,

      CDESCP     VARCHAR(25)    NOT NULL,

      CRED       INTEGER,

      CLABFEE    DECIMAL (5,2),

      CDEPT      CHAR(4)        NOT NULL,

PRIMARY KEY (CNO),

FOREIGN KEY (CDEPT)

         REFERENCES DEPARTMENT

         ON DELETE RESTRICT)
```

System Response

You should receive a system-generated message which states that the statement was successful. Note, however, that execution would fail if the DEPARTMENT did not exist. It would also fail if the DEPARTMENT table was created without a primary key.

Comments

1. The PRIMARY KEY clause identified CNO. Sometimes this clause can specify multiple columns. For example, the PRIMARY KEY clause for the CLASS table would be specified as shown below.

   ```
   PRIMARY KEY (CNO, SEC)
   ```

   The inclusion of this clause in a CREATE TABLE statement will cause DB2/400 to automatically create a unique index on the primary key column(s).

2. The FOREIGN KEY identified CDEPT as referencing the DEPARTMENT table. In particular, this means that each CDEPT value in the COURSE table must match some existing primary key (DEPT) value in the DEPARTMENT table. Some tables can have multiple foreign keys. Sometimes a foreign key can be composite. For example, the REGISTRAT table would have two FOREIGN KEY clauses as shown below.

   ```
   FOREIGN KEY (SNO) REFERENCES STUDENT
   FOREIGN KEY (CNO, SEC) REFERENCES CLASS
   ```

3. The FOREIGN KEY clause may also specify constraints. The current example shows ON DELETE RESTRICT. This means that any attempt to delete a "parent" row in the DEPARTMENT table would be rejected. For example, an attempt to delete the CIS row from the DEPARTMENT table would be rejected under the assumption that there are "CIS" values in the CDEPT column of the COURSE table. However, deleting the "MGT" row would be allowed. DB2/400 allows the specification of other constraint definitions. Other constraints are described on the following page.

4. The current example assumes that the COURSE table does not already exist. Sample Statement 23.2 illustrates the definition of primary and foreign keys for an existing table.

5. Although not an integrity issue, DB2/400 now supports longer column names and table names. These names can be up to 30 characters.

FOREIGN KEY CONSTRAINTS

We describe some but not all of the constraints which can be specified when you declare a FOREIGN KEY clause in a CREATE TABLE statement.

ON UPDATE RESTRICT. An UPDATE statement which modifies the primary key in the parent table is not allowed if a foreign key exists in the child table which matches that primary key.

ON DELETE CASCADE. Assume a DELETE operation is applied to a row in the parent table. This DELETE statement will automatically delete all rows in child table having a foreign key that matches the primary key of the row deleted in the parent table. For example, this clause would allow the deletion of the CIS department row from the DEPARTMENT table. It would also automatically delete all rows in the COURSE table with a "CIS" value in the CDEPT column.

ON DELETE SET NULL. Assume a DELETE operation is applied to a row in the parent table. This constraint option automatically sets any matching foreign key to NULL if the related primary key row in the parent table is deleted. Note that this does not remove the child table row. Furthermore, the column must not have been defined as NOT NULL at time of table creation.

ALTER TABLE STATEMENT

Assume the COURSE table already exists because we previously executed the CREATE TABLE statement in Sample Statement 12.1 (without any key definitions). DB2/400 now supports the ALTER TABLE statement. This statement allows you to add constraint definitions to existing tables.

Sample Statement 23.2   Alter the definition of the COURSE table to include the same primary-key and foreign-key constraints specified in the previous sample statement.

ALTER TABLE SQLTST/COURSE

ADD PRIMARY KEY (CNO)

ADD FOREIGN KEY (CDEPT)

    REFERENCES DEPARTMENT

System Response

You should receive a system-generated message which states that the statement was successful. However, execution would fail if the DEPARTMENT table did not exist or it was created without a primary key.

Comment

Other DB2 products provide additional capabilities through the ALTER TABLE statement. For example, you can use this statement to add new columns to an existing table. We expect DB2/400 to provide comparable support in the future.

SUMMARY

There are many integrity constraints which are not addressed by entity or referential integrity. For example, there may be a business rule which states that the average lab fee for a given department cannot exceed $300. Such rules are often called *user-defined* integrity rules.

DB2/400 has no general-purpose declarative mechanism for supporting user-defined integrity rules. The traditional approach is to have those programs which update the database perform edit processing to enforce these rules. However, DB2/400 does provide a procedural mechanism called a *trigger* which can be very useful in the enforcement of user-defined integrity rules. Because a trigger is actually a program, we postpone discussion of this topic until Chap. 25.

DB2/400: A Client-Server DBMS

Throughout this text we have focused on the syntax and semantics of SQL statements. (This is consistent with our primary objective as described in the Preface.) Except for a brief discussion of Query Manager, we have paid little attention to the hardware/software environment used to submit and examine the result of an SQL statement. However, because of (1) the recent popularity of *client-server* database management systems and (2) the new DB2/400 features which support client-server processing, we feel that it would be appropriate and helpful to present a brief overview of this topic. We will first explain the basic client-server concepts. Then we will describe how these concepts apply within the AS/400 world.

We begin by examining the notion of a *time-share* system. This will lay the foundation for our discussion of the distinct features and advantages of a client-server system. We conclude with a brief examination of distributed database management.

TIME-SHARE SYSTEMS

A time-share computing system allows multiple users to simultaneously access a computer. Time-share processing allows each user's interactive program to share time on the computer. A conventional AS/400 system supports time-share processing. Each user can enter commands from a terminal or a PC operating in terminal-emulation mode. The terminals/PCs use a communications network to request the services of the time-share system. The communications network can be a local area network (LAN) or a wide area network (WAN). Figure 24.1 shows the basic architecture of a time-share system. In the AS/400 world, the data could be an SQL/400 database and Query Manager could be one of the programs used to execute SQL statements. We make the following observations about this architecture.

- All programs are executed on the time-share computer. Specifically, the DBMS and application programs all utilize the resources of the time-share computer.
- Because a PC operates in terminal emulation mode, its primary responsibility is to handle the network communication message processing and information display. It does not perform any application processing. This means that much of the user's PC computing power is under-utilized.
- The entire database resides on the time-share computer.

There are three potential problems associated with a time-share architecture. The first two problems have a negative impact on response time. The third problem reduces throughput. All three can have a negative impact on people productivity.

1. If many programs are executing, or, if a particular program is using a considerable amount of the computer's resources, then each program requires more time to complete its processing.
2. Communication network costs can be considerable, especially if a large amount of data is transmitted from the computer to the user's terminal/PC.
3. If a time-share computer goes down, all programs halt, and all users wait.

Many AS/400 users have suffered these problems. We will see that a client-server system can reduce, but not eliminate, such problems.

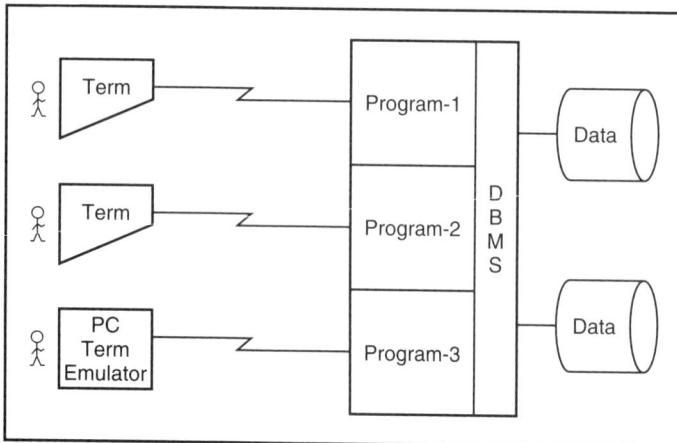

Figure 24.1 Time-share system.

CLIENT-SERVER SYSTEM

"Client-server" is a computing architecture used in many different systems. It is not a product per se. A client-server DBMS is really just a DBMS which uses a client-server architecture to provide database services. We note that the "client-server" aspect of a system is usually transparent ("under the hood") with respect to the user.

A client-server architecture specifies two processes: (1) a client process and (2) a server process. Each process usually resides on a separate computer. The client process usually executes on the user's PC. The server process usually executes on a time-share computer. Therefore, a client-server system includes time-share processing. Like a time-share system, the computers are connected using a communications network. A client requests a service from the server via the network.

In the database world, a special kind of server, called a *database server,* will run a DBMS (e.g., DB2/400). Users operate client computers (e.g., IBM PCs) to execute application programs which request database services. A database request is usually specified using SQL. An SQL statement (e.g., SELECT) is sent to the server for execution. After execution a response (e.g., a result table) is returned to the client.

Figure 24.2 illustrates the architecture of a typical client-server DBMS. We make the following observations about this architecture.

1. A user operates a client computer, often called a *workstation.* Unlike a pure time-share environment, a "dumb" terminal is not used. This relates to the next observation.

2. A user's client computer actually performs real computing, unlike a dumb terminal. The client computer may perform complex processing of data sent to/from the database server. (Note that in the time-share mode, this processing could not be done on the user's computer.) Also, a client may provide a graphical user interface (GUI). In a client-server environment, a considerable amount of work can be removed from the time-share server and processed on client machines.

3. The server may be devoted to just one special task: the operation of the DBMS. This can be achieved by executing all application programs on client computers. The server operates in time-share mode allowing many clients access to the DBMS. (We note that a client-server architecture has been used to support other kinds of specialized servers such as file servers and print servers.)

4. Client-server processing is a form of "distributed processing." This implies that the processing for a given application is distributed across multiple computers. The client-server version of distributed processing does not allow the database server to initiate work. Rather, a server merely responds to requests from clients.

5. Client-server processing is also a form of "parallel processing." Even a simple client-server system has multiple computers (one server and some number of clients). These computers operate in parallel. Some number of clients may simultaneously process data previously sent to them by the server while the server is processing data for some other client.

6. A client-server system provides a modest level of system reliability because one client can continue processing even if another client is down.

In effect, the distribution of processing across multiple computers helps address some problems associated with time-share systems. More work can be done on the client machines, thus reducing the potential bottleneck in the server machine. If a database server goes down, each client can continue to operate by performing non-database processing. Also, some database applications permit copying a subset of data from the server to the client. Then the client can disconnect from the server and perform queries on the local copy of the data.

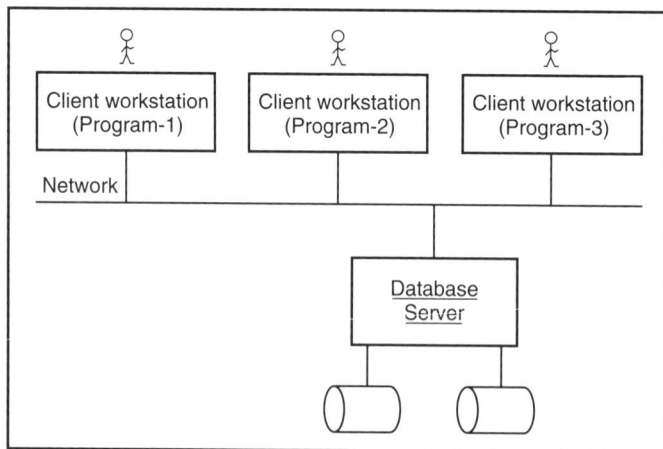

Figure 24.2 Client-server DBMS.

SQL IN THE CLIENT-SERVER WORLD

Communication between a client and a server requires that each process understand the same language. In the database world, this language is SQL. Figure 24.3a illustrates this fact. Clients can pass SQL statements to a server by running a variety of different "front-end" programs. In general, a front-end program may be:

1. An interactive tool which allows a user to enter SQL statements, display results, format reports, and perform some housekeeping tasks like saving a query. (This tool would behave like Query Manager, but we note that Query Manager itself cannot be executed as a client process.)

2. A traditional application program written in some 3GL (e.g., RPG, COBOL) which contains embedded SQL statements. (The next chapter will provide more detail on embedded SQL.)

3. A GUI which allows a user to "point and shoot" at graphical icons which represent tables or objects found in the application domain. The GUI converts the users point-and-shoot actions into SQL statements for transmission to the database server. It could be argued that GUIs are one of the primary reasons for the recent popularity of client-server systems.

Figure 24.3b illustrates the different types of client programs which generate SQL. We note that DB2/400 supports a variety of such tools.

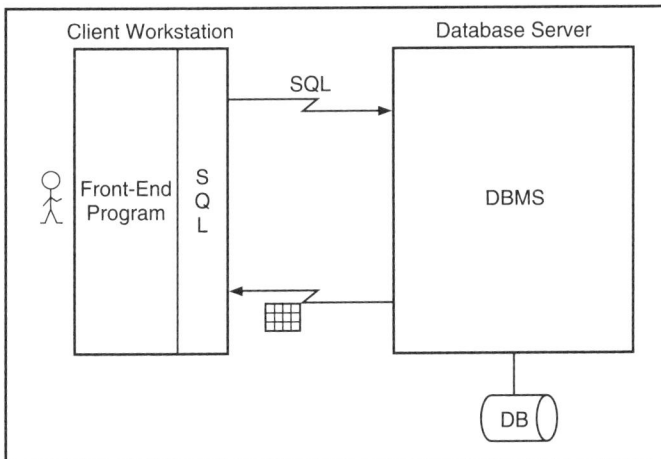

Figure 24.3a   Client programs send SQL to a database server.

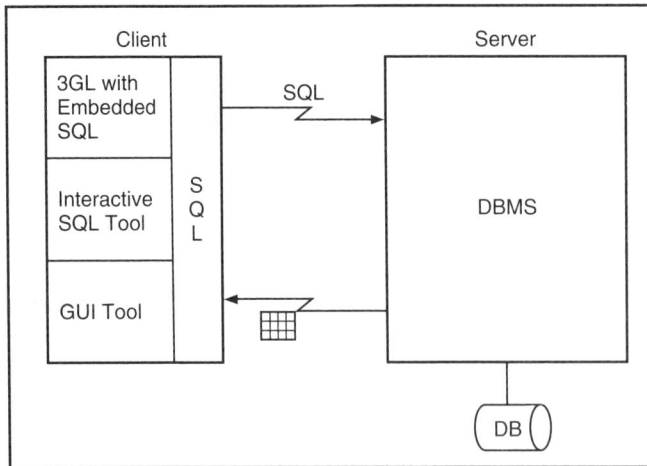

Figure 24.3*b* Different types of client software tools send SQL to a database server.

COMMUNICATIONS SOFTWARE
IN THE CLIENT-SERVER WORLD

We need to say a little more about the communications network between a client and a server. A communications network requires that the communications software be present on both the client and server. Also, this network software has its own language called a *protocol* (e.g., TCP/IP, SNA). You do not need to know the details of any network software or its protocol. All we need to know, is that any message, which is sent across a network, needs to be "packaged" into this protocol before it is sent to the server, and it needs to be "unpackaged" on arrival at the server. Likewise, any result sent from a server to a client needs to be packaged and unpackaged according to the rules of the specific protocol.

In particular, if an SQL statement is sent from a client program (unlike a program executing on a server), then the SQL statement must be packaged and unpackaged according to the rules of the protocol. A client-server DBMS must provide a software module which performs this packaging and unpackaging of SQL statements and results. Figure 24.3*c* adds more detail to Fig. 24.3*b* by illustrating the network software and the module (shown as X) which handles the packaging and unpackaging.

CLIENT-SERVER ARCHITECTURE FOR DB2/400

We can now use Fig. 24.3*c* as a basis for describing the basic components of a client-server system using DB2/400. We list some choices available for the technology infrastructure. We emphasize that the following list of hardware and software is not complete and we expect that it will grow rapidly in the near future.

```
            Client                              Server
┌─────────────┬───┬───┬───┐          ┌───┬───┬──────────┐
│ 3GL with    │   │   │ C │    SQL   │ C │   │          │
│ Embedded    │   │   │ o │ ──────▶  │ o │   │          │
│ SQL         │   │   │ m │          │ m │   │          │
│             │ S │   │ m.│          │ m.│   │          │
├─────────────┤ Q │ X │   │          │   │ X │  DBMS    │
│ Interactive │ L │   │ S │          │ S │   │          │
│ SQL Tool    │   │   │ o │          │ o │   │          │
│             │   │   │ f │          │ f │   │          │
├─────────────┤   │   │ t │          │ t │   │          │
│ GUI Tool    │   │   │ w │  ◀────── │ w │   │          │
│             │   │   │ a │          │ a │   │          │
│             │   │   │ r │          │ r │   │          │
│             │   │   │ e │          │ e │   │          │
└─────────────┴───┴───┴───┘          └───┴───┴────┬─────┘
                                              ┌───┴──┐
                                              │ DB   )
                                              └──────┘
```

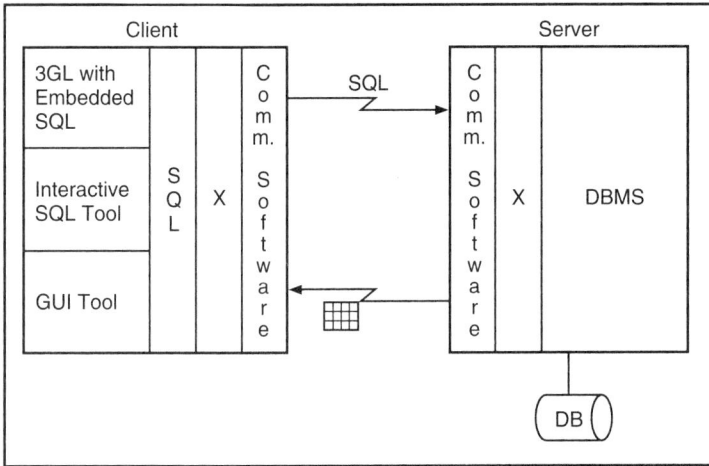

Figure 24.3c *X* represents software module to package and unpackage SQL for the network protocol.

Database server. DB2/400 running on an AS/400 machine.

Client machine. Wide variety of different processors.

- IBM PC or comparable processor
- IBM, SUN, HP workstation processors
- Apple Macintosh

Client operating system

- DOS Windows and OS/2 on PCs
- UNIX, AIX on workstations

Communication networks. APPN and TCP/IP.

Communications protocol

- an IBM proprietary protocol
- DRDA: an IBM "standard" protocol

Network "packing" programs. Depends on OS and protocols.

- Client Access/400 product (if using DOS Windows or OS/2 with the proprietary protocol)
- DDCS/2 product (if using OS/2 with the DRDA protocol)
- ODBC (Open Data Base Connectivity)

Again, we reemphasize an important point. After the system administrator and database administrator determine and install the appropriate hardware and software for the technology infrastructure, it becomes transparent to the user. Users and application programmers interface with one of the aforementioned front-end client tools which generate some variation of "good old" SQL.

Also, it is worth noting that many third-party vendors have developed versions of their GUI products (e.g., Quest, Forest and Trees, Q+E) to communicate with DB2/400. It is expected that many more such products will be available in the near future.

MULTIPLE DATABASE SERVERS

It is possible to have multiple database servers on the same communications network as illustrated in Fig. 24.4. In particular, multiple DB2/400 servers can be connected to the same network. This configuration has advantages if your organization has two major application domains which are not closely integrated.

We emphasize that this approach is not a "distributed database" (to be described below) because the database servers operate independent of each other. Each server supports a distinct application, has its own catalog, and may be managed by a different database administrator. Some users or programs may access both servers. However, such users and programs would have to explicitly sign onto the specific server they would like to access. After signing onto a specific server, the user/program can only manipulate the data located on that server.

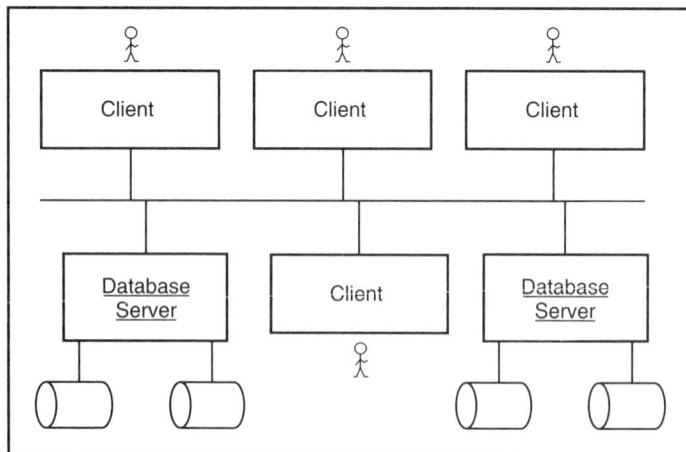

Figure 24.4   Multiple database servers.

DISTRIBUTED DATABASE

A Distributed Database Management System (DDBMS) physically looks like Fig. 24.4. There are multiple database servers connected via a communications network. The key difference is logical. *A DDBMS allows users and programs to perceive the data stored on the separate servers as a single global integrated database.*

A user on a client workstation might forward a transaction to a database server. However, the transaction might reference data which resides on a second server. To satisfy this request the first server would transparently access and obtain the data from the second server. Under this circumstance, the first server would operate as a client of the second server.

Building a DDBMS is a monumental task. Again, a detail description of the technology behind a DDBMS is beyond the scope of this text. We will simply note that the initial version of DB2/400 will not provide full DDBMS support.

IBM uses the following terms to describe different levels of support for distributed database processing.

- Remote request
- Remote unit of work
- Distributed unit of work
- Distributed request

DB2/400 should be able to support the first three levels. The initial version will not support a distributed request. We will use SQL pseudocode to present examples to describe each of these levels.

We begin by specifying the physical location of a table by using its location as a prefix to its name. For example, if the COURSE table is in HARTFORD, we reference it as "HARTFORD.COURSE". (We note that this notation ignores the important issues of location transparency and proper naming techniques.)

Example 1:   Remote request

Assume: You are on Machine-1 (M1) and TABLE1 is stored on M1. You would like to access tables TABLE2 and TABLE3 which are located on Machine-2 (M2).

You can submit the following statement (remote request) from M1.

```
SELECT ....
FROM   M2.TABLE2, M2.TABLE3
WHERE  ....
```

Comment: This example is a *single statement* (request) which references tables on a remote machine. It makes no difference if the statement is a query or an update operation. Multiple remote tables can be referenced *as long as they reside on the same machine.*

Example 2:   Remote unit of work

Assume: You would like to define a database transaction (a logical "unit of work") consisting of multiple SQL statements where each statement references one or more tables on the same remote machine.

With a remote unit of work you can execute the same kind of SQL statement applicable to a remote request. Furthermore, you can execute the following statements which constitute a logical unit of work.

```
{previous sync. point}

UPDATE M2.TABLE2
SET    ....
WHERE  ....

UPDATE M2.TABLE3
SET    ....
WHERE  ....

COMMIT
```

Comment: The primary restriction is that all tables referenced in the transaction (TABLE2 and TABLE3) must be located on the same machine.

Example 3:   Distributed unit of work

Assume: Like a remote unit of work, you would like to be able to define a transaction (a logical "unit of work"). However, you would also like different SQL statements to be able to reference different machines.

Under distributed unit of work, you can execute the same kind of SQL statements applicable to remote unit of work. Furthermore, you can execute the following statements which constitute a logical unit of work involving tables at different machines.

```
{previous sync. point}
UPDATE M2.TABLE2
SET    ....
WHERE  ....

UPDATE M3.TABLE3
SET    ....
WHERE  ....

COMMIT
```

Comments

1. The referenced tables, TABLE2 and TABLE3, may be located on different machines. *However, there is a restriction that each individual statement can only reference tables which reside on the same machine.* The system will pass each statement to the appropriate machine for processing.

2. This type of transaction is more complex because it requires special internal processing to handle situations where one machine successfully completes its work, while another fails because the machine or network goes down. (This internal processing includes the application of a two-phase commit recovery protocol. Discussion of this topic is beyond the scope of this text.)

Example 4:   Distributed request

Assume: You can remove the restriction associated with a distributed unit of work. You would like to formulate a single SQL statement which references tables located on different machines. The statement may or may not be part of a multiple statement transaction.

With a distributed request you can execute the same kind of SQL statements applicable to a distributed unit of work. Furthermore, you can execute SQL statements where each individual statement may reference multiple tables located on different machines. For example, you can join TABLE1 on machine M1 with TABLE2 on machine M2.

```
SELECT ....
FROM   M1.TABLE1, M2.TABLE2
WHERE  ....
```

Also, you can have a distributed unit of work containing a distributed request.

```
{previous sync. point}

UPDATE M2.TABLE2
SET    ....
WHERE  ....

DELETE
FROM M3.TABLE3
WHERE ACCTNO = (SELECT ACCTNO
               FROM M1.TABLE1
               WHERE ....)

COMMIT
```

Comments

1. A fully distributed DBMS should be able to support distributed requests.

2. The initial version of DB2/400 will *not* support distributed requests. There are many reasons why supporting distributed requests is extremely difficult. (These reasons include the global data dictionary and global query optimization problems. A discussion of these problems is beyond the scope of this text.) Figures 24.5*a* through 24.5*d* summarize the previously described levels of distributed database processing.

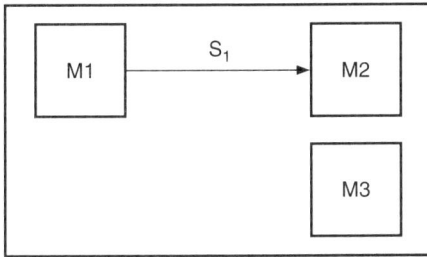

Figure 24.5a Remote request: S1 is a single statement.

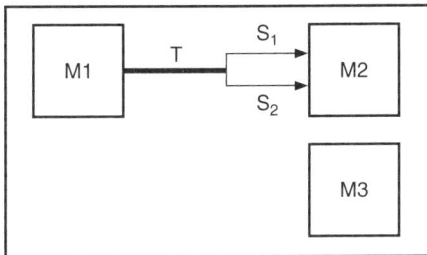

Figure 24.5b Remote unit of work: T is a transaction with two statements, S1 and S2.

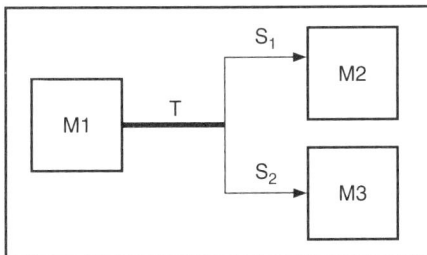

Figure 24.5c Distributed unit of work: T is a transaction with two statements, S1 and S2.

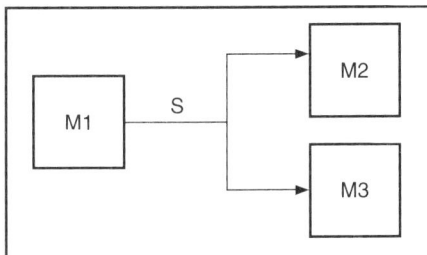

Figure 24.5d Distributed request: S is a single statement.

HETEROGENEOUS DISTRIBUTED DATABASE

In the previous section we tacitly assumed that each of the database servers had the same kind of DBMS, presumably DB2/400. This was a "homogeneous" DDBMS. If we remove this assumption, then we arrive at yet another level of complexity. Figure 24.6 illustrates multiple different database servers connected via a communications network. This kind of configuration is called a "heterogeneous" DDBMS. (It may also be called a "multidatabase system.")

It is expected that DB2/400 will be able to communicate with other DB2 systems. Also, it is expected that vendors will build gateways which allow some kind of interface with non-IBM database products.

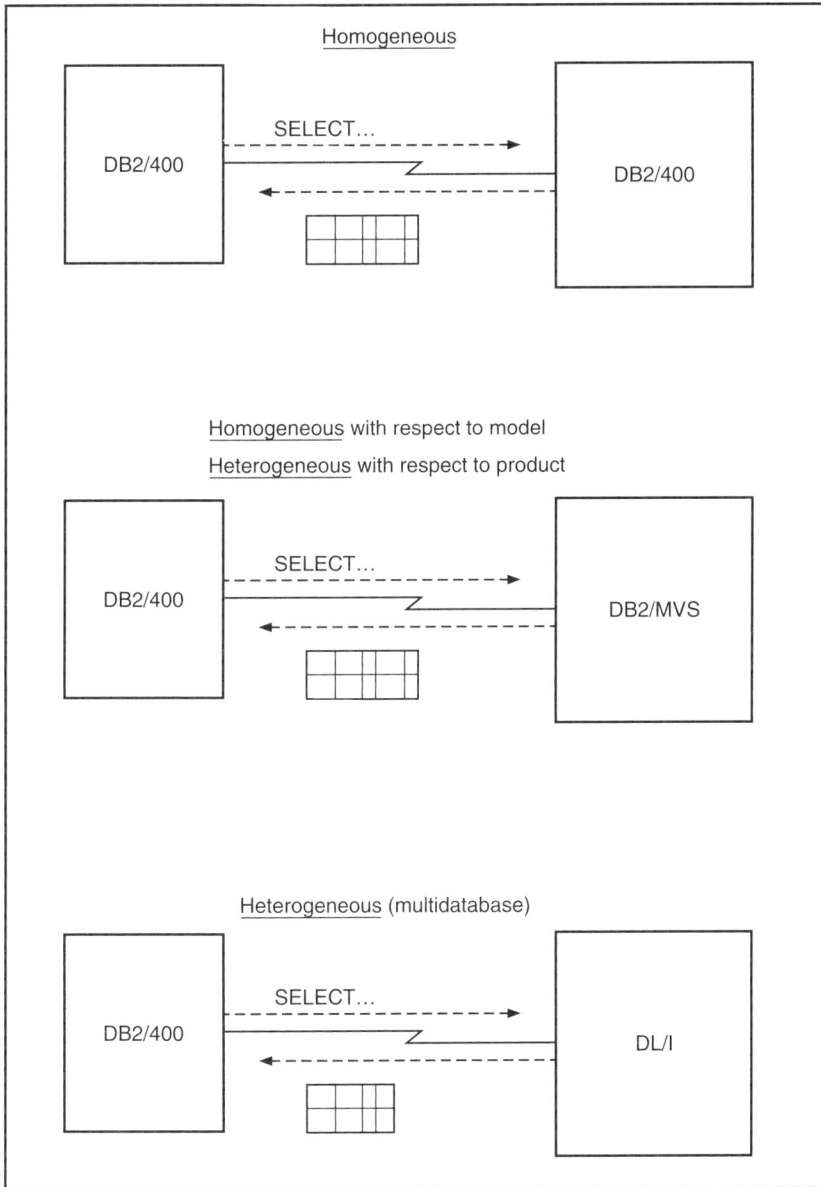

Figure 24.6   Homogeneous and heterogeneous distributed database systems.

SUMMARY

This chapter presented a very brief overview of client-server and distributed database systems with commentary on DB2/400. The bad news is the internal complexity of such systems. Such complexity surely means that there will most likely be some imperfections in the initial version of DB2/400. The good news is that this complexity will generally be transparent to users and application programmers.

Overview of DB2/400 API

The current version of SQL/400 allows the embedding of SQL statements in traditional procedural languages such as RPG and COBOL. This is a very broad topic which is beyond the scope of this text. In fact, an entire book could be written on this topic. Accordingly, this chapter is strictly conceptual. Its objective is to present a very brief overview to a very big topic. It is included for the sake of completeness and to provide a background for discussion of DB2/400 stored procedures and triggers.

Most of the ideas presented in this book are understandable by a computer literate user who may not have the knowledge of a traditional (3GL) programming language (e.g., RPG, COBOL). This chapter, unlike previous chapters, is written for the professional programmer in that it presumes that the reader has a working knowledge of any such 3GL.

EMBEDDED SQL

Consider embedding an SQL statement in a host program written in RPG (or any other traditional 3GL). Conceptually speaking, we usually embed SQL in a host language with the intention of substituting a SELECT statement where we would normally have a "read" command, or an INSERT or UPDATE statement where we would normally have a "write" command.

Embedding SQL into RPG presumes that the programmer knows both SQL and RPG. This book has provided the reader with the necessary SQL knowledge. Presumably the programmer already knows RPG. However, knowing both SQL and RPG is not sufficient for the task of embedding SQL inside RPG because there are a number of concepts and special embedded SQL statements (e.g., OPEN CURSOR) which are not relevant to interactive SQL. These ideas and statements are not necessarily difficult for the professional programmer. However, the concepts and syntax are not elegant. The process is analogous to shoving a square peg into a round hole. In fact, some authors have referred to this problem as the "impedance mismatch" problem.

One aspect of the impedance mismatch problem is the correspondence between the data types of the host language and the data types of the database system. Another aspect pertains to the "chunks" of data processed by the host language and the DBMS. A traditional programming language manipulates data on a record-at-a-time basis while SQL manipulates data on a set-level.

The concepts of syntax related to embedded SQL are beyond the scope of this text. However, a firm knowledge of SQL as described in this text is a necessary prerequisite. We present an example using pseudocode to illustrate the process of retrieving multiple rows from the COURSE table and returning them to a host program.

Step 1.   Declare a cursor.

```
DECLARE CURSOR C1 FOR
    SELECT CNAME, CRED FROM COURSE
    WHERE CLABFEE > 100
```

Step 2.   Execute using the OPEN statement.

```
OPEN CURSOR C1
```

Step 3.   Retrieve the next row into a memory variables called *cname* and *cred* using the FETCH statement.

```
FETCH C1 INTO :cname, :cred
```

Step 4.   Process the first row.

Step 5.   Iterate on steps 3 and 4 until there is a "no hit" condition.

Step 6.   Conclude processing by using the CLOSE statement.

```
CLOSE CURSOR C1
```

Comments

1. For set-level processing, embedded SQL requires the declaration of a *cursor* which roughly corresponds to a pointer to a row in a result table produced by the execution of a SELECT statement. You need a DECLARE CURSOR statement at the beginning of your host program to associate the cursor (C1) with the SELECT statement. We note that declaring the cursor does not execute the statement.

2. The OPEN CURSOR statement actually executes the SELECT statement associated with the cursor. This causes the DBMS to execute the SELECT statement and store the result in a temporary result table. Your host program has no direct access to this result table. You must fetch each row from the result table one at a time.

3. The FETCH statement is used to retrieve the "next" row from the result table and bring it into memory. The INTO clause specifies the memory variable(s) which will contain the values found in this row.

4. Process the host variables using standard host language commands. This process could entail complex computations or displaying the data in graphical format.

5. Iteration on steps 3 and 4 has the same logic as iterating on traditional "read-process-write" logic. The elegance of set-level processing is absent. As previously mentioned, this is a fundamental part of the impedance mismatch problem.

6. The CLOSE CURSOR statement will release any resources associated with the query.

7. Each of the above SQL statements would be embedded within delimiters to identify them at distinct from the host language commands. A language precompiler would scan the program to replace the SQL statements with conventional host language commands in preparation for conventional compile, link, and execution.

CLIENT-SERVER CONSIDERATIONS

In a conventional time-share environment, programs with embedded SQL are (1) written in a traditional programming language and (2) executed on the time-share computer. However, in a client-server environment, there are other options.

GUI Tools for Users

In a client-server environment most users who desire to perform ad hoc queries against their database will use a GUI instead of entering raw SELECT statements. It could be argued that the presence of such tools will eliminate the need for users to learn SQL. This may be true for those users whose queries are very simple. However, *it can also be argued that users should be capable of reading the SQL statements which are generated by the GUI.* This is especially true if the user's query is complex. One of the primary objectives of this text has been to illustrate and sensitize the reader to the logical (not just the syntactical) issues associated with writing correct SELECT statements. A GUI can only generate the SELECT statement that you tell it to generate via pointing and clicking on graphical icons. You can be certain that the syntax of the generated SELECT statement will be correct. However, what about the logic of the statement? It will not necessarily generate the statement that you *intended*. (Currently, there is no magic button which will tell the GUI to "do what I mean, not what I say.")

Application-Generation Tools for Developers

The evolution of application development tools for clients will result in the automatic generation of application programs which contain embedded SQL. The successful application of such tools will mean that only a relatively few professional programmers will have to confront the "impedance mismatch" complexity associated with embedded SQL. However, again, we believe that developers should be capable of reading the SQL generated by such tools.

Processing on the Server versus the Client

As indicated in the previous chapter, application programs containing embedded SQL will usually be executed on the client machine. However, there are occasions when it is advantageous to execute procedural code on the server. For example, assume you need to perform a complex calculation which is beyond the capabilities of SQL (e.g., net present value, multiple regression). Each row/record would need to be transferred from the server to the client in order to perform the calculations on the client. However, if the user only wanted the final result—not the raw data stored in these rows/records—then transferring such a large amount of data to the client would unnecessarily incur considerable network cost. The obvious solution is to perform the calculations on the server and simply pass the final result back to the client. This objective can be realized by using stored procedures.

STORED PROCEDURES

A stored procedure is simply a program which (unlike conventional SQL/400 programs) can be invoked by the DB2/400 database server. The process involves the execution of the procedure via a "call" statement which may pass any required parameters.

The impact of this powerful addition will be most felt in the client-server environment using embedded SQL programs. In such an environment the application programs are usually executed on the client. However, as noted above, there may be circumstances when the developer would like to control where certain processing should occur. Stored procedures will allow the developer to specify execution of the program on the server. This has potential performance advantages and enhances program reusability.

The availability of a stored procedure on the server would allow the client to call the procedure to perform the calculations and just return the result. This would eliminate the need to transfer the rows/records leading to a reduction in network communication traffic.

It should be noted that a stored procedure can be written in any 3GL programming language or the REXX procedural language. This differs from other non-IBM products that use a special proprietary language to create a stored procedure.

DATABASE TRIGGERS

Triggers are similar in concept to stored procedures. They are programs written in some 3GL which are stored and executed on the server. The major difference is that, unlike stored procedures, they are automatically invoked by an update operation on a specified table. (Recall that a stored procedure is explicitly invoked by a "CALL" statement in the application program.) A trigger is activated as a byproduct of a row-level change to a database table. The trigger can be "fired" before or after an INSERT, UPDATE, or DELETE request.

Triggers are often used to support user-defined integrity. Consider the rule that the average lab fee for a given department cannot exceed $300. Enforcing such a rule would require recalculating the average for each DELETE where the lab fee is less than $300 and each INSERT where the lab fee exceeds $300. A trigger could be used to automatically examine each update operation to test for the $300 condition, recalculate the average, and provide feedback to the application program. This saves the program the effort of explicitly testing for the integrity constraint. Furthermore, it ensures that it is impossible for a careless programmer to circumvent the integrity constraint.

Instead of using declarative referential integrity, triggers can also be used to implement a do-it-yourself version of referential integrity. This can be useful when the declarative version is inappropriate due to special processing requirements or when you want to selectively enforce just certain constraints in an existing application.

Finally, we note that triggers and procedures are not defined using SQL. (This differs from some other client-server products which support proprietary CREATE PROCEDURE and CREATE TRIGGER statements.) Writing the stored procedures in a conventional 3GL provides greater portability and may provide opportunities for greater efficiency.

QUERY OPTIMIZATION AND THE EXPLAIN COMMAND

Earlier in the text we indicated that the primary objective of the user is to write semantically correct SQL statements. In other words, the user specifies "what" and the system figures out "how to" efficiently satisfy the user's request. The DBMS has a component called an optimizer which, in the ideal, should be able to generate the most efficient access path to the necessary data. Creating potential access paths for possible selection by the optimizer is the responsibility of the DBA who must perform physical database design.

We do not emphasize efficiency when users execute one-time ad hoc queries in a decision support system. However, an application programmer may write a program which is executed 1000 times per day. Under such circumstances, efficiency becomes a real consideration. The programmer may need to "second guess" the optimizer to verify its choice of access path and/or suggest alternative access paths to the DBA. DB2/400 will support an "EXPLAIN" command which will allow a programmer to ask the optimizer to indicate the access path it would choose for a specified SELECT statement.

SUMMARY

This chapter introduced the fundamental concepts associated with embedded SQL, stored procedures, and triggers. Again, we note that a detailed discussion of these topics is far beyond the scope of this text. However, we emphasize that a knowledge of the basic SQL language, as described in this text, is a necessary prerequisite for understanding these topics.

Entering and Exiting Query Manager

This appendix describes the sign-on and sign-off procedures used to execute SQL statements using SQL/400 Query Manager.

PRELIMINARY COMMENTS

1. If this is your first experience with SQL/400, we recommend that you read Chap. 1 and the first section (Entering SQL Statements) of Chap. 2 before you actually sign-on to Query Manager.

2. Make sure that you have obtained the proper operating system and Query Manager profiles and passwords.

3. If you plan to execute the sample queries and exercises in this text, then you (or your DBA) needs to create the sample educational database. This process is described in App. C.

THE SIGN-ON PROCESS

1. Access your AS/400 session. This process may also require that you enter a specific library list and have specific security rights. This step is specific to your system. This means that rookie users may have to ask their DBA to describe this process.

2. Sign-on to SQL/400 Query Manager

   a. Enter "STRQM" and press the Enter key (Return key).

   b. The system should respond with some self-identifying information and then display:

```
        SQL/400 Query Manager

  Select one of the following:

    1. Work with Query Manager queries
    2. Work with Query Manager report forms
    3. Work with Query Manager tables
                 .
                 .
                 .
   10. Work with Query Manager profiles
```

The main options for Query Manager provide you with several tools.

(1) Work with Query Manager queries provides access to the SQL editor and related options. This is where you will do the majority of your work.

(2) Work with Query Manager report forms allows you to create report forms (formats) for your interactive or batch output.

(3) Work with Query Manager tables provides a prompt-based method for creating tables and entering initial data.

(4) Work with Query Manager profiles gives you access to your default setup parameters for using SQL/400 Query Manager. (Please see comment 3.)

Comments

1. Sometimes your System Manager will make the sign-on process easier by establishing a menu which starts the SQL/400 Query Manager environment. This effectively allows you to skip step 2.

2. The AS/400 has built-in help for every field and screen. You can access that by positioning your cursor to the area in question and then pressing the F1 key. The F2 key provides general screen-related help. By pressing the F11 key you can do a search on a "keyword." This capability is very helpful in learning SQL/400 Query Manager.

3. The authors recommend that you have your Default query creation mode set to "SQL." The prompted option is a convenient way to learn SQL statement formatting, but becomes somewhat inconvenient as your proficiency grows. Above all, SQL creation mode allows you to interact with SQL in a more generic industry mode.

4. The AS/400 screens are very informative. By reading the function keys and utilizing the help system you should be able to function in Query Manager with very little assistance.

THE SIGN-OFF PROCESS

1. By pressing the F3 key you will exit each screen until you have reached the point where you started Query Manager.

2. Follow the standard procedure to exit your AS/400 session. (Again, you may have to ask your DBA or System Manager to describe this process.)

Educational Database

The design shown in Fig. B.1 represents the basic content and structure of the sample tables used throughout this text. Only the conceptual primary key and foreign key columns are shown in Fig. B.1. The primary key columns are underlined. Sample data are shown in Figs. B.2a and B.2b.

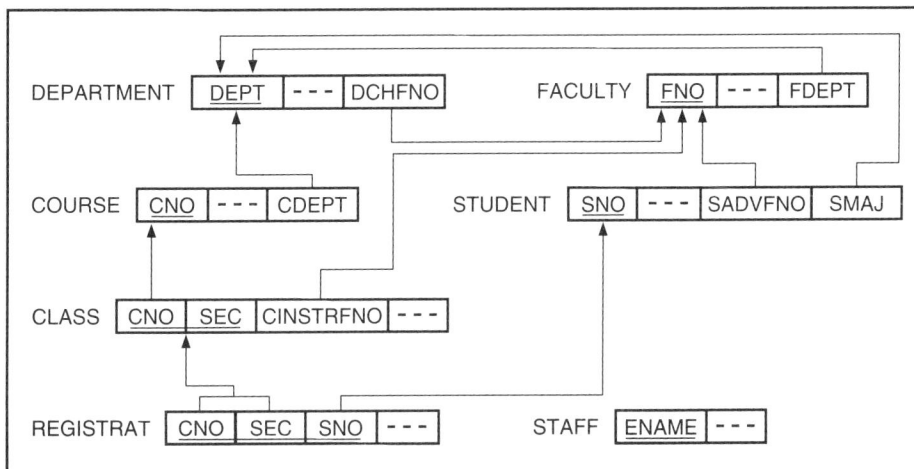

Figure B.1 Educational database design.

DEPARTMENT

DEPT	DBLD	DROOM	DCHFNO
THEO	HU	200	10
CIS	SC	300	80
MGT	SC	100	–
PHIL	HU	100	60

STAFF

ENAME	ETITLE	ESALARY	DEPT
LUKE	EVANGLIST3	53	THEO
MARK	EVANGLIST2	52	THEO
MATTHEW	EVANGLIST1	51	THEO
DICK NIX	CROOK	25001	PHIL
HANK KISS	JESTER	25000	PHIL
JOHN	EVANGLIST4	54	THEO
EUCLID	LAB ASSIST	1000	MATH
ARCHIMEDES	LAB ASSIST	200	ENG
DA VINCI	LAB ASSIST	500	–

COURSE

CNO	CNAME	CDESCP	CRED	CLABFEE	CDEPT
C11	INTRO TO CS	FOR ROOKIES	3	100.00	CIS
C22	DATA STRUCTURES	VERY USEFUL	3	50.00	CIS
C33	DISCRETE MATHEMATICS	ABSOLUTELY NECESSARY	3	.00	CIS
C44	DIGITAL CIRCUITS	AH HA!	3	.00	CIS
C55	COMPUTER ARCH.	VON NEUMANN'S MACH.	3	100.00	CIS
C66	RELATIONAL DATABASE	THE ONLY WAY TO GO	3	500.00	CIS
P11	EMPIRICISM	SEE IT-BELIEVE IT	3	100.00	PHIL
P22	RATIONALISM	FOR CIS MAJORS	3	50.00	PHIL
P33	EXISTENTIALISM	FOR CIS MAJORS	3	200.00	PHIL
P44	SOLIPSISM	ME MYSELF AND I	6	.00	PHIL
T11	SCHOLASTICISM	FOR THE PIOUS	3	150.00	THEO
T12	FUNDAMENTALISM	FOR THE CAREFREE	3	90.00	THEO
T33	HEDONISM	FOR THE SANE	3	.00	THEO
T44	COMMUNISM	FOR THE GREEDY	6	200.00	THEO

CLASS

CNO	SEC	CINSTRFNO	CDAY	CTIME	CBLD	CROOM
C11	01	08	MO	08:00–09:00A.M.	SC	305
C11	02	08	TU	08:00–09:00A.M.	SC	306
C33	01	80	WE	09:00–10:30A.M.	SC	305
C55	01	85	TH	11:00–12:00A.M.	HU	306
P11	01	06	TH	09:00–10:00A.M.	HU	102
P33	01	06	FR	11:00–12:00A.M.	HU	201
T11	01	10	MO	10:00–11:00A.M.	HU	101
T11	02	65	MO	10:00–11:00A.M.	HU	102
T33	01	65	WE	11:00–12:00A.M.	HU	101

Figure B.2a Educational database.

REGISTRATION

CNO	SEC	SNO	REG_DATE
C11	01	325	04-JAN-1988
C11	01	800	15-DEC-1987
C11	02	100	17-DEC-1987
C11	02	150	17-DEC-1987
P33	01	100	23-DEC-1987
P33	01	800	23-DEC-1987
T11	01	100	23-DEC-1987
T11	01	150	15-DEC-1987
T11	01	800	15-DEC-1987

FACULTY

FNO	FNAME	FADDR	FHIRE_DATE	FNUM_DEP	FSALARY	FDEPT
06	KATHY PEPE	7 STONERIDGE RD	15-JAN-1979	2	35000.00	PHIL
10	JESSIE MARTYN	2135 EAST DR	01-SEP-1969	1	45000.00	THEO
08	JOE COHN	BOX 1138	09-JUL-1979	2	35000.00	CIS
85	AL HARTLEY	SILVER STREET	05-SEP-1979	7	45000.00	CIS
60	JULIE MARTYN	2135 EAST DR	01-SEP-1969	1	45000.00	PHIL
65	LISA BOBAK	77 LAUGHING LN	06-SEP-1981	–	36000.00	THEO
80	BARB HLAVATY	489 SOUTH ROAD	16-JAN-1982	3	35000.00	CIS

STUDENT

SNO	SNAME	SADDR	SPHNO	SBDATE	SIQ	SADVFNO	SMAJ
325	CURLEY DUBAY	CONNECTICUT	203-123-4567	780517	122	10	THEO
150	LARRY DUBAY	CONNECTICUT	203-123-4567	780517	121	80	CIS
100	MOE DUBAY	CONNECTICUT	203-123-4567	780517	120	10	THEO
800	ROCKY BALBOA	PENNSYLVANIA	112-112-1122	461004	99	60	PHIL

Figure B.2*b* Educational database.

Using the Educational Database

This appendix describes how to set up the educational database so that you can execute the sample queries and exercises in this text. To create the sample data you would enter each SQL statement in the SQL/400 Query Manager editor and execute each individual statement. Rookie users may have to ask their DBA or System Manager to perform this task for them.

We present a conceptual overview of these files. Then we present the mechanics of loading the files. From a practical point of view, the mechanics is the important thing. To understand the content of the SQLLoad file requires reading this text. However, we believe it is helpful to present a little information about the purpose and content of these files. Again, we note that you really don't need to understand the content of these files to follow the mechanical steps necessary to load them.

THE SQLLOAD FILE

Chapter 1 of this text begins by describing the SELECT statement which is used to retrieve data from tables. This chapter presumes that the tables have already been created and loaded with sample data. To establish this situation, the appropriate CREATE TABLE and INSERT statements (described in Chaps. 12 and 13) need to be executed. These statements are present in the SQLLoad file shown in Fig. C.1.

Figure C.1 SQLLoad file.

```
--------------------------------------------------------------------
CREATE TABLE SQLTST/COURSE
(CNO     CHAR(3)     NOT NULL,
 CNAME   VARCHAR(22) NOT NULL,
 CDESCP  VARCHAR(25) NOT NULL,
 CRED    INTEGER,
 CLABFEE DECIMAL(5,2),
 CDEPT   CHAR(4)     NOT NULL)
--------------------------------------------------------------------

INSERT INTO COURSE VALUES
    ('C11','INTRO TO CS','FOR ROOKIES',3, 100,'CIS')
--------------------------------------------------------------------
INSERT INTO COURSE VALUES
    ('C22','DATA STRUCTURES','VERY USEFUL',3, 50,'CIS')
--------------------------------------------------------------------
INSERT INTO COURSE VALUES
    ('C33','DISCRETE MATHEMATICS','ABSOLUTELY NECESSARY',3, 0,'CIS')
--------------------------------------------------------------------
INSERT INTO COURSE VALUES
    ('C44','DIGITAL CIRCUITS','AH HA!',3, 0,'CIS')
--------------------------------------------------------------------
INSERT INTO COURSE VALUES
    ('C55','COMPUTER ARCH.','VON NEUMANN''S MACH.',3, 100,'CIS')
--------------------------------------------------------------------
INSERT INTO COURSE VALUES
    ('C66','RELATIONAL DATABASE','THE ONLY WAY TO GO',3, 500,'CIS')
--------------------------------------------------------------------
INSERT INTO COURSE VALUES
    ('P11','EMPIRICISM','SEE IT-BELIEVE IT',3, 100,'PHIL')
--------------------------------------------------------------------
INSERT INTO COURSE VALUES
    ('P22','RATIONALISM','FOR CIS MAJORS',3, 50,'PHIL')
--------------------------------------------------------------------
INSERT INTO COURSE VALUES
    ('P33','EXISTENTIALISM','FOR CIS MAJORS',3, 200,'PHIL')
--------------------------------------------------------------------
INSERT INTO COURSE VALUES
    ('P44','SOLIPSISM','ME MYSELF AND I',6, 0,'PHIL')
--------------------------------------------------------------------
INSERT INTO COURSE VALUES
    ('T11','SCHOLASTICISM','FOR THE PIOUS',3,150,'THEO')
--------------------------------------------------------------------
INSERT INTO COURSE VALUES
    ('T12','FUNDAMENTALISM','FOR THE CAREFREE',3,90,'THEO')
--------------------------------------------------------------------
```

Figure C.1 *(Continued)*

```
INSERT INTO COURSE VALUES
    ('T33','HEDONISM','FOR THE SANE',3,0,'THEO')
------------------------------------------------------------
INSERT INTO COURSE VALUES
    ('T44','COMMUNISM','FOR THE GREEDY',6,200,'THEO')
------------------------------------------------------------


CREATE TABLE SQLTST/DEPARTMENT
(DEPT    CHAR(4)     NOT NULL,
 DBLD    CHAR(2),
 DROOM   CHAR(3),
 DCHFNO  CHAR(2))

------------------------------------------------------------
INSERT INTO DEPARTMENT VALUES ('THEO','HU','200','10')
------------------------------------------------------------
INSERT INTO DEPARTMENT VALUES ('CIS', 'SC','300','80')
------------------------------------------------------------
INSERT INTO DEPARTMENT VALUES ('MGT', 'SC','100', NULL)
------------------------------------------------------------
INSERT INTO DEPARTMENT VALUES ('PHIL','HU','100','60')



CREATE TABLE SQLTST/STAFF
(ENAME   CHAR(10)    NOT NULL,
 ETITLE  CHAR(10),
 ESALARY INTEGER,
 DEPT    CHAR(4))

------------------------------------------------------------
INSERT INTO STAFF VALUES ('LUKE', 'EVANGLIST3', 53, 'THEO')
------------------------------------------------------------
INSERT INTO STAFF VALUES ('MARK', 'EVANGLIST2', 52, 'THEO')
------------------------------------------------------------
INSERT INTO STAFF VALUES ('MATTHEW', 'EVANGLIST1', 51, 'THEO')
------------------------------------------------------------
INSERT INTO STAFF VALUES ('DICK NIX', 'CROOK', 25001, 'PHIL')
------------------------------------------------------------
INSERT INTO STAFF VALUES ('HANK KISS', 'JESTER', 25000, 'PHIL')
------------------------------------------------------------
INSERT INTO STAFF VALUES ('JOHN', 'EVANGLIST4', 54, 'THEO')
------------------------------------------------------------
INSERT INTO STAFF VALUES ('EUCLID', 'LAB ASSIST', 1000,  'MATH')
------------------------------------------------------------
```

Figure C.1   (*Continued*)

```
INSERT INTO STAFF VALUES ('ARCHIMEDES', 'LAB ASSIST', 200, 'ENG')
-----------------------------------------------------------------
INSERT INTO STAFF VALUES ('DA VINCI', 'LAB ASSIST', 500, NULL)
-----------------------------------------------------------------


CREATE TABLE SQLTST/STUDENT
(SNO     CHAR(3)      NOT NULL,
 SNAME   CHAR(25)     NOT NULL,
 SADDR   CHAR(25),
 SPHNO   CHAR(12),
 SBDATE  CHAR(6),
 SIQ     INTEGER,
 SADVFNO CHAR(2),
 SMAJ    CHAR(4)      NOT NULL)


-----------------------------------------------------------------
INSERT INTO STUDENT VALUES ('325','CURLEY DUBAY', 'CONNECTICUT',
'203-123-4567','780517',122,'10', 'THEO')
-----------------------------------------------------------------
INSERT INTO STUDENT VALUES ('150','LARRY DUBAY', 'CONNECTICUT',
'203-123-4567','780517',121,'80','CIS')
-----------------------------------------------------------------
INSERT INTO STUDENT VALUES ('100','MOE DUBAY', 'CONNECTICUT',
'203-123-4567','780517',120,'10','THEO')
-----------------------------------------------------------------
INSERT INTO STUDENT VALUES ('800','ROCKY BALBOA', 'PENNSYLVANIA',
'112-112-1122','461004',99, '60','PHIL')
-----------------------------------------------------------------


CREATE TABLE SQLTST/CLASS
(CNO       CHAR(3)      NOT NULL,
 SEC       CHAR(2)      NOT NULL,
 CINSTRFNO CHAR(2),
 CDAY      CHAR(2),
 CTIME     CHAR(15),
 CBLD      CHAR(2),
 CROOM     CHAR(3))


-----------------------------------------------------------------
INSERT INTO CLASS VALUES
     ('C33','01','80','WE','09:00-10:30A.M.','SC','305')
-----------------------------------------------------------------
INSERT INTO CLASS VALUES
     ('C55','01','85','TH','11:00-12:00A.M.','SC','306')
-----------------------------------------------------------------
```

Figure C.1 *(Continued)*

```
INSERT INTO CLASS VALUES
     ('C11','01','08','MO','08:00-09:00A.M.','SC','305')
-------------------------------------------------------------------
INSERT INTO CLASS VALUES
     ('C11','02','08','TU','08:00-09:00A.M.','SC','306')
-------------------------------------------------------------------
INSERT INTO CLASS VALUES
     ('P11','01','06','TH','09:00-10:00A.M.','HU','102')
-------------------------------------------------------------------
INSERT INTO CLASS VALUES
     ('P33', 01','06','FR','11:00-12:00A.M.','HU','201')
-------------------------------------------------------------------
INSERT INTO CLASS VALUES
     ('T11','01','10','MO','10:00-11:00A.M.','HU','101')
-------------------------------------------------------------------
INSERT INTO CLASS VALUES
     ('T11','02','65','MO','10:00-11:00A.M.','HU','102')
-------------------------------------------------------------------
INSERT INTO CLASS VALUES
     ('T33','01','65','WE','11:00-12:00A.M.','HU','101')
-------------------------------------------------------------------


CREATE TABLE SQLTST/FACULTY
(FNO         CHAR(2)    NOT NULL,
 FNAME       CHAR(20)   NOT NULL,
 FADDR       CHAR(25),
 FHIRE_DATE CHAR(10),
 FNUM_DEP    INTEGER,
 FSALARY     DECIMAL(7,2),
 FDEPT       CHAR(4))

-------------------------------------------------------------------
INSERT INTO FACULTY VALUES
('06','KATHY PEPE','7 STONERIDGE RD', '1979-01-15', 2, 35000, 'PHIL')
-------------------------------------------------------------------
INSERT INTO FACULTY VALUES
('10','JESSIE MARTYN','2135 EAST DR', '1982-03-07', 1, 45000,'THEO')
-------------------------------------------------------------------
INSERT INTO FACULTY VALUES
('08','JOE COHN','BOX 1138', '1979-07-09', 2, 35000, 'CIS')
-------------------------------------------------------------------
INSERT INTO FACULTY VALUES
('85','AL HARTLEY','SILVER STREET', '1979-09-05', 7, 45000, 'CIS')
-------------------------------------------------------------------
```

Figure C.1 (*Continued*)

```
INSERT INTO FACULTY VALUES
('60','JULIE MARTYN','2135 EAST DR', '1978-05-17', 1, 45000, 'PHIL')
-----------------------------------------------------------------------
INSERT INTO FACULTY VALUES
('65','LISA BOBAK','77 LAUGHING LN', '1981-09-06', 1, 36000, 'THEO')
-----------------------------------------------------------------------
INSERT INTO FACULTY VALUES
('80','BARB HLAVATY','489 SOUTH ROAD', '1982-01-16', 3, 35000, 'CIS')
-----------------------------------------------------------------------


CREATE TABLE SQLTST/REGISTRAT
(CNO       CHAR(3)    NOT NULL,
 SEC       CHAR(2)    NOT NULL,
 SNO       CHAR(3)    NOT NULL,
 REG_DATE  DATE,
 REG_TIME  TIME)

-----------------------------------------------------------------------
INSERT INTO REGISTRAT VALUES
    ('C11', '01', '325', '02/04/88', '11:35:00')
-----------------------------------------------------------------------
INSERT INTO REGISTRAT VALUES
    ('C11', '01', '800', '12/15/87', '10:00:00')
-----------------------------------------------------------------------
INSERT INTO REGISTRAT VALUES
    ('C11', '02', '150', '12/17/87', '12:12:00')
-----------------------------------------------------------------------
INSERT INTO REGISTRAT VALUES
    ('P33', '01', '100', '12/23/87', '13:18:00')
-----------------------------------------------------------------------
INSERT INTO REGISTRAT VALUES
    ('P33', '01', '800', '12/23/87', '16:00:00')
-----------------------------------------------------------------------
INSERT INTO REGISTRAT VALUES
    ('T11', '01', '100', '12/23/87', '16:35:00')
-----------------------------------------------------------------------
INSERT INTO REGISTRAT VALUES
    ('T11', '01', '150', '12/15/87', '17:00:00')
-----------------------------------------------------------------------
INSERT INTO REGISTRAT VALUES
    ('T11', '01', '800', '12/15/87', '19:00:00')
-----------------------------------------------------------------------
INSERT INTO REGISTRAT VALUES
    ('C11', '01', '111', '12/26/92', '19:21:00')
-----------------------------------------------------------------------
```

Figure C.1 *(Continued)*

```
INSERT INTO REGISTRAT VALUES
    ('T33', '01', '325', '09/19/91', '12:23:00')
-------------------------------------------------------
INSERT INTO REGISTRAT VALUES
    ('T33', '01', '100', '09/19/91', '13:22:00')
-------------------------------------------------------
INSERT INTO REGISTRAT VALUES
    ('T33', '01', '150', '08/19/91', '14:44:00')
-------------------------------------------------------
INSERT INTO REGISTRAT VALUES
    ('C66', '01', '200', '10/02/93', '22:22:00')
-------------------------------------------------------


CREATE TABLE SQLTST/NULLTAB
(PKEY      INTEGER,
 COLA      INTEGER,
 COLB      INTEGER,
 COLC      INTEGER)

-------------------------------------------------------
INSERT INTO NULLTAB VALUES (1,    10,    20,   5)
-------------------------------------------------------
INSERT INTO NULLTAB VALUES (2,    30,    30,   5)
-------------------------------------------------------
INSERT INTO NULLTAB VALUES (3,    160,  NULL, 10)
-------------------------------------------------------
INSERT INTO NULLTAB VALUES (4,    NULL, 170,   5)
-------------------------------------------------------
INSERT INTO NULLTAB VALUES (5,    NULL, NULL, 10)
-------------------------------------------------------
INSERT INTO NULLTAB VALUES (6,    10,    40,   5)
-------------------------------------------------------
INSERT INTO NULLTAB VALUES (7,    30,    60,   5)
-------------------------------------------------------
INSERT INTO NULLTAB VALUES (8,    NULL, NULL, NULL)
-------------------------------------------------------
INSERT INTO NULLTAB VALUES (NULL, NULL, NULL, NULL)
-------------------------------------------------------
INSERT INTO NULLTAB VALUES (NULL, NULL, NULL, NULL)
-------------------------------------------------------
INSERT INTO NULLTAB VALUES (NULL, NULL, NULL, NULL)
```

MECHANICS OF LOADING FILES

Entering SQLLoad File with the SQL/400 Query Manager Editor

1. Sign onto SQL/400 Query Manager by entering "STRQM". Appendix A describes this step in more detail.

2. Select option 1 (Work with Query Manager queries) from the main menu of the SQL/400 Query Manager menu. When you get the SQL editor enter each SQL statement separately as shown below.

```
                              Edit Query
Columns . . . : 1 70                          Query . . . :
QM . .

Type SQL Statement
    ************************* Beginning of Data ************************
'''''''  INSERT INTO COURSE VALUES
'''''''  ('C1', 'INTRO TO CS', 'FOR ROOKIES', 3, 100, 'CIS')
'''''''
'''''''
'''''''
'''''''
'''''''
'''''''
'''''''
'''''''
'''''''
'''''''
    ************************* End of Data ************************
F2=Alternate keys    F3=Exit       F4=Prompt   F5=Run report   F6=Run sample
F9=Retrieve          F15=Check syntax          F24=More keys
```

Press function key "F5" to execute the SQL statement. You must type in each statement separately. The system will respond by executing each of the statements.

3. Assuming the previous step was successful, all of the tables described in App. B are now available for processing. You are ready to start executing the sample queries and exercises.

Answers to Exercises

CHAPTER 1

A. SELECT * FROM COURSE WHERE CLABFEE < 150

B. SELECT * FROM COURSE WHERE CRED > 3

C. SELECT * FROM COURSE WHERE CDEPT = 'THEO'

D. SELECT * FROM COURSE WHERE CNAME = 'RELATIONAL DATABASE'

E. SELECT * FROM COURSE WHERE CNO = 'P44'

F. SELECT * FROM COURSE WHERE CNO < 'P01'

G. SELECT * FROM COURSE WHERE CNAME > 'RATIONALISM'

H. SELECT CNAME, CDESCP FROM COURSE

I. SELECT CDEPT, CNO, CLABFEE, CRED FROM COURSE

J. SELECT CNO, CLABFEE FROM COURSE WHERE CLABFEE > 100

K. SELECT CNAME FROM COURSE WHERE CDEPT = 'CIS'

L. SELECT CLABFEE FROM COURSE

M. SELECT DISTINCT CLABFEE FROM COURSE

N. SELECT CRED, CLABFEE FROM COURSE WHERE CDEPT = 'CIS'

O. SELECT DISTINCT CRED, CLABFEE FROM COURSE WHERE CDEPT = 'CIS'

P. SELECT * FROM STAFF

Q. SELECT * FROM STAFF WHERE ESALARY < 1000

R. SELECT * FROM STAFF WHERE DEPT = 'THEO'

S. SELECT ENAME, ETITLE FROM STAFF

T. SELECT ENAME, ESALARY FROM STAFF WHERE ESALARY > 1000

U. SELECT ENAME, ETITLE FROM STAFF WHERE ENAME < 'MARK'

V. SELECT DISTINCT ETITLE FROM STAFF

CHAPTER 3

A. SELECT * FROM COURSE ORDER BY CDEPT

B. SELECT CNAME, CLABFEE FROM COURSE WHERE CDEPT = 'PHIL'
ORDER BY CNAME DESC

C. SELECT CNAME, CNO, CRED, CLABFEE FROM COURSE ORDER BY
CLABFEE, CNO

D. SELECT * FROM COURSE ORDER BY 3 DESC

E. SELECT CDEPT, CLABFEE, CNAME FROM COURSE WHERE CRED = 3
ORDER BY CDEPT, CLABFEE DESC, CNAME

F. SELECT * FROM STAFF ORDER BY ENAME

G. SELECT ENAME, ESALARY FROM STAFF WHERE ESALARY < 1000 ORDER
BY ESALARY DESC

H. SELECT * FROM STAFF WHERE DEPT = 'THEO' ORDER BY ETITLE

I. SELECT DEPT, ENAME, ESALARY FROM STAFF ORDER BY DEPT,
ESALARY

J. SELECT DEPT, ETITLE, ESALARY FROM STAFF ORDER BY DEPT,
ESALARY DESC

CHAPTER 4

A. SELECT * FROM COURSE WHERE CRED = 3 AND CDEPT = 'PHIL'

B. SELECT * FROM COURSE WHERE CLABFEE >= 100 AND CLABFEE <= 500

C. SELECT * FROM COURSE WHERE CRED = 3 AND CDEPT = 'THEO' AND
CLABFEE >= 100 AND CLABFEE <= 400

D. SELECT * FROM COURSE WHERE CDEPT = 'PHIL' OR CDEPT = 'THEO'

E. SELECT * FROM COURSE WHERE CDEPT = 'THEO' OR CRED = 6

F. SELECT * FROM COURSE WHERE CLABFEE = 0.00 OR CLABFEE = 90.00 OR CLABFEE = 150.00

G. SELECT CNO, CNAME, CLABFEE FROM COURSE WHERE NOT CLABFEE = 100

or

SELECT CNO, CNAME, CLABFEE FROM COURSE WHERE CLABFEE <> 100

H. SELECT CNO, CLABFEE FROM COURSE WHERE NOT CLABFEE = 100 AND NOT CLABFEE = 200

I. SELECT * FROM COURSE WHERE (CRED = 6 AND CDEPT = 'PHIL') OR CLABFEE > 200

J. SELECT * FROM COURSE WHERE CRED = 3 AND (CLABFEE < 100 OR CLABFEE > 300)

K. SELECT * FROM COURSE WHERE NOT CLABFEE > 100 OR (CDEPT = 'THEO' AND CRED = 6)

L. SELECT * FROM COURSE WHERE NOT (CRED = 3 AND CDEPT = 'PHIL')

M. SELECT * FROM COURSE WHERE CLABFEE IN (12.12, 50.00, 75.00, 90.00, 100.00, 500.00)

N. SELECT * FROM COURSE WHERE CLABFEE NOT IN (12.12, 50.00, 75.00, 90.00, 100.00, 500.00)

O. SELECT CNO, CLABFEE FROM COURSE WHERE CLABFEE BETWEEN 50.00 AND 400.00

P. SELECT CNO, CLABFEE FROM COURSE WHERE CLABFEE NOT BETWEEN 50.00 AND 400.00

Q. SELECT CNAME, CDESCP FROM COURSE WHERE CDESCP BETWEEN 'FOR' AND 'FORZ'

R. SELECT CDEPT, CNO, CDESCP FROM COURSE WHERE CDEPT IN ('CIS', 'THEO') AND CLABFEE NOT BETWEEN 100 AND 400 ORDER BY CDEPT, CNO

S. SELECT * FROM STAFF WHERE DEPT = 'PHIL' OR DEPT = 'THEO'

T. SELECT * FROM STAFF WHERE DEPT = 'THEO' AND ESALARY > 52

U. SELECT ENAME FROM STAFF WHERE ESALARY >= 52 AND ESALARY <= 1000

or

SELECT ENAME FROM STAFF WHERE ESALARY BETWEEN 52 AND 1000

V. SELECT ENAME, ETITLE FROM STAFF WHERE DEPT = 'THEO' AND (ESALARY = 51 OR ESALARY = 54)

W. SELECT ENAME, ESALARY FROM STAFF WHERE ESALARY IN (51, 53, 100, 200, 25000)

X. SELECT ENAME, ESALARY FROM STAFF WHERE ESALARY NOT BETWEEN 100 AND 1000 ORDER BY ENAME
or
SELECT ENAME, ESALARY FROM STAFF WHERE ESALARY < 100 OR ESALARY > 1000 ORDER BY ENAME

Y. SELECT DISTINCT DEPT FROM STAFF WHERE ESALARY > 5000

CHAPTER 5

A. SELECT * FROM COURSE WHERE CDESCP LIKE 'FOR THE%'

B. SELECT CNAME, CDESCP FROM COURSE WHERE CDESCP LIKE '%E'

C. SELECT CNAME, CDESCP FROM COURSE WHERE CDESCP LIKE '%.%' OR CDESCP LIKE '%-%' OR CDESCP LIKE '%!%'

D. SELECT DISTINCT CDEPT FROM COURSE WHERE CDEPT LIKE'%IL'

E. SELECT CNAME, CDEPT FROM COURSE WHERE CDEPT LIKE '_ _ _'

F. SELECT CNAME, CDESCP FROM COURSE WHERE CDESCP LIKE '_ _ _ _THE_ _A%'

G. SELECT CNAME, CDESCP FROM COURSE WHERE CNAME NOT LIKE '%E' AND CNAME NOT LIKE '%S'

H. SELECT * FROM STAFF WHERE ENAME LIKE 'MA%'

I. SELECT * FROM STAFF WHERE ETITLE LIKE '%1' OR ETITLE LIKE '%2' OR ETITLE LIKE '%3'

J. SELECT ENAME, ETITLE FROM STAFF WHERE ENAME LIKE '%S%' AND ETITLE LIKE '%S%'

K. SELECT DISTINCT DEPT FROM STAFF WHERE DEPT LIKE '_ _E%'

L. SELECT ENAME FROM STAFF WHERE ENAME LIKE '_ _ _ _I%' ORDER BY ENAME

CHAPTER 6

A. SELECT CNO, CRED, CRED * 2 FROM COURSE WHERE CDEPT = 'PHIL'

B. SELECT CNO, CRED * 10.50 FROM COURSE WHERE CDEPT = 'THEO'

C. SELECT CNO, CLABFEE, CLABFEE / 2.0 FROM COURSE WHERE CLABFEE > 0.00

D. SELECT CNO, (CLABFEE * 1.50) + 35 FROM COURSE WHERE CLABFEE < 200

E. SELECT ENAME, ESALARY + 100 FROM STAFF

F. SELECT ENAME, ESALARY, ESALARY * 1.15 FROM STAFF

G. SELECT ENAME, ESALARY – 100 FROM STAFF WHERE ESALARY – 100 < 25000

H. SELECT ENAME, ESALARY + 1000 FROM STAFF WHERE ESALARY < 25000 ORDER BY 2 DESC

CHAPTER 7

A. SELECT MIN(CNAME) FROM COURSE

B. SELECT SUM(CLABFEE) FROM COURSE WHERE CDEPT = 'PHIL'

C. SELECT AVG(CLABFEE), MAX(CLABFEE), MIN(CLABFEE) FROM COURSE WHERE CDEPT = 'CIS' AND CLABFEE <> 0

D. SELECT COUNT (*) FROM COURSE

E. SELECT COUNT (*) FROM COURSE
WHERE CNAME LIKE 'E%'

F. SELECT AVG(CRED * 50.0) FROM COURSE WHERE CDEPT = 'THEO'

G. SELECT CDEPT, SUM(CRED) FROM COURSE GROUP BY CDEPT

H. SELECT CDEPT, COUNT(*) FROM COURSE GROUP BY CDEPT ORDER BY CDEPT

I. SELECT CDEPT, SUM(CLABFEE) FROM COURSE WHERE CRED <> 6 GROUP BY CDEPT ORDER BY 2 DESC

J. SELECT CDEPT, MAX(CLABFEE) FROM COURSE GROUP BY CDEPT HAVING MAX(CLABFEE) > 300
or
SELECT CDEPT, MAX(CLABFEE) FROM COURSE WHERE CLABFEE > 300 GROUP BY CDEPT

K. SELECT CDEPT, SUM(CRED) FROM COURSE GROUP BY CDEPT HAVING SUM(CRED) > 15

L. SELECT CDEPT, SUM(CLABFEE) FROM COURSE WHERE CRED = 3 GROUP BY CDEPT HAVING SUM(CLABFEE) <= 150

M. SELECT CDEPT, MAX(CLABFEE) FROM COURSE WHERE CLABFEE <= 400
GROUP BY CDEPT HAVING MAX(CLABFEE) > 175

O. SELECT SUM(ESALARY), AVG(ESALARY), MAX(ESALARY), MIN(ESALARY)
FROM STAFF

P. SELECT COUNT(*) FROM STAFF WHERE DEPT = 'THEO'

Q. SELECT SUM(ESALARY) + 5000 FROM STAFF

R. SELECT DEPT, AVG(ESALARY) FROM STAFF GROUP BY DEPT

S. SELECT DEPT, SUM(ESALARY) FROM STAFF WHERE ESALARY > 600
GROUP BY DEPT ORDER BY 2

CHAPTER 8

A. SELECT INTEGER(CLABFEE) FROM COURSE

B. SELECT CNO, ROUND(CLABFEE/CRED,2) FROM COURSE

C. SELECT SUBSTR(CNO,2), SUBSTR(CNAME,1,5), SUBSTR(CDESCP,4,2)
FROM COURSE WHERE CDEPT = 'PHIL'

D. SELECT LENGTH(CNAME) FROM COURSE

E. SELECT DISTINCT CDEPT, LENGTH(CDEPT) FROM COURSE

F. SELECT CNO, CDESCP FROM COURSE WHERE LENGTH(CDESCP) < 15

G. SELECT CDESCP ¦¦ CNO FROM COURSE

CHAPTER 9

A. SET REG_DATE EDIT CODE TO TDM–

B. SET CURRENT DATE EDIT CODE TO TDMA/
SET CURRENT TIME EDIT CODE TO TTU:

C. SELECT HOUR(CURRENT TIME), MINUTE(CURRENT TIME),
SECOND(CURRENT TIME)
EDIT HEADINGS FOR EACH FIELD

D. SELECT SNO, REG_DATE, REG_DATE + 90 DAYS
FROM REGISTRAT WHERE SNO = '325'

E. SELECT REG_DATE, CNO, SEC, SNO
FROM REGISTRAT WHERE REG_DATE > '12/31/87'

F. SELECT SNO REG_DATE
FROM REGISTRAT WHERE MONTH(REG_DATE) = 12

CHAPTER 10

A. CHANGE "CNO" HEADING TEXT TO "COURSE NUMBER"
    ENLARGE THE WIDTH OF CNO TO 14
    ENTER A USAGE CODE OF 'DO2' FOR CLABFEE
    ENLARGE THE WIDTH OF CLABFEE TO 9

B. ENTER A 'BREAK2' FOR THE CRED COLUMN
    ADD A USAGE CODE OF AVERAGE FOR CRED

C. SELECT ENAME, ETITLE, ESALARY, DEPT FROM STAFF
    ORDER BY DEPT
    SET ESALARY USAGE TO MAX
    SET DEPT USAGE TO BREAK1
    SET BREAK TEXT FOOTING FOR BREAK1 TO "MAX DEPT SALARY"
    SET BREAK TEXT FOOTING LINES AFTER TO 3
    SET FINAL TEXT TO "HIGHEST SALARY"

CHAPTER 12

A. SEE CREATE TABLE STATEMENTS IN APP. C.

B. CREATE TABLE SQLTST/JUNK (C1 CHAR (10) NOT NULL, C2 INTEGER, C3
    DECIMAL (7,2) NOT NULL)

C. CREATE UNIQUE INDEX XSTUDENT ON SQLTST/STUDENT (SNO)

D. CREATE TABLE SQLTST/CISCOURSE
    (CISCNO CHAR (3) NOT NULL,
    CISCNAME VARCHAR (22) NOT NULL,
    CISCRED INTEGER,
    CISCLABFEE DECIMAL (5, 2))
    CREATE UNIQUE INDEX XCCOURSE ON SQLTST/CISCOURSE (CISCNO)

CHAPTER 13

A. INSERT INTO STAFF (ENAME, ETITLE, ESALARY, DEPT)
    VALUES ('ALAN', 'LAB ASSIST', 3000, 'CIS')

B. INSERT INTO STAFF (DEPT, ENAME)
    VALUES ('CIS', 'GEORGE')

C. UPDATE STAFF SET ESALARY = 4000 WHERE DEPT = 'CIS'

D. DELETE FROM STAFF WHERE DEPT = 'CIS'

E. CREATE TABLE EXPENSIVE

   (EXPCNO CHAR(3),

   EXPCNAME   CHAR(22),

   EXPCLABFEE   DECIMAL(5,2),

   EXPDEPT CHAR(4))

   INSERT INTO EXPENSIVE

   SELECT CNO, CNAME, CLABFEE, CDEPT FROM COURSE WHERE

   CLABFEE > 100

F. UPDATE EXPENSIVE

   SET EXPCLABFEE = EXPCLABFEE – 50

   WHERE EXPCLABFEE > 400

G. DELETE FROM EXPENSIVE WHERE EXPDEPT = 'THEO'

H. INSERT INTO EXPENSIVE (XCNO, XDEPT) VALUES ('X99', 'XXX')

I. UPDATE EXPENSIVE SET EXPCNAME = 'JUNK'

J. DELETE FROM EXPENSIVE

K. DROP TABLE EXPENSIVE

CHAPTER 14

A. SELECT AVG(FNUM_DEP), SUM(FNUM_DEP), COUNT(*) FROM FACULTY

B. SELECT SUM(FSALARY + (250 * FNUM_DEP)) FROM FACULTY

C. SELECT * FROM NULLTAB WHERE COLA <> COLB

D. SELECT FNAME, FNO, FNUM_DEP FROM FACULTY ORDER BY
   FNUM_DEP DESC

E. SELECT AVG(FSALARY) FROM FACULTY GROUP BY FNUM_DEP

F. SELECT FNAME, FNUM_DEP, FDEPT FROM FACULTY WHERE
   FNUM_DEP IS NULL

G. SELECT ENAME, DEPT FROM STAFF WHERE DEPT IS NULL

H. SELECT DEPT, COUNT(*) FROM STAFF GROUP BY DEPT

CHAPTER 15

A. SELECT * FROM COURSE, DEPARTMENT WHERE CDEPT = DEPT

B. SELECT CNO, CNAME, CDESCP, CRED, CLABFEE, CDEPT, DBLD,
   DROOM, DCHFNO FROM COURSE, DEPARTMENT WHERE CDEPT = DEPT

C. SELECT CNAME, CLABFEE, DCHFNO FROM COURSE, DEPARTMENT WHERE CDEPT = DEPT AND CLABFEE > 100.00

D. SELECT CNO, CNAME FROM COURSE, DEPARTMENT WHERE CDEPT = DEPT AND DCHFNO = '60' ORDER BY CNO DESC

E. SELECT ENAME, ESALARY FROM STAFF, DEPARTMENT WHERE STAFF.DEPT = DEPARTMENT.DEPT AND DBLD = 'SC'

F. SELECT DISTINCT DBLD, DROOM FROM DEPARTMENT, STAFF WHERE DEPARTMENT.DEPT = STAFF.DEPT AND ESALARY > 200

G. SELECT MIN(CLABFEE), MAX(CLABFEE) FROM COURSE, DEPARTMENT WHERE CDEPT = DEPT AND DBLD = 'SC'

H. SELECT COUNT(*) FROM STAFF, DEPARTMENT WHERE STAFF.DEPT = DEPARTMENT.DEPT

I. SELECT ENAME, ESALARY, CLABFEE, CLABFEE – ESALARY FROM STAFF, COURSE WHERE DEPT = CDEPT AND (CLABFEE – ESALARY) >= 52

J. SELECT DEPARTMENT.DEPT, SUM(ESALARY), AVG(ESALARY) FROM STAFF, DEPARTMENT WHERE DEPARTMENT.DEPT = STAFF.DEPT GROUP BY DEPARTMENT.DEPT

K. SELECT CNAME, COUNT(*) FROM STAFF, COURSE WHERE DEPT = CDEPT GROUP BY CNAME

L. SELECT DEPARTMENT.DEPT FROM DEPARTMENT, STAFF WHERE DEPARTMENT.DEPT = STAFF.DEPT GROUP BY DEPARTMENT.DEPT HAVING COUNT(*) >= 3

M. SELECT DEPARTMENT.DEPT, COUNT(*) FROM DEPARTMENT, STAFF WHERE DEPARTMENT.DEPT = STAFF.DEPT GROUP BY DEPARTMENT.DEPT

N. SELECT DCHFNO FROM DEPARTMENT, COURSE WHERE DEPT = CDEPT AND CRED = 6

O. SELECT COURSE.CNO, CNAME, SEC FROM COURSE, CLASS WHERE COURSE.CNO = CLASS.CNO AND CDAY = 'MO'

P. SELECT COURSE.CNO, CNAME FROM REGISTRAT, COURSE WHERE REGISTRAT.CNO = COURSE.CNO AND SNO = '800'

Q. SELECT COURSE.CNO, SEC, CINSTRFNO, CDAY, CTIME, CBLD, CROOM FROM CLASS, COURSE WHERE CLASS.CNO = COURSE.CNO AND CLABFEE < 100.00 AND CDAY <> 'FR'

R. SELECT SNO, REG_DATE FROM REGISTRAT, COURSE
   WHERE REGISTRAT.CNO = COURSE.CNO AND CDEPT = 'THEO'

S. SELECT COUNT(*) FROM COURSE, REGISTRAT
   WHERE REGISTRAT.CNO = COURSE.CNO
   AND CNAME = 'EXISTENTIALISM'

T. SELECT COUNT(*) FROM REGISTRAT, COURSE
   WHERE REGISTRAT.CNO = COURSE.CNO AND CDEPT = 'PHIL'

U. SELECT DISTINCT FNO, FNAME FROM FACULTY, CLASS WHERE
   FNO = CINSTRFNO AND CDAY IN ('MO', 'FR')

V. SELECT FNAME FROM FACULTY, DEPARTMENT, COURSE
   WHERE FNO = DCHFNO AND DEPT = CDEPT AND CRED = 6

Wa. SELECT COURSE.CNO, CLASS.SEC, CNAME, CINSTRFNO, SNO
    FROM REGISTRAT, COURSE, CLASS
    WHERE COURSE.CNO = CLASS.CNO
    AND CLASS.CNO = REGISTRAT.CNO
    AND REGISTRAT.SEC = CLASS.SEC
    AND REGISTRAT.SEC = '01' AND CNAME = 'EXISTENTIALISM'

Wb. SELECT COURSE.CNO, CLASS.SEC, CNAME, CINSTRFNO, STUDENT.SNO,
    SNAME FROM REGISTRAT, COURSE,
    CLASS, STUDENT WHERE COURSE.CNO = CLASS.CNO
    AND CLASS.CNO = REGISTRAT.CNO AND REGISTRAT.SEC =
    CLASS.SEC AND REGISTRAT.SEC = '01'
    AND REGISTRAT.SNO = STUDENT.SNO
    AND CNAME = 'EXISTENTIALISM'

Wc. SELECT COURSE.CNO, CLASS.SEC, CNAME, FNAME,
    STUDENT.SNO, SNAME FROM REGISTRAT, COURSE, CLASS,
    STUDENT, FACULTY
    WHERE COURSE.CNO = CLASS.CNO
    AND CLASS.CNO = REGISTRAT.CNO
    AND REGISTRAT.SEC = CLASS.SEC
    AND REGISTRAT.SEC = '01'
    AND REGISTRAT.SNO = STUDENT.SNO AND CINSTRFNO = FNO
    AND CNAME = 'EXISTENTIALISM'

X. "paper and pencil exercise" –––

Y. SELECT * FROM COURSE, FACULTY

Za. SELECT D1.DEPT, D2.DEPT FROM DEPARTMENT D1, DEPARTMENT D2
   WHERE D1.DBLD = D2.DBLD AND D1.DEPT < D2.DEPT

Zb. SELECT S1.ENAME, S1.ESALARY, S2.ENAME, S2.ESALARY, S1.ESALARY –
   S2.ESALARY FROM STAFF S1, STAFF S2 WHERE (S1.ESALARY –
   S2.ESALARY) > 1000

Zc. SELECT S1.ENAME, S1.ESALARY, S2.ENAME, S2.ESALARY, S1.ESALARY –
   S2.ESALARY FROM STAFF S1, STAFF S2 WHERE (S1.ESALARY –
   S2.ESALARY) > 1000 AND S1.DEPT = S2.DEPT

Zd. SELECT S1.ENAME, S1.ESALARY, S2.ENAME, S2.ESALARY,
   S1.ESALARY – S2.ESALARY
   FROM STAFF S1, STAFF S2, DEPARTMENT
   WHERE S1.DEPT = S2.DEPT AND DEPARTMENT.DEPT = S1.DEPT
   AND (S1.ESALARY – S2.ESALARY) > 1000 AND DBLD = 'HU'

CHAPTER 16

A. SELECT CNO, CNAME, CDEPT FROM COURSE
   WHERE CLABFEE = (SELECT MIN(CLABFEE) FROM COURSE)

B. SELECT CNO, CNAME, CDEPT, CLABFEE FROM COURSE
   WHERE CLABFEE = (SELECT MAX(CLABFEE) FROM COURSE WHERE
   CLABFEE < 500.00)

C. SELECT CNO, CNAME, CDEPT, CLABFEE FROM COURSE WHERE
   CLABFEE = (SELECT MIN(CLABFEE) FROM COURSE WHERE CLABFEE
   > 0)

D. SELECT CNO, CNAME, CDEPT, CLABFEE FROM COURSE
   WHERE CRED = 6
   AND CLABFEE = (SELECT MAX(CLABFEE) FROM COURSE WHERE CRED
   = 6)

E. SELECT CNO, CNAME, CLABFEE FROM COURSE WHERE CLABFEE <
   (SELECT AVG(CLABFEE) FROM COURSE WHERE CDEPT = 'THEO')

F. SELECT * FROM COURSE WHERE CLABFEE >
   (SELECT MAX(CLABFEE) FROM COURSE
   WHERE CDEPT IN ('THEO', 'PHIL'))

G. SELECT ENAME, ESALARY FROM STAFF
   WHERE ESALARY >= (SELECT MAX(CLABFEE) FROM COURSE)

H. SELECT * FROM COURSE WHERE CDEPT = 'CIS' AND CLABFEE <
(SELECT AVG(ESALARY) FROM STAFF WHERE DEPT = 'THEO')

I. SELECT DEPT, DCHFNO FROM DEPARTMENT WHERE DEPT IN
(SELECT CDEPT FROM COURSE WHERE CRED = 6)

J. SELECT DISTINCT CNO, SEC, CBLD FROM CLASS
WHERE CBLD IN (SELECT DBLD FROM DEPARTMENT WHERE DEPT IN
(SELECT DEPT FROM STAFF WHERE ENAME = 'DICK NIX'))

K. SELECT FNAME, FDEPT FROM FACULTY WHERE FNO NOT IN
(SELECT CINSTRFNO FROM CLASS)

L. SELECT FNAME, FNUM_DEP FROM FACULTY
WHERE FNUM_DEP = ANY (SELECT CRED FROM COURSE)

M. SELECT CNO, CNAME FROM COURSE WHERE CNO IN
(SELECT CNO FROM REGISTRAT WHERE SNO = '800')

N. SELECT * FROM CLASS WHERE CNO IN
(SELECT CNO FROM COURSE
WHERE CLABFEE < 100.00 AND CDAY <> 'FR')

O. SELECT CNO, REG_DATE FROM REGISTRAT
WHERE CNO IN
(SELECT CNO FROM COURSE
WHERE CDEPT IN
(SELECT DEPT FROM DEPARTMENT WHERE DBLD = 'SC'))

P. SELECT CNO, CNAME, CDEPT, CLABFEE FROM COURSE
WHERE CLABFEE = (SELECT MAX(CLABFEE) FROM COURSE
WHERE CLABFEE <> (SELECT MAX(CLABFEE) FROM COURSE))

Q. SELECT FNAME, FNUM_DEP FROM FACULTY
WHERE FNUM_DEP < (SELECT MIN(CRED) FROM COURSE)

CHAPTER 17

A. SELECT ESALARY FROM STAFF
UNION
SELECT FSALARY FROM FACULTY

B. SELECT CDEPT, CRED, CDESCP FROM COURSE
WHERE CDEPT = 'PHIL'
UNION

SELECT FDEPT, FNUM_DEP, FADDR FROM FACULTY

WHERE FDEPT = 'PHIL'

C. SELECT CLABFEE, CRED, 'COURSE' FROM COURSE

WHERE CDEPT = 'CIS'

UNION ALL

SELECT FSALARY, FNUM_DEP, 'FACULTY' FROM FACULTY

WHERE FDEPT = 'CIS'

D. SELECT CNAME, CDEPT, CLABFEE, 'EXPENSIVE' FROM COURSE

WHERE CLABFEE >= 200.00

UNION ALL

SELECT CNAME, CDEPT, CLABFEE, 'CHEAP' FROM COURSE

WHERE CLABFEE <= 50.00

E. SELECT ESALARY FROM STAFF

UNION ALL

SELECT FSALARY FROM FACULTY

CHAPTER 18

A. SELECT FNAME, FDEPT, FSALARY FROM FACULTY FX WHERE
FSALARY > (SELECT AVG(FSALARY) FROM FACULTY WHERE FDEPT = FX.FDEPT)

B. SELECT FNAME, FDEPT FROM FACULTY FX

WHERE FNUM_DEP >

(SELECT AVG(CRED) FROM COURSE WHERE CDEPT = FX.FDEPT)

C. SELECT FNAME, FDEPT FROM FACULTY WHERE EXISTS

(SELECT * FROM COURSE

WHERE CDEPT = FACULTY.FDEPT AND CRED = 6)

or

SELECT FNAME, FDEPT FROM FACULTY WHERE FDEPT IN

(SELECT CDEPT FROM COURSE WHERE CRED = 6)

or

SELECT FNAME, FDEPT FROM FACULTY, COURSE

WHERE FDEPT = CDEPT AND CRED = 6

D. SELECT CNO, CNAME, CLABFEE FROM COURSE WHERE CLABFEE >
(SELECT MIN(ESALARY) FROM STAFF)

or

SELECT DISTINCT CNO, CNAME, CLABFEE FROM COURSE, STAFF
WHERE CLABFEE > ESALARY

E. SELECT FNAME, FDEPT FROM FACULTY WHERE NOT EXISTS
    (SELECT * FROM COURSE WHERE FACULTY.FDEPT = CDEPT AND CRED
    = 6)

F. SELECT CNAME, CDEPT, CLABFEE FROM COURSE CX WHERE CLABFEE =
    (SELECT MAX(CLABFEE) FROM COURSE WHERE CDEPT = CX.CDEPT)

G. SELECT DEPT, DBLD, DROOM, COURSE.CNO, CNAME, SEC, CDAY
    FROM DEPARTMENT, COURSE, CLASS
    WHERE DEPT = CDEPT AND COURSE.CNO = CLASS.CNO
    UNION
    SELECT DEPT, DBLD, DROOM, COURSE.CNO, CNAME, ' ', ' '
    FROM DEPARTMENT, COURSE WHERE DEPT = CDEPT AND NOT
    EXISTS
    (SELECT * FROM CLASS WHERE CNO = COURSE.CNO)
    UNION
    SELECT DEPT, DBLD, DROOM, ' ', ' ', ' ', ' '
    FROM DEPARTMENT WHERE NOT EXISTS
    (SELECT * FROM COURSE WHERE CDEPT = DEPARTMENT.DEPT)
    FROM FACULTY, COURSE, CLASS
    WHERE COURSE.CNO = CLASS.CNO AND FNO = CINSTRFNO

CHAPTER 19

A. CREATE VIEW FPAYROLL
    AS SELECT FNAME, FSALARY, PHIRE_DATE, FNUM_DEP FROM FACULTY

B. CREATE VIEW FPAYROLL2 (F2N, F2S, F2H)
    AS SELECT FNAME, FSALARY, FHIRE_DATE FROM FACULTY

C. CREATE VIEW VFSAL
    (DEPARTMENT, HIGH_SAL, LOW_SAL)
    AS SELECT FDEPT, MAX(FSALARY), MIN(FSALARY) FROM FACULTY
    GROUP BY FDEPT

D. CREATE VIEW FAVERAGES (FAVG_SAL, FAVG_DEP) AS SELECT
    AVG(FSALARY), AVG(FNUM_DEP) FROM FPAYROLL

E. DROP VIEW VFSAL

   ("SELECT * FROM VFSAL" will now cause an error)

F. DROP VIEW FPAYROLL

   ("SELECT * FROM FAVERAGES" will now cause an error)

G. CREATE VIEW VTHEOSTAFF

   AS SELECT ENAME, ESALARY, ETITLE

   FROM STAFF WHERE DEPT = 'THEO'

H. CREATE VIEW VAVG_STAFF (DEPT, AVG_SAL)

   AS SELECT DEPT, AVG(ESALARY) FROM STAFF GROUP BY DEPT

I. CREATE VIEW MYVIEW (TOTAL)

   AS SELECT SUM(ESALARY) FROM VTHEOSTAFF

J. CREATE VIEW VINSTR (INSTR, COURSE_NME)

   AS SELECT DISTINCT FNAME, CNAME

   FROM FACULTY, COURSE, CLASS

   WHERE COURSE.CNO = CLASS.CNO AND FNO = CINSTRFNO

K. DROP VIEW VTHEOSTAFF

L. No. View is defined on multiple tables.

CHAPTER 20

A. GRANT INSERT, SELECT ON STAFF TO CURLEY

B. GRANT ALL ON DEPARTMENT TO PUBLIC

C. REVOKE ALL ON DEPARTMENT FROM PUBLIC

CHAPTER 21

A. SELECT NAME FROM SYSTABLES WHERE NAME LIKE 'SYS%'

B. SELECT NAME, TBNAME FROM SYSCOLUMNS WHERE TBNAME LIKE 'SYS%' ORDER BY NAME

CHAPTER 22

A. DELETE FROM COURSE WHERE CDEPT = 'CIS'

   ROLLBACK

Index

ABOUT THE AUTHORS

TIM MARTYN has over 20 years experience as a consultant and instructor for professional training seminars. His clients have included IBM, Aetna, Texas Instruments, and many other companies. He is a member of the computer science faculty at the University of Hartford.

TIM HARTLEY is also a member of the computer science faculty at the University of Hartford and has been active as a consultant for Westinghouse, IBM, Travelers, and other companies. He and Tim Martyn are the co-authors of *DB2/SQL: A Professional Programmer's Guide* and *ORACLE/SQL: A Professional Programmer's Guide,* both published by McGraw-Hill.

RICHARD JOHNSON is Director of MIS at Backus Hospital, Norwich, Connecticut and has over 15 years experience working with database management systems.

ABOUT THE SERIES

The J. Ranade IBM and DEC Series are McGraw-Hill's primary vehicles for providing mini- and mainframe computing professionals with practical and timely concepts, solutions, and applications. Jay Ranade is also Editor in Chief of the J. Ranade Workstation Series and Series Advisor to the McGraw-Hill Series on Computer Communications.

Jay Ranade, Series Editor in Chief and best-selling computer author, is a consultant and Assistant V.P. at Merrill Lynch.